THE PALESTINIAN NATIONAL REVIVAL

PERSPECTIVES ON ISRAEL STUDIES

S. Ilan Troen, Natan Aridan, Donna Divine, David Ellenson, and Arieh Saposnik, *editors*

Sponsored by the Ben-Gurion Research Institute for the Study of Israel and Zionism of the Ben-Gurion University of the Negev and the Schusterman Center for Israel Studies of Brandeis University

THE PALESTINIAN NATIONAL REVIVAL
In the Shadow of the Leadership Crisis, 1937–1967

Moshe Shemesh

Indiana University Press

This book is a publication of

Indiana University Press
Office of Scholarly Publishing
Herman B Wells Library 350
1320 East 10th Street
Bloomington, Indiana 47405 USA

iupress.org

First paperback edition, 2025
© 2018 by Moshe Shemesh

All rights reserved
No part of this book may be reproduced or utilized in any form or
by any means, electronic or mechanical, including photocopying
and recording, or by any information storage and retrieval
system, without permission in writing from the publisher.

First printing 2025

Cataloging information is available from the Library of Congress.

ISBN 978-0-253-03659-9 (cloth)
ISBN 978-0-253-07174-3 (pbk.)
ISBN 978-0-253-03660-5 (web PDF)

To my beloved family:
 Rachel, Yahel, and Yasaf; Oren, Shirley, and Carmel,
 my first granddaughter (May 15, 2018)

Contents

Acknowledgments ... ix
Preface: Aims and Scope ... xi

Part I: The Leadership Crisis of the Palestinian National Movement, 1937–63: The Decline from Power of Mufti Haj Amin al-Husayni

1. En Route to a Crisis of Leadership: The 1930s through World War II ... 3
2. Return of the Mufti and Increased Arab Involvement in the Filastin Issue ... 23
3. The All-Palestine Government, September 1948: Historical Failure of Leadership or Default Option? ... 44
4. The Palestinians in the Absence of Leadership, 1949–63 ... 60

Part II: National Revival: The 1950s as the Formative Years of the New Palestinian National Movement

5. The Nakba Generation ... 79
6. The "Sons of the Nakba" Generation: Emergent Leadership of the New Palestinian National Movement ... 106
7. Manifestations of the Palestinian National Awakening: The Arab Nationalists Movement, Fatah, the Ba'th Party, and the General Union of Palestinian Students ... 124
8. The Palestinians of the Gaza Strip under the Egyptian Government ... 152

Part III: The West Bank Palestinians under Hashemite Rule: The "Palestinization" Process in the Shadow of Egyptian Subversion and Influence

9. The Palestinians under the Hashemite Regime ... 165

10.	First Crisis: Aftermath of the Israel Defense Forces Raid on Qibya	175
11.	Second Crisis: In the Shadow of Egyptian Subversion, December 1955–April 1957	179
12.	The Crisis of April 1963: West Bank Palestinians and the Revival of a Palestinian Entity	196
13.	The Palestinians of Jordan, 1965–66: Between Shuqayri, Husayn, and the Emergence of Fatah	204
14.	The Crisis of November 1966: The Aftermath of the Israel Defense Forces Raid on Samu'	213

Part IV: Ahmad al-Shuqayri: Between the Arab Hammer and Palestinian Anvil, 1964–67: A Predictable Failure of Leadership and the Peak of a Leadership Crisis

15.	Ahmad al-Shuqayri's Path to PLO Leadership: A Role Awaiting a Hero versus a Leader Imposed from Above	223
16.	The Struggle over Leadership of the PLO: Emergence of Fatah and Decline in Shuqayri's Status, 1965–66	236
17.	The Leadership Crisis Escalates, June 1966–May 1967	254
18.	Shuqayri: The End of the Road, June–December 1967	271
	Conclusion	287
	Bibliography	297
	Name Index	309
	Subject Index	315

Acknowledgments

I WOULD LIKE TO thank the Ben-Gurion Institute for the Study of Israel and Zionism at Ben-Gurion University of the Negev, where I am a senior researcher, for its collegial atmosphere, and thank the directors for their support, especially Paula Kabalo, who expedited the completion of my research.

This book constitutes the second part of my research trilogy surveying and documenting the history of the Arab-Israeli conflict and the chronicles of the new Palestinian national movement between the years 1949 and 1974. The research began with my master's thesis, which I completed under the supervision of the late historian Jacob Talmon at the Hebrew University of Jerusalem, "The Palestinian National Re-Awakening, 1964–1974: The Background, Components, and Achievements of Its Revival."

I am grateful to the late Benjamin Pinkus, who was my colleague at Ben-Gurion Institute, for reading the first draft of this book and providing helpful comments. The book's third part was written with his warm recommendation. Special thanks to Avi Shlaim at Oxford University for his valuable comments. I am thankful to Israel Gershoni and Haggai Erlich at Tel Aviv University for their constructive remarks; to Yezid Sayigh who provided me with original sources regarding the Fatah organization; and to Moshe Efrat, who provided me with material from his research on Palestinian refugees. Also to Natan Aridan for his valuable editorial remarks.

I am indebted to Dee Mortensen, editorial director at Indiana University Press and Ilan Troen, editor, Indiana University Press Series Perspectives on Israel Studies for their invaluable support, encouragement, and suggestions in expediting publication of this book.

My deep thanks to the staff of the unit within the Israel Defense Forces Intelligence Branch known during the period of the research as "Intelligence 5" and later as "Hatzav," for the wealth of material that was very valuable in researching the 1950s and 1960s, during which they translated Arab radio broadcasts and Arab press items; to the library staff of the Truman Institute at the Hebrew University of Jerusalem; and to staff members of the Israel State Archives and of the Israel Defense Forces Archives for their assistance and guidance in locating materials. Thanks to the staff of the Ben-Gurion Archives in Sede Boker, to the head of archives, Hana Pinshow, and to Leana Feldman for their dedicated service. Thanks to the Ben-Gurion Research Institute library staff, headed by Lily Adar, and to Yefim Magarill in addition Yosef Litus for his computerization assistance. Thanks to Hadas Blum for preparing the index.

I am indebted to the Israel Academy of Sciences and Humanities of the Israel Science Foundation, which helped support research of the second part of this book.

Last but not least, my gratitude to Merav Datan for her dedicated, professional translation and editing work.

Preface: Aims and Scope

THIS BOOK CONTRIBUTES to a deeper understanding of the Palestinian national movement in the twentieth century, especially the roots of the national revival in the 1950s and the emergence of the Palestine Liberation Organization (PLO) in the 1960s. It addresses the Palestinian leadership crisis of those years, with special emphasis on the Palestinian position vis-à-vis the Arab-Israeli conflict.

The four parts of this book constitute a single unit based on a well-defined chronological framework. They are mutually linked, with later developments shedding light on earlier ones.

This volume makes a scholarly contribution to the literature by

1. Identifying the 1950s as the formative years of the new Palestinian national movement as it emerged in the aftermath of the 1948 Arab-Israeli War. It begins with a discussion of the Palestinian leadership crisis from the 1930s through the 1950s. It offers a new perspective on Palestinian society and its leadership and on the dilemmas, difficulties, and crises they confronted. The leadership of al-Haj Amin al-Husayni (the mufti) and his successor, Ahmad al-Shuqayri, are examined in the context of contemporary regional and international events.
2. Aiming to present an objective, balanced, and multidimensional approach that distinguishes between individual leadership and the development of the Palestinian national movement before and after 1948. It stresses the close correlation between the Palestinian leadership crisis, or rather lack of leadership, and the Palestinian national reawakening and revival during the 1950s. It attempts to resolve the apparent contradiction between the dominant narrative of Palestinian historians, which places emphasis on the leadership crisis and the leadership's failure to achieve the objectives of the Palestinian national movement, and the conclusion that emerges from this analysis, according to which the Palestinian national reawakening actually took place during the 1950s. The reawakening was characterized by social solidarity, resilience, survival, and determination. Practically out of nothing, it generated a national revival, which in turn led to many achievements. I examine the parts played by the mufti and Shuqayri in the national revival and conclude that, despite their failures, they were not nonentities as presented in most historical studies of the period. This book discusses the lack of Palestinian leadership with authority in the lead-up to the 1948 Arab-Israeli War and during the course of this war, the lack of a leadership recognized by

Arab states and the international community as the legitimate representative of the Palestinian people. Without a deep understanding of the Palestinian leadership crisis and its impact on the Palestinian cause, any analysis of the policy of King ʿAbdulla of Jordan regarding the Palestinian issue will be incomplete. So too is any analysis of Israel's policy on this issue in the aftermath of the 1948 War.

3. Addressing the question: Why were decisions relating to the Palestinian people and the Palestinian territories during the critical years before, during, and after the 1948 War taken by Arab leaders rather than by the Palestinian leadership headed by the mufti? This phenomenon cannot be understood without reviewing the Palestinian leadership from the early 1930s. The leadership was in a state of perpetual crisis, even though to all appearances the Husaynis' leadership, with the mufti as its head, seemed stable. The discussion concludes that the lack of an authoritative, recognized Palestinian leadership actually made it easier for Israel to decide on the "Jordanian option"—to conduct negotiations with Jordan over the future of the Palestinian territories under its control and to reach an agreement by which the West Bank would be part of the Hashemite Kingdom. Thus, the lack of a "Palestinian option" enabled King ʿAbdulla to realize his ambition of annexing the West Bank to his kingdom with Israeli acquiescence. Under these circumstances, Egypt had no alternative but to maintain control over the Gaza Strip as a "deposit"—a pledge of safekeeping.

4. Revealing that Arab involvement in the fate of Palestine (or Filastin) steadily increased at the request of the Palestinian leadership itself—in contrast to the salient view among Arab scholars that the Arab states appropriated the Palestinian issue from the Palestinians in the late 1940s. The leadership's need for Arab involvement stemmed from its weakness and inability to cope with the challenges posed by the Zionist movement and the British government. The increasing Arab involvement gave rise to a commitment to help the Palestinians, which peaked with the Arab armies' invasion of the territory of the newly born state of Israel on May 15, 1948. The Palestinians were never as dependent on Arab states as they were during the period after the World War II; in the words of the Palestinian researcher Bayan Nuwayhid al-Hut, ʿUrubat al-maʿraka wa-ʿUrubat al-qadiyya ("the Arabness of the campaign and the Arabness of the problem").

5. Concluding differently from Palestinian and Israeli scholars, including Yehoshafat Harkabi, regarding the conditions of Palestinians during the 1950s. These historians have tended to view the 1950s as a dormant period, during which there was no evident significant, independent Palestinian political activity. They identify the mid-1960s as the starting point of the Palestinian national movement on a meaningful and visible scale. In contrast to the conventional view, I maintain that the 1950s were the formative years

during which the objectives of the new Palestinian national movement crystallized, in the form of a national revival.
6. Outlining the social and political forces that facilitated the emergence of a "new" Palestinian national movement. The Palestinian national reawakening after the 1948 War generated a deadlock and even caused regression in the "old" Palestinian national movement. Its most salient manifestation was the appearance of *fida'iyyun* (guerrilla organizations) in the mid-1960s and Fatah's first military operation on January 1, 1965, against Israel's National Water Carrier. This operation marked the onset of a lengthy Palestinian armed struggle against Israel.
7. Evaluating the social circumstances of the "Nakba Generation" (Jeel al-Nakba, the generation of the parents) and the heritage it bequeathed to the second generation of the Nakba—the "Sons of the Nakba" (Jeel Abna' al-Nakba). Toward this end, it applies Karl Manheim's perspective regarding "political generations." Within this framework, the book surveys the factors behind the national awakening of the "sons of the Nakba" generation, which gave rise to a new Palestinian leadership, more authentic than its predecessors, having emerged from the bottom up. It addresses the following key questions: How did a socially, economically, and politically disintegrated refugee society generate a new national movement, militant in both character and deed? How should one understand the near-total enlistment of the Palestinian masses in support of the national objective and the overall popular support for the new movement? Moreover, how did the Palestinians achieve such a high level of solidarity—a solidarity that served as one of the essential elements of the national revival and enabled the new Palestinian national movement to withstand the crises it confronted after 1965?
8. Providing evidence in support of my main thesis regarding the 1950s with research into the relatively widespread political activity on the part of Palestinian intelligentsia—initially within existing Arab political frameworks and later through independent political Palestinian self-organization. Toward this end, the book surveys the activities of Palestinian intelligentsia, especially students at Beirut University, during the early 1950s within the framework of the Arab Nationalists Movement (Harakat al-Qawmiyyin al-'Arab), which they helped found. These activists underwent an accelerated process of "Palestinization"—reinforcement of the Palestinian identity and awareness, which led them at a later stage (in December 1967) to establish the Popular Front for the Liberation of Palestine (PFLP).
9. Reviewing the process of the Fatah organization's establishment, from its inception in 1956 and 1957, through the crystallization of its ideological program in 1958 and its organizational structure in 1959, until its public emergence with its first guerilla action in January 1965. Fatah was considered the first Palestinian movement, in the full sense of the term, since 1948. An

important and unique contribution to research on Fatah is provided by a summary of the contents of the movement's monthly magazine, *Filastinuna*, which was first published in Beirut in October 1959 and continued through November 1964. It also examines the activities of Palestinian student unions from the early 1950s, especially the activities of the General Union of Palestinian Students, which was established in 1959. Fatah's leaders—mostly from the Gaza Strip and refugee camps therein—emerged from this student association. In sum, the book presents a picture of a vibrant political society, which cannot be described as dormant.

10. Providing a distinct contribution to research on the Palestinian national movement in the section dealing with the process of Palestinization—the reinforcement of Palestinian national identity and awareness on the part of Palestinians in the West Bank under the rule of King Husayn. This book concludes that the process of "Jordanization," which the Hashemite Kingdom tried to impose on the Palestinian population of the West Bank, failed. Jordan's rulers aspired toward the assimilation of the Palestinian population within Jordanian identity and the reframing of Jordan as the representative of the Palestinian cause. In contrast to the assessment of Jordanian researchers and authorities, who viewed the establishment of the Palestine Liberation Organization in 1964 as a turning point in relations between the Palestinian population of the West Bank and the Hashemite Kingdom, this book argues that the kingdom's Palestinian population did not abandon their Palestinian identity and historical past but, rather, maintained a collective memory throughout the period of Jordanian rule over the West Bank. Furthermore, it maintains that, paradoxically, the gradual disengagement of the West Bank from the East Bank of the kingdom of Jordan actually began with the former's annexation in 1950.

11. Surveying the crises that erupted between the regime and the population of the West Bank during the period of Hashemite rule in order to understand the Palestinization process that the West Bank residents underwent. These crises escalated over the years, beginning with the Israel Defense Forces (IDF) attack on Qibya in October 1953, through the crisis of the Baghdad Pact in December 1955 and the crises of April 1957 and April 1963, and concluding with the nadir in relations between the two sides during the crisis of November 1966, after the IDF operation in Samu'. This book concludes that the period between December 1955 and April 1957 was decisive for the history of the Jordanian kingdom leading up to the Six Day War. This was a period of ongoing crisis that touched upon all the elements of the kingdom's domestic and inter-Arab foreign policy—a formative period for the regime of the young King Husayn. Similarly, the book reviews the important issue of political and military subversion in Jordan on the part of Egypt and Syria and the influence these subversive activities had on the conduct of

Palestinians in the West Bank. And it discusses the related phenomenon of recruitment and activation of fida'i cells by Egypt in Jordan that were to be deployed against Israel.
12. Concluding that Ahmad al-Shuqayri's leadership crisis, which culminated in his resignation in December 1967, resulted not only from his management style but also from the processes that Palestinian society was undergoing, including the emergence of a new, authentic Palestinian leadership. It surveys the developments that led to his decline from power and eventual disappearance from the Palestinian political arena after the Six Day War.

Part I
The Leadership Crisis of the Palestinian National Movement, 1937–63

The Decline from Power of Mufti Haj Amin al-Husayni

1 En Route to a Crisis of Leadership
The 1930s through World War II

Characteristics of the Crisis—1937 to 1948

A core issue in discussions of the role and influence of Palestinians in relation to the crisis between Israel and the Arab states during the years 1948–49 is the absence of a Palestinian leadership with the authority and political sway necessary to advance and steer the Palestinian cause. There was no leadership capable of making executable decisions in all matters relating to the future of the Palestinian problem and Palestinian territories or recognized by Arab states and the international community as the legitimate representative of the Palestinian people.

Where was the Palestinian leadership during the critical crisis of the 1948 Arab-Israeli War (hereinafter, the 1948 war) and the regional crisis that occurred in its aftermath, when the term "Filastin" (Palestine) disappeared from the geopolitical map of the Middle East? How did this leadership lose its standing to such an extent that it had no discernable influence on even the most crucial matters relating to the future of the Palestinian cause and fate of the Palestinians? How did it happen that decisions regarding the Palestinian people and Palestinian territories were in fact made by Arab states?

One cannot understand the circumstances and standing of the Palestinian leadership during and even before the 1948 war without first reviewing the crises it underwent beginning in the early 1930s, which were actually Mufti Haj Amin al-Husayni's glory days as leader of the Palestinian national movement. This was a leadership in a perpetual state of crisis, although it appeared to be stable because it was headed by the Husayni family, with the mufti at the helm.

The Arab states—first and foremost Egypt and Jordan—began to play an increasingly important role in shaping the struggle of the Palestinian national movement and, after World War II, in determining the composition of its leadership and the future of the Palestinian territories that remained under the control of Arab states. As a consequence, the Palestinians had no role in the armistice agreements between Arab states and Israel (with Egypt—February 3, 1949; Lebanon—March 23, 1949; Jordan—April 3, 1949 and Syria—July 20, 1949). This absence of Palestinian representatives from the armistice talks made it easier for Israel to conduct negotiations with Jordan regarding the future of territories under the latter's control and a possible agreement under which the West Bank would be annexed by and become part of the kingdom of Jordan.[1] Indeed, at the time there was no Palestinian leader or institution with the authority and legitimate standing to participate in negotiations with Israel.

Arab States' Commitment to Resolution of the Palestinian Problem

In contrast to the prevailing opinion among Western and Palestinian researchers, which holds that Arab states appropriated the Palestinian issue from the Palestinians,[2] Arab involvement in shaping the Palestinian cause steadily increased because, in fact, the Palestinian leadership itself requested and encouraged it. The leadership's need for Arab involvement stemmed from its own weakness and inability to cope with challenges posed by the Zionist movement and British government and from crises triggered by its chronic state of division. The ever-increasing Arab involvement generated a parallel process of commitment to provide assistance to the Palestinians, a process that culminated in the Arab military invasion of the newly established state of Israel on May 14, 1948. This process was described by Bayan al-Hut as a transformation of the Palestinian problem into an Arab problem (*'urubat al-ma'raka wa 'urubat al-qadiyya*),[3] as manifested after 1948 when the Palestinian problem became a facet of the Arab-Israeli conflict, whereas previously it had been an Arab-Palestinian versus Jewish-Zionist issue.

The origin of the Arab-Israeli conflict, accordingly, lies in the Arab involvement with and commitment to Palestine that actually preceded the 1948 war and benefited the Palestinian national movement. The 1948 Palestinian exodus known as the Nakba was, in fact, an Arab Nakba just as much as it was Palestinian, and long after 1948 it continued to be perceived as such.[4] Indeed, the Arab commitment to resolution of the Palestinian problem grew stronger with the emergence of the Arab-Israeli conflict after the Nakba and the transformation of the Arabs into a primary and active party to this conflict.[5] Nothing could substitute for this Arab support, and it became an integral aspect of the evolution of the new Palestinian national movement that emerged in January 1965 in the form of *fida'i* (guerrilla) organizations.

The Dominant Husayni Influence on the Leadership of the Palestinian National Movement

From its emergence in the 1920s through the end of the British Mandate era, the Husayni family, headed by Haj Amin al-Husayni, was the manifestly dominant influence in the leadership of the Palestinian national movement. This leadership remained in place despite the decline in the mufti's status after he fled the country in 1937, and its standing remained generally intact despite the crises it faced beginning in the 1930s. Consequently, and given the weakness of the opposition, the continuity and decisive influence of the Husaynis' leadership succeeded in forestalling the emergence of an alternative, rival leadership, even with the mufti's absence from Filastin during 1937–1946. This prolonged crisis of leadership was one of the main reasons that the Palestinian movement failed to achieve its aims.[6] The crisis enabled King 'Abdulla to annex the West Bank to his kingdom, thereby also sealing the fate of the Gaza Strip—that part of Filastin that remained under Egyptian control.

The Palestinian Leadership's Expectations and Demands versus Its Ability

A vast gap existed between the expectations and demands of the Palestinian leadership, on the one hand, and its ability to achieve them, on the other. Specifically, the Palestinians demanded that the Balfour Declaration be revoked, that Jewish immigration to Palestine be halted, that independent Palestinian rule be established over the entire territory of the mandate, and that the sale of lands to Jews be ceased.

The Palestinian leadership operated with a sense of frustration and disappointment, including vis-à-vis Arab states. Thus, paradoxically, it became even more entrenched in its extremist positions, which were characterized by absolute rejection of any compromise or accurate portrayal of political reality. With the support of Palestinian opposition, Arab states made efforts to soften the mufti's position, even as a tactical matter, but these efforts bore no fruit. The extremism of the leadership's positions became more than a means to achieve the national objectives of the Palestinian national movement; it became an end in itself: "The negative [stances] would inevitably lead to a decision that would result in confrontation and entrenchment (*mujabaha wa-sumood*)."[7] Consequently, armed confrontation (with the British and with the Jewish population of Palestine) became unavoidable.

Frustrated and unable to achieve its national objectives through political means—in contrast to the successes of the Zionist movement and the British government's adherence to the objectives of the mandate—the Palestinian national movement across nearly all of its factions turned toward violent, armed struggle, at times infused with a religious Islamic dimension, in pursuit of its objectives. This Palestinian struggle peaked with the 1936–39 revolt.

The Nakba gained historic significance when the state of Israel was founded despite expectations of the Palestinian leadership and Arab states. It grew in significance when the new state succeeded in militarily defeating the Arab states that had forcibly tried to prevent its establishment.

The Absence of Palestinian Governing Institutions

During the British Mandate era, the Palestinian leadership, in contrast to the Zionist movement, never established any governing entities that could serve as institutions for a state in the making. The leadership opposed on principle the formation of institutions for self-government in cooperation with Jewish representative bodies operating on the basis of the Balfour Declaration and the charter of the mandate. For example, the Palestinian leadership objected to the establishment of a legislative council as proposed by the British government in 1923 and later in 1935. In October 1923, the British high commissioner recommended to a delegation of Palestinian leaders headed by Kazim al-Husayni, chairman of the Palestinian Executive Committee, that an "Arab Agency" be established along the lines of the Jewish Agency. Kazim al-Husayni categorically rejected the proposal, arguing against "setting up an Arab Agency in the model of the Jewish Agency, [which would] make our status equal to that of the Zionists, by giving us this present." Palestinian negotiators had already rejected proposals for a legislative council and an advisory council that would have had much greater authority than the proposed agency and whose composition would have reflected the Arab majority in Palestine.[8] Evidently, the Palestinian leadership was concerned that acceptance of this proposal would be interpreted as recognition of the Jewish Agency and legal approval of its existence, and therefore as recognition of the Jews' rights over Palestine. In contrast, the leadership of the Palestinian national movement did have institutional bodies that served as representatives of the Arab-Palestinian population before the British government and directed the movement's struggle.

The Mufti Joins the Axis Powers

The mufti's affiliation with the Axis powers and his strong interest in assisting Nazi Germany in its war against the Allies played an important part in shaping the attitude of Arab states toward him and in determining his standing in the international arena during the critical years of the Palestinian struggle after World War II. Interestingly, though not surprisingly, the entry for Muhammad Amin al-Husayni in the Palestinian encyclopedia (*Al-Mawsu'a al-Filastiniyya*) completely ignores the period of the mufti's stay in Nazi Germany as well as his ties with it during World War II.[9]

The mufti's collaboration with Nazi Germany was, in effect, a gamble whose negative impact could not be prevented by the Palestinian national movement or its leader. At the same time, the Palestinian public, who were in general politically opposed to the Allies, did not penalize the mufti or view his activities as a reason to depose him. Indeed, the public waited eagerly for the German army to arrive in Palestine, and it cheered for Rommel when he reached the outskirts of Egypt.

The Arab League and the Mufti: A Severe Crisis of Confidence

The mufti returned from exile in 1946 to lead the Palestinian national movement, at a time when the Filastin problem had become the central issue on the agenda of the newly formed Arab League, established in 1945. Its establishment granted Iraq and Jordan special importance with respect to the Palestinian issue, as Article 7 of the Arab League Charter gave each Arab state the right to veto its resolutions.[10] Thus a Hashemite front was created, which opposed the mufti and played a decisive role in discussions regarding the Filastin question. This front further compounded the hostility of the Arab League toward the mufti and the league's nearly automatic rejection of any demand he posed. As the Filastin problem became increasingly central, so too hostility toward the mufti increased and with it the need for greater Arab involvement.

Opposition to the mufti and objection to the Palestinian national movement on the part of Jordan and Iraq had the effect of weakening the Palestinian leadership and undermining its importance and standing, in particular the status of the mufti. In fact, the mufti was not actively included in any political or military process undertaken by the Arab League regarding the Filastin question during the years following World War II. Consequently, the mufti's status also declined significantly in the international arena.

Institutions of the Palestinian National Movement: 1920–34

Until the collapse of King Faysal's government in Damascus (July 24, 1920), political activists in the Arab community of Palestine tended to view Filastin as part of Syria, specifically as "southern Syria." Palestinian figures even participated in the Syrian General Congress that took place in Damascus in 1919 as representatives of southern Syria.[11] The collapse of Faysal's government and abandonment of the idea of southern Syria, alongside establishment of the British Mandate over Palestine, obliged local political activists to begin setting up Palestinian institutions to lead the national struggle, while also relying on existing institutions, salient among which were the Muslim-Christian Associations founded in 1918.[12]

During the mandate era there were four national institutions through which members of the Palestinian leadership operated and in whose name most political resolutions relating to the Palestinian national movement were officially published: the Palestinian Arab Congress (al-Mu'tamar al-'Arabi al-Filastini); the Executive Committee (al-Lajna al-Tanfidhiyya), which was elected by the congress; the Arab Higher Committee (AHC; al-Lajna al-'Arabiyya al-'Ulya), which replaced the Executive Committee; and the Arab Higher Hay'a ("Authority"; al-Hay'a al-'Arabiyya al-'Ulya). This book uses the term "Arab Higher Hay'a," or "hay'a," in order to distinguish it from its predecessor, the Arab Higher Committee, or AHC.

Another important institution was the Supreme Muslim Council (al-Majlis al-Islami al-A'la), headed by the mufti. This council did not succeed in becoming a countrywide leadership body, as it was a government body appointed and funded by the high commissioner. Indeed, it was a tool in the mufti's hands to reinforce his standing.

In all, a total of seven Palestinian Arab congresses were held, with the last one taking place in June 1927. The First Palestinian Arab Congress (al-Mu'tamar al-'Arabi al-Filastini al-'Awal) took place in Jerusalem from January 27 to February 9, 1919, with twenty-seven delegates representing various regions and cities of Filastin. The congress was held in the framework of the concept of "Filastin–southern Syria."[13]

With respect to the Second Palestinian Arab Congress, there are a number of versions regarding its timing and actual occurrence. 'Izzat Darwaza writes in his memoirs that it was "decided to hold the second congress in Jerusalem in May 1920 to protest the confirmation of the British Mandate over Palestine and the incorporation of the Balfour Declaration in the instrument of the Mandate at the San Remo Conference [in April 1920]. However, the Palestine government forbade its convening." Yehoshua Porath accepts this version, which was further affirmed by Bayan Nuwayhid al-Hut. Her conclusion was that the British authorities succeeded in erasing all traces of what was supposed to be the second congress.[14]

The Third Palestinian Arab Congress took place December 13–19, 1920, in Haifa. A total of thirty-one delegates participated in the first session, out of forty-six expected participants. The congress was presented as the representative body for the entire Palestinian population in Filastin, and Amin al-Husayni participated actively in its discussions. Musa Kazim al-Husayni was elected as chairman of the congress.

The congress decided that every time it convened, it would elect an Executive Committee composed of nine members and tasked with implementation of the congress's resolutions. Additionally, Kazim al-Husayni was elected as chairman of the Executive Committee, which in turn became the leading body of the Palestinian national movement and struggle.

The congress also approved a charter for Filastin based on "rejection of the Balfour Declaration, rejection of Jewish immigration, rejection of the sale of land to Jews, and the establishment of an independent constitutional national government." It demanded that the British government "establish a native (*wataniyya*) government responsible to a representative assembly (*majlis niyaabi*), whose members would be chosen from the populace that was Arabic-speaking and had resided in Palestine before the [First World] War." Muslih concludes, "The Palestinian Arab nationalist movement had for the first time defined its objectives, from both an ideological and organizational perspective, in distinct Palestinian terms."[15]

The Fourth Palestinian Arab Congress, which convened in Jerusalem from May 29 to June 4, 1921, took place against the background of the May 1, 1921, riots and the election of Amin al-Husayni as mufti of Jerusalem. The congress decided that its term would continue for a full year and that Musa Kazim al-Husayni would serve as permanent chairman. The congress elected a new thirteen-member Executive Committee.[16]

The Fifth Palestinian Arab Congress took place in Nablus on August 20, 1922, against the background of the authorization for the British Mandate over Palestine, which included authorization of the Balfour Declaration as well. Among its resolutions were the following: rejection of the mandate, a general boycott of the Jews, rejection of the proposed constitution for Filastin, and a boycott of the elections to the legislative council. With respect to these resolutions, the fifth congress was characterized by extremism to a greater extent than its predecessors.[17]

The Sixth Palestinian Arab Congress convened June 16–20, 1923, in Jaffa.

The Interim Period, 1923–28: The Rise to Power of the Mufti and Emergence of the Opposition

Five years elapsed between the sixth and seventh Palestinian Arab congresses (June 20–27, 1928). A number of important developments related to the issue of Palestinian leadership took place during these years: the Executive Committee emerged as the official representative of the Palestinian national movement, Mufti Amin al-Husayni rose to power, and the opposition emerged as part of the Palestinian leadership.

The Executive Committee that was elected by the various congresses became the official representative of the Palestinian national movement and led its struggle, be it against the British government or against the Zionist movement, with the Husaynis as the dominant shapers of its policy. The election of Musa Kazim al-Husayni as chairman of the Executive Committee—a position he filled as long as it existed—made him, at least formally, the leader of the Palestinian national movement, earning him the titles "the shaykh of the problem" (*shaykh al-qadiyya*) and "al-pasha."[18] In May 1921, when he was only twenty-six years old, Husayni was appointed mufti of Jerusalem, and in January 1922 he was elected chairman of the Supreme Muslim Council.

Husayni's leadership developed gradually and continuously in conjunction with the establishment of the Supreme Muslim Council in 1921, which served as a very effective tool for him to wield political influence. Because of their family connection, during the 1920s, Amin al-Husayni did not pose a threat to the standing of the Grand Shaykh Kazim al-Husayni. Bayan al-Hut describes the mufti's characteristics:

> Although al-Haj enjoyed religious respect as the mufti of Jerusalem and chairman of the Supreme Muslim Council, and despite the cloak of a [religious] wise man on his shoulders and the turban on his head, the truth behind the honorable religious appearance began to emerge, [namely] the fact that he is

a political figure of the highest order; accordingly, as the practical political power of Haj Amin increased, so too did the power of his political opponents, and the hostility was severe from the outset.... Among the salient characteristics of Haj Amin was his political cunning.[19]

The mufti's supporters were called *majlisiyyin* (from "al-Majlis al Islami al-A'la") because the mufti was the chairman of the Supreme Muslim Council. This was a united, consolidated group that surrounded the mufti's leadership and, because of his political and practical influence, became the political foundation for his activities.

Researchers concur that the rise of the opposition (*mu'arada*) to the *majlisiyyin*'s policy had its roots in fundamental elements related to the internal political division within Palestinian society. Bayan al-Hut notes another factor: "The most powerful factor was always the interest of the Mandatory government in creating a split in the political national movement, and therefore it supported the rival oppositionist group known as *al-mu'arada*."[20] The Nashashibi family led the opposition, and the political struggle within the national movement was now concentrated primarily between the Husaynis and the Nashashibis. This struggle, which was most extreme in Jerusalem, left its mark on the activities and functioning of the Palestinian leadership.

The status of the Nashashibi family was first and foremost an outcome of the status of its leader, Raghib al-Nashashibi, who had served in the past as delegate in the Ottoman parliament and as chief engineer of the Jerusalem district. The opposition extended beyond the narrow scope of family, encompassing a broader public that included individuals who had held offices from the time of the Ottoman era and remained without a role to play, as well as others who had been removed from office by the Husaynis.

Leaders of the Palestinian opposition of the 1920s were not infused with the revolutionary Palestinian spirit expressed by the Executive Committee and Supreme Muslim Council. Naturally, "the wealthy of Palestine tended to align with the opposition camp more than with the Executive Committee camp, whereas the few members of the intelligentsia in the country tended more towards the Executive Committee camp than vice versa."[21]

The Nashashibis emerged from the 1927 municipal elections with a number of significant successes. Their victory in Jerusalem was particularly striking: out of eight Arab representatives in the municipality (five Muslims and three Christians), six were Nashashibi supporters (three Muslims and three Christians). Jewish votes also contributed to the Nashashibis' victory, and Raghib al-Nashashibi was elected mayor. The opposition was victorious throughout the country in the 1927 elections, as its candidates succeeded in most cities. Thus the opposition became an important factor that had to be taken into account in the development and management of the Palestinian national movement. The influence of the opposition under Raghib al-Nashashibi's leadership fluctuated but was never decisive. Only rarely, in fact, did the opposition achieve a position of real influence, as most of its power remained in the realm of municipal councils.

The Seventh Palestinian Arab Congress took place June 20–27, 1928, in Jerusalem. Its composition reflected the new political scene. The number of participants reached nearly two hundred fifty, and consequently the number of Executive Committee members increased as well, reaching forty-eight. This was the last Executive Committee, and it continued to serve as the official representative body of the Palestinian movement until the death of Kazim al-Husayni in 1934.

The seventh congress foreshadowed the Husayni camp's loss of dominance, within the congress as well as in the Executive Committee. This time the opposition participated as an equal partner, and for every *majlisi* from one or another city there was a participating *mu'arid*.

The congress refrained from passing a resolution directly addressing the right of independence or rejecting the Balfour Declaration or the British Mandate, presumably because of the prevailing interest among members of the Palestinian leadership in promoting the idea of convening a representative legislative body for the country. Bayan al-Hut asserts that the congress "adopted a general resolution affirming the resolutions of previous congresses. It was clear that rejection of the Balfour Declaration was not explicit this time, nor did it receive its own special paragraph, but rather was included within the resolution that called for the establishment of a national parliamentary government." The congress adopted the following resolution: "The Palestinian Arab Congress . . . unanimously decided to call for the establishment of a parliamentary government in Filastin . . . and calls for the revocation of the tithe and the establishment of an agricultural bank, for the education budget to be doubled, and for the passing of legislation to cease until a parliamentary government is established. [The congress] elected a committee to implement the resolutions and direct the national movement."[22]

Early Signs of Crisis in the Mufti's Leadership, 1929–37: The Decline of the Executive Committee and Establishment of the Arab Higher Committee

The August 1929 Western Wall riots constituted a turning point not only in terms of the mufti's status but also for the history of the Palestinian national movement and, naturally, relations between the Jewish community of Palestine and the Palestinian Arabs. Thereafter, significant changes took place in the Palestinian political system: the mufti's status as leader was reinforced, as he had led the religious struggle surrounding the Western Wall issue. At the same time, the status of the Executive Committee and its leader declined, against the background of the weakened standing of the Executive Committee chairman. The mufti aspired to eliminate this body and become the only figure leading the Palestinian national movement. Political circumstances and the feebleness of the Nashashibi opposition helped him in the pursuit of this goal.

Three parallel processes characterize this period of the mufti's leadership, each one of which complemented the other two, with all three reinforcing one another. The first process was the radicalization of the Palestinian national movement and its ideological and organizational crystallization, as young cadres with radical opinions appeared on the scene. The second process was the rise of the nationalist stream within the Arab national movement in its various forms. As a result of these two processes, the status of the mufti was reinforced and he became the undisputed leader of the Palestinian national movement. The third process was the decline in the status of the Executive Committee and of the Nashashibi opposition, which in turn made it possible to establish the AHC, headed by the mufti. Indeed, during the years 1921–31, the Supreme Muslim Council became a religious tool for reinforcement of the mufti's influence and, in effect, the religious Islamic wing of the Palestinian national movement.

The Executive Committee began to lose standing in 1930, and its status steadily declined until it completely collapsed in 1934, with the death of Musa Kazim al-Husayni, who had headed it since its establishment in late 1920. Its decline paralleled the continuously rising leadership status of the mufti. The composition of the Executive Committee that had been elected during the Seventh Palestinian Arab Congress—half *majlisiyyin* and half *mu'arideen*—only exacerbated the internal strife, which was naturally influenced by the political arena as well. The end of the Executive Committee was therefore only a matter of time.

The death of the Executive Committee chairman on March 26, 1934, expedited the collapse of this body. It also brought an end to the Executive Committee front headed by Kazim al-Husayni and the Nashashibis following the seventh congress, and it contributed to their decline in standing. Raghib Nashashibi's failure to be appointed as head of the Jerusalem municipality following the 1934 elections constituted a severe blow to the opposition, from which it was unable to recover during the years that followed.

The death of Musa Kazim al-Husayni in March 1934 and collapse of the Executive Committee provided the opportunity for which the mufti had been waiting to seize the reins of the Palestinian national movement in practical terms. This development correlated well with the radicalization process that the Palestinian population, particularly the intelligentsia, was undergoing—a process in which the rise of an educated younger generation who generally supported the mufti was particularly evident. The atmosphere that prevailed in the country after the events of August 1929 served as fertile ground for these radicals, and after 1931 their voice and views could be heard throughout the country. Against this background, radical Palestinian organizations that revolted against the traditional, moderate leadership also emerged. Simultaneously, new political parties that changed the composition of the political struggle within the Palestinian leadership also arose. Nevertheless, the Husayni camp still remained the dominant one within the leadership.

The radicalization of Palestinian politics gave rise, among other things, to a general strike in April 1936, alongside acts of violence against the Jewish community and the British government and, later, to the Arab revolt. At this critical stage for Palestinian politics, the Palestinian national movement had no official leadership, as no such leadership had emerged since the death of Musa Kazim al-Husayni and collapse of the Executive Committee he had headed. The establishment of a new Palestinian national leadership, particularly one that could lead the general strike, was now an urgent agenda item. On April 25, 1936, Palestinian delegations from various parts of the country convened to discuss the leadership crisis.

As a consequence of the pressure applied by young militants and the press, Raghib al-Nashashibi and Amin al-Husayni backed down from their earlier positions, thereby making it possible to establish the AHC on April 25, 1936. It was agreed that the mufti would serve as chairman of the new entity and that the five political party leaders would be members: Raghib al-Nashashibi, head of the National Defense Party (Hizb al-Difa' al-Watani); Jamal al-Husayni, head of the Palestinian Arab Party (al-Hizb al-'Arabi al-Filastini); Ya'qub al-Ghusayn, head of the Youth Congress (Hizb-Mu'tamar al-Shabab al-Filastini); 'Abd al-Latif Salah, head of the National Bloc (al-Kutla al-Watiniyya); and Husayn al-Khalidi, head of the Reform Party (Hizb al-'Islah al-'Arabi). In addition, 'Awni 'Abd al-Hadi, leader of al-Istiqlal Party, was appointed as secretary of the AHC, and Ahmad Hilmi 'Abd al-Baqi, also from al-Istiqlal, was appointed as treasurer. Alfred Rok, a Greek Catholic and one of the leaders of the Palestinian Arab Party, was appointed as representative of the Christians alongside Ya'qub Farraj, a Greek Orthodox and one of the leaders of the National Defense Party. Thus, three members represented the Husayni camp, and each of the three remaining parties was represented by its leader. Al-Istiqlal was, accordingly, overrepresented given that this party had, in fact, ceased to exist two years earlier. Presumably, their increased representation stemmed from the central part played by Istiqlal members in organizing the strike, planning the national committees, and establishing the AHC.[23]

In her assessment of the AHC's composition, Bayan al-Hut writes, "This composition of the AHC seemingly comprised one representative from each political party and from a few communities, but in fact the three main political parties were each given two seats: Jamal al-Husayni and Alfred Rok (representing the Catholics) of the Arab Party; Raghib al-Nashashibi and Ya'qub Farraj (representing the Orthodox) of the Defense Party; and 'Awni 'Abd al-Hadi and Ahmad Hilmi 'Abd al-Baqi (independent) of al-Istiqlal. This composition created some form of balance within the AHC."[24]

The failure of the general strike, especially the need for Arab states' intervention in order to end it, was an indication of the standing and authority of the Palestinian leadership and the AHC. This was a political turning point—not only in the approach of the Palestinian leadership but also, in particular, in terms of Arab receptivity to the leadership's request for intervention, which resulted in a commitment on the part of Arab states to assist the Palestinian national movement in times of need. It was also an important expression of the dependence of the Palestinian national movement on the support and assistance of Arab states. This dynamic of Arab involvement, sometimes at the request of the Palestinian leadership, would increase over time, especially after World War II. "The AHC, which was established within a week of the start of the strike, did its best to foster Arab countries' involvement in the struggle over Palestine on behalf of the Palestinian Arabs. In September 1936, when it became evident that there were shortcomings in the ability to sustain the strike, the AHC asked Arab leaders to call on their Palestinian brothers to end the strike." The call to end the strike was issued on October 8, 1936, by King Sa'ud, King Ghazi, and Amir 'Abdulla. Their calls were published in the Palestinian press on October 11, 1936, and on the following day the AHC statement regarding the end of the strike was published.[25]

Throughout this period, the mufti continued to serve as both chairman of the Supreme Muslim Council and chairman of the AHC. The mufti's departure to Saudi Arabia for the hajj (pilgrimage to Mecca) and to Syria for a visit, in July 1937, served as an excuse for the National Defense Party to leave the AHC, on the pretext that the mufti had left precisely when the situation in the country was critically serious, and without informing AHC members of his departure.

Crisis of Leadership and Rejection of the White Paper, 1937–39

The measures taken by the government following the assassination of Lewis Andrews, acting British district commissioner for Galilee, on September 26, 1937, dealt a severe blow to the Palestinian national leadership. This was the first assassination of a high-ranking British official, and it was regarded as a declaration of revolt against British rule. On September 30, the government decided to arrest Amin al-Husayni if he left his place of refuge in al-Haram al-Sharif and to arrange as quickly and secretly as possible for the arrest of the Supreme Muslim Council members and their deportation to the islands of the Seychelles. The AHC and the national committees were declared illegal. Arrest warrants were issued against AHC members, and the mufti was dismissed from his position as chairman of the Supreme Muslim Council. Arrest warrants were also issued against

AHC members who were outside of Palestine at the time, as was an injunction prohibiting their return to the country: 'Awni 'Abd al-Hadi and Alfred Rok were staying in Geneva, 'Abd al-Latif Salah was staying in Europe, and 'Izzat Darwaza was in Baghdad. Jamal al-Husayni succeeded in escaping to Lebanon. The British authorities managed to arrest AHC members Ahmad Hilmi 'Abd al-Baqi, Fu'ad Saba, Ya'qub al-Ghusayn, and Husayn al-Khalidi, as well as Rashid al-Haj Ibrahim, the Istiqlal leader from Haifa. These five were deported to the Seychelles.[26] Likewise, various clergymen, dignitaries, and activists from national organizations were arrested but remained in the country.

The mufti, fearing that the authorities would enter al-Haram al-Sharif, where he had found refuge, decided to escape while dressed as a Bedouin on the night between October 12 and 13. He was driven by car to Jaffa, and from there he sailed by boat to Lebanon. French Mandate authorities arrested him on the shore of Lebanon but decided to grant him asylum while also restricting his movement.[27] Amin al-Husayni remained in Lebanon for two years, until World War II broke out. His escape from the country seemingly cleared the way for more moderate Palestinian leaders, but these remained passive for two reasons: the National Defense Party had already lost its standing and influence for the most part, and Amin al-Husayni's escape sparked a large-scale revival of the Arab revolt.

On November 7, 1938, the British government announced its intention to convene an Arab-Jewish conference that would include representatives from Arab states in order to find a solution to the question of Palestine. The issue of the mufti's participation in the congress became a stumbling block between him and the AHC members who were brought back from the Seychelles. Amin al-Husayni and his supporters insisted that no one participate in the conference without him, whereas the Seychelles deportees claimed that participation in itself was more important than the mufti's personal problem. The dispute was resolved by deciding that Amin al-Husayni would be appointed to head a delegation but would "freely choose" to remain in Beirut. In official documents of the delegation, the mufti is listed as chairman, with Jamal al-Husayni acting in his place.[28]

From Arab states, representatives of Egypt, Iraq, Saudi Arabia, Jordan, and Yemen participated. 'Abd al-Rahman 'Azzam, secretary general of the Arab League, was appointed an adviser to the Arab delegation and became a full member, and George Antonius served as secretary general for all the Arab delegations.[29]

The Arab delegations' rejection of the British White Paper of 1939 (published May 17) was the main topic under discussion at the conference, with conflicting factors and interests at play. As it turned out, there were differences of opinion on this matter, even among close associates of the mufti. In Bayan al-Hut's assessment, "The openly stated positions of those who rejected the White Paper were not the true positions."[30] In his memoirs, 'Awni 'Abd al-Hadi writes of the

London congress that "all the representatives of Arab states at the congress preferred to accept the White Paper, but they said that they had come to the congress in order to advise the Palestinian delegation, and that the last word belonged to the Palestinian delegation, whatever its position.... I must say that I was among those who called for the White Paper to be accepted, because I believed that the government of Britain could not go along with the Arabs any more than it had."[31] Later 'Awni 'Abd al-Hadi adopted a different position. In a letter he wrote to 'Ali Mahir on November 4, 1939, he stated, "The White Paper does not in its current formulation accord with Arab national principles and it should not be accepted in its entirety . . . as most of its articles are unclear."[32] Bayan al-Hut adds, "The special papers of 'Izzat Tannus make it clear that most AHC members accepted the White Paper after discussing it in detail during a special meeting in . . . the mufti's place of residence in Lebanon, but the mufti rejected it because of the lack of clarity in some of its articles."[33]

Bayan al-Hut sums up the issue, not without attempting to justify the mufti's stance:

> Supporters of the White Paper, did not honestly voice their views, whether out of respect for or fear of the mufti. And those who accepted it based their opinion on realistic political considerations, especially given that the domestic situation had reached a nadir and driven the average citizen to bitter despair.... The mufti based his opinion on the percentage of objectives that the White Paper would achieve out of [the totality of] national demands and political rights for his people. As this percentage was small, and as confidence in the British government was lacking even when it came to implementing this small percentage, he rejected it.[34]

When the AHC published its resolution regarding rejection of the white paper, all the Arab states adopted its position, with the exception of Jordan. Because of the internal debate, this declaration was published only two weeks later (on May 30, 1939). The Nashashibis for their part published their response, which was affirmative, on May 29, 1939. They even announced their intention to cooperate with the government in implementing the new policy. Other personalities, such as Musa al-'Alami, George Antonius, Ahmad al-Shuqayri, and 'Izzat Tannus, expressed their reservations about the AHC resolution in private conversations.[35]

There was one, unequivocal lesson that Palestinian Arabs could draw from the London congress, in the words of Yehoshua Porath:

> Only owing to the intervention of the Arab States in Palestine affairs had they achieved their most important political victory since the beginning of the Mandate. By the end of the Second World War this lesson may have driven them to rely more and more upon the Arab States' support and less and less upon themselves.... Therefore it was to the advantage of the Palestinian Arabs that their case should be presented to the victorious Allies by Nahas Pasha of

Egypt or Nuri al-Saʻid of Iraq rather than by their leader Amin al-Husayni who had stayed in Berlin during the War and recruited Arab and Muslim public opinion for the Axis powers. This tactical consideration may also have played a role in the various factors which in 1945–48 led the Palestinian Arabs to almost total reliance upon the Arab States.[36]

Lack of Leadership: The War Years, 1939–45

In concluding his study, Yosef Nevo writes,

> The factor with the greatest influence on the political development of the Arab movement in the country [Palestine] during the years 1939–45 was the lack of leadership.... A functional pan-national body that shaped policy and ensured its implementation existed only for short, non-continuous periods (between 1939 and 1941); even then it did not operate within [Mandatory Palestine]. The leader best known to a majority of the country's Arabs and the heads of the largest political party were outside the borders of the country for the entire period. Other political party heads and accepted leaders were [also] away from the country for a long time.[37]

In 1942 members of the AHC were geographically distributed as follows: the mufti was in Germany; Jamal al-Husayni was in Rhodesia; ʻIzzat Darwaza was in Turkey; Ahmad Hilmi ʻAbd al-Baqi, Fuʼad Saba, Alfred Rok, and Husayn Fakhri al-Khalidi were in Lebanon; and ʻAwni ʻAbd al-Hadi, Yaʻqub al-Ghusayn, and ʻAbd al-Latif Salah were in Egypt. This situation reflected the failure of attempts undertaken to establish a consensus on Palestinian leadership during the war years as well as the nadir that the Palestinian national movement and its leadership had reached. Bayan al-Hut summarizes the situation as follows: "The power of the national movement of the Palestinian people was at its lowest.... A general comparison between the power of the Jews and the power of the Arabs in the land of Filastin reveals that the Jews were never stronger politically and militarily than they were after the war, and the Arabs were never weaker than they were during that time."[38]

Despite the opportunity it now had to fill the vacuum created by the absence of the Husayni leadership in Palestine, the Palestinian opposition was also at its nadir. Opposition groups became politically active only in 1943, at the initiative of Istiqlal leaders, but their efforts were also fruitless. The National Defense Party under Nashashibi's leadership, which served as the flagship of the opposition, was disintegrating during the war years and lacked any organizational structure. Although the British government did not prevent the party from operating, Raghib al-Nashashibi preferred to suspend his political activism during the first years of the war, having concluded that it would not be possible to change the political situation. The National Defense Party, having aligned itself with the British authorities, had no standing in the eyes of the Palestinian public, who viewed it as serving the British. The party leaders officially resumed the party's activities in mid-1944 under the leadership of its long-standing president, Raghib al-Nashashibi, after a strong need for the Palestinian national leadership to have a representative structure became evident. Despite the wishes of its leaders, even then the National Defense Party did not succeed in becoming a political force, and most of its supporters remained passive.[39]

Throughout this time, Husayni activists made efforts to obstruct any activity liable to undermine their leader's status, the Husaynis' status, or the status of their party—the Arab Party—as leaders of the Palestinian national movement and its struggle. While the Husaynis as a party or movement were stagnant and their leader was preoccupied with his relations with Germany, his supporters in the country made efforts—even by means of violence—to prevent any organizing that could endanger the standing of his party or leadership. The party's main objective at the time was to freeze the general political situation while simultaneously establishing party chapters and preparing them for their leader's return. At the same time, however, the party's local leaders could not make any new measures or decisions on major political issues because of the absence of the mufti.

The mufti's standing in the eyes of the Palestinian public—which expected the Axis states to be victorious and the mufti to return to the country with them—was strong enough to prevent the emergence of any alternative to his leadership. Indeed, there was no such alternative. The Husaynis were determined not to relinquish the political status they had secured by 1937, and their motivation and organizational skills deserve mention for helping them achieve their objective, albeit through the use of violence against their opponents at times. They managed to fend off every type of effort by the opposition to achieve political standing and undermine their own dominance over the political arena. The Husaynis also succeeded in thwarting every attempt to establish a representative Palestinian institution in which they would not have a majority or superior standing. Eventually, toward the end of the war, the Husaynis emerged as the best organized political body.[40]

In light of the mufti's close relations with the Axis states, especially Nazi Germany where he spent most of the war, and his efforts to enlist Arab and Muslim support in these countries, it was only natural that his political standing declined significantly, particularly in the Arab arena and among Arab states that had good relations with Britain (such as Egypt, Iraq, and Jordan). Consequently, after the war ended with the defeat of the Axis states, the mufti was unable to reclaim the power he had enjoyed before the war, when the extent of that power had been a source of concern for Britain.

The war years widened the gaps between the two movements struggling over Palestine—the Zionist movement and the Palestinian national movement.

These gaps were manifested in leadership institutions and infrastructures for the establishment of national governance as well as in the support of the superpowers and the international community for the Zionist movement, its leadership, and the right of Jews to self-determination alongside the Arabs' right to self-determination. The divided nature of this support meant that a solution would entail dividing Palestine.

Notes

1. See Avraham Sela', *Memaga'im le-Masa 'u-Mattan* [From talks to negotiations] (Tel Aviv: Moshe Dayan Center, 1985); Avi Shlaim, *Collusion across the Jordan* (Oxford: Clarendon Press, 1988); Itamar Rabinovich, *Ha-Shalom Shehamak: Yahse Yisra'el-Arav, 1949–1952* [Elusive peace: Israel-Arab relations, 1949–1952] (Tel Aviv: Keter, 1991), published in English as *The Road Not Taken: Early Arab-Israeli Relations* (New York: Oxford University Press, 1991); see also *Documents on Foreign Policy of Israel*, vol. 8, ed. Yemima Rosenthal (Jerusalem: Ha-Madpis ha-Memshalti, 1995).

2. See Me'ir Pa'il, "Hafka'at ha-Ribonut ha-Medinit 'al Falastin mi-Yede ha-Falastinim 'al Yede Medinot Arav bi-Tkufat Milhemet ha-'Asma'ut 1947–1948" [Expropriation of political sovereignty over Palestine from the Palestinians by Arab states during the War of Independence, 1947–1948], *Hasiyyonut* 3 (1974); 'Isam Sakhnini, "Al-Kiyan al-Filastini 1964–1974," *Shu'un Filastiniyya* 40–41 (February–March 1975); Samih Shabib, "Muqadamat al-Musadara al-Rasmiyya lil-Shakhsiyya al-Wataniyya al-Filastiniyya 1948–1950," *Shu'un Filastiniyya* 129–31 (August–October 1982). Avraham Sela' supports this position: "Although Arab governments did commit themselves to providing material and political assistance to Palestinian Arabs in order to achieve their political objectives, their unfortunate political circumstances meant that this commitment entailed a tendency to expropriate the right to have the final word in their own affairs"; see "Ha-'Aravim ha-Falastinim be-Milhemet 1948" [The Palestinian Arabs during the 1948 war], in *Ha-Tnu'a ha-Le'umit ha-Falastinit: Me-'Imut le-Hashlama?* [The Palestinian national movement: From confrontation to reconciliation?], ed. Moshe Ma'oz and Benjamin Z. Kedar (Tel Aviv: Ministry of Defense, 1996), 128.

3. Bayan Nuwayhid al-Hut, *Al-Qiyadat wa al-Mu'assasat al-Siyasiyya fi Filastin, 1917–1948* (Beirut: Mu'assasat al-Dirasat al-Filastiniyya, 1986), 639.

4. See, for example, Qustantin Zurayq, *Ma'na al-Nakba* (Beirut: Dar al-'Ilm le al-Malayeen, 1948); Qadri Hafiz Tuqan, *Ba'da al-Nakba* (Beirut: Dar al-'Ilm le al-Malayeen, 1950); Musa al-'Alami, *'Ibrat Filastin* (Beirut: Dar al-Kashshaf, 1949); 'Arif al-'Arif, *Al-Nakba Nakbat Bayt al-Maqdis wa al-Firdaws al-Mafqud, 1947–1952*, 6 vols. (Sidon: al-Maktaba al-'Asriyya, 1956–1960); Walid al-Qamhawi, *Al-Nakba wa al-Bina' fi al-Watan al-'Arabi*, 2 vols. (Beirut: Dar al-'Ilm le al-Malayeen, 1962).

5. On the Arab commitment to resolving the Palestinian problem, see Moshe Shemesh, *Arab Politics, Palestinian Nationalism and the Six Day War: The Crystallization of Arab Strategy and Nasir's Descent to War, 1957–1967* (Brighton, UK: Sussex, 2008).

6. On the development of the Husaynis' leadership, the Nashashibis' opposition, and the struggle between them, see Yehoshua Porath, *The Emergence of the Palestinian-Arab National Movement, 1918–1929* (London: Frank Cass, 1974); Yehoshua Porath, *The Palestinian-Arab*

National Movement: From Riots to Rebellion, 1929–1939 (London: Frank Cass, 1977); Joseph Nevo, "Ha-Hitpathut ha-Politit shel ha-Tnua'a ha-Le'umit ha-'Aravit ha-Falastinit, 1939–1945" [The Political development of the Palestinian Arab national movement, 1939–1945] (PhD diss., Tel Aviv University, 1977); Joseph Nevo, "Ha-Tnua'a ha-Le'umit ha-'Aravit ha-Falastinit be-Milhemet ha-'Olam ha-Shniyya" [The Arab-Palestinian national movement during the Second World War], in Ma'oz and Kedar, *The Palestinian National Movement*.

7. Bayan al-Hut, *Al-Qiyadat*, 638.
8. According to Porath, *The Emergence*, 176–77:

> The Cabinet Committee concluded its debates on 27th July 1923, and four days later the Cabinet approved its recommendations. . . . [It concluded that] steps should be taken to allay the Arab impression—however incorrect it might be—that the Jews had a preferential position. Therefore the Committee recommended the establishment of an 'Arab Agency' parallel to the Jewish Agency to act as an advisory body to the Government with respect to all non-Jewish interests in Palestine. . . . Nevertheless, this proposal too was rejected by the Arab representatives when the [High Commissioner] mentioned it unofficially on 5th November 1923, and again several days later, when it was officially and publicly suggested."

See also Yehoshua Porath, *Ma'avak ha-'Aravim ha-Falastinim, 1918–1939: Kovetz Te'udot* [The Palestinian-Arab struggle, 1918–1939: Collected documents] (Jerusalem: The Hebrew University of Jerusalem, 1981), 96–98. The text of the "Response of the Arab Executive Committee to the Proposal of the High Commissioner regarding the Establishment of an Arab Agency along the Lines of the Jewish Agency in Palestine" is taken from the version published in the Jaffa newspaper *Filastin* on November 20, 1923.

9. On the mufti's ties with Nazi Germany, see Yig'al Carmon, "Mufti Yerushalayim, Haj Amin al-Husayni, ve-Germania ha-Nazit be-Tkufat Milhemet ha-'Olam ha-Shniyya" [The Mufti of Jerusalem, Haj Amin al-Husayni, and Nazi Germany during World War II] (MA thesis, Hebrew University of Jerusalem, 1988); Zvi Elpeleg, *Ha-Mufti ha-Gadol* [The Grand Mufti] (Tel Aviv: Ministry of Defense, 1989); Lukas Hirschowitz, *Ha-Reich ha-Shlishi ve-ha-Mizrah ha-'Aravi* [The Third Reich and the Arab East] (Merhavia: Sifriat Poalim, 1965); Daniel Carpi, "Ha-Mufti shel Yerushalayim, Amin al-Husayni ve-Pe'iluto ha-Medinit be-Yemei Milhemet ha-Olam ha-Shniyya" [The Mufti of Jerusalem, Amin al-Husayni, and his political activities during World War II], *Hasiyyonut* 9 (1984); David Yisraeli, *Ha-Reich ha-Germani ve-Eretz Yisra'el, Be'ayot Eretz Yisra'el ba-Mediniyut ha-Germanit ba-Shanim, 1889–1945* [The German Reich and Palestine: The problems of Palestine in German Policy, 1889–1945] (Ramat Gan: Bar-Ilan University, 1974). On the mufti's own views of his ties with the Nazis, see "The Mufti's Memoirs," *'Akhir Sa'a*, September 20, 1972, September 27, 1972, November 8, 1972, November 29, 1972, and December 11, 1972. Another explanation for the mufti's cooperation with the Nazis is offered in an interview with Khayriyya Qasimiyya, in 'Ammad Shakur and Khayriyya Qasimiyya, "Muqabalatan ma'a al-Haj Amin al-Husayni," *Shu'un Filastiniyya* 26 (August 1974): 12–18; see also the entry "Muhammad Amin al-Husayni," in *Al-Mawsu'a al-Filastiniyya* 1 (Damascus: al-Hay'a al-Mawsu'a al-Filastiniyya, 1984), 141.

10. See Asher Goren, *Ha-Liga ha-'Aravit* [The Arab League] (Tel Aviv: Ma'yanot, 1954), 377–82.
11. Bayan al-Hut, *Al-Qiyadat*, 85.
12. On the establishment of the Muslim-Christian Associations, see Porath, *The Emergence*, 32–33; Bayan al-Hut, *Al-Qiyadat*, 80–84.

13. Bayan al-Hut, *Al-Qiyadat*, 95, citing Akram Zu'aytir, Private Papers preserved in the Institution for Palestinian Studies, 1st collection, doc. 15 (hereinafter "Zu'aytir, Private Papers"); 'Izzat Darwaza, *Mudhakirat* 1 (Beirut: Dar al-Gharb al Islami, 1993), 329; Porath, *The Emergence*, 23-25, 79-85.

14. See Bayan al-Hut, *Al-Qiyadat*, 123-24, citing Ahmad al-Imam; Muhammad Muslih, *The Origins of Palestinian Nationalism* (New York: Columbia University Press, 1988), 204-5; Darwaza, *Mudhakirat*, 497-98. Muslih supports Bayan's claim that the second congress never took place. He cites Bayan and Ahmad al-Imam regarding the background and reason for its convening. In Muslih's words, "Some historians therefore erred when they wrote that the third congress had been designated as such because it followed the General Syrian Congress and what they called the Second Palestinian Arab Congress, which was held in Damascus at the end of February 1920," *The Origins*, 204-5.

15. For details on the third congress, see Bayan al-Hut, *Al-Qiyadat*, 138-42; Muslih, *The Origins*, 9, 204-10; Porath, *The Emergence*, 108-10; Porath, *Documents*, 3-15; Zu'aytir, Private Papers, doc. 61, pp. 3-15; Darwaza, *Mudhakirat*, 497-98; see also the protocol of all the sessions of the congress in Arabic, in Porath, *Documents*, 15-32; see also 'Awni 'Abd al-Hadi, *Awraq Khassa*, ed. Khayriyya Qasimiyya (Beirut: PLO Markaz al-Abhath, 1974), 57-58.

16. For the protocol in Arabic of the fourth congress, see Porath, *Documents*, 37-48; Porath, *The Emergence*, 110; Bayan al-Hut, *Al-Qiyadat*, 209, 852-53; Zu'aytir, Private Papers; Darwaza, *Mudhakirat*, 512-14.

17. Porath, *The Emergence*, 110-11; Porath, *Documents*, 78-82; 'Abd al-Hadi, *Awraq Khassa*, 59-60; Darwaza, *Mudhakirat*, 558-660; Bayan al-Hut, *Al-Qiyadat*, 163.

18. Bayan al-Hut, *Al-Qiyadat*, 143-45.

19. Ibid., 175-77; on the election of the mufti to both positions, see Porath, *The Emergence*, 184-207.

20. Bayan al-Hut, *Al-Qiyadat*, 175-79.

21. On the rise of the Nashashibi opposition, see Porath, *The Emergence*, 213-30.

22. Porath, *The Emergence*, 253-54; Porath, *Documents*, 107-13; Bayan al-Hut, *Al-Qiyadat*, 195-96.

23. Bayan al-Hut, *Al-Qiyadat*, 335-37, citing Husayn Fakhri al-Khalidi, *Mudhakirat Khasa* (Beirut, 1949), 222 (in special library in Beirut); see also Darwaza, *Hawla al-Haraka*, 118.

24. Bayan al-Hut, *Al-Qiyadat*, 336.

25. Porath, *From Riots to Rebellion*, 176-77; see also Porath, *Documents*, 244-45.

26. Bayan al-Hut, *Al-Qiyadat*, 373, citing 'Abd al-Hadi, *Awraq Khassa*, letter from 'Adil Arsalan to 'Awni 'Abd al-Hadi, October 7, 1937, PLO Research Center; see also Darwaza, *Hawla al-Haraka*, 3:183; Porath, *From Riots to Rebellion*, 235.

27. On the story of the mufti's escape, see his memoir, Amin al-Husayni, *Haqa'iq 'An Qadiyat Filastin* (Cairo: Maktab al-Hay'a al-'Arabiyya al-'Ulya li-Filastin, 1954); Porath, *From Riots to Rebellion*, 236.

28. See Porath, *Documents*, 391-92; Porath, *From Riots to Rebellion*, 281-84; Bayan al-Hut, *Al-Qiyadat*, 388-90.

29. Bayan al-Hut, *Al-Qiyadat*, 390, 398; 'Abd al-Hadi, *Awraq Khassa*, 111.

30. Bayan al-Hut, *Al-Qiyadat*, 396.

31. 'Abd al-Hadi, *Awraq Khassa*.

32. Ibid., letter to 'Ali Mahir, November 4, 1937.

33. Bayan al-Hut, *Al-Qiyadat*, 397, citing 'Izzat Tanus, *Awraq Khassa* (in a special library).

34. Bayan al-Hut, *Al-Qiyadat*, 397.

35. Porath, *From Riots to Rebellion*, 292–93; see also Ahmad al-Shuqayri, *Arba'un 'Amman fi al-Hayat al—'Arabiyya wa al-Duwaliyya* (Beirut: Dar Al-Nahar, 1969), 190.
36. Porath, *From Riots to Rebellion*, 302–3.
37. Nevo, "The political development," 437–40.
38. Bayan al-Hut, *Al-Qiyadat*, 447.
39. Nevo, "The Arab-Palestinian national movement," 106.
40. Bayan al-Hut, *Al-Qiyadat*, 470–77; Nevo, "The Arab-Palestinian national movement," 105–6; Khalidi, *Mudhakirat*, 417–20.

2 Return of the Mufti and Increased Arab Involvement in the Filastin Issue

The Question of Filastin and the Palestinian Leadership Crisis
in Arab League Debates before the Return of the Mufti

From the moment the Arab League was established and through the 1948 Arab-Israeli War, and indeed after the war as well, it engaged intensively in the question of Filastin in addition to the issue of Arab unity. In fact, through its various institutions—the League Council or its political committee—the Arab League replaced the Palestinian leadership in determining how to address fateful questions related to the Palestinians and the Filastin problem. It did so because of the weakness of and divisions within the Palestinian leadership, among other reasons, particularly the absence of an agreed-upon leadership. The Arab League's representation of Palestinian interests was also an outcome of the weak standing of the mufti and the hostility that had formed against him among Arab leaders, to the point that all his demands were rejected, including the demand to establish a Palestinian government under his leadership within the territory of Mandatory Palestine.

Because it was not considered a state, Filastin did not receive an official invitation to participate in the preparatory talks for the establishment of the Arab League, which took place from September 25 to October 7, 1944, in Alexandria, Egypt. Egypt's Prime Minister Nahas Pasha, who oversaw the preparatory talks, issued an informal invitation, however, notifying the Egyptian consul in Jerusalem, Mahmud Fawzi, that he would like to have the Palestinian parties send a delegation to participate in the talks. The invitation prompted discussions on the question of Palestinian leadership and attempts to establish a new leadership, but given the differences of opinion that emerged among the parties, forming a delegation was not a simple matter. The Husayni Arab Party demanded that it have a majority of representatives in the delegation and that the party leaders under arrest in Rhodesia be released. Under pressure from Egypt and Iraq, and given that the Filastin issue was to be a focus of the talks, the Palestinian parties eventually accepted a compromise: it was decided to send a single representative who did not belong to any political party. This individual would not be authorized to participate in the voting on resolutions and would only be authorized to make a speech about the Palestinian problem. The elected representative was

Musa al-'Alami.¹ The Palestinan parties agreed that 'Alami would participate in meeting sessions as a representative of the Arabs of Filastin, not as a representative of Filastin or the government of Filastin, and his remarks would address only the question of Filastin. Musa al-'Alami made a speech at the preparatory committee on October 5, 1944, two days before its sessions came to a close. He presented an extensive survey of the development of the Filastin problem, with emphasis on the dire circumstances of Filastin's Arabs.²

The conference concluded with the production of the Alexandria Protocol regarding establishment of the Arab League. Article 5 of the protocol included a Resolution on Filastin, which held among other things that "Filastin constitutes one of the important pillars of Arab states" and expressed sorrow over the tragedies and suffering inflicted on European Jews, while asserting that "there is no injustice or injury more severe than the resolution of their problem through the infliction of another injustice upon the Arabs of Filastin."³

Between affirmation of the Alexandria Protocol on October 7, 1944, and affirmation of the text of the Arab League Charter on March 22, 1945, the subcommittee that was mandated to formulate the text of the charter discussed the nature of participation and status that would apply to the Palestinian delegate in meetings of the league. Differences of opinion emerged among Arab state representatives regarding 'Alami's role in the sub-committee. Eventually a formulation was agreed on for the text that would be incorporated into the Arab League Charter under the heading "Special Annex on Filastin," assigning the authority to decide this matter to the council. According to this formulation, "Noting the special circumstances of Filastin, and until it enjoys independence in practice, the League Council will elect the representative of Filastin Arabs, who will participate in its work."⁴

During the first meeting of the League Council's second session, on October 31, 1945, the secretary general reported on the mission to Filastin undertaken by Taqi al-Din al-Sulh, a member of the Lebanese delegation in Cairo, in order to ascertain the various positions of Palestinian leaders. In late July 1945, Sulh arrived in Filastin, where he "met with all the leaders . . . as well as government officials, and clandestinely visited a number of villages and met with observers and opinion-makers. He returned with extensive reports about everyone's opinions, including those who wanted to remain anonymous. After discussing these reports, the committee decided on its plan."⁵ Tawfiq al-Suwaydi, who headed the committee on economic matters, visited Filastin with the same objective—the plan for saving lands in Filastin—on his way back from London in August 1945. He made an attempt at reconciliation among the leaders, but was not successful in this regard.

The second session of the Arab League Council took place in Cairo from October 31 to December 14, 1945, under the leadership of Jamil Mardam, the

Syrian delegate in Cairo. The focus of talks during this rather lengthy session was on various issues related to the Filastin problem. The talks addressed the need for Palestinian participation for the sake of consultation on relevant issues, and on November 8, the council decided to establish an eight-member subcommittee to formulate policy recommendations regarding Filastin. Simultaneously, the council decided "to assign responsibility to Jamil Mardam and his associates in the council to establish contact with the heads of Palestinian political parties and groups in order to agree on a course of action for the coordination of propaganda on behalf of Filastin." The council decided that Mardam's mission would also include "aligning the positions of the Palestinian political parties to the extent possible."[6]

On November 15, 1945, Jamil Mardam traveled to Jerusalem accompanied by Taqi al-Din al-Sulh and Khayr al-Din al-Zirikli, the Saudi Arabian delegate to the Arab League. The Palestinian Arab Party continued to insist on its right to majority representation within any Palestinian leadership entity established. The ensuing deadlock resulted in the three delegates reaching a compromise on returning to the old formulation of the Arab Higher Committee (AHC). The heads of the six Palestinian political parties and other leaders authorized Mardam in writing "to appoint 12 members who will comprise the Arab Higher Committee, with a view to having a united front." The written authorization was signed by Tawfiq Salih al-Husayni, Husayn Fakhri al-Khalidi, Ya'qub al-Ghusayn, Sulayman Tuqan, 'Awni 'Abd al-Hadi, 'Abd al-Latif Salah, and Ahmad Hilmi 'Abd al-Baqi. The day after the meeting with Mardam "everyone agreed on the revival of the Arab High Committee that had existed in 1937 and had been disbanded in light of well-known developments." In his report on this matter to the League Council at its November 24 meeting, Mardam stated, "During our meeting a number of participants suggested that the council itself elect its Filastin delegate." This recommendation undoubtedly resulted from differences of opinion on this issue and the Husaynis' position.[7]

Following Mardam's survey, the council held a meeting on December 4 at which it resolved the following:

- Filastin would be represented by one or more delegates on the condition that the delegation comprise no more than three members. The delegation will participate in all council deliberations, as noted in the Filastin Annex of the league's charter.
- The process by which representatives are to be elected is as follows: The AHC will nominate candidates, and the council will then appoint them.

The council's December 12 meeting opened with the chairman's announcement that the AHC had, in accordance with the council's request, proposed that the

Filastin delegation to the council include Musa al-'Alami, Ya'qub al-Ghusayn, and Amil al-Ghuri. The council affirmed their membership, and they were immediately invited to participate in its deliberations.[8]

The political party affiliations of the twelve AHC members as determined by Mardam were identical to the those of the previous AHC members: the six heads of the parties represented in the previous AHC—Tawfiq Salih al-Husayni (filling in for his brother Jamal, who was in exile in Rhodesia, as chairman of the Arab Party), Raghib al-Nashashibi, 'Awni 'Abd al-Hadi, Husayn al-Khalidi, 'Abd al-Latif Salah, and Ya'qub al-Ghusayn—were joined by Kamal al-Dajani, Ahmad Hilmi 'Abd al-Baqi, Rafiq al-Tamimi, Musa al-'Alami, Amil al-Ghuri, and Yusif Sahyun (three of whom were regarded as Arab Party appointees). The new AHC, which was identical to its predecessor not only in terms of political party composition but also in terms of its name—al-Lajna al-'Arabiyya al-'Ulya—decided during its very first meeting to send a delegation to Cairo for the continuation of the league's second session. 'Izzat Darwaza, who was staying in Damascus at the time, wrote about the formation of the new AHC: "The situation [before the formation of the new AHC] was undoubtedly woeful. The empty void resulting from the lack of such a committee was very bad for the reputation and cause of Filastin. All we expect is that there will be coordination and cooperation among the parties to the committee and that all fighting and scheming, whatever its cause, come to an end."[9]

The agreement to retain the previous political composition resulted more from external Arab pressure than from self-convictions of the Palestinian leaders. By establishing the AHC, the Arab League was replacing the local Palestinian leadership. This move reflected the deteriorating situation of Palestinian leadership and its inability to reach an agreement on fundamental issues as well as the increasing Arab involvement in developments related to leadership of the Palestinian movement and the Filastin issue.

In late 1945, the Palestinian detainees in Rhodesia were released. On his return to Palestine in February 1946, Jamal al-Husayni declared that he would "change the negative political thinking that has shaped how matters have been handled in the country since the occupation." It emerged later that Husayni's assertion was "based on recognition of the Arab Party becoming the nearly exclusive leadership; otherwise . . . there is no solidarity."[10] He was appointed chairman of the AHC and became the dominant figure therein. Under his leadership, however, no change occurred in the policy of the Arab Party—a policy characterized by "stubbornness and arrogance, with no regard for the importance of other parties."[11]

During the final week of March 1946, Jamal al-Husayni took a number of measures that were intended, in his words, "to strengthen and coordinate" the AHC but, in fact, aimed to reinforce the status of the Husaynis and the standing of the Arab Party within this body. In this context, he proposed the inclusion of additional representatives to the AHC: one from each of the five other political parties, two from the Arab Party, and another ten. He also summoned the twelve members of the current AHC and the seventeen new members, all of whom supported him. Only sixteen—all supporters of Husayni—attended the meeting. Representatives of the other political parties boycotted the gathering. The attendees elected Jamal al-Husayni chairman of the committee and acting *ra'is* (president)—a title reserved for the mufti. The newly formed committee also elected Jamal al-Husayni, 'Izzat Tannus, and Ahmad al-Shuqayri to represent Filastin in the Arab League Council. In addressing Jamal al-Husayni's reorganization of the AHC, 'Izzat Darwaza described it as a hasty move and asserted that Husayni was obligated to consult with the political party heads and receive their agreement. According to 'Awni 'Abd al-Hadi, "Despite the severity of the situation with respect to the Filastin problem, division increased among the Palestinian political parties and the new AHC did not succeed in bringing about the desired coordination."[12]

The issue of Palestinian representation in the Arab League, the standing and composition of the AHC, and internal Palestinian disputes became subjects of deliberations once again during the third session of the Arab League Council in Cairo from March 25 to April 13, 1946. Changes made by Jamal al-Husayni to the composition of the AHC and the disputes within the Palestinian leadership did not escape the attention of the council members. The issue of Palestinian representation arose when the league addressed the question of "saving Arab lands in Filastin" without the presence of any Palestinian representative. During the opening assembly the league's secretary general, 'Azzam, announced that the AHC chairman had informed him in a cable that the AHC "elected Jamal al-Husayni, Ahmad al-Shuqayri, and Dr. Tannus as the Filastin delegates to the League Council," noting that "the AHC has no right to appoint members to represent Filastin in the league. The league's charter holds that only the league has the authority to appoint the Filastin delegate. We were lenient in the past and granted the AHC the authority to nominate candidates, with the council appointing the AHC's candidates." The secretary general added, "Between the conclusion of the previous session and opening of the current session, differences of opinion emerged among members of the committee [AHC]. A new committee with new members was formed. I understand that this new committee is composed of 23 or more members. Undoubtedly, the committee to which we now turn for candidates to represent Filastin must be recognized by us and we must feel that the people of Filastin are satisfied with it."[13]

At the same time, the heads of the five other political parties refused to cooperate with the AHC formed by Jamal al-Husayni and dominated by the Arab Party, and, eventually, in March 1946, issued a statement criticizing him and asserting that they did not recognize the new committee or the delegation to the League Council.¹⁴ In late May 1946, before the council convened in Bloudan, Syria, to discuss the Filastin problem, the heads of these five political parties organized a political conference in Jerusalem with the participation of party representatives from various regions of Filastin. Additional participants included leftist labor representatives, neutrals, and educated young people. Among the leaders who participated were Husayn al-Khalidi, 'Awni 'Abd al-Hadi, Sulayman Tuqan, Ya'qub al-Ghusayn, Ahmad Hilmi 'Abd al-Baqi, and Kamal Hanun. The conference participants decided to establish the Arab Higher Front (al-Jabha al-'Arabiyya al-'Ulya), to be composed of heads of the five political parties and other figureheads, such as Sulayman Tuqan from the Defense Party and Ahmad Hilmi 'Abd al-Baqi. The front's executive committee immediately sent notification to the secretariat of the Arab League objecting to any resolutions that were to be passed in Bloudan unless the front were represented during league meetings and participated in its discussions on Filastin. Simultaneously, in light of the front's activities, Jamal al-Husayni called on a group of his supporters, in the name of the AHC, to expand his formal base of support and reinforce his status.¹⁵

Consequently, the Arab League Council, which convened for its fourth session in Bloudan from June 8 to 12, 1946, witnessed the division of the Palestinian leadership into two camps: the Arab Higher Front, which represented five political parties, and the AHC, now fully representing the Husayni camp. Jamal al-Husayni participated in the opening session meeting as the undisputed Filastin delegate. This session of the league was devoted completely to the Filastin problem. During the session's first meeting (on June 8), the ALC affirmed Jamil Mardam's recommendation for the establishment of two subcommittees: one for foreign affairs, to discuss measures to be taken in the international arena; and the second for internal affairs, to discuss the actual assistance that Arab states would provide to Filastin Arabs. For our purposes, the internal affairs subcommittee is of particular importance. This body included representatives of all Arab states as well as Jamal al-Husayni, with Sa'ib Salam of Lebanon elected secretary. A report presented by the subcommittee to the League Council on June 10, 1946, found that two essential matters needed to be addressed in practical and decisive terms in order to assist the Palestinian cause in a meaningful way:

- The establishment of an Arab Higher Hay'a ("Authority"), to be affirmed by the Arab League: the subcommittee recommended inviting some of the Palestinian leaders who had been absent from the gathering to come to Bloudan and consult on ways of achieving Palestinian unity and enabling the establishment of the new hay'a.
- Securing the funding needed to address the Palestinian problem.

The subcommittee's position was that "the issue should be referred back to the League Council in order to establish the Palestinian hay'a ... because it is not possible to make progress in carrying out the measures on behalf of Filastin unless the hay'a is established and [the league] gives final approval for its establishment." Likewise, the subcommittee recommended that "the League Council appoint a special permanent committee, to be composed of three or five members from among Arab state representatives, whose seat will be in Cairo, at the [league's general] secretariat, and to be called 'the Filastin Committee,' which will oversee all the problems of Filastin in the name of the League Council."[16]

Its role would also be to approve financial plans, to determine funding allocation processes, and to oversee them.

At the sixth gathering of the Arab League's special session in Bloudan, on June 12, Sa'ib Salam reported on a meeting he had held on the previous day with Palestinian leaders: "We met until late yesterday with the leaders of Filastin, each one of whom presented his position very openly. Sadly, we did not achieve any result during this lengthy meeting. Today we will continue the talks." Ramadan Pasha, who had also participated in the talks, added his impressions: "I am convinced that the leaders of Filastin agree on the principles and the goals, but there are personal disputes among them, making their reconciliation nearly impossible. [The personal disputes revolve around] who will be a member of the hay'a and who will be the chairman. I therefore propose casting lots to decide who to appoint." The council resumed deliberations on the internal affairs report on the evening of June 12. At the outset of these deliberations, Sa'ib Salam surprised the council with the following "good news":

1. The committee recommends that the League Council authorize the following [four] figureheads to serve as "al-Hay'a al-Filastiniyya al-'Arabiyya al-'Ulya," which [it recommends] the Arab League decide to establish in Filastin: Jamal al-Husayni, Ahmad Hilmi 'Abd al-Baqi, Dr. Husayn al-Khalidi, and Amil al-Ghuri.
2. The committee is convinced that for organizational purposes, Jamal al-Husayni should serve as deputy chairman of the hay'a and Dr. Khalidi should serve as secretary [of the hay'a].
3. The committee is convinced that the Arab League should recommend the dissolution of the current AHC.

Jamal al-Husayni welcomed the recommendation that the Palestinian representative body operate under the auspices of the league. He even added, "What will guarantee the realization of the Council's wish for unity of positions and a fruitful outcome thereof is, in my opinion that the Council now pass a resolution, *which the League will impose on us*, thereby enabling us to persuade the organizations in Filastin to abide by it." Regarding the name of the new body about to be established, he noted, "I advise retaining the name 'al-Lajna al-'Arabiyya al-'Ulya' (AHC) because the government recognizes this name." This recommendation was not adopted. The impression that emerged in the council was one of deep division and dispute within the Palestinian leadership, between the Husaynis and the heads of the Arab Higher Front. Council members were furious about the split and divisiveness among Palestinians, whose arguments and mutual accusations even carried over into the corridors of the council building. Despite the impression of differences of opinion among Palestinian representatives, or perhaps because of it, Salam's announcement regarding agreement on the establishment of the hay'a earned the support of all the Arab delegations, "even though the plan was vague regarding the hay'a's mode of operation."[17] Ultimately, the hay'a was composed of four members—two from the AHC and two from the Arab Higher Front. Ahmad Hilmi 'Abd al-Baqi and Husayn al-Khalidi were from the front, and Jamal al-Husayni and Amil al-Ghuri from the AHC. It was agreed that the chairman's position would remain vacant until the mufti returned from Europe.

Following these appointments and the League Council's recommendation, members of the front and members of the AHC met in Jerusalem and declared their acceptance of the establishment of the Arab Higher Hay'a. Likewise, they announced the dissolution of the AHC and the Arab Higher Front as well as cessation of their activities. The leaders of the political parties, with the exception of the Arab Party leadership (the Husaynis), decided to disband their parties.[18]

The helplessness of the Palestinian leadership and its inability to reach an agreement about representation for the Palestinian cause were more evident at the League Council session in Bloudan than at any previous Arab forum. The result was a request—if not plea—for Arab intervention in the search for an acceptable solution. The situation became so tense that Jamal al-Husayni asked the council to impose a solution on all the Palestinian factions. In the end, the parties affiliated with the Arab Higher Front abided by the League Council's resolution and disbanded, while the Arab Party to which Husayni belonged continued to exist and even continued, on its own and under the mufti's leadership, to lead the Palestinian national movement. The Husaynis' leadership role was further buttressed by the municipal elections of January–February 1946, from which their candidates emerged victorious in Nablus, formerly a stronghold of the Defense Party (the Nashashibis).

The Return of the Mufti, June 1946: The Decline of His Status and the Rejection of His Demands by the Arab League

The mufti returned from France to the region (Egypt) on June 19, 1946, and resumed his political activities in July 1946 with Cairo as his base. At the same time, he began organizing the internal institutions of the Arab Higher Hay'a, assuming the role of chairman on his return and thus once again becoming the official leader of the Palestinians in practice.

The problem of Palestinian representation in the Arab League did not surface again as a topic of discussion: the Arab Higher Hay'a (or, more accurately, the mufti) continued to represent the Palestinians in the league, but without effectively influencing its resolutions on the Filastin issue. Simultaneously, a dramatic shift in the mufti's status as leader occurred within the Arab arena: whereas it had been difficult to bypass, ignore, or confront him in the Arab arena before September 1937, it was now possible to ignore him, clash with him, bypass him, and even reject his demands. Undoubtedly, his support for Nazi Germany and his stay in Berlin during the war contributed to this situation. Direct and open clashes took place, in particular, between the mufti and the governments of Jordan and Iraq. One may conclude that after returning to the region from Germany, the mufti was the wrong person to lead the Palestinian cause.

Despite the decline in the mufti's status within the Arab arena, the internal disagreement over the composition of the Palestinian leadership was actually resolved in a way that favored recognition of the Husaynis' dominance. The mufti's problematic standing in the Arab and international arenas galvanized the Husayni leadership to act to prevent any effort to undermine the mufti's dominance as leader of the Palestinian national movement, generally, and of the Arab Higher Hay'a that replaced the AHC, specifically. To this end, the Husayni leadership became more aggressive and, indeed, violent toward opposition members and did not even shy away from acts of domestic terror.

In light of the deteriorating condition of the Palestinian leadership and the increasing involvement of Arab states in the Filastin question, the mufti decided to try to turn the clock back at all costs, to regain the standing he had enjoyed when he fled the country. He did not acknowledge the changes that had taken place in the Arab and Palestinian arenas since his departure. Seeking to reinforce his status as leader of the Palestinians, and specifically to reclaim his position as guardian of the Filastin issue, he took two broad courses of action. First, he added five new members to the Arab Higher Hay'a, including Mu'in al-Madi (who resigned in 1947) and 'Izzat Darwaza (who also resigned in mid-1947). Second, he took measures to establish national representative ruling institutions that he hoped would provide maneuverability for him and perhaps even independence of action in the Palestinian arena. Specifically, he strove to establish a civil administration or provisional government for the territories under British or Arab rule, and the key measure he took toward this end was establishment of the All-Palestine Government. In the military realm, he strove for command over the Palestinian units and, beyond that, an active role in the overall Arab military command; these measures were not successful.

The Arab League Council's Political Committee Meeting in Sawfar, September 16–19, 1947

Following the publication of a report by the United Nations Special Committee on Palestine (UNSCOP), the Arab League Council's Political Committee convened in the village of Sawfar in Lebanon.[19] The Palestinian participants to these talks were members of the Arab Higher Hay'a after its expansion by the mufti: Mu'in al-Madi, 'Izzat Darwaza, and Amil al-Ghuri. The committee's secret resolution addressed the establishment of a permanent technical committee composed of representatives of league members as well as representatives of Filastin, with its seat in Cairo. Its function would be to supervise the allocation of funds raised by Arab states and to organize assistance for the defense of Filastin.[20]

The Arab League Session in 'Aley, October 1947

The Arab League's session in 'Aley, moderated by Riyad al-Sulh of Lebanon, took place October 7–9, 1947. The main agenda item of the session was the question of Filastin's future and Arab follow-up measures relating to the Sawfar conference resolutions. It is significant that despite inclusion of this agenda item, the mufti was not invited to the gathering, although the Filastin delegate, Mu'in al-Madi, did attend the debates.[21]

The mufti surprised the conference attendees by showing up uninvited, knowing that his status had eroded in the eyes of Arab states since his return to Cairo. The Iraqi delegate Salih Jaber headed the opposition to the mufti. He requested that Riyad al-Sulh, as chairman of the session, prevent the mufti's participation, but Sulh refused on the grounds that the mufti was a guest of the government.[22] Thus the mufti succeeded in addressing the conference attendees and presenting his plan for the establishment of an Arab government in Filastin under his leadership. The Iraqi and Jordanian delegates firmly opposed his proposal. Iraq emerged as the strongest opponent of the mufti and as a full supporter of King 'Abdulla in all matters relating to the fate of the Palestinian cause, in particular his struggle against the mufti.

Salih Jaber claimed that "Iraq cannot cooperate with the mufti in any way whatsoever because it is convinced that he seriously failed the Palestinian cause and led it from one failure to another. He was personally responsible for this disaster. Thus my opposition to the establishment of this government was accepted, as was the decision to postpone discussion of the matter until after Filastin is redeemed and its owners are given the opportunity to decide their fate." Regarding the mufti's proposal, Jaber reported, "His objective in showing up and holding talks [with members of the Arab delegations to the conference] was to promote the establishment of a government in Filastin under his leadership. I objected to the idea and fought against it because it is provocative toward international opinion at the UN and other nations that have resisted his activities and leadership with all their might."[23] The fierce Iraqi-Jordanian opposition and negative attitude toward the mufti himself resulted in the rejection of his proposal.[24]

The mufti's failed efforts at the 'Aley conference reflected his new status among Arab states. The deterioration of his status was further evident in late 1947, after the UN passed its resolution on the partition of Palestine into Jewish and Arab states, with the commencement of Arab preparations to recruit Palestinian and Arab volunteers to assist the Arab population in Filastin. The mufti was interested in launching an uprising as an extension of the violent riots that had already broken out in the country. Most Arab governments as well as the league's secretary general favored preventing the mufti from seizing command over the irregular forces. Their position that was further supported by delegations of dignitaries who opposed the mufti and conducted demarches in Arab capitals during October and November 1947, in an effort to persuade the government of Syria and secretary general of the Arab League not to allow him to lead the war in Filastin. Other participants in this process included AHC members from al-Istiqlal Party, 'Izzat Darwaza, Mu'in al-Madi, and Subhi al-Khadra, who were based in Damascus and often leveled harsh criticism against the mufti personally. All these personalities repeatedly emphasized to Arab statesmen that it would be dangerous to grant the mufti authority to lead the war because he was unfit for the role and because such authorization would result in renewed domestic terrorism within the Palestinian camp.[25]

Conference of Heads of Arab Governments—Cairo, December 8-12, 1947

Following adoption of the UN resolution on the partition of Palestine, a special gathering of the heads of Arab governments convened to discuss the consequences of the resolution and the Arab response to it. No Filastin delegate attended this conference. All debates were conducted in secret, and they produced a number of secret resolutions regarding military preparations aimed at preventing implementation of the UN resolution. Toward the end of the session, the league's secretary general, 'Azzam, raised the issue of local administration in Filastin and explained its importance. Jamil Mardam, the Syrian representative, supported him. Egypt's delegate, Mahmud Fahmi al-Nuqrashi, enthusiastically supported the idea and even underscored the need to place the mufti at the head of this administration. He noted that he was aware that Iraq and Jordan disagreed, but he requested that they compromise. The response of Iraq's Salih Jaber, as reported by him, was as follows:

> It is not necessary to establish a civil administration for Filastin when it is in a state of war, and when the military commander is responsible for appointing

local officials such as the mayor and others, as needed. The mufti is unfit for this role, as I explained at the 'Aley conference.... Iraq does not agree to have him appointed to head the administration and strives to prevent such a move.... It is not the role of this congress to discuss this important issue, which belongs only to *ahl* [the people of] Filastin.[26]

Like the gathering in 'Aley, the Cairo conference did not adopt a resolution on a civil administration in Filastin. Rather, it adopted resolutions opposing the mufti's position. Among the secret resolutions adopted that are relevant to our discussion were the following:

- To take action to thwart the partition plan; to prevent the establishment of a Jewish state in Filastin; and to keep Filastin Arab, independent, and united.
- To establish a military technical committee within the secretariat under the supervision of the secretary general. The duties of this committee will include supervising the organization, training and arming volunteers, securing the required weapons and equipment, and ensuring that relations are maintained between the league's secretariat and the volunteers from various Arab countries.
- Liwa' [Major General] Isma'il Safwat [from Iraq] will assume command over the national forces composed of Filastin Arabs and volunteers from other countries for operations related to the defense of Filastin.[27]

As with the 'Aley conference, the resolutions clearly reflected the negative attitude of most Arab states, especially Iraq and Jordan, to the mufti and his demands. The resolutions were, accordingly, another expression of mistrust of the mufti and his leadership. In practical terms, the resolutions denied the mufti any military or financial connection—direct or indirect—to the Arab volunteers in general and the Palestinian volunteers in particular, that is, to all irregular forces intended to fight in Filastin and, above all, to any military command over them. Command over volunteer and Palestinian forces was assigned to an Iraqi officer (Isma'il Safwat) who was at the time the Iraqi deputy chief of staff.

Naturally, these secret resolutions of the Arab League did not please the mufti or his close associates. Yet the mufti was not dissuaded by the rejection of his proposals for a civil administration in Filastin under his leadership or by the shackling of his hands with respect to Palestinian volunteers. Indeed, he continued trying to find a way to reclaim his historical status. Among other things, he "strove to establish facts that would obligate Arab states to act vigorously, through efforts to prevent the lull in action from spreading and working to encourage rioting in the country. Amil al-Ghouri, on returning from a visit with the mufti, conveyed instructions in this regard: more encouragement of those elements that seek to continue the violence." Indeed, encouraged by the positions of several Arab states including Egypt, as well as the Arab League secretary general, the Arab Higher Hay'a (as expanded by the mufti) developed a proposed plan for a civil administration in Filastin that would declare "an independent, democratic Arab state in Filastin" on termination of the British Mandate on May 15, 1948. This plan was formulated at a meeting of the expanded hay'a in Cairo, which began in early January 1948 and lasted for two weeks, in advance of the meeting of the Arab League's Political Committee that was scheduled to convene in February 1948. The hay'a's plan called for the establishment of a National Council and Executive Committee. Most Arab states did not support the hay'a plan, especially after it became known that Britain did not.[28]

The Seventh Session of the League Council, Cairo, February 7–22, 1948

On February 7, 1948, the League Council convened in Cairo for a session that lasted two weeks. The prime minister of Lebanon, Riyad al-Sulh, chaired the session. In reviewing the council's agenda, it was decided to shift discussions of the Filastin question to the Political Committee, which was composed of the heads of delegations. Once again, the mufti was not officially invited to participate in council or political committee debates. Sulh proposed that the council elect a Filastin delegate who would be accompanied by advisers. He also reported that in talks between the league's secretariat and the Arab Higher Hay'a—which the league viewed as representing Filastin in this regard—the hay'a proposed its chairman, the mufti Amin al-Husayni, as the Filastin delegate to the League Council's session. Likewise, the hay'a proposed appointing Jamal al-Husayni, Mu'in al-Madi, Rafiq al-Tamimi, and Amil al-Ghuri as advisers. The League Council approved the hay'a's recommendations and invited its candidates to participate in the session meetings. The mufti also participated in discussions of the Political Committee.[29]

Iraqi foreign minister Hamdi al-Pachachi, head of Iraq's delegation to the session, reported on the resolutions of the Political Committee regarding the Palestinian problem. His report surveyed the political and military aspects of the secret resolutions of the committee. Significantly for our purposes, Pachachi describes the Political Committee's resolutions regarding the mufti's demands as follows:

1. [The mufti proposed] appointing a representative from the Arab Higher Hay'a alongside the General Command, whose role would be to address Filastin's civil and political problems. After debating the matter, the committee rejected this proposal.
2. The mufti demanded transferring to the national committees (that is, the Arab Higher Hay'a) [sic] the administration of Filastin in those areas from

which the British forces and administration have withdrawn. The matter was discussed and it was decided to refer the issue to [the decision of] the high command, which meant that this proposal too was rejected.

3. The mufti demanded that the Political Committee reach a decision about the establishment of a local administration in Filastin, which would have responsibility to act after the British withdrawal on May 15, 1948, or sooner. This was in accordance with the wishes of the Arab Higher Hay'a. He was told that it was necessary first to unite the Palestinians and strengthen the Arab Higher Hay'a by including a number of prominent figureheads [whose views] differed [that is, they would not be from the Husayni camp]. This would ensure that the Hay'a fully represents *ahl Filastin*. It would then be possible to discuss the Hay'a's proposal for the establishment of a local administration in Filastin. In any event, it is premature to discuss this proposal. Discussion of the demand is postponed to the next session.
4. The mufti demanded that the Political Committee lend the Arab Higher Hay'a enough money to enable it to carry out the functions assigned to the local administration as proposed in the previous paragraph. It was decided to view this demand as premature.
5. The mufti demanded that the Political Committee allocate a certain sum of money to the Arab Higher Hay'a for the purpose of payments [reparations] to victims of the events in Filastin—those whose homes had been destroyed or who had lost family members. After a lengthy discussion it was decided to reject this demand, on the grounds that it was the duty of Palestinians to make these payments, drawing on the contributions that they collect from *ahl Filastin*.[30]

To complete the picture of the mufti's lowly status and isolation within the Arab arena, it is worth citing a number of additional secret resolutions that were adopted by the Political Committee during this session of the Arab League Council on February 16, 1948. These included the following measures, among others:

1. The Political Committee will assemble a committee, to be named the "Filastin Committee," which will carry out arrangements on its behalf for the defense of Filastin and oversight over these matters. This committee will operate under the supervision of the Political Committee, within the limits that it determines.
2. The Filastin Committee will be headed by the secretary general or someone on his behalf and members nominated by Arab states as well as the Filastin delegate. All will be appointed by the Political Committee. The committee's mandate will be to undertake all the preparations necessary for the defense of Filastin and to outline the overarching policy for this defense. This committee will be the source of authority for the General Command.
3. [Major General] Liwa' Isma'il Safwat is appointed as commander-in-chief of defense operations for Filastin. The department heads of the General

Command will be appointed by the Filastin Committee on the basis of recommendations of the commander-in-chief. The commander-in-chief has full authority to direct and oversee military operations in Filastin. He has the authority to take any measure he deems necessary for the success of these operations. All forces fighting in Filastin are subordinate to him.
4. Alongside the secretariat a Permanent Military Committee will be established, composed of representatives of [member] states. Its function will be to ensure military cooperation among the Arab states and to carry out the duties assigned to it by the League Council. Isma'il Safwat, a member of the Filastin Committee, was appointed as chairman of this committee.[31]

What emerges clearly from these political and military resolutions is that the mufti was not assigned any type of position that would identify him as the leader of the Palestinians, particularly given that the entire political and military system was geared toward supporting Filastin and the Palestinians. Moreover, all military operations in Filastin were to be overseen by a commander appointed by the Political Committee, and all the Arab forces, including Palestinian volunteer forces, were to be subordinate to him. Thus the mufti was excluded from any position of influence over political measures and military operations in Filastin.

This was a critical period for the Palestinian cause, in the aftermath of the UN partition resolution and in advance of British withdrawal, during which time Arab states were discussing a comprehensive military mobilization. The rejection of all the mufti's proposals and demands at this critical time reflected a new nadir for him within the Arab arena. In fact, he was excluded from any position, political or military, related to Arab measures to address the Palestinian problem. This state of affairs was a major achievement for Iraq and Jordan.

Bayan al-Hut depicts the situation as follows: "The Palestinian problem came under the exclusive purview of the Arab League. The leadership of the chairman of the Arab Higher Hay'a, the great Palestinian leader, was diminished to the point that his authority and responsibility were as limited as those of every other member of the Filastin Committee."[32]

Rejection of the Mufti's Demand to Serve as Commander of the Irregular Military Units

In light of the league's position, the only sphere that remained available to the mufti was that of the irregular Palestinian volunteer units, which is where he now sought to exert his authority. Given his frustration in the aftermath of league resolutions denying him any means of influence, and seeking to remain relevant in the context of the Palestinian struggle, the mufti allowed himself to violate the Arab League resolutions and the instructions of the commander-in-chief of the Arab forces in Filastin, including the orders regarding command over volunteer units. The mufti's conduct served only to fuel the flames among those who were pulling away from him and were unwilling to comply with his political and military demands.

The October 9, 1947, report submitted by Major General Isma'il Safwat to the Arab League secretariat, as a member of the Permanent Military Committee of the League, already addressed the question of the irregular Palestinian forces and command over them. It recommended "the establishment of an Arab General Command as soon as possible, to link all the special command centers. This [body] would have command over all the forces concentrated near Filastin or within Filastin itself, whether regular or irregular." In a report he submitted on November 27, 1947, to the Iraqi chief of staff regarding the military measures that had been taken and needed to be taken, Safwat addressed the question of volunteer units in Filastin and Arab countries. He reiterated the recommendation he had made in October, adding, "the command center that will be mandated to mobilize the Palestinian forces [needs to be] subordinate to the Arab General Command, as would be the other command centers."[33] The mufti's conduct should be understood as stemming from his desire to force his leadership on the military sphere, given that he had been sidelined in the political sphere.

Major General Safwat's negative view of the mufti's conduct is reflected in an especially harsh report that he submitted to the Filastin Committee on March 11, 1948, under the title "On the Involvement of the Mufti of Filastin." At the outset of his report, Safwat states, "Even though the secret resolutions [of the Political Committee] of February 1948 clearly gave full authorization to the commander-in-chief for the guidance supervision of military operations in Filastin and made all the fighting forces subordinate to him and subject to his control, nonetheless associates of the mufti did not recognize the General Command or obey its orders, and they continue carrying out their separate, anarchistic activities, without regard for or adherence to these resolutions."

In a report on "The Mufti's Involvement and Continued Insistence on Establishing an Armed Force under His Command," which Safwat prepared in July 1949, he harshly criticizes the mufti's conduct during the war, including his disregard for orders that he had agreed to follow. Safwat adds, "Following discussion of this issue, the Filastin Committee demanded that the mufti cease these activities and not create any more difficulties in addition to those already facing the General Command and encumbering its principal mission. However, His Honor [the mufti] continued as before—promising but not acting, promising but not implementing. He carried on with his activities, thereby exacerbating the military situation and compounding the difficulties."[34]

The Mufti and the Domestic Arena

Although the mufti's status after returning to Cairo deteriorated in the Arab arena, particularly within the league's institutions where he had no real influence, he maintained the reins of leadership in the domestic Palestinian arena. The Arab Party and Husayni camp retained near-absolute dominance.

One of the factors that influenced domestic Palestinian politics and helped maintain the mufti's status in the domestic Palestinian arena was a decision by political party leaders to disband their parties in accordance with the recommendation of the league's Political Committee and to establish the Arab Higher Hay'a. Their aim was to foster "national unity" and create an umbrella organization of Palestinians that could operate without the differences of opinion and internal dispute prevalent among the Palestinian leadership. Bayan al-Hut reached the conclusion that the decision to disband their parties stemmed from "their being sick and tired of the stubbornness and arrogance of the Arab Party, and ultimately from their failure to regain national unity." She adds, "Possibly they thought that the mufti was more broad-minded than his close associates and supporters, so that when he stood at the head of the Arab Higher Hay'a he would have no choice but to return some measure of respect to these leaders; instead, some months after returning to the region, the mufti announced his decision to add five new members to the hay'a."[35]

The Palestinian leaders who constituted the core of the opposition to the Husaynis could not provide an alternative to the mufti's leadership and status among the Palestinian public or to the standing of his party. The traditional opposition no longer existed, especially after the political parties had disbanded themselves. In fact, its leader, Raghib al-Nashashibi, preferred to isolate and distance himself from the political arena. The new political parties that emerged did not oppose the mufti, and the most salient among them, 'Usbat al-Tahrir al-Watani (the National Liberation Group), even supported the mufti. The new leaders of labor and youth associations also saw the mufti as the one and only leader of the Palestinian national movement.

According to the Egyptian consul in Jerusalem, the Arabs of Filastin began to recoil from the oft-repeated declarations of Arab leaders regarding their decision to help Filastin. Many members of the public in Filastin began to believe that the heads of Arab governments and of political parties in Arab countries were exploiting the Filastin Catastrophe as a political propaganda tool.[36]

The most salient and important characteristic of the Palestinian domestic system after World War II, and especially after the mufti's return, was the absence of a majority of the Palestinian leadership from the main theater of operations—Filastin. This leadership was *mutanaqqila*, that is, mobile, moving from place to place outside of Filastin. Until 1948 Filastin, in fact, lacked local leadership.[37]

This state of affairs is reflected in the testimonies of two leaders, members of the Arab Higher Hay'a, who had been associates of the mufti many years earlier, during his glory days, and had cooperated closely with him: Husayn Fakhri al-Khalidi and 'Izzat Darwaza. In his memoirs Khalidi relates that in the summer of 1947, only three hay'a members staffed its office in Jerusalem—Jamal al-Husayni,

'Abd al-Baqi, and Khalidi himself. Khalidi noted critically that during the year preceding the Nakba, only two hay'a members were in Filastin—'Abd al-Baqi and Khalidi himself—both ministers "without portfolios." In his words, "In fact, the center of gravity of the hay'a was in other offices, outside Jerusalem. The importance of the Jerusalem office steadily declined, until it included one clerk alongside the two authorized members." Indeed, the general consensus did not view Jerusalem as the seat of the hay'a.[38]

Khalidi's testimony is supplemented by that of the Egyptian consul in Jerusalem, Ahmad Farraj Ta'i', in a report submitted to his government on January 21, 1948:

> The Arab Higher Hay'a has become the subject of harsh criticism by the people. Its two members who remained in Jerusalem, Ahmad Hilmi 'Abd al-Baqi and Husayn al-Khalidi, are strongly rebuked by people on a daily basis, at times cursed, and are being asked where the weapons and other hay'a members are, and what they are doing in Cairo or Beirut.... It should be noted that, unfortunately, the hay'a is managing the Filastin struggle terribly, and everything its leaders say to the contrary is not true.... [Even] if there is a reason for the mufti to be absent, the absence from Filastin of most of the hay'a members was a serious mistake.[39]

The leadership—that is, the mufti or the hay'a—conducted its discussions and meetings in Cairo or Damascus. The mufti had not visited Jerusalem since he fled in 1937, and he returned only in March 1967.[40] From the moment he returned to Egypt, took charge of the Arab Higher Hay'a, and seized the reins of leadership, the mufti reassumed the personal style of leadership that had been characteristic of him during his glory days. After returning, he took measures to shape the hay'a in accordance with his wishes, in a way that would grant near-absolute control to the Husaynis while neutralizing the two members who represented the oppositionist front. Toward this end, he appointed five of his supporters and close associates: Rafiq al-Tamimi, Is-haq Darwish, and Shaykh Hasan Abu al-Sa'ud of the Arab Party (Darwish and Sa'ud had been with him in Europe), Mu'in al-Madi, and 'Izzat Darwaza. The latter two had formerly belonged to al-Istiqlal Party but earned his trust because of the close ties they had forged with him by cooperating closely during the revolt, when Darwaza was the mufti's right-hand man. The hay'a's work, however, differed from their cooperative efforts during the revolt, and as such Darwaza and Madi disagreed with the mufti on many issues. They both found it difficult to cooperate with him or to accede to his wishes and eventually resigned from the hay'a, in 1947.[41] On their resignation, the hay'a's composition changed, such that it then comprised the mufti's closest associates from among the leaders of the Arab Party as well as two independents who did not oppose his policy—Husayn Fakhri al-Khalidi, a founder of the Reform Party, and Ahmad Hilmi 'Abd al-Baqi, who was regarded as leaning toward al-Istiqlal Party. As these two parties had disbanded, the two members were considered independents.

Darwaza's memoirs contain very harsh criticism of the mufti and his methods. Summarizing his impressions of the mufti's conduct, Darwaza observes, "I noticed that he maintained his old ways, as during the years of the revolt, including his personal balance of considerations. It seemed to me that the mufti had not changed in terms of his style of conversing or making inquiries. He continued twisting things frequently and giving much weight to his personal considerations. Hesitation and suspicion were still in his nature."[42]

Notes

1. Khalidi, *Mudhakirat*, 423–25, cited in Bayan al-Hut, *Al-Qiyadat*, 536–38, 540.
2. For text of 'Alami's speech, see Bayan al-Hut, *Al-Qiyadat*, 809–15.
3. Goren, *Ha-Liga ha-'Aravit*, 376.
4. Bayan al-Hut, *Al-Qiyadat*, 539–40; for the wording of the article, see Goren, *Ha-Liga ha-'Aravit*, 382; Bayan al-Hut, *Al-Qiyadat*, 816. The Filastin annex of the Arab League Charter—using very cautious language and invoking the Treaty of Lausanne as well as the League of Nations Covenant—asserts Filastin's legal right of independence. This right, according to the annex, is also the basis for the resolution to include Filastin's Arabs in league activities.
5. Jami'at al-Duwal al-'Arabiyya, *Al-Mahadiral al-Khitamiyya li-Jalasat Dawr al-'Ijtima'al-'Adi al-Thani li- Majlis al-Jami'a, 31 October 1945–14 December 1945* (Cairo, 1949), 8.
6. Jami'at al-Duwal al-'Arabiyya, *Al-Amana al-'Ama, Fahras Muqarrarat Majlis al-Duwal al-'Arabiyya min al-Dawra al-'Ula Hatta al-Dawra al-Tasi'a 'Ashara, June 1945–September 1953* (Cairo), sess. 4, November 8, 1945, and sess. 6, November 12, 1945, 3; see also Jami'at al-Duwal al-'Arabiyya, *Al-'Ijtima' al-'Adi al-Thani*.
7. Ibid.
8. Jami'at al-Duwal al-'Arabiyya, *Al-'Ijtima' al-'Adi al-Thani*.
9. Darwaza, *Mudhakirat*, 138–39, letter from 'Izzat Darwaza to 'Awni 'Abd al-Hadi on the significance of the composition of the new committee; see also the assessment of its composition by Nevo in "The Arab-Palestinian National Movement," 110: "The new AHC was composed of five Husaynis, the five heads of the other parties, and Musa 'Alami and Ahmad Hilmi (an economist closely affiliated with al-Istiqlal) as nonpartisan representatives. A coalition of yesterday's rivals quickly took shape within the AHC: The Arab Palestinian Party and al-Istiqlal neutralized the other representatives and made themselves at home within the AHC."
10. Bayan al-Hut, *Al-Qiyadat*, 479.
11. Ibid.
12. 'Abd al-Hadi, *Awraq Khassa*, 141. In a letter he sent from Damascus to 'Awni 'Abd al-Hadi on April 6, 1946, 'Izzat Darwaza examined the causes of internal tension. Darwaza wrote to Jamal al-Husayni while still in Rhodesia, calling for solidarity and elimination of the causes of tension. It came as a surprise to him when Jamal announced the addition of new members to the AHC, all of whom were his associates.

13. Jami'at al-Duwal al-'Arabiyya, *Mazabit Jalasat Dawr al-'Ijtima' al-'Adi al-Thalith li-Majlis al-Jami'a, 25 March 1946–13 April 1946* (Cairo, 1946).

14. Khalidi, *Mudhakirat*, 508–9, cited in Bayan al-Hut, *Al-Qiyadat*, 543.

15. 'Abd al-Hadi, *Awraq Khassa*, 142.

16. For details of the debates of the fourth session, see Jami'at al-Duwal al-'Arabiyya, *Mazabit Dawrat al-'Ijtima' al-Rabi'a Ghayr al-'Adiya, 8 June 1946–12 June 1946* (Cairo, 1946).

17. Ibid. (emphasis added); see also Khalidi, *Mudhakirat*, 509, cited in Bayan al-Hut, *Al-Qiyadat*, 543; 'Abd al-Hadi, *Awraq Khassa*, 142–43. 'Awni wrote a letter from Jerusalem to his friend on June 16, 1946.

18. Darwaza, *Hawla al-Haraka*, 4:54 ; Khalidi, *Mudhakirat*, 513, cited in Bayan al-Hut, *Al-Qiyadat*, 545.

19. The United Nations Special Committee on Palestine (UNSCOP) was mandated by the UN in May 1947 to examine the "question of Palestine," after the British government referred the Mandate for Palestine back to the UN.

20. *Taqrir Lajnat al-Tahqiq al-Niyabiyya fi Qadiyat Filastin*, an official Iraqi publication (Baghdad, 1948); Protocol of the Sawfar Arab League conference, 90–93; see also the secret discussions of this conference, 75–76, and Salih Jaber's report, 18–20.

21. *Taqrir Lajnat al-Tahqiq*, 59–65, 79.

22. Ibid., 67; 'Arif al-'Arif, *Al-Nakba, Nakbat Bayt al-Maqdis wa Al-Firdaws al-Mafqud, 1947–1952*, vol. 1 (Sidon, 1956–1960), 16; Bayan al-Hut, *Al-Qiyadat*, 580.

23. *Taqrir Lajnat al-Tahqiq*, Salih Jaber's report, 67.

24. Ibid., 67–68; 'Arif, *Al-Nakba*, 1:16; Bayan al-Hut, *Al-Qiyadat*, 580.

25. Sela', "The Palestinian Arabs during the 1948 War," 149.

26. *Taqrir Lajnat al-Tahqiq*, Salih Jaber's report, 77–78.

27. Ibid., 69–70; see also *Taqrir Lajnat al-Tahqiq*, Annex 13, 95–96.

28. Israel Foreign Ministry (IFM), *Ba-Mahane ha-'Aravi, Sikum Yedi'ot* [Summary of information], December 28, 1947, January 11, 1948, January 18, 1948; IFM, *Intelligence Report*, January 17, 1948; Shabib, "Muqadamat al-Musadara"; Samih Shabib, *Hukumat 'Umum Filastin Muqadamat wa Nata'ij* (Algiers, 1988), 35–36.

29. Jami'at al-Duwal al-'Arabiyya, *Mazabit Dawr al-'Ijtima' al-'Adi al-Sabi' li-Majlis al-Jami'a, 7 February 1948–22 February 1948* (Cairo, 1946), 142; *Taqrir Lajnat al-Tahqiq*, Annex 14, Hamdi Pachachi's Report, 100–102.

30. *Taqrir Lajnat al-Tahqiq*, Pachachi's Report on the Political Committee of the Arab League Council, 7th sess., February 7, 1948, 101–2. According to Bayan al-Hut, the mufti presented military, political, and material demands, and all were categorically rejected on the grounds that the hay'a did not represent all the Palestinians. This was the publicly stated reason, whereas the real reasons were the ongoing dispute between the mufti and the military committee in Damascus, on the one hand, and the rising star of his rival, King 'Abdulla, on the other. Bayan al-Hut, *Al-Qiyadat*, 583.

31. *Taqrir Lajnat al-Tahqiq*, 146–48; for a list of the military committee members, see Bayan al-Hut, *Al-Qiyadat*, 905.

32. Bayan al-Hut, *Al-Qiyadat*, 584.

33. *Taqrir Lajnat al-Tahqiq*, 127, 132–33, 143.

34. Ibid., 128, 149–50.

35. Bayan al-Hut, *Al-Qiyadat*, 585–86.

36. Ahmad Farraj Ta'i', *Safahat Matwiyya 'An Filastin*, 68, cited in Bayan al-Hut, *Al-Qiyadat*, 591.

37. Bayan al-Hut, *Al-Qiyadat*, 596.
38. Khalidi, *Mudhakirat*, 526–28, 647–48; Bayan al-Hut, *Al-Qiyadat*, 589–90.
39. Farraj, *Safahat*, 96–97; Bayan al-Hut, *Al-Qiyadat*, 592–593, 607.
40. On the visit of the mufti to Jerusalem, see Moshe Shemesh, *The Palestinian Entity 1959–1974: Arab Politics and the PLO*, 2nd ed. (London: Frank Cass, 1996), 52.
41. Darwaza, *Hawla al-Haraka*, 4:158; Khalidi, *Mudhakirat*, 523–24; Bayan al-Hut, *Al-Qiyadat*, 586.
42. Darwaza, *Mudhakirat*, 5:568–84.

3 The All-Palestine Government, September 1948

Historical Failure of Leadership or Default Option?

The Arab League Changes Its Stance: The Resolution Establishing a Civil Administration in Filastin

As the termination of the British Mandate over Palestine drew near, the mufti tried once again to secure an Arab resolution establishing a Palestinian civil administration in the territories expected to be captured by Arab armies or transferred to emergent Arab states. Of course, King 'Abdulla's aspiration to rule over the territories of Filastin under Jordanian military occupation would presage his continued objection to the mufti's proposal.

At a meeting with the Arab League's Political Committee on April 12, 1948, King Faruq of Egypt presented a new proposal regarding the status of Palestinian territories captured by Egypt and Jordan. During the course of the meeting an announcement in his name was , stating that "should Arab armies enter Palestine, I want it clearly understood that this measure should be looked upon as a temporary one, unrelated to any attempt at permanent occupation or fragmentation."[1] Undoubtedly, this stance (or warning) was directed at King 'Abdulla. Indeed, besides rejecting the mufti's proposal regarding establishment of a civil administration, the Arab League's Political Committee adopted a resolution stating that "the arrival of Arab armies in Filastin in order to save it should be seen as a temporary measure that in no way indicates the occupation or division of Filastin. After its liberation is completed, [Filastin] will be transferred to its owners to rule it as they wish."[2] In effect, this resolution meant that a decisive stance would not be adopted regarding the territories of Filastin that remain in Arab hands at the end of the war. The resolution directly addressed only Egypt and Jordan, which had captured Palestinian territories and appointed military governors to administer them. On May 20, 1948, the Jordanian Legion announced the establishment of a civil administration, under the command of military governors, and appointed Ahmad Hilmi 'Abd al-Baqi governor of Jerusalem. However,

'Abd al-Baqi did not step into this role, as he was also appointed to head the All-Palestine Government established in Gaza.

The May 14, 1948, declaration on the establishment of the state of Israel to include part of Filastin put the Arab states in an uncomfortable position, especially when the newly founded state received international recognition while the Palestinians had no real, or even nominal, governing body that could claim to represent Filastin and the Palestinian population. The Arab Higher Hay'a was not perceived as fulfilling this role, particularly given that the person who headed it, Amin al-Husayni, had cooperated with the Nazis. In light of the lack of a Palestinian entity equivalent to the state of Israel, the need to address and fill the void became apparent. Moreover, Arab states, including the Political Committee of the Arab League Council itself, were at the time examining the still-unpublished Bernadotte Plan—a plan that included annexation of the Arab portion of Filastin by Jordan—which they eventually rejected. The lowest common denominator that could be reached through pan-Arab consensus without Jordanian opposition was the establishment of a civil administration in the Palestinian territories under Arab control, without any political or military authority.

Indeed, the official position of the Arab League regarding a civil administration in Filastin underwent a discernable shift at a meeting of the Political Committee on July 8, 1948, the final day of the first truce during the 1948 Arab-Israeli War. The committee decided to establish a "provisional civil administration" in the territories captured by Arab armed forces. According to Darwaza, "The motivation behind this resolution was the demand of the Arab Higher Hay'a to declare the establishment of a Palestinian Arab state following announcement of the mandate's termination and the Arab military invasion, as the Jews had done, as well as the importance that the Arab Palestinian delegation and other Arab delegations in New York ascribed to this need." Darwaza adds that Jordan's objection during the Political Committee's discussions resulted in "amendment of the term [Palestinian Arab state], with the committee deciding to use the term 'civil administration' and, apparently as a consequence [of this], the placement of limitations on this body."[3]

The Political Committee adopted this resolution on July 8, 1948, following discussions that included the participation of Palestinian representatives Ahmad Hilmi 'Abd al-Baqi and Husayn al-Khalidi, who were committee members, as well as Henry Katan and Ahmad al-Shuqayri, who served as advisers. The resolution's main provisions held as follows:

1. A provisional civil administration shall be established in Filastin. At the present time its responsibilities shall not include political affairs.
2. The administration's apparatus shall comprise a chairman and nine members, each one of whom shall be responsible for one of the following civil

ministries: justice, health services, social affairs, transportation, finance, national economic affairs, agricultural affairs, general internal security, and public relations.
3. The authority of the administration's council shall apply to all territories that have been captured by Arab armed forces and those that will be captured, until all of Arab Filastin is included.
4. The Arab League Council and associated Arab governments shall determine the responsibilities of the administration's council and its members as well as the authority of military governors who might be appointed by the ruling Arab armies in various regions.
5. The civil administration's council shall operate in accordance with the resolutions or instructions of the Arab League Council or the Political Committee.[4]

Unsurprisingly, this resolution was adopted without any consultation with the Arab Higher Hay'a, neither the mufti nor his close associates. As a matter of substance, the resolution lacked any operational value, as it denied the civil administration council any authority over political affairs or even other important affairs; in these areas, it had to abide by the guidelines and instructions of the Political Committee. It was clear that Jordan and Iraq would oppose the granting of any ruling power to the civil administration council. Thus, the Political Committee resolutions on this matter remained on paper only.

The Arab Higher Hay'a and the mufti were, of course, dissatisfied with the resolution. For tactical reasons, however, they decided to refrain from expressing any positive or negative views openly. Amil al-Ghuri addresses this point: "[The Hay'a] saw the establishment of such an administration as a blow to its very existence. Some of its members viewed it as an effort to be rid of [the Hay'a] and distance it from the leadership of the Palestinian national movement. Recognition by the Hay'a of the proposed administration and support for its establishment meant self-dissolution."[5] In a letter of September 1948, the mufti expressed—albeit not openly—his objection to the civil administration, arguing that its establishment was "not based on the views of the Arab Higher Hay'a.... We have been and are continuing to work to amend the resolution."[6]

The secretariat of the Arab League published the substance of the resolution on the night between July 9 and 10, 1948. The following day, the League's secretary general announced the composition of the Palestinian civil administration council. According to Jamal al-Husayni, the council was structured as follows: three members of the Arab Party (Jamal al-Husayni, Raja' al-Husayni, and Yusif Sahyun); three members of the other parties ('Awni 'Abd al-Hadi, Husayn Fakhri al-Khalidi, and Sulayman Tuqan); and three neutral members (Michel Abqaryus, 'Ali Hasana, and Amin 'Aql). In his view, its chair Ahmad Hilmi and Hasana had leanings toward the mufti.[7]

Establishment of the All-Palestine Government

The League's Political Committee reconvened from September 6 to 9 to discuss the Palestinian problem in advance of the UN General Assembly review of the report by its representative, Count Folke Bernadotte of Sweden. The salient view that emerged during the discussion tended toward voting in favor of Filastin's territorial integrity, thereby undermining the state of Israel's right to exist as well as its military successes during ten days of fighting. The mufti continued with his efforts to establish an independent Palestinian government and, toward this end, sent Jamal al-Husayni to visit Arab states and secure their support. This time, Egypt, Syria, Lebanon, and the Arab League's secretary general listened to his position, and, ultimately, the Arab states, excluding Jordan, agreed on a proposal for the establishment of a Filastin government.

Even though most Arab governments accepted the logic of establishing a Palestinian government, the league's Political Committee only went so far as to issue a general resolution regarding "the reasonability, legitimacy, and necessity of the concept, a natural right of the people (*ahl*) of Filastin, whose implementation depends on the will and aspiration of the Palestinians. If they actualize it, Arab governments will recognize it and assist it materially and morally."[8] The committee thus left the establishment of a Palestinian government in the hands of the mufti and his close associates. Interestingly, the Political Committee deliberately refrained from passing a resolution supporting the establishment of a Palestinian government, even though it was clear that the mufti was intent on establishing it and would use the resolution toward this end. Presumably, the resolution was formulated in such a way as to avoid confrontation with King 'Abdulla and perhaps even secure his support. It was already made clear during the committee's discussions that the Palestinian government to be declared would encompass all of Filastin and that the mufti would neither head nor serve as a member of the government. This understanding, which was reached with Egypt's consent as well, was intended to prevent objection by 'Abdulla and the Iraqi leadership to the extent possible.

Encouraged by the support of the Arab League, the Arab Higher Hay'a turned to Ahmad Hilmi and demanded that he expedite preparations toward an announcement regarding the establishment of this government.[9] And indeed, on September 23, 1948, the All-Palestine Government was announced.

During this period, several factors relating to Mandatory Palestine spurred Arab leaders, with the exception of King 'Abdulla, to take practical steps toward the establishment of a Palestinian government. Those factors included the forthcoming debate on the Bernadotte report in the UN General Assembly; the need to demonstrate to the General Assembly that a Palestinian Arab government that is capable of ruling (Mandatory) Palestine exists and is comparable to the government of Israel; the need to discuss the territories under Arab occupation and to determine their future; and Egypt's special interest in obstructing King 'Abdulla, who intended to annex the Arab portion of Mandatory Palestine to Jordan by underscoring the territorial unity of Filastin. Egypt and other Arab states feared a political arrangement between 'Abdulla and Israel.[10]

The Arab Higher Hay'a convened September 15, 1948, in Cairo, under the chairmanship of the mufti. All civil administration members were invited.[11] The Hay'a decided, in coordination with the league's Political Committee and secretary general, to actualize the July 1948 resolution of the Political Committee. Subsequently, on September 22, all members of the civil administration who were staying in Egypt met in Gaza and declared themselves to be the "All-Palestine Government" (Hukumat 'Umum Filastin). The emphasis on "All-Palestine" was meant to express rejection of the division of Filastin and preservation of its unity. The government's composition was identical to the composition of the civil administration council as confirmed by the league's Political Committee in July 1948, and Ahmad Hilmi 'Abd al-Baqi became prime minister. Following the declaration, Ahmad Hilmi 'Abd al-Baqi sent a memorandum to Arab governments and the Arab League secretary general, which stated,

> Given that the people of Filastin (*ahl Filastin*) have a natural right to self-determination, and on the basis of resolutions and discussions of the Political Committee, it was decided to declare the whole of Filastin, within the recognized borders prior to termination of the British Mandate (May 15, 1948), as an independent state and to establish therein, on a democratic basis, the All-Palestine Government, which will be responsible to a representative National Council. Until a preparatory committee can be elected in order to approve the constitution of the country, with Jerusalem as its capital, Gaza will be the provisional seat of the government.[12]

In consultation with members of the Political Committee and the Arab League secretary general, and of course the mufti and members of the Arab Higher Hay'a, Ahmad Hilmi 'Abd al-Baqi convened the Palestinian National Council in Gaza on September 30, 1948. The objective of this meeting was to ascribe a general representative character to the council and to grant legitimacy to the entire process of establishing the Palestinian government. Toward this end, 150 people from various sectors were invited to the council gathering: members of the Arab Higher Hay'a; members of government; heads of municipal councils, local and village councils, and trade unions; members of national committees; heads of associations of physicians, pharmacists, lawyers, and engineers; heads of extended families and tribes; members of political delegations that had represented Filastin since 1948; heads of political parties; and representatives of religious community organizations such as the Supreme

Muslim Council, the Orthodox Executive Committee, and the Union of Christian Churches.[13]

The opening session of the Palestinian National Council took place on September 30, 1948, in an atmosphere of festivity. Khalil al-Sakakini, the eldest council member, was elected as acting chairman. Amin al-Husayni was elected as president of the council. A radio announcer for Near East Radio (al-Sharq al-Adna) in Cairo reported that the election of the mufti was received with reservation in Egypt.[14]

After his election, the mufti delivered a speech,[15] following which the government received the council's vote of confidence, with a majority of sixty-four in support and eight opposed. Eleven demanded that the vote of confidence be postponed until after discussion of the constitution. The new government was composed of the following ministers: Ahmad Hilmi 'Abd al-Baqi—prime minister, Jamal al-Husayni—foreign affairs, Husayn al-Khalidi—health, Akram Zu'aytir—education, 'Ali Hasana—justice, 'Awni 'Abd al-Hadi—social affairs, Michel Abqaryus—finance (treasury), Raja' al-Husayni—defense, Yusif Sahyun—propaganda and public relations, Futi Frayj—economic affairs, and Amin 'Aql—agriculture. Anwar Nusayba was elected government secretary. The government platform that was approved included, among other provisions, "a declaration of Filastin within the recognized borders of May 15, 1948, [as] an independent, democratic state with national sovereignty and Jerusalem as its capital . . . [with the] guarantee of religious, civil, and individual freedom for citizens of all religious communities [including] preservation of holy sites and the guarantee of freedom of worship for all religious communities."

The second meeting of the council took place in the afternoon of the following day, Friday, October 1, and was also chaired by the mufti. Seven invitees who had not attended the first meeting arrived this time, resulting in a total of ninety participants. These seven included Akram Zu'aytir, 'Awni 'Abd al-Hadi, and Mu'in al-Madi. During the meeting, the provisional constitution for the All-Palestine Government was approved. The terms of the constitution provided that the Palestinian National Council would convene every six months, as summoned by the chairman; the All-Palestine Government is to be considered a legal apparatus for discharging the duties of all the authorities—judicial, executive, and legislative—throughout Filastin, as they existed before termination of the British Mandate on May 15, 1948; the government and ministers are the executive authority; the legislative authority is manifested in the Palestinian National Council; and the city of Jerusalem is the government capital.[16]

The closing session of the Palestinian National Council took place on October 3, when the conference resolutions were affirmed. These included the October 1, 1948, declaration of independence for Filastin, which states,

> In accordance with the Palestinian Arab people's natural and historical right of freedom and independence, the sacred right for which it has sacrificed its purest blood and most honorable *shahids* who fought against the forces of imperialism and Zionism that rose up to defeat it, we, members of the Palestinian National Council that convened in Gaza on this day, the first of October 1948, declare the independence of the whole of Filastin, which borders on Syria and Lebanon in the north, Syria and Transjordan in the east, the Mediterranean Sea in the west, and Egypt in the south; [we declare] full independence and the establishment of a free, democratic, and sovereign state, all of whose citizens will enjoy their liberties and rights.[17]

It was further decided during the council's closing session that the flag of the Arab revolt would be the flag of the government of Filastin, that Jerusalem would be its capital, and that the Bernadotte Plan and the concept of dividing Filastin were absolutely rejected. (See table 3.1.)

On October 1, 1948, in his capacity as the newly appointed prime minister of the All-Palestine Government, Ahmad Hilmi 'Abd al-Baqi informed the UN secretary general and the governments of Great Britain and the United States of the establishment of his government as the official representative of the Arabs of Filastin. He requested that a delegation of the All-Palestine Government be allowed to participate in the UN General Assembly discussion of Bernadotte's recommendations for a resolution of the Palestinian problem. Strong opposition to this request on the part of Britain and the United States, combined with lack of significant Arab support, resulted in the General Assembly rejecting the request, on the grounds this was a fictitious rather than officially recognized government.[18]

An October 2 telegram circulated by the American acting secretary of state to US diplomatic offices in Arab capitals, London, Paris, and Tel Aviv outlined US policy regarding the "Arab Palestine Government":

> US Govt considers establishment of "Arab Palestine Govt" under present circumstances prejudicial to successful solution of the Palestine problem as well as to best interests Arab States and Arab inhabitants Palestine. "Govt" [sic] apparently being set up without prior consultation wishes Arab Palestinians. Also appears dominated by Mufti, an adventurer, whose reprehensible wartime activities in association with our enemies cannot be forgotten or forgiven by US. Best interests Arab States being prejudiced by published indications that Arab unity disturbed by formation of "Govt." Moreover by claiming speak for all Palestine "Govt" affords ready pretext to Jewish revisionists to make similar claims for right [of] PGI [Provisional Government of Israel] control all Palestine.
>
> If asked re US attitude on future of Arab Palestine you should recall to questioners that US Govt has announced its support of all Bernadotte's conclusions.[19]

Table 3.1. Composition of the Palestinian National Council

Representatives	Present	Regrets	Absent
Arab Hay'a	6	3	–
Government members	8	–	–
City mayors	7	6	3
Heads of local councils	13	5	4
Delegation members	10	6	4
Chambers of commerce	7	5	–
National committees	20	9	2
Tribal and family leaders	16	10	6
Subtotal	87	44	19
Invitations not received			7
TOTAL	87	44	12

Source: *Shabib, Hukumat 'Umum*, 48.

Arab State Positions on the All-Palestine Government

In assessing Egypt's position on the All-Palestine Government, it is necessary to distinguish between its negative view of the mufti personally and of his past, on the one hand, and its positive view regarding establishment of the All-Palestine Government, on the other hand. As noted, Egypt conditioned its support for the government on the mufti having no part in it. Indeed, Egypt made a concerted effort to minimize as much as possible the prominence of the mufti at events marking the establishment of the government and at the gathering of the Palestinian National Council in Gaza. The Egyptians were well aware of the hostile stances of Great Britain and the United States toward the mufti because of his relations with the Nazis during World War II. Prime Minister Nuqrashi was confronted with a dilemma: on the one hand, for the sake of Arab public opinion he was interested in demonstrating Egypt's support for the Palestinian issue and making up for military failures during the war in Mandatory Palestine while, on the other hand, he was concerned that the establishment of a Palestinian government could encourage King 'Abdulla to annex Palestinian territories to his kingdom. Furthermore, Nuqrashi was concerned about the mufti's political activities given his and King Faruq's lack of confidence in the mufti, among other reasons because of the latter's ties with the Muslim Brotherhood, which at the time was declared illegal in Egypt.[20]

After agreeing to and even urging establishment of the All-Palestine Government, Egypt sought to prevent the mufti's arrival in Gaza, or at least to keep it as short as possible, primarily in order to reduce the significance of this development in the eyes of King 'Abdulla and Britain. In a meeting on September 27 with the mufti, Nuqrashi promised that Egypt would recognize the new government in the very near future and fully support it. The mufti received a similar promise from Muhsin al-Barazi of Syria, who had arrived in Cairo on the same day.[21] At the same time, as he told the British ambassador in Cairo after Britain had also pressed King Faruq to prevent the mufti's arrival in Filastin, Nuqrashi tried to discourage the mufti from traveling to Gaza. He also informed the British ambassador that, in his opinion, there was no intention of having the Palestinian government operate an army or conduct independent foreign relations. In the assessment of the British ambassador, the Egyptian response to the mufti's arrival in Gaza would be either to expel him to Be'er Sheva or to persuade him to return to Egypt.[22] Nuqrashi was also involved in the decision of the Egyptian government not to permit entry into Gaza for members of the mufti's guard, who sought to arrive in cars filled with uniforms and equipment.[23]

Conceivably, the mufti did not want to miss an event that symbolized the peak of his political achievements, at which he expected to be in the spotlight, as in fact happened. Indeed, the Egyptians did not try to disrupt him during the course of the Palestinian National Council and declaration of the All-Palestine Government's establishment. Only a few days after the conference concluded did the Egyptians decide to bring the mufti back from Gaza to Cairo "by force" (or to compel him to return to Cairo). The mufti reached the Egyptian capital on the afternoon of October 7. Once in Cairo, he was placed under house arrest and heavy guard.[24] Henceforth he was prevented from engaging in any political activity in Egypt relating to the Palestinian problem and, of course, from traveling to the Gaza Strip.[25]

Egypt officially recognized the All-Palestine Government relatively late (on October 12, 1948), and Nuqrashi informed the prime minister, Ahmad Hilmi 'Abd al-Baqi. On the same day, the government of Iraq also recognized the All-Palestine Government. The governments of Syria and Lebanon followed suit as well, as in time did the remaining Arab states, with the exception of Jordan, naturally.[26]

It was expected that Iraq, being a Hashemite kingdom, would fully support King 'Abdulla's position, as it had during the rule of Salih Jaber. However, when Muzahim al-Pachachi was appointed prime minister and the political atmosphere in Iraq changed—against the background of the war in Filastin and the nationalist pan-Arab mood that accompanied this war—it was difficult for the regent and the new prime minister to maintain the policy declared by Salih Jaber. When Pachachi was about to leave for Cairo to attend a meeting of the League Council's Political Committee on June 29, 1948, the Iraqi parliament expressed its concerns regarding the Palestinian question. The parliament demanded that he explicitly promise not to commit to anything but the establishment of an independent Arab state in all of Filastin, and Pachachi replied that he sees the Filastin problem as an Iraqi problem.[27]

Pachachi's approach to the Filastin issue, and specifically to the question of the All-Palestine Government's standing, was characterized by skilled statesmanship and diplomatic tactics within a practical and realistic framework. In statements of position and conversations with associates of the mufti, the Iraqi prime minister expressed full support for the All-Palestine Government, having coordinated his stances with Egyptian Prime Minister Nuqrashi and thereby angering King 'Abdulla. In the spirit of the Arab League's Political Committee resolution regarding establishment of the All-Palestine Government, Pachachi told the mufti's representative in Baghdad that "establishment of an Arab government in Filastin is the right of Filastin's residents, which no one may deny. They are free to form a government any time they want, without waiting for decisions or instructions from someone else, being lords of their land. Iraq will not interfere in the establishment of such a government."[28] By contrast, in conversations with the British and Jordanians, Pachachi demanded that they remain patient and expressed doubt regarding the fate of the All-Palestine Government.

On October 6 the British ambassador in Cairo reported on a conversation with Pachachi, conveying that Pachachi again pleaded with the British to be patient and not apply too much pressure. According to the ambassador, Pachachi repeatedly urged patience and expressed the following opinions: the Arabs are disappointed; their involvement in Filastin was a failure and, for the Palestinians, a catastrophe; these are known facts; the Palestinians must be granted what is termed a government of their own for the time being; it will not last long; the Arabs will, inevitably, go through a process of accepting the existence of a Jewish state; there is no need to be concerned about what is called the government of Filastin; it is not significant and will remain insignificant; sooner or later the territory will be annexed by Transjordan or Egypt.[29]

Thus Pachachi viewed recognition of the All-Palestine Government as a tactical measure to address the immediate need of presenting a pan-Arab position indicating commitment to the Palestinians and the Palestinian problem, in response to the demands of nationalists in Iraq. The delayed recognition—on October 12, 1948—should not be interpreted as hesitation on the part of Pachachi but, rather, as an act of patience in expectation of developments, including military, in the Palestinian-Israeli arena. Pachachi admonished the Jordanians and British alike not to act hastily and press the matter, urging patience and incremental steps in formulating a position toward the mufti and the All-Palestine Government. Indeed, he was ultimately proved right in this regard.

* * *

In conclusion, Iraq played an important part in all matters relating to configuration of the Palestinian leadership and Palestinian institutions. Unlike his predecessor, Iraq's new prime minister, Muzahim al-Pachachi, adopted pan-Arab positions that reflected increased closeness with Egypt and Syria, especially in supporting the Palestinian struggle. His position with respect to the All-Palestine Government and Jordan should be understood in this light. Differences of opinion regarding the All-Palestine Government emerged within the Iraqi leadership. Particularly salient were the different approaches of the regent and Pachachi. The regent's position on this matter was hesitant, and his stance toward the mufti was categorically negative. Concerns about his own and the government's domestic image influenced the formulation of his policy on this issue, as he sought to protect the interests of the Hashemite family. Pachachi, in contrast, advocated a favorable position toward the Palestinian demands for self-government, although he was simultaneously very pessimistic about the possibility of this goal being actualized. Recognition by Egypt and Iraq did not improve the All-Palestine Government's chances of survival. Rather, it increased King 'Abdulla's determination to continue undermining its existence and to render it meaningless. Evidently, 'Abdulla and the British overestimated the importance of the All-Palestine Government and its capacity to survive.

The British and King 'Abdulla were very concerned about the possible establishment of the All-Palestine Government, viewing such a government and its recognition on the part of Arab states as posing a real menace to the Hashemite family. They acted out of obsession, with no sense of proportionality regarding the government's importance or capacity for survival. Presumably, their aggravation and concern stemmed from the traumas that Britain and Jordan had experienced in the past as a consequence of the mufti's actions against them, including his connection with Rashid 'Ali al-Kaylani's 1941 coup in Iraq and with the Nazis during World War II.

Britain and Jordan conducted a harsh, unremitting campaign against the mufti and the establishment of the All-Palestine Government. They saw every success on the part of the mufti as a blow to their vital interests and a threat to the continued existence of the Hashemite regimes in Iraq and Jordan. The main catalyzer in this struggle against the mufti and All-Palestine Government was the British ambassador in Amman, Alec Kirkbride, who even devoted a special chapter to this government in his autobiography.[30] The Hashemite Kingdom of Jordan presented the following arguments against the All-Palestine Government:

- Its establishment conflicts with the resolution of the league's Political Committee.
- It undermines the war effort against Israel and the authority of Arab armed forces fighting Israel. It pretends to rule over areas actually held by the armed forces of Egypt, Jordan, Iraq, and Syria as well as the Salvation Army (Jaysh al-Inqadh) of Qawuqji, which has been placed under Lebanese command. It also claims to rule in Israel and territories held by the Israeli army.
- Its establishment means a reversion to the situation that existed on May 15, 1948.

- It constitutes initial acceptance of the partition plan because the world will not recognize it without also recognizing Israel.
- It does not represent Filastin Arabs and it goes against their will. Its founders are no more than power-hungry authority seekers.

King 'Abdulla and his spokesmen further asserted that "a Palestinian government can only be established after the enemy is defeated," that it must be elected by the Palestinian people themselves, and that its capital must be Jerusalem, that under no circumstances can it be Gaza.[31]

King 'Abdulla was concerned about the relationship and loyalty of Palestinian West Bank residents to his kingdom rather than about the verity of the government's existence. Evidence of 'Abdulla's difficult situation and anxiety is provided by a report by Kirkbride, the British ambassador to Amman, who described a conversation he had with the king on October 2, 1948, during which the king was in a "bad mood." Regarding difficulties surrounding the future of the Arab territories of Filastin, the king said, according to the ambassador's report, that organized opposition to the inclusion of the Arab territories of Palestine as part of Transjordan was directed against Britain to the same extent that it was directed against Transjordan, and that maneuvers by Arab supporters in this context could lead to a war among the Arabs themselves. The ambassador added that 'Abdulla had requested a guarantee that the Anglo-Transjordanian Treaty would be invoked if other Arab states attack the country.[32] This rather pessimistic assessment on the part of the king was unrealistic, an indication of his mood and sense of disappointment more than a true assessment of reality.

Interestingly, even the measured Ambassador Kirkbride, who was well versed in matters relating to Jordan and the Arab world, was infected by the mood of crisis afflicting the king and his prime minister. On October 4, two days after his conversation with them, he submitted an assessment stating that he believed the government of Transjordan would soon have to revisit its policy regarding membership in the Arab League and cooperation with other Arab governments in Palestine, a likely development if Iraq decided to recognize the Arab government in Palestine. He reported that he believed the prime minister was considering adopting one of two approaches: leaving the Arab League and withdrawing the legion from Palestine, or only withdrawing the legion while remaining in the league. According to the ambassador, the king felt that it would be pointless for Transjordan alone to voice opposition to a Palestinian Arab government that was recognized by the other Arab states. The king also reportedly feared that removing the Arab League from Palestine after such a government began operating risked setting in motion events that could lead to clashes between this force and the volunteers controlled by the new government. Apparently, according to the ambassador, the king also feared a large Jewish offensive backed by a UN resolution, which Arab armies would be unable to repel.[33]

Kirkbride's assessment and reports failed the test of reality following Iraq's and Egypt's recognition of the government in Gaza on October 12. Possibly Israeli undertakings during this time (Operation Yoav on October 15) and the UN's nonrecognition of the All-Palestine Government, as well as the mufti's lack of success in playing any sort of military role, quieted concerns of King 'Abdulla and his prime minister and reduced their anxiety regarding the Palestinian government.[34]

In his campaign against the government of Gaza, King 'Abdulla made an effort to provoke the Arabs of Filastin within his jurisdiction. Toward this end, large-scale protests were organized and the mufti's objectors, including those beyond 'Abdulla's sphere of influence, received added encouragement. On the ground, Jordanian authorities tried to prevent or delay the departure of Palestinian National Council members to Gaza, and some indeed sent notices expressing support for the council's resolutions but stating that they could not attend. An armored vehicle of the legion was stationed at the crossroads between Bethlehem and Jericho in order to check the identity of people traveling to Gaza through Amman. Jamal al-Husayni's tour of West Bank cities (Ramalla, Bir Zayt, 'Anabta, Tulkarm, Qalqilya), during which he heard expressions of support for a Palestinian government, was deliberately cut short when he was summoned to a meeting with the king on September 28. He was also delayed in Jericho for an entire day on October 2, along with city representatives who were not permitted to travel to Gaza.[35]

Throughout October and November of 1948, King 'Abdulla continued his campaign to enlist the support of the Arab portion of Filastin that was under his rule, with a view to paving the way toward a resolution on its annexation to Transjordan. He did so, among other means, by dispatching supportive delegations from throughout this strip of land. Delegations of Palestinians who reached Amman openly called for Jordanian annexation of the areas in which they resided and declared 'Abdulla their king—the king of Filastin and Transjordan. During November, the king even visited Filastin a number of times, and during his visit to Jerusalem on November 15, the Coptic bishop crowned him king of Jerusalem.

The high point of Jordanian government activity was a Palestinian conference in Jericho, which opened on December 1, 1948. Its main focus was the adoption of resolutions that were unequivocally supportive of unification of the two banks of the Jordan River. The objectives of the conference in Jericho were clear: to declare the unification of Arab Filastin with Transjordan under the rule of King 'Abdulla, to remove the issue of resolution of the Palestinian problem from the purview of the Arab League, and to authorize the king, as the official representative of Filastin's Arabs, to achieve a resolution of the Palestinian problem.[36]

Notes

1. From a memorandum about a meeting between the Political Committee and King Faruq on April 12, 1948, in Cairo, Mardam Documents, Institute of Palestinian Studies, Beirut, cited in Walid Khalidi, "The Arab Perspective," in *The End of the Palestine Mandate*, ed. William Roger Louis and Robert W. Stookey (London: Tauris, 1986), 129.
2. Jami'at al-Duwal al-'Arabiyya, *Fahras Muqarrarat*, 68. The text of the resolution was reaffirmed by the Political Committee on April 13, 1950.
3. Muhamad 'Izzat Darwaza, *Al-Qadiyya al-Filastiniyya*, vol. 2 (Sidon), 190–94; see also Darwaza, *Hawla al-Haraka*, vols. 4, 5.
4. Political Committee resolution adopted July 8, 1948, in Darwaza, *Al-Qadiyya*, 191–93; Shabib, "Muqadamat al-Musadara"; Shabib, *Hukumat 'Umum Filastin*, 37–38.
5. Shabib, "Muqadamat al-Musadara," citing a letter from Amil al-Ghuri to Mufti Amin al-Husayni, dated July 11, 1947.
6. Shabib, "Muqadamat al-Musadara," citing a letter from Amin al-Husayni to 'Isa 'Isa in Beirut, dated September 8, 1948.
7. Israel Foreign Ministry (IFM), Research Department, Daily Summary of Information, July 19, 1948, July 23, 1948; see also Nimr al-Hawari's version of the election of Hilmi as the head of the Civil Administration, *Sir al-Nakba* (Nazareth, 1955), 270–72.
8. Darwaza, *Al-Qadiyya*, 211.
9. Shabib, *Hukumat 'Umum Filastin*, 39, citing a letter from Amil al-Ghuri to Ahmad Hilmi 'Abd al-Baqi, dated September 23, 1948, and a letter from the mufti to Amil al-Ghuri, dated September 26, 1948. Both letters are in the archives of the PLO Research Center, Beirut.
10. Shabib, "Muqadamat al-Musadara"; Shabib, *Hukumat 'Umum Filastin*, 40; Darwaza, *Al-Qadiyya*, 210–11; IFM, Daily Summary of Information, September 26, 1948; IFM, Middle East Department, News from Middle East Countries, Inter-Arab Policy, Assessment by Asher Goren on the background for the establishment of the All-Palestine Government, dated October 14, 1948; see also report by the British Ambassador in Amman, Kirkbride, October 6, 1948, in which he included the assessment of Glubb titled "Trans-Jordan and Palestine Situation Today, 5th October 1948," in Kirkbride, Amman, to Burrowe, London, National Archives of the United Kingdom (formerly Public Relations Office, hereinafter PRO), FO, 371/68642E96, October 6, 1948; on the negative US attitude, see FRUS, 1948, vol. 5, pt. 2, Washington DC, 1976, p. 1447, note 1 by the editor. See also Avi Shlaim, "The Rise and Fall of the All-Palestine Government in Gaza," *Journal of Palestine Studies* 20, no. 1 (1990).
11. IFM, Middle East Department, Daily Summary of Arab Radio Stations, Beirut Radio, September 16–17, 1948.
12. 'Arif, *Al-Nakba*, 3:705–6; Darwaza, *Al-Qadiyya*, 211.
13. Shabib, *Hukumat 'Umum Filastin*, 41–42; Shabib, "Muqadamat al-Musadara," 75; 'Arif, *Al-Nakba*, 3:703–4; see also Mahdi 'Abd al-Hadi, *Al-Mas'ala al-Filastiniyya wa Mashari' al-Hulul al-Siyasiyya, 1934–1974* (Beirut: al-Maktaba al-'Asriyya, 1975), 75, quoting a total of eighty-five attendees; Darwaza, *Al-Qadiyya*, 212, quoting a total of nearly ninety attendees.
14. For details of the first and second sessions of the council, see IFM, Daily Summary of Arab Radio Stations, October 1–2, 1948, Beirut Radio and Near East Radio (Al-Sharq al-Adna, a British radio station), October 3, 1948.
15. For the text of the mufti's speech, see Shabib, *Hukumat 'Umum Filastin*, 42.

16. Ibid., 43–44, 78–80 (text of the constitution—Al-Nizam al-Muwaqat li-Hukumat 'Umum Filastin).

17. Ibid., 80 (text of Filastin Declaration of Independence).

18. Ibid., 53–54; for the text of Hilmi's letter to the State Department, see FRUS, 1948, vol. 5, pt. 2, Washington, DC, 1976, p. 1447; see also editor's note 1, according to which London informed the State Department on October 7, 1948, that Britain had no intention of acknowledging "what is called government."

19. FRUS, 1948, vol. 5, pt. 2, Washington, DC, 1976, 1447–48.

20. On December 8, 1948, Nuqrashi issued an order to disband the Muslim Brotherhood in Egypt, to prohibit all its activities, and to confiscate all its assets.

21. IFM, Daily Summary of Information, September 28, 1948.

22. PRO, Andrews, Cairo to Foreign Office, London, 371/58642/ E12703, September 29, 1948; see also Foreign Office, 371/68642/ E12654, September 28, 1948.

23. IFM, Daily Summary of Information, October 1, 1948.

24. Husayni, *Haqa'iq*, 84–86. It is interesting to note the version of the mufti's transfer to Cairo that appears under the entry "Hukumat 'Amum Filastin" in *Al-Mawsu'a al-Filastiniyya*, vol. 3 (Damascus: al-Hay'a al-Mawsu'a al-Filastiniyya, 1984), 343–44:

> A few days after the Palestinians began preparations and mobilization of the *mujahidin*, the Egyptian authorities intervened and transferred the mufti by force to Cairo, and compelled a number of the National Council members to leave Gaza for Cairo. The prime minister and government members remained in Gaza, but the Egyptian authorities quickly forced them to transfer to Egypt. The government continued to exist in Cairo, without carrying out its mandated mission, especially in the political sphere. At the same time, the Egyptian authorities blockaded the building of the Arab Higher Hay'a in Cairo. The mufti was strictly monitored, and his freedom to work and freedom of movement were revoked.

See also *Filastin* [monthly magazine of the mufti] 30 (August 1963): 6–11.

25. 'Arif, *Al-Nakba*, 3:709.

26. IFM, Daily Summary of Arab Radio Stations, October 11–14, 1948, and Daily Summary of Information, September 22, 1948.

27. IFM, Daily Summary of Arab Radio Stations, Cairo Radio, September 28–29, 1948.

28. IFM, Daily Summary of Information, September 26, 1948, October 10, 1948.

29. Andrews, Cairo to London, PRO, FO 371/68642 E12792, October 2, 1948; Andrews, Cairo to London, PRO, FO 371/68642 13042, October 6, 1948.

30. Alec Kirkbride, *From the Wings: Amman Memoirs, 1947–1951* (London: Frank Cass, 1976); see chap. 5, "The Government of All-Palestine."

31. For the details of Jordan's arguments, see IFM, Middle East Department, Information from Arab Countries, no. 16, October 14, 1948.

32. Kirkbride, Amman to London, PRO, FO 371/68842 E12899, October 2, 1948.

33. Kirkbride, Amman to London, PRO, FO 371/68862 E12925, October 4, 1948.

34. Kirkbride later changed his version, claiming that neither he nor the king were in a state of panic regarding this issue and that his ministers viewed the establishment of the Palestinian government as a joke. According to Kirkbride's memoirs, "King Abdullah and his Ministers treated the move as a joke. Some of the Arab states went through the motion of formal recognition, but His Majesty's Government and other powers followed the lead set by the United Nations Organisation and ignored the so-called Government of All-Palestine"; Kirkbride, *Amman Memoirs*, 58–59.

35. IFM, Middle East Department, News from Middle East Countries, Inter-Arab Policy, Assessment by Asher Goren on the background of the establishment of the All-Palestine Government, October 14, 1948; IFM, Daily Summary of Information, September 28, 1948, October 1, 1948, October 6, 1948.

36. Kirkbride commented that it was apparent from the decisions of the conference that only the first aim was achieved. Kirkbride, Amman to London, PRO, FO 371/68644 E15789, December 8, 1948.

4 The Palestinians in the Absence of Leadership, 1949–63

After the All-Palestine Government exhausted its potential and the mufti's status reached its nadir, the Palestinians remained without leadership. Even the inter-Arab circumstances had changed: armistice agreements between Israel and Egypt as well as Jordan were signed without any Palestinian representation, and, in effect, the curtain came down on the Palestinian cause as an acute problem of a people who seek self-determination. It was clear, at least to Arab leaders, that eventually the territory captured by Jordan would be annexed to the Hashemite kingdom and that the All-Palestine Government would not last long. The mufti Haj Amin al-Husayni, for his part, continued to play the part he had scripted for himself—namely, chairman of the Arab Higher Hay'a—as if nothing had changed. Likewise, Ahmad Hilmi 'Abd al-Baqi maintained his insignificant, virtual role as prime minister of the All-Palestine Government and in this capacity also served as the Filastin delegate to the Arab League.

The End of the All-Palestine Government

During the ninth session of the Arab League Council in Cairo, which was held from September 30 to November 15, 1948, after the establishment of the All-Palestine Government, Ahmad Hilmi 'Abd al-Baqi and Jamal al-Husayni were invited to participate as prime minister and as foreign minister, respectively. On January 27, 1949, the Foreign Ministry of the All-Palestine Government sent a memorandum to the league's secretariat, protesting the fact that the League had not fulfilled its promise "to provide financial assistance so as to enable the government to carry out its mission." The memorandum noted that "Arab states, with the exception of Jordan, promised to provide the All-Palestine Government with the sum of 25,000 liras in order to commence operations," adding that "the government has acquired debts in excess of 12,000 Egyptian liras, and requests to date have yielded no results."[1]

In his capacity as prime minister of the All-Palestine Government, 'Abd al-Baqi participated in the tenth session of the League Council in Cairo held March 17–21, 1949.[2] Presumably, the All-Palestine Government was invited to participate in the session because of its recent establishment and recognition and because its representation in the international arena was important, especially given that the dispute with Jordan had not yet peaked. This dispute steadily intensified as it became increasingly apparent that King ʻAbdulla was intent on annexing the West Bank to Jordan. Indeed, Ahmad Hilmi was not invited to the eleventh session of the League Council, held from October 17, 1949 to February 15, 1950, mainly because Jordan objected, although the Syrian delegation did include two Palestinian advisers: Akram Zuʻaytir and Henry Katan.[3] On October 17, 1949, the day the session opened, the Foreign Ministry of the All-Palestine Government sent the league secretariat a memorandum strongly protesting that it had not been invited to the league's session.[4] The league's secretary general, who made an announcement concerning this memorandum during the second gathering of this session, noted that "this memorandum relates to the wording of the charter [of the Arab League, the Filastin Annex], which requires the election of a delegate to represent the Arabs of Filastin. The council has the right, if it wishes, to discuss this memorandum in order to elect the Palestinian delegate, or to view it as a political Arab problem and therefore to defer discussion to a later time."[5]

The Egyptian delegate proposed that discussions be held regarding the election of a representative of Filastin Arabs to participate in League Council debates. Iraqi Prime Minister Nuri al-Saʻid, who also represented Jordanian interests, sought to have this discussion postponed. He requested that a decision be deferred until the league's members reached a consensus. In his opinion, implementation of the relevant charter provision was conditional on a unanimous decision regarding the chosen representative of Filastin's Arabs.[6] Nuri al-Saʻid was referring to Article 7 of the Arab League Charter, which requires unanimity on any resolution that obligates all league members. The Egyptian delegate agreed on this point and therefore deferred the discussion. On October 30, the All-Palestine Government again protested "the continuing insistence of the Arab League not to invite it to the League Council, which discusses the Filastin issue and adopts crucial resolutions that are important to Palestinians."[7]

The Filastin delegate was, once again, not invited when the twelfth session of the League Council convened from March 25 to June 17, 1950, because of the objection of "one of the Arab states," presumably Jordan.[8] This session did, however, officially address the issue of Palestinian representation. Egyptian Prime Minister Mustafa al-Nahas, head of the Egyptian delegation, raised this issue for discussion at the opening meeting of the session. He suggested that the council elect a Filastin delegate to participate in its deliberations in accordance with the Filastin Annex of the Arab League Charter, which he cited. The Jordanian representative, Jordan's ambassador in Cairo, objected to any discussion of this issue and requested that the council defer such discussion to the next meeting, when the Jordanian delegation to the league would be present. Nahas agreed to postpone the discussion. During interim deliberations, it was agreed that if the council affirms the appointment of a Filastin delegate, he would participate in Political

Committee debates when it addressed Palestinian issues. The second meeting of the council, on May 27, took place without any Jordanian participation. Nahas insisted that the issue of Palestinian representation be addressed immediately.

The league's secretary general requested that the council "pay attention to the difference between electing someone to represent Filastin Arabs and electing someone to represent the Filastin government." To which the Lebanese prime minister replied that "the council is free to elect whomever it wishes." Egyptian Foreign Minister Muhammad Salah al-Din joined those who supported the election of Filastin delegates.

After a lengthy, in-depth debate, in light of the position of Jordan and Iraq, the council eventually approved an invitation to be issued to the Palestinians based on a formulation by the Egyptian delegation. As summed up by the league's secretary general, "The council unanimously agrees to invite the All-Palestine Government to send delegates to participate in the council meetings." The council also affirmed "the participation of a Filastin delegate in Political Committee meetings when it debates Palestinian issues." Indeed, - 'Abd al-Baqi, prime minister of the All-Palestine Government, and two additional members—Raja' al-Husayni and Futi Frayj—participated in a council meeting on March 29, 1950.[9]

Following the March 1950 resolution of the League Council, the issue of Palestinian representation in the league did not arise again, and Ahmad Hilmi 'Abd al-Baqi continued to serve as "the Filastin delegate to the Arab League" until his death in June 1963. He alone represented Filastin at the thirteenth session of the Arab League Council, convened October 13, 1950–February 2, 1951,[10] but during the fourteenth session of the council, held March 17–May 19, 1951, three additional Palestinian delegates joined him: Futi Frayj, Amin 'Aql, and Rafiq al-Lababidi.[11]

At the fifteenth session of the League Council, which met October 3–13, 1951, in Alexandria, Ahmad Hilmi was once again the sole representative of the Palestinians. On the eve of the gathering, he sent a request to the session's chairman, asking that the council agree to include a delegate from the All-Palestine Government in the Permanent Filastin Committee that was meant to address the issues of Filastin and the Palestinian refugees, and which the League Council had decided to establish in October 1949.[12]

Iraq's representative in Cairo, Najib al-Rawi, suggested that the request be referred for discussion in the Political Committee so that when it addresses the refugee problem, it consults with Filastin delegates. Ibrahim Farraj, a member of the Egyptian delegation, stated in this context, "If resolutions are adopted unanimously, then there is no obstacle to the Filastin government being represented in the committee, as long as its delegate does not participate in voting, given that this government lacks [the capability and authority] to implement the committee's resolutions." Ahmad Hilmi 'Abd al-Baqi responded, "We have already submitted the request to the Political Committee, and we were told to submit it to the League Council. It is unreasonable not to have the Filastin government represented in a committee that addresses issues relating to Filastin." Hilmi added, provocatively, "Why would the Filastin government not be represented in this committee when it is a stakeholder, and what prevents [its representation]? If the league does not recognize this government, why not disband this government [and thereby] put an end to the matter?" A member of the Egyptian delegation, Fu'ad Saraj al-Din, proposed that the question be referred for consideration by the Political Committee, and his proposal was accepted.[13]

During the course of 1951, the All-Palestine Government continued to disintegrate, as most or all of its members resigned and found other positions in Arab states: Minister of Agriculture Amin 'Aql was appointed to a position in the Arab League; the health minister, Futi Frayj, opened a clinic in Egypt; Finance Minister Michel Abqaryus was appointed as a lecturer at Beirut University; Defense Minister Raja' al-Husayni became a transportation adviser in Saudi Arabia; Minister of Public Relations Yusif Sahyun opened a store for medicines in Cairo; Secretary General Anwar Nusayba was appointed defense minister in the Jordanian government; Minister of Justice 'Ali Hasana was appointed deputy minister of internal affairs in the West Bank; Foreign Minister Jamal al-Husayni became an adviser to the Saudi government; Minister of Social Affairs 'Awni 'Abd al-Hadi was appointed the Jordanian ambassador to Cairo and presented his letter of credentials to King Faruq on October 11, 1951.[14]

Against the background of these developments, the Arab League Council resolved on March 29, 1952, that "in light of the cessation of activities on the part of the All-Palestine Government under the current circumstances, the prime minister shall serve as the Filastin delegate to the Arab League Council. He shall be allocated a budget of 1,500 Egyptian liras for his bureau's expenses in 1952." This was an empty title, lacking any mention of Filastin's Arabs or the All-Palestine Government. Moreover, the resolution reduced the number of Palestinian delegates to just one—the prime minister. On April 9, 1953, the League Council approved the budget of the All-Palestine Government, that is, Ahmad Hilmi's budget.[15]

While the All-Palestine Government was disappearing from the Arab and Palestinian political arenas, the mufti continued to carry the title of chairman of the Arab Higher Hay'a even though this body no longer had any significance, standing, or influence whatsoever. He continued, as well, to insist on his right to serve as the legal representative of the Palestinian people and to speak on their behalf. In this context, the mufti also continued to make extremist statements regarding the Palestinian issue in the face of increasingly harsh criticism against him.

The Status and Activities of the Mufti, 1959–63: Impact of Inter-Arab Debates on Revival of the Palestinian Entity

Egypt—Character Assassination of the Mufti

An Egyptian initiative in March 1959 to revive the Palestinian entity (*al-kiyan al-Filastini*) marked an important turning point for the mufti in terms of status. Egypt raised this issue for the first time at the thirty-first session of the Arab League Council on March 29. The council decided on a high-level Arab conference to deal with "the stages of development of the Palestinian problem" and to formulate a unified Arab policy that all league members would be obligated to implement. Additionally, the council decided on "the reorganization of the Palestinian people, highlighting its entity as a unified people rather than mere refugees, so their voice will be heard in the inter-Arab arena (*al-majal al-qawmi*) and international arena through representatives elected by the Palestinian people."[16]

The purpose of reviving the Palestinian entity was to establish independent political institutions that would represent the Palestinians as a people. For tactical reasons, the Egyptians refrained at this stage from officially discussing "self-determination" or the establishment of a "Palestinian state." Emphasis was placed on the existence of a Palestinian *people* and its political representation as such.

It was evident from the moment Egypt initiated its efforts to establish new Palestinian representative institutions that it would be striving to eliminate the traditional, anachronistic Palestinian institution, namely, the Arab Higher Hay'a headed by Mufti Haj Amin al-Husayni. Egypt had long disapproved of the mufti, who constituted an obstacle to the implementation of Egypt's plans regarding the Palestinian problem.

In July 1959, Egypt embarked on a drastic, systematic, and vicious campaign to undermine the mufti's status by maligning his past and his personality with the assistance of Mamduh Rida, political reporter for the weekly *Ruz al-Yusif*.[17] Presumably Rida was briefed by Egyptian intelligence services in the context of this campaign. For example, in an article of July 6, 1959, Rida expressed sorrow that "Filastin is represented today by the very people who caused the catastrophe that befell it" and accused the mufti of taking action "to establish a free government for Filastin, a dangerous idea whose objective is to undermine the plan for resolving the issue of the Palestinian people that was adopted by the league in March 1959." He also accused the mufti of corruption, specifically, for having "misused funds that were transferred to him from the Arab League for the benefit of refugees," and he called on young Palestinians "to demand an audit of [the mufti's] accounts." He argued that "behind [the mufti] stands a foreign superpower that is interested in freezing the current situation of the refugees" and advised him to understand that "he is no longer wanted as a leader and he should exit the stage . . . before the audience starts booing him and pelting him with eggs and tomatoes."

Rida's verbal assault peaked with a lengthy article on August 17, 1959, in which he detailed "all of the mufti's crimes" throughout his political career. The article described the mufti in the following terms: he is a man who plots against the Palestinian people and trades in its rights, whose goal is his own well-being, satisfying his selfish desires, and surrounding himself with a group of yes-men; he has placed most members of the Arab Higher Hay'a "in his pocket," and he managed it with a view to his personal benefit, while wheeling and dealing in the Palestinian interest and maintaining a ceasefire with the Zionist and British endeavor; later, when he realized that everyone views him as bearing primary responsibility for the Filastin Catastrophe, he published a ridiculous editorial in which he held that direct responsibility for the expulsion of Filastin's Arabs from their country and their homes rests on the shoulders of the British and Jews, thereby shirking responsibility himself; the mufti's duties gave him full control over assets and funds that derived from various taxes and incomes, including financial assistance from the Arab League, donations, and funds for orphans.

Mamduh Rida accused "His Holiness" of usurping these funds for himself and his associates and of collaboration in the sale of Palestinian lands to Jews. Rida reminded his readers that it was the British high commissioner, Herbert Samuel, a Jew, who appointed the mufti to this position, with the assistance of Chaim Weizmann and King 'Abdulla. As such, he was serving the interests of those who appointed him while deceiving the Palestinian people. The series of articles concluded with an accusation that the mufti was trying to establish a government composed of his supporters in Arab states, in response to the Egyptian plan for organization of the Palestinian people, and he did this, among other means, through the assistance of a "foreign superpower" supportive of the idea.[18]

Egyptian campaign against the mufti aimed to make him abandon the Palestinian political stage in general and Cairo in particular, in order to prevent any possibility of his acting to derail the Egyptian process as well as any perceived link between him and the new Egyptian policy on revival of the Palestinian entity. Indeed, the mufti did leave Cairo in mid-August 1959 and settle in Lebanon, but he refused to exit the political stage. In fact, it appears that, fundamentally misjudging the extent of his influence among the Palestinian population, he was determined to fight for his position.

In August 1959, a Commission of Experts on Filastin convened in Sawfar, Lebanon. The commission had been established by a March 1959 resolution of the Arab League Council with the aim of continuing the debate on a Palestinian entity. The mufti sought to appear before the commission, but Egypt took measures to thwart his efforts and prevent his attendance. It also accused him of seeking to foment division within the commission. The Egyptians found a like-minded partner in Jordan, whose delegates also opposed the mufti's participation in their deliberations.

The mufti continued working to enlist support among Palestinians in Lebanon, Kuwait, and to some extent Jordan as well. These efforts, in addition to his relations with the new Iraqi leader, 'Abd al-Karim Qasim, who came to power through the coup of July 1958, fueled the continuing Egyptian campaign against him, through both the press in Egypt and the pro-Egyptian press in Lebanon. For example, the Lebanese newspaper *al-Kifah* (January 15, 1960) called on him to leave the political arena, and the pro-Egyptian *al-Anwar* cited a memorandum of December 30, 1962, which it received from Palestinian students in Lebanon, demanding "an end to the activities of the mufti and his associates." The Egyptian press, too, repeatedly maligned the mufti, and Nasir al-Din al-Nashashibi called on him from the pages of *al-Jumhuriyya* (October 19, 1963) to leave the political arena. On December 5, 1963, *al-Jumhuriyya* reported on talks between the mufti and the Syrian Ba'th Party after the Ba'th coup that same year and asserted that he had tried to enlist Saudi Arabia in his efforts against the initiative to revive the Palestinian entity. The Egyptian press continued to attack the mufti when he expressed objection to Ahmad al-Shuqayri's plan to establish a Palestinian entity. The independent Lebanese newspaper *al-Jarida* (August 21, 1959) summed up the mufti's situation: "The mufti lives in another world, insisting on personally charting an old political course, of which he was the architect and which resulted in the loss of Filastin and shame for the Arabs."

Egypt's attacks on the mufti continued from 1964 through 1966 as well, after the establishment of the new Palestinian entity (the PLO). Egypt continued to defame the mufti and disparage him through its media outlets and the pro-Egyptian press in Lebanon. As in previous years, it did this systematically and consistently by repeatedly underscoring his guilt in the "great betrayal" and even "an attempt on the life of Hikmat al-Masri" of Nablus. The Egyptians also reiterated their calls "to silence him somehow." Egypt's attacks on the mufti intensified further in the context of the crisis that erupted between Egypt and Jordan during the second half of 1966 and the mufti's visit to the kingdom, which was described in the Egyptian media as "intended to demolish the Palestinian cause and thwart fida'iyyun actions."[19]

The Last Resort: The Mufti Turns to Qasim

The Egyptian campaign for the character assassination of the mufti and his expulsion from the Palestinian political arena, in combination with his failure to reassert his standing, had the effect of drastically curtailing his maneuverability. The limited capacity for action that remained for him resulted more from prevailing conditions in the inter-Arab arena than from support for his position as chairman of the Arab Higher Hay'a. There was a vacuum in terms of representative Palestinian institutions as a consequence of the Arab League's inability to reach a decision regarding revival of the Palestinian entity during 1959 through 1963, and the mufti sought to take advantage of these circumstances by offering his services to someone willing to accept them. Given that Egypt was taking measures to remove him and that the king of Jordan despised him, there remained the Iraqi leader, Colonel 'Abd al-Karim Qasim, his only savior.

Qasim responded to the initiative of Egypt's President Nasir regarding a Palestinian entity relatively late. Only in mid-December 1959 did he suggest the opposing idea of an "eternal Palestinian republic" (*khalida*). He first raised the notion of establishing such a republic during a December 15 speech before a conference of Iraqi physicians:

> Arab Filastin will not be revived unless an Arab state is established, encompassing all the stolen parts of the homeland and ruled by its residents.... Who assaulted Filastin? Three gangs and states did so. The criminal gangs of Israel, who stole the lion's share, Jordan, which stole another part and added it to its own territory, and Egypt, which during Faruq's rule tore off another part of Filastin. It would be better if those who trade in the name of Filastin would call for the establishment of a Palestinian state to be ruled by its residents.[20]

Qasim presented his plan for the establishment of an "eternal Palestinian republic" as the solution to the Palestinian problem and a framework for Palestinian self-determination: "A [Palestinian] republic should be established in all the territory of Filastin as a whole. We believe that all parts of Filastin are Arab and must be returned to the owners. The Palestinian Arab people do not recognize a Jewish right to the land of Filastin, and we will not agree to the establishment of an Israeli state in an Arab country."[21]

Qasim saw the mufti as a means of advancing his own plans for the Palestinian entity in the context of his struggle against Nasir. The mufti had very little to offer Qasim, and what he did have was almost entirely insignificant. The mufti paid him back primarily through open support for his plans and positions vis-à-vis the Palestinian issue. In January 1960, the mufti openly voiced his support for Qasim's plan for the establishment of a Palestinian republic, and in July 1961 he met with Qasim during a visit to Baghdad as a guest of the Iraqi government.[22] Following this visit, an office of the Arab Higher Hay'a was opened in Baghdad in August 1961, with Ziyad al-Khatib as its head.[23] Amil al-Ghuri, a member of the hay'a and assistant to the mufti, who met with Qasim during a February 1962 visit to Baghdad, praised him for "taking on the Palestinian cause after it had been at a standstill, and for calling for its return to its owners." Ghuri also praised the establishment of the Palestinian Liberation Army in Iraq.[24]

On May 2, 1962, the mufti, accompanied by Amil al-Ghuri, arrived in Baghdad for a visit that lasted until May 8. On May 5, the mufti met with Qasim. Reporting on this meeting, Baghdad Radio stated, "The mufti received praise for his honest efforts on behalf of Filastin, Arabs, and Islam from the prime minister [Qasim]. Qasim discussed the Filastin problem with him."[25]

On conclusion of his visit to Baghdad, the mufti expressed his view that "Qasim's plan for the liberation of Filastin, according to which the Palestinian people themselves will assume the responsibility for liberating their country with the support of Arab states, is the right plan and corresponds fully with the will of the Palestinian people. The Palestinians concur with the authorities in Iraq regarding the liberation of Filastin."[26]

Qasim provided the mufti with financial assistance that, in combination with the aid he received from Saudi Arabia, enabled him to maintain a propaganda machine. In this context, the mufti published *Filastin*, the monthly magazine of the Arab Higher Hay'a, and oversaw open as well as clandestine political activities in areas of high Palestinian concentration in Arab states, including Jordan and Lebanon. In August 1960, Qasim announced an annual allocation of 250,000 dinar to the hay'a, and in May 1962 granted it an additional 350,000 dinar.[27] Iraqi media outlets gave extensive coverage to the mufti's political activity and his many announcements. The mufti, for his part, employed his longstanding agents to carry out clandestine activities in support of Qasim and King Sa'ud. After the fall of Qasim's regime in February 1963, hay'a activities in Iraq were suspended, its office in Baghdad was shut down, and Iraqi financial assistance was terminated.

The Mufti's Struggle against Shuqayri: The Final Downfall

The overthrow of Qasim's regime in Iraq on February 8, 1963, curtailed the mufti's freedom of action and undercut support for him. After the offices of the Arab Higher Hay'a in Cairo and Baghdad were shut down, only five remained: in Rabat, Jedda, Beirut, Damascus, and New York. The hay'a had to make do with the material and political support of Saudi Arabia and the passive and reluctant support of the Ba'th Party in Syria. A January 1964 resolution of the first Arab Summit, addressing revival of the Palestinian entity, paved the way for Shuqayri to convene the Jerusalem Congress from May to June 1964, at which the PLO would be officially established. This resolution caused the mufti's struggle to become more bitter and violent. He was not averse to employing any available means in his efforts to cause Shuqayri to fail. Yet his efforts did not bear fruit.

The mufti's efforts included a boycott of the Jerusalem Congress and an intense public relations campaign condemning plans to turn the PLO into the representative of Palestinians. The Arab Higher Hay'a even termed the Jerusalem Congress "an imperialist Zionist plot aimed at annihilating the Palestinian cause."[28]

The mufti also directed activities to be undertaken in areas where Palestinians were concentrated in Arab states, with a view to undermining the activities of Shuqayri. The mufti focused his activities on the West Bank and the refugees in Syria. In February, May, and October 1964, he sent delegations on his behalf to the West Bank to meet with Palestinian political activists and enlist their support. He also sent the text of his statements against Shuqayri by mail from Beirut to dozens of dignitaries and political activists in the West Bank, including Jordanian members of parliament. Reactions of the Palestinian public were typically very negative, and support for the mufti dwindled down to a very small group of elderly veteran supporters who had no influence.[29]

In addition, the mufti carried out subversive actions against Shuqayri. These actions were, for many Palestinians, reminiscent of his past activities. Among other measures, he distributed funds in Jerusalem in order to "buy" supporters and established a fictitious organization, "the Palestinian National Movement" (Al-Haraka al-Wataniyya al-Filastiniyya). In May 1964, while Amil al-Ghuri was visiting Jordan, the mufti tried to "raise [ethnic-religious] issues in order to persuade Christians to support the position of the Arab Higher Hay'a." On May 27, 1964, the eve of the Palestinian congress in Jerusalem, the mufti took his most extreme action: one of his agents fired a round of bullets at the home of Hikmat al-Masri, a Nablus dignitary, in an effort to deter political activists from cooperating with Shuqayri, and thereby to undermine the congress.[30]

In sum, the mufti's efforts to exert influence in the Arab and Palestinian arenas failed. Eventually, he remained isolated, with only Saudi support. His complete removal from the political scene was only a matter of time. The Egyptians now pinned their hopes on another Palestinian personality, whom they promoted and placed on the Arab political stage—Ahmad al-Shuqayri. This development, alongside resolutions of the Arab League Council from September 1963 and, later, the first Arab Summit in January 1964, effectively closed this chapter of history on the Palestinian national movement. The outcome of the Six Day War and the increased strength of militant Palestinian organizations led to the mufti's complete exclusion from any sphere of Palestinian activity and relegated him solely to the Islamic religious sphere. The Arab Higher Hay'a tried to sustain its existence by expressing support for the new Palestinian organizations and their guerilla operations.[31]

The mufti died in 1974, closing the chapter on the institution of the Arab Higher Hay'a.

* * *

In conclusion, under the British Mandate, what most characterized the Palestinian national movement in all its forms, from the mid-1930s onward, was the political vacuum created by the absence of any Palestinian leadership with the authority to impose its view or shape decisions regarding resolution of the Palestinian problem. Initially this was a physical vacuum—that is, the absence of leadership in Filastin during World War II—with political repercussions that Ahmad al-Shuqayri described as "a national vacuum, with no activity and no leadership."[32] After the mufti returned to the region in 1946, it became a political vacuum because of the inability of Palestinian leadership—namely, the mufti—to guide the Palestinian cause. In practice, then, the Arab states determined the course of this cause. The increasing involvement of Arab states in the Palestinian problem and its resolution and the near-total dependence of the Palestinian national movement on these states in pursuit of its goal transformed the Palestinian problem into an inter-Arab problem, at times even more the latter than the former.

As a result of the political vacuum in Palestinian leadership, responsibility for determining the fate of Palestinians shifted to Egypt, which controlled the Gaza Strip, and to Jordan, which controlled the West Bank. As such, the steps taken by Egypt and Jordan, as well as the resolutions adopted by the Arab League under their influence, cannot be understood without taking into account the lack of Palestinian leadership.

Specifically, no analysis of the policies of King 'Abdulla toward the Palestinian question, the Arab arena, or Israel can be complete unless it explores the significance of the Palestinian leadership crisis and its impact on the Palestinian cause and on the leeway it gave King 'Abdulla. The same applies to analysis of Israel's policy on the Palestinian problem and its relations with King 'Abdulla. Jordan, which strove to prevent any Palestinian representation or the establishment of representative institutions for Palestinians, benefited the most from the lack of influential Palestinian leadership. This situation helped 'Abdulla present the Arab world with a "done deal" by annexing the West Bank, without any Arab state imposing the sanctions that had been threatened against the king should he do so and without being able to block the annexation. It also enabled 'Abdulla to try to reach an agreement with Israel. Indirectly, it shaped the fate of the Gaza Strip as well.

In the drama of the inter-Arab struggle against Abdullah's annexation of the West Bank, the mufti and his leadership apparatus were marginal. The king of Jordan could therefore successfully annex the West Bank without any significant reaction or objection on the part of the Husayni Palestinian leadership or any other Palestinian constituency.[33] The struggle against annexation was primarily guided by Egypt through the Arab League, and it was not successful. Without the leeway he had, 'Abdulla's efforts to reach an agreement with Israel before and after the war would not have been possible. In fact, 'Abdulla had near-complete freedom of maneuverability, within certain limits stemming from the influence of the inter-Arab world and of the Palestinians who were part of Jordanian leadership. This is the background against which to understand the rapprochement between Israel and Jordan.

The lack of a Palestinian entity with pan-Arab and Palestinian authority was a very convenient situation for Israel, as it offered an opportunity to reach an agreement with King 'Abdulla. Most of the king's efforts were focused on ensuring his rule in the West Bank—an aspiration that made him a desirable partner for Israel. The lack of authoritative Palestinian leadership in fact eliminated the possibility of any reasonable "Palestinian option" as an alternative to the "Jordanian option" along the eastern border of the state of Israel. It also paved the way for political arrangements with the Jordanian king that were based on his annexation of the West Bank. Although Arab states, Egypt foremost among them, made a concerted effort to derail 'Abdulla's annexation measures, it was actually close Palestinian associates of the king who thwarted his attempts to reach an agreement with Israel after the 1948 Arab-Israeli War.

Arab involvement in the Palestinian issue and determination of the Palestinians' fate increased, to the extent that Arab states began assuming direct responsibility for the cause. Their involvement became especially significant with the convening of the Preparatory Committee for the Arab League in Alexandria in 1944. It further intensified over the years to the point that the Palestinian problem, alongside the question of Arab unity, became the main topic of Arab League debates. "'Urubat Filastin" (the "Arabness" of Filastin) found full expression with the Arab states' military invasion of Palestine on May 15, 1948. The Palestinian national movement was finally and fully intrinsically linked with the Arab world, to the extent that in practice it became the core of the Arab-Israeli conflict.

The Palestinians had never been as dependent on Arab states as they were during the period following World War II. Indeed, they had no alternative other than Arab support, given their own weakness and the vast disparity between their leader's aspirations and his ability to actualize these aspirations. The mufti proved unable to lead a struggle against the Zionist movement and the British Mandate or engage in regular warfare as May 15, 1948, approached. Arab states were aware of this problem and tried to meet their obligations vis-à-vis the Palestinians while also protecting their own national interests. This paradox is, to this day, characteristic of the history of the Palestinian national movement and its relations with Arab states: ever since the Arab League took on the Palestinian problem, the dilemma for Arabs has been how to bridge the contradiction between their commitment to the Palestinian cause and Palestinians, on the one hand, and the national interests and national security of each Arab state, on the other. As such, to understand the achievements of the new Palestinian national movement, one must take into account the commitment and support it received from the Arab world.

Filastin became the magnetic core for two opposing "poles" of leaders—the mufti at one end, and King 'Abdulla at the other. This polarization was also manifest at two parallel Palestinian conferences—in Gaza and in Jericho. 'Abdulla, who ruled over part of Arab Filastin, had attained a major achievement and, in fact, launched the struggle over Palestinian representation and, later, over control of the West Bank. This struggle was between two entities: the Palestinian entity that took the form of the Palestine Liberation Organization in 1964 and the Jordanian entity, namely, the Hashemite Kingdom of Jordan. It became an existential struggle and remained a focal point in the Arab arena until it was resolved at the Arab Summit in Rabat in October 1974.

The failure of the Palestinian national movement to achieve its goals is attributable, first and foremost, to the mufti's domineering style of leadership. The deteriorating status and disintegration of the Palestinian leadership and, above all, of the mufti's status in the Palestinian and Arab arenas are evidenced by the fate of the All-Palestine Government and its members, in particular the attitude of the Arab League to this government. The factors that shifted the league's position toward favoring the establishment of the All-Palestine Government were more external than intra-Arab: Arab recognition of the need to establish this government and grant the mufti a means of control. This was a final, perhaps desperate, attempt on the part of Egypt and Syria to prevent Jordan's annexation of the West Bank. This fact is crucial to understanding the rapid disintegration of the Palestinian government: it was established for a specific purpose, and when that purpose became irrelevant, there was no longer a need for such a government. The establishment of this government was also a gesture toward the Palestinians and a measure designed to improve the image of Arab leaders after their military failures in Filastin. The gesture did not, in effect, greatly benefit the Palestinians; it only demonstrated the incompetence of their leadership.

In line with its position on the Palestinian issue and its attitude toward the mufti, Egypt refrained from suggesting that the Gaza Strip serve as the base of activities for the All-Palestine Government; indeed, it took measures to locate the mufti and his government in Cairo, where they were closely watched by Egyptian security authorities. Toward Ahmad al-Shuqayri, however, it adopted a completely different attitude: it granted him freedom of travel to the Gaza Strip, as the base of the Palestinian entity after the establishment of the PLO in 1964, when this served Egyptian interests.

In their writings about this period, Arab leaders and leaders of the new Palestinian national movement, as well as Palestinian researchers, harshly criticized the establishment of the All-Palestine Government. Over time, this government came to be viewed as a negative example of any idea or proposal regarding the establishment of a Palestinian government in exile or a provisional Palestinian government. In his memoirs (1986), Abu Jihad (Khalil al-Wazir, a leader and founder of Fatah) criticized the timing of the announcement on establishment of the All-Palestine Government.[34]

Ahmad al-Shuqayri, who at the time closely followed developments related to establishment of the All-Palestine Government, later criticized it harshly. He cited it as a negative example in arguing against a government in exile when the issue was raised during the first Arab Summit. In answer to King Saʻud's query as to why he was not establishing a Palestinian government, Shuqayri replied, "The experience of the All-Palestine Government, which Arab states and Afghanistan recognized, was a failure, and nothing remained of it in the end except its head, [and he too] has already died and there is no need to revive [dead] bones."[35]

The mufti's efforts during the 1950s and 1960s to exert influence in the Arab and Palestinian arenas and to secure recognition of his status failed. This failure further underscored his previous failures, before and during the 1948 war. The criticism leveled against him increased over time. Despite his failures, however, the mufti did have a key role in the history of the Palestinian national movement. He played the part of heroic leader of the Palestinian national awakening and emerging Palestinian national movement during the era of the British Mandate in Palestine. He was responsible for its achievements and failures, and especially for establishing its extremist and violent approach. His survival as a leader is attributable, in part, to the fact that no one could rival his status, personality, or charisma.

Notes

1. Shabib, *Hukumat ʻUmum Filastin*, 55.
2. ʻAbd al-Hadi, *Awraq Khassa*, 182.
3. Jamiʻat al-Duwal al-ʻArabiyya, *Al-Amana al-ʻAma, Mazabit Jalasat Dawr al-'Ijtimaʻ al-ʻAdi al-Hadi ʻAshar li-Majlis al-Jamiʻa, 17 October 1949–15 February 1950* (Cairo).
4. Shabib, *Hukumat ʻUmum Filastin*, 56–57.
5. Jamiʻat al-Duwal al-ʻArabiyya, *Al-Amana al-ʻAma, Mazabit Jalasat Dawr al-'Ijtimaʻ al-ʻAdi al-Hadi ʻAshar li-Majlis al-Jamiʻa, 17 October 1949–15 February 1950* (Cairo).
6. Shabib, *Hukumat ʻUmum Filastin*, 56–57.
7. Ibid., 57–58.
8. ʻAbd al-Hadi, *Awraq Khassa*, 182.
9. Jamiʻat al-Duwal al-ʻArabiyya, *Al-Amana al-ʻAma, Mazabit Jalasat Dawr al-'Ijtimaʻ al-ʻAdi al-Thani ʻAshar li-Majlis al-Jamiʻa, 25 March 1950–17 June 1950* (Cairo); see also Jamiʻat al-Duwal al-ʻArabiyya, *Fahras Muqarrarat*, 59 (March 27, 1950), 68 (April 13, 1950), 69 (June 12, 1950).
10. Jamiʻat al-Duwal al-ʻArabiyya, *Al-Amana al-ʻAma, Mazabit Jalasat Dawr al-'Ijtimaʻ al-ʻAdi al-Thalith ʻAshar li-Majlis Jamiʻat al-Duwal al-ʻArabiyya, 23 October 1950–2 February 1951* (n.p., n.d.).
11. Jamiʻat al-Duwal al-ʻArabiyya, *Al-Amana al-ʻAma, Mazabit Jalasat Dawr al-'Ijtimaʻ al-ʻAdi al-Rabiʻ ʻAshar li-Majlis Jamiʻat al-Duwal al-ʻArabiyya, 17 March 1951–19 May 1951* (n.p., n.d.).
12. Jamiʻat al-Duwal al-ʻArabiyya, *Fahras Muqarrarat*, 54.

13. Jami'at al-Duwal al-'Arabiyya, *Al-Amana al-'Ama, Mazabit Jalasat Dawr al-'Ijtima' al-'Adi al-Khamis 'Ashar li-Majlis Jami'at al-Duwal al-'Arabiyya, 3 October 1951–13 October 1951* (n.p., n.d.).

14. 'Arif, *Al-Nakba*, 3:711.

15. Jami'at al-Duwal al-'Arabiyya, *Fahras Muqarrarat*, 123.

16. On the Egyptian initiative and the Arab League Council resolution on revival of the Palestinian entity, see Shemesh, *The Palestinian Entity*, 1–8; on the Egyptian perception, see *al-Musawar*, July 10, 1959; *Akhbar al-Yawm*, December 31, 1960; *al-Akhbar* (Cairo), August 14, 1959; *al-Ahram*, August 14, 1959, August 27, 1959, February 14, 1960, December 15, 1960; *Ruz al-Yusif*, September 5, 1960.

17. On the Egyptian campaign against the mufti, see articles by Mamduh Rida in *Ruz al-Yusif*, July 6, 1959, July 20, 1959, July 27, 1959, August 3, 1959, August 10, 1959, August 17, 1959.

18. Ibid.

19. On the persecution of the mufti by the Egyptians, see *al-Jumhuriyya*, April 15, 1964, April 16, 1964, October 11, 1964, March 13, 1967, March 23, 1967; *Akhir Sa'a*, June 24, 1964, November 16, 1966; *Ruz al-Yusif*, March 23, 1964, April 13, 1964, June 5, 1964; *al-Akhbar* (Cairo), January 26, 1964, June 15, 1964; *al-Musawar*, April 24, 1964, March 9, 1967, March 23, 1967, April 6, 1967; *al-Huriyya* (Beirut), May 16, 1966.

20. Qasim, Baghdad Radio, December 15, 1959.

21. On Qasim's perception of "the eternal Palestinian republic," see Qasim, Baghdad Radio, December 15, 1959, December 18, 1959, July 29, 1960, February 2, 1961; *al-Thawra* (Baghdad), September 6, 1960, April 9, 1962, May 7, 1962, May 13, 1962; *al-Zaman* (Baghdad), May 20, 1962, August 12, 1962; see also Shemesh, *The Palestinian Entity*, 8–13.

22. Husayni, *al-Hayat*, January 12, 1960.

23. See *al-Zaman*, July 9, 1961, August 14, 1961, August 28, 1961.

24. Baghdad Radio, February 16, 1962, citing Amil al-Ghuri in his interview with the Iraqi News Agency.

25. Baghdad Radio, May 8, 1962, May 9, 1962; *al-Thawra*, May 6, 1962.

26. Husayni, Baghdad Radio, May 9, 1962.

27. On Qasim's support for the mufti, see *al-Zaman* 4, May 8, 1962; *al-Thawra* 18, May 24, 1962; ibid. 5, May 7, 1962; *al-Hawadith*, May 11, 1962, June 21, 1962.

28. See *Filastin* (magazine of the mufti) 37, March 1, 1964; ibid. 38, April 1, 1964; ibid. 40, June 1, 1964; ibid. 41, July 1, 1964; ibid. 44, October 1, 1964; ibid. 46, December 1, 1964; ibid. 47, January 1, 1965, ibid. 51, June 1, 1965; see also "Al-Hay'a al-'Arabiyya al-'Ulya," March 1964, from the private collection of documents and files from Jordanian government in the West Bank (hereinafter DJG), including Security and Intelligence Services files, 1962–64, captured by the IDF in the Six Day War, and residing at the Ben-Gurion Archives, Sede Boker, Israel; *al-Hayat*, January 8, 1964, February 19, 1964, March 3 and 12, 1964, June 26, 1964, July 17 and 21, 1964.

29. DJG, documents from file titled "Al-Hay'a al-'Arabiyya al-'Ulya," January, February, March, May, and October 1964; *al-Hayat*, January 11, 1964; February 22, 1964.

30. See *al-Akhbar* (Cairo), June 15, 1964; *al-Musawar*, June 5, 1964; see also DJG, *al-Wahda*, magazine of the ANM (Jordan), June 1964; on the mufti's activities, see DJG, documents from the years 1964–1965.

31. *Filastin* 49, March 1, 1965; *al-Hayat*, June 16, 1965; November 19, 1965; April 21, 1967; *al-Difa'*, September 14, 1967.

32. Ahmad al-Shuqayri, *Arba'un 'Aman fi al-Hayat al-'Arabiyya wa al-Duwaliyya* (Beirut, 1969), 203.

33. 'Isa al-Shu'aybi, *Al-Kiyaniyya al-Filastiniyya, 1947–1977* (Beirut: PLO Markaz al-Abhath, 1979), 33–39.

34. See Khalil al-Wazir (Abu Jihad), *Harakat Fatah, al-Nushu', al-Irtiqa', al-Tatawwur, al-Mumathil al-Shar'i, al-Bidayat* 1 (unpublished internal publication of Fatah, January 1986). (I would like to thank Yezid Sayigh for sending me a copy of this document); see also Shemesh, *The Palestinian Entity*, 246–48.

35. Ahmad al-Shuqayri, *Min al-Qimma 'Ila al-Hazima Ma'a al-Muluk wa al-Ru'asa'* (Beirut: Dar al-'Awda, 1971), 47.

PART II
NATIONAL REVIVAL

*The 1950s as the Formative Years of the
New Palestinian National Movement*

5 The Nakba Generation

It is no coincidence that the new Palestinian national movement that emerged in the mid-1960s was violent in nature. Its seeds had sprouted in the 1950s, and it grew against the background of social and political developments within Palestinian society itself, in the Arab world, and in the context of the Arab-Israeli conflict. Of particular significance were the founding of the state of Israel, the fulfillment of Zionism, and the refugee problem that resulted from the 1948 Arab-Israeli War. Events outside the region that shaped the growth of the movement included developments in the international arena in the aftermath of World War II, primarily the advance of liberalism and the intense decolonization process that took place among African and Asian nations.

Historians, who include Israelis and Palestinians who have researched the Palestinian national movement, tend to view the 1950s as a dormant period, during which no significant independent Palestinian political activity occurred. They regard the mid-1960s (1965) as the starting point for the Palestinian national awakening in its overt and concrete manifestation.

In his scholarly study "The Palestinians in the Fifties and Their Awakening as Reflected in their Literature,"[1] Yehoshafat Harkabi surveys writings by Palestinian authors published between 1961 and 1966 who addressed the issue of Palestinian society after the 1948 Nakba. Among the writers whose works Harkabi surveys are Mustafa al-Dabbagh, Niqola al-Dur, Subhi Yasin, Lutf Ghantus, Walid al-Qamhawi, Nasir al-Din al-Nashashibi, and Naji 'Alush. According to Harkabi, these writers sought to answer the following questions:

- What happened after 1948 to the various groups into which Palestinian society split?
- What social and political processes did they undergo? How did their expectations and hopes evolve? What was the prevailing mood and how did it change?
- How did the Palestinians manifest as a political factor in the Arab-Israeli conflict?[2]

Harkabi summarizes the writers' responses as follows:

> Thus from the establishment of the ephemeral "All-Palestine Government" in Gaza in October 1948 until the founding of the Palestinian Liberation Organization (PLO) in 1964, the voice of Palestinians as an organized political group

was muted.... In the fifties there was little inclination on the part of the Palestinians to organize themselves.... It seems that the Palestinian awakening must be related not to the revolutionary mood of 1956 but to the later period of regression [that is, the regression of Arab nationalism during the early 1960s].[3]

Harkabi's conclusion, ascribing the Palestinian awakening to the later period of regression, is only one side of the coin. In my opinion, a process of regression or a decline in Arab nationalism by itself would not have generated such powerful emotions and intense activity as those that erupted within a short period of time. Indeed, it was the fierce confrontation between the aspirations of Arab nationalism and the Palestinians during the 1950s—on the one hand—and Arab reality and the conflict with the state of Israel, which dashed these aspirations—on the other hand—that led to the intense outburst of Palestinian national awakening, causing it to emerge at that particular time rather than later.

In contrast to the opinions of Harkabi and Palestinian researchers, I argue that the 1950s (1949–59) were not characterized by political dormancy on the part of Palestinians. On the contrary, the 1950s were formative years during which the elements, substance, and objectives of the new Palestinian national movement took shape in the form of a national reawakening. Most elements of this national awakening differed from those of the "old" movement that had emerged during the 1920s under the leadership of Mufti Haj Amin al-Husayni. This part of the book seeks to explore the roots of the reawakening, which transpired after the outcome of the 1948 war interrupted the evolution of the "old" Palestinian national movement, and to prove that the social and political processes that Palestinian society underwent during the 1950s in fact enabled the new Palestinian national movement to emerge. This movement manifested itself in the form of the fida'iyyun (or fida'i organizations) that emerged during the mid-1960s and, more explicitly, on January 1, 1965, when the organization Fatah carried out its first guerrilla action—against Israel's National Water Carrier.

The founding of the state of Israel and the military defeat of Arab countries in the 1948 war constitute the most traumatic event that the Arab world has experienced since that time. Within the Arab world, this military defeat was described in such harsh terms as "the Filastin Catastrophe" (Nakbat Filastin or Karithat Filastin). Thirty years of intensive political and military Palestinian efforts, supported by Arab states, to prevent implementation of the Balfour Declaration and the establishment of a national homeland for the Jewish people had ultimately been ineffective.

Nakbat Filastin and the lessons to be learned from it became a key theme within social and political life in the Arab world, as well as the starting point for all matters relating to Israel, its status, and its fate in the region. Thus the "Palestinian problem" was created and it became the core issue of the Arab-Israeli conflict, replacing the Jewish Zionist–Arab Palestinian conflict that existed before the 1948 war.

The Arab world could not come to terms with its military defeat following the 1948 war or with the establishment of the state of Israel on the ground within the region, despite the armistice agreements it had signed with Israel. Arab leaders did not hide their ambitions of undoing the disgrace of defeat, and their stated intent was to wipe out the new state. In time this objective was presented as one of the fundamental goals of Arab nationalism. The struggle against Israel during this period exacerbated relations between Arab states (especially Egypt) and the state of Israel, as manifested in three central areas: the stated Arab position, with its declared aim of abolishing the state of Israel as the representative Zionist entity; an economic boycott of Israel and, in particular, prevention of the transit of Israeli ships through the Suez Canal and Straits of Tiran; and deliberate deterioration of the situation within Israel's borders, epitomized by Egypt's deployment of fida'i cells via the Gaza Strip, and from Jordan and Lebanon, in order to carry out acts of murder and guerrilla actions inside Israel.

A review of Israeli intelligence reports and surveys from the years preceding the Sinai War ("Operation Kadesh"—October 1956), which are based on reliable information, reveals that during these years Arab states had a very real and nearly obsessive fear that Israel would attack in order to expand its territory. These states even adopted emergency measures aimed at withstanding a potential Israeli assault.[4] The claims regarding Israel's "expansionist nature" as well as the talk about a second round of war were based, at least in part, on a deeply held belief that Israel had expansionist intentions. This view, for example, was prevalent among Jordanians in the period leading up to the raid on Qibya (October 1953) and after border skirmishes or retaliatory action by the Israel Defense Forces. Presumably, these concerns would have tempered the Arabs' position on matters of war and peace, but, paradoxically, the reverse occurred: the fear of peace with Israel was greater than the fear of a second round of war with Israel. Moreover, peace with Israel was perceived not only as an admission of defeat in 1948, as a public concession to the disgrace of defeat, and as capitulation on the return of refugees but also increasingly as opening the gates to an Israeli, primarily economic, invasion of the Middle East. According to this view, peace would enable Israel to expand, conduct a "cold" stealthy takeover, conquer Arab markets, eliminate Arab industry, concentrate all trade in its own hands, and so on. Thus peace came to be seen in terms of loss, and hence it was wrong to shy away from the risk of war.

In an internal report from March 20, 1950, the Arab League's secretary general summarized the Arab position on the Palestinian problem (or the Arab-Israeli conflict) to the League Council during its twelfth session:

> The Arab states are committed to the return of all the refugees who wish to return and to the granting of reparations for the property and homes of those who do not wish to return. Regarding a territorial solution, the Arab

states adhere to the position that the territory of the Jewish state as defined in the UN resolution of 1947 serves as the basis for this solution alongside territorial reparations, in accordance with two principles: first, the seizure of areas of the Jewish state for the settlement of refugees who are not returning; and second, if Israel maintains control over parts of the territories that it now occupies, which were not part of its territory under the [UN] Partition Plan, then it should supplement the Arab territory [under the Partition Plan] through compensation using [other] parts of its territory in accordance with the above-mentioned Partition Plan. In light of these considerations, the need for a territorial link between Arab states, and security considerations, the Arab delegations demanded that the [UN] Conciliation Commission include within the Arab part of Filastin [according to the Partition Plan] the remaining portions of the Negev and the Eastern Galilee, return Lydda, Ramle, Jaffa, and Be'er Sheva, [create] a corridor between Jerusalem and the Arab Jaffa Port, and make the Haifa Port a freely accessible port.[5]

Approved by the most authoritative Arab forum of the time, the provisions of this report served as the official, accepted stance of the Arab states during the period surveyed in this part. Indeed, Arab heads of states adhered to it in their public declarations, although they refrained from providing details as the secretary general had in his report. This position also served as a guideline for Arab leaders, including Nasir, in their talks with Western statesmen.

The period after the Sinai War was a formative one for the Arab world in general and for the Arab-Israeli conflict in particular. It strongly influenced the Palestinian national reawakening, which was actually a product of this period in all respects, especially the Arab-Israeli conflict as manifested at the time. The period is marked by the prominence, dominance, and undisputed leadership of Nasir following his strategic and political victory in the Sinai and Suez campaigns, which directly paved the way for the unification of Egypt and Syria and establishment of the United Arab Republic (UAR) in February 1958. This union became a driving force within Arab politics until the dissolution of the UAR in September 1961, which in turn gave rise to a "unification trauma" from which the Arab world has not yet recovered. Naturally, the Arab-Israeli conflict was influenced by these two defining events, and in its context the Palestinians, too, were affected. Indeed, the dissolution of the UAR was a great source of disappointment among educated Palestinians and constituted one of the driving forces behind Palestinian self-organization.

During this period, the Arab world gained experience in most aspects of classic Arab nationalism as it underwent challenging trials and tribulations: regime changes, revolutions, and shattered myths regarding Arab revolutions and Arab unity. Also during this time, the Arab world's perception of the elements of the Arab-Israeli conflict and its resolution took shape. Arab society in general and Palestinian society in particular underwent unprecedented formative processes with long-lasting effects. It was a new era—an era of changing goals and objectives.

The Aftershock of the Nakba

The most salient and significant phenomenon that appears in studies of the period following the Sinai War and its outcome is the depth of the trauma of the 1948 Nakba in the public consciousness and collective memory of Arabs generally and Palestinians specifically. The phenomenon is evident in Arab society to this day. For the Arab public, the aftershock of the Nakba intensified after the Sinai War. The vast multitude of publications condemning Israel and Zionism after the campaign, articles and reports in the Arab press, Arab broadcasts, and, above all, the impassioned speeches of Arab leaders themselves combined to fan the flames of hostility toward Israel and toward its very existence in the region.[6] A competition emerged among Arab states aiming for the most extreme expressions against Israel, to the point that extremism became an end in itself.

The Nakba of Filastin made a deep impression on the political consciousness of Egypt's leader, Nasir, and was an important core element in the formation of his strategy for a solution.[7] To appreciate the significance of the Nakba for Arabs and their obsessive aspiration to be liberated from it through a decisive victory over Israel, one must review the Arab press and transcripts of Arab broadcasts from the period, such as those of Egyptian commentator Ahmad Sa'id, and the speeches of Nasir and other Arab leaders, including during the May 1967 crisis. Nasir's famous line in the event that Israel were to launch a war—"ahlan wa sahlan" ("welcome")—was delivered during a speech on May 22, 1967, in which he announced the closure of the Tiran Straits to Israeli vessels.[8] His message resonated like thunder throughout the Arab world and brought Arab expectations of a victory and redemption from the disgrace of 1948 to a peak. In light of the cumulative anti-Israel sentiments that had built up since 1948 and resurged after 1956, a mere catalyst was enough to spark a fire in the form of all-out war between Israel and the Arab world. Indeed, the overall sentiment within the Arab public during the crisis period preceding the Six Day War was that the Arab world, under the leadership of Nasir, was finally advancing toward a solution to the problem of 1948, that is, the Palestinian problem.[9]

The Sinai War had two major consequences that influenced the Arab arena, the Arab-Israeli conflict, and the Palestinian national reawakening. Both of these stemmed from the emergence of Nasir as the undisputed leader of Egypt and the Arab world: his sweeping campaign for the political conquest of the Arab world, and the positioning of the Palestinian problem at the center of political discourse within this world.

The concept of Arab nationalism was at the core of Nasir's campaign to conquer the Arab world, a campaign he launched in a speech on November 7,

1956. The period between 1957 and 1961 was the golden age of Arab nationalism in general and Nasirism in particular. The principles of Arab nationalism that Nasir advocated formed the essence of Nasirism.[10] He advocated active, militant Arab nationalism using all means, including force, to implement its principles. Nasir identified a number of goals for Arab nationalism, foremost among them the liberation of the Arab world in political, social, and economic terms and the abolition of imperialism and of Arab reactionism.[11]

The second consequence of Nasir's political victory in the Sinai War was his intensive effort to raise Arab consciousness regarding the Palestinian problem and its solution. During this time, Nasir promoted the "problem of Filastin" and the "liberation of Filastin" to the status of central agenda items for the Arab world. He viewed the Palestinian problem as an integral part of his perspective of Arab nationalism, that is, the perspective of Nasirism. For him, the lessons of the 1948 war were a starting point in the formulation of a strategy to address the conflict. The struggle against Zionism was as important to him as the struggle against imperialism. During the victorious aftermath of the campaign—and particularly during the time of the Egyptian-Syrian union, which constituted the height of his success in the Arab arena—he greatly advanced Arab consciousness of the Filastin problem. Immediately after the Sinai War, Nasir began to attack Israel in his speeches more harshly than he had ever previously. He asserted that all his actions in Egypt and within the Arab arena were directed toward the liberation of Filastin and argued that this problem was the most salient driving force behind developments in the Arab East. He even portrayed his military intervention in Yemen as a step toward the liberation of Filastin.[12]

The Sinai War resulted in a change in Egypt's strategy toward a solution to the Palestinian problem. As part of this new strategy, Nasir used the campaign to position the Palestinians as a principal party to the conflict by depicting the Palestinian problem as the national problem of a people aspiring to self-determination, thus making it a permanent problem until its goal were to be achieved. The concrete manifestation of this process was the 1959 Egyptian initiative to revive the Palestinian entity after it had "disappeared" following the 1948 war.

Having turned the Palestinian problem into the core issue of Arab nationalism, Nasir set out to demonstrate his commitment to a solution, thereby raising expectations among Arabs in general and Palestinians in particular that under his leadership the Arab world would indeed liberate Filastin. Nasir's commitment to solving the Palestinian problem was revalidated during the years 1964–67. As an expression of his commitment, Nasir placed the Palestinian problem at the center of Arab world divisions and called for a united effort toward its resolution. Arab unity became, in his words "the path to the liberation of Filastin." He presented the unification of Egypt and Syria as a union for the sake of Filastin, and its dissolution as a disaster for the Filastin problem. Besides the Yemen war, the war against Arab reactionism and Western imperialism were also depicted as serving the cause of Filastin. Nasir went so far as to assert that all his actions were aimed at solving the problem of Filastin.

An analysis of Nasir's policy reveals, among other things, that the outcomes of the Sinai War significantly exacerbated the Arab-Israeli conflict, or what Arab states called "the problem of Filastin." This conclusion contradicts the assumption that has prevailed for years among Israeli researchers and statesmen, which holds that the campaign was followed by a period of calm, as conveyed by the biblical phrase "and the land was quiet" for eleven years. In fact, only along the border with Egypt did calm prevail, as the border with Jordan and especially the border with Syria were not quiet. The deteriorating state of security along these two borders was one of the aggravating factors leading to the Six Day War. Additional factors that exacerbated the Arab-Israeli conflict in the aftermath of the Sinai War included the Palestinian problem and its resolution as a focus of political discourse in the Arab world and the Palestinian national reawakening as manifested in the appearance of fida'i organizations, foremost among which was Fatah. Nasir and his perspective of Arab nationalism left their mark on these two phenomena. Exacerbation of the Arab-Israeli conflict, in turn, had a significant influence on the Palestinian national reawakening and contributed to reemergence of the issue of a Palestinian entity and its revival.

The struggle over water between Israel and the Arab states, which had begun in 1959, was another salient factor that aggravated the Arab-Israeli conflict and worsened the security situation, which in turn led to the breakout of the Six Day War. The struggle over water hastened Arab action and even resulted in the Arab states, for the first time, preparing a military plan for the destruction of the state of Israel and defining a long-term strategic goal in their conflict with Israel.[13]

Nasir's handling of the water problem and of the conflict with Israel was the main impetus for his call on December 23, 1963, to convene an Arab summit meeting. That summit would once again address the question of a Palestinian entity, and as such, the Arab debate on the water issue benefited the issue of a Palestinian entity.[14] The first Arab Summit took place in January 1964.

From this point forward, historical developments had the effect of further highlighting the Palestinian problem: Arab League discussions during the years 1959–63 that addressed elements of the Arab-Israeli conflict and how to resolve it paved the way to resolutions of the first Arab Summit regarding the revival of the Palestinian entity; these resolutions in turn paved the way for the founding of the PLO by Ahmad al-Shuqayri; the discussions and resolutions of the Khartoum Summit of August–September 1967 then sealed Shuqayri's fate, thereby paving the way for Palestinian fida'i organizations to take control of the Palestinian establishment; and the resolutions of the Rabat Summit of October 1974 recognized the PLO as the sole legal representative of the Palestinian people, that is, they recognized it as a principal party to the conflict and, effectively, denied Jordan the possibility of regaining the West Bank.

Applying a historical perspective today makes it possible to identify the two most important events of that period in the transformation of the Palestinian problem into the core issue in the Arab-Israeli conflict: the founding of the Palestine Liberation Organization in June 1964 and the emergence of the Palestine National Liberation Movement (Fatah) in January 1965. Fatah's emergence was a sign that fida'i organizations had become the leaders of the new Palestinian national movement. These two events constituted turning points in the development of the Palestinian national movement and in the part it played within the Arab-Israeli conflict.

The founding of the PLO, the emergence of Fatah, Arab activities aimed at reviving the Palestinian entity, and the struggle between King Husayn and Shuqayri, in combination, reinforced national consciousness among Palestinians generally and West Bank residents specifically and heralded the Palestinian national reawakening. This reawakening, in turn, was a key contributing factor to the increasing centrality of the Palestinian issue within the Arab-Israeli conflict, as strongly evidenced after the IDF raid on the village of Samu' on November 13, 1966. As a consequence of the raid, for the first time since Jordan's official annexation of the West Bank in April 1950, the Jordanian leadership reevaluated relations between the Hashemite regime and the Palestinian population of the West Bank and began to formulate options regarding the extent of autonomy to be granted to West Bank residents.[15]

During this time, the influence of pan-Arab nationalist, leftist political movements—such as the Arab Nationalists Movement (ANM), the Ba'th Party, and pro-Nasir movements—reached its peak. The Palestinian intelligentsia and the young generation of Palestinians found fertile ground in these movements for their political activities and promotion of their agenda.

The founders of Fatah and other *fida'i* (guerilla) organizations were shaped by the Arab nationalism that Nasir advocated after the Sinai War. In July 1956, reacting to Nasir's speech about the nationalization of the Suez Canal, Abu Iyad, one of Fatah's founders, said, "Henceforth Nasir has become the leader of the struggle against imperialism. . . . Nasir has reclaimed the honor and self-confidence of Arabs and all Third World peoples. Anything is now possible, including the liberation of Filastin."[16]

The dissolution of the union between Egypt and Syria (September 1961), a union that provided the military and political basis for the "liberation of Filastin," derailed the Palestinians' hopes of achieving liberation through Arab unity. The renowned Palestinian researcher, 'Isam Sakhnini, addressed this issue in 1972: "The unification of the two states, at a minimum . . . constituted the foundation on which Palestinians based their hopes and dreams for the liberation of their homeland. The dissolution [of the UAR] sowed doubts among Palestinians regarding the value of waiting for Arab unification. They therefore began to seek independent forms of Palestinian action through which the Palestinian people could act directly, with no intermediary."[17]

The Palestinian Arena: National Awakening in the Shadow of Social Disintegration

During the 1950s, Palestinian society experienced two fundamental and seemingly contradictory processes. At the level of leadership, Palestinians underwent a general crisis, manifested by their political disappearance from the Arab arena and disappearance of the term "Filastin" from the geopolitical map of the Middle East. At the popular level, Palestinian society underwent far-reaching changes in the aftermath of the 1948 war and emergence of the refugee problem. The result of these sociopolitical processes was a Palestinian national reawakening. It is not possible to understand the emergence of the new Palestinian national movement without understanding the processes that Palestinian society underwent. This Palestinian awakening served as the background, and perhaps also the driving force, for the leadership crisis that befell the Palestinian leader who entered the spotlight within the Palestinian and Arab arena in the early 1960s—Ahmad al-Shuqayri.

The Palestinians held high expectations that Arab countries would take action for the sake of *al-'awda* (the return). The reality of the Arab world not only failed to meet their expectations, it even dashed any hope of achieving their dream of returning. This gap between expectations and reality generated a deep sense of frustration among the second generation of Palestinians after 1948, and that frustration is what drove the second generation to take matters into its own hands and seek to pursue its interests on its own.

The seeds of the new Palestinian national movement had already sprouted by the time Israel captured the Gaza Strip in the course of the Sinai War. Fatah leaders ascribe the initial conception of their organization to this period of Israeli conquest, and some even claim to have taken part in the struggle against that conquest. It is not surprising, therefore, that a large portion of Fatah's founders were originally from Gaza. Moreover, by 1958, shortly after Israel had completed its withdrawal from Gaza, the ideology of Fatah's founders who had studied at Cairo University already began to take shape.[18] By 1959, the organizational structure had already been established and additional Palestinian organizations were beginning to appear.[19]

Disappointment with the Arab world was compounded by the persecution of Fatah members, during their early days, at the hands of Arab states. These factors became a source of trauma whose scars were long evident and, in fact, are visible to this day. For example, during a speech on January 6, 1976, Abu Iyad spoke out against Arab states because they had not provided assistance to Palestinians during the 1958 civil war in Lebanon. In his words,

> The Arab states deceived us after 1948. As they have deceived us in the past, so too they are deceiving us now. The [Arab] leaders deceived us then, after the [Palestinian] masses believed them [and then] began to feel that the eight days needed for the Arab armies and governments to save them turned into forty years, during which they suffered all manner of humiliation. We were treated like slaves. The Arab intelligence [services] pursued us in order to smother us. . . . Arab governments fought us. . . . The Palestinian revolution broke out after our people grew tired of words and chatter.[20]

Research into the history of the Palestinian national reawakening raises a number of salient questions, which subsequent chapters will attempt to answer:

- How did it happen that a scattered society of refugees produced a national movement that is militant in both character and action?
- How should one seek to understand the near-total recruitment of Palestinians for the national cause and the overall popular support for the Palestinian national movement?
- How did a scattered and divided society of refugees attain such a high degree of social solidarity—a solidarity that proved essential to its national reawakening, a solidarity that drew universal support and enabled the continuing survival of this society and its achievements in the face of the most difficult crises it had endured since its emergence in the regional political arena?

The Nakba Generation

From a historical perspective, the 1948 Nakba was and remains the worst trauma that the Palestinians experienced since the Palestinian national awakening of the 1920s. The term "Nakba" was originally applied to the 1948 Arab defeat, encompassing the catastrophe that befell the Palestinians and the consequent refugee problem. Books and articles published during the 1950s analyzed the causes of the overall Arab defeat, pointing to social and cultural reasons as well as technological inferiority, among others.

Qustantin Zurayq's *Ma'na al-Nakba* (The significance of the Nakba), whose first edition was published as early as August 1948, was a pioneering study that explored the roots of the Nakba. Zurayq argues that the near-term remedy for the Nakba should be based on five elements: "reinforcing the sense of danger and the will to struggle, material mobilization in all sectors of industry, the highest degree of unification possible among Arab states, inclusion of popular forces in battle, [and] Arab willingness to reach internal agreements and sacrifice some of their own interests for the sake of repelling the greatest danger of all." Despite his recommendations, the Arabs suffered another military defeat with the Six Day War, which drove him to write another book, *Ma'na al-Nakba Mujddadan* (The significance of the Nakba Renewed). In so doing, he was seeking to make the point that the Arabs had not learned the lessons of the 1948 Nakba.[21]

Two Palestinian writers also responded immediately to the Nakba. The first was Musa al-'Alami, whose book *'Ibrat Filastin* (The lesson of Filastin) was published in 1949, and the second was Qadri Tuqan, whose book *Ba'da al-Nakba* (Following the Nakba) was published in 1950. 'Alami's book begins by attributing full responsibility for the Nakba to Britain because of the Balfour Declaration. He divides the Nakba between the phase of Palestinian defense and the later phase of Arab defense. In his opinion, "We failed in both phases because we were fighting a divided war, whereas the Jews were fighting an inclusive war. They were well armed and we were poorly armed. Their goal was clearly defined and ours—not coordinated." 'Alami saw Arab unity as the solution to the Nakba. He called for a change to Arab regimes, the creation of a "strong and inclusive cultural regime," and the implementation of a comprehensive plan to make use of Arab resources and establish a national defense mechanism.[22]

In contrast to Musa al-'Alami's political and military outlook, the starting point for Qadri Tuqan, as an educator, was educational and cultural. Tuqan's book opens by calling on Arabs to rediscover the vulnerabilities in their national structure and rewrite Arab history, with special attention to Arab contributions in the fields of science and culture, rather than settling for a record of history based on fighting and struggles. He devotes an entire chapter to the need for a renewed discussion of cultural programs as a basis for any response to the Nakba. He also speaks of the need to formulate a new philosophy of culture that will, for example, transform the study of history into the study of industrial, conceptual, cultural, and educational history. Tuqan emphasizes the need to employ a scientific methodology in all aspects of life, and he adopts the approach of Zurayq and 'Alami, according to whom the Jews defeated the Arabs through the weapons of science and organization, which the Arabs did not possess.[23]

The impact of the Nakba on the Arab public was compounded by the Sinai War, which sparked a multitude of books, articles, papers, and broadcasts in the Arab world denouncing Israel and Zionism. Above all, it fueled impassioned speeches by Arab leaders, who promoted hostility toward Israel and the denial of its very existence in the region.

In time, and in particular after the Six Day War and emergence of the Palestinian factor as a core issue in the Arab-Israeli conflict, the meaning of the term "Nakba" shifted from serving as a description of the all-Arab catastrophe to serving as an exclusive description of the disaster that befell the Palestinians after the 1948 war, and it retains this meaning today.

The Nakba became the most important aspect of the collective memory of Palestinians, and especially of refugees descended from the 1948 generation. Its outcome shaped the new Palestinian identity, and its impact is evident among the Palestinian generations that followed, having been transmitted from one generation to the next. Activists from the second generation, which came to be known as the Generation of Liberation (Jeel al-Tahrir), became leaders of the new Palestinian movement and founders of the Palestinian organizations that emerged during the late 1950s and early 1960s.

As more time passed, the trauma of the Nakba intensified and turned into a myth on which future Palestinian generations were raised. Like any myth, it acquired new attributes over time. It became an integral part of every Palestinian's life, even those whose parents had not personally experienced the event, such as residents of the West Bank who became subjects of the Hashemite Kingdom of Jordan.

The Parents' Generation: Disintegration of the Social Structure

The quintessential social phenomenon among the Palestinians after the 1948 war and the Nakba was the emergence of Palestinian refugees and refugee camps in Arab countries, especially in Jordan, Lebanon, the Gaza Strip, and Syria, as well as Iraq and Egypt. The number of Palestinian refugees who left or were expelled from territories under Israel's control is a matter of dispute among researchers from Israel, the West, Palestinian communities, and Arab states.

In his study, Moshe Efrat, an expert in Middle Eastern economics, concluded that the number of Palestinian refugees in 1949 stood at 666,000.[24] In contrast, a study by Janet Abu-Lughod arrived at a higher figure—780,000 refugees in 1949.[25] The UN-sponsored Clapp Mission, for its part, recorded 716,000 refugees.[26]

Efrat compared his estimates with those of the United Nations Relief and Works Agency for Palestine Refugees in the Near East (UNRWA), using figures for the distribution of refugees by location of the camps in which they resided in various countries in 1949.[27] (See table 5.1.)

The "generational structure" that developed among refugees and within Palestinian society more generally after 1948 is an important aspect of any effort to understand the background of the Palestinian national reawakening. The basic premises established by Karl Mannheim for identifying the characteristics of a "political generation" are also applicable to the problem of generations that emerged within the Palestinian population.[28] Indeed, Arab and Palestinian literature on the period after 1948 views the social side effects of the refugee phenomenon as an important contributing factor in shaping the principles and goals of the new Palestinian national movement. The national awakening is regarded as the protest of the "younger generation" against the injustice to which the parents'

Table 5.1. Actual number of refugees (in thousands) as recorded (including camps)

	Efrat's estimate	UNRWA data
East Bank of the Jordan River	65	158
West Bank (including East Jerusalem)	249	335
Gaza Strip	165	193
Lebanon	71	124
Syria	70	80
Israel	46	46
TOTAL	666	936

generation was subjected and against the hostile treatment of this population in exile by Arab society, as well as an expression of the disintegration of the social structure of the traditional Palestinian community.

The parents' generation included the heads of uprooted families, who had moved with their families to Arab countries, the West Bank, or the Gaza Strip. These heads of families were at least in their late twenties. Drawing on Karl Mannheim's findings regarding the formative years of an individual, the parents' generation of Palestinian refugees was shaped by the historical events and social changes of the 1930s or 1940s, that is, the events in Palestine during the 1930s and World War II.

This generation experienced an upheaval in terms of its social status as a consequence of the disintegration of the old social class structure and its own inability to construct a new foundation on its ruins. Although it was present during the social changes that took place within Palestinian society after 1948, because of this generation's advanced average age and the social and economic changes that took place after being uprooted, it did not have the means to respond actively to the revolutionary changes taking place within society. The immediate upheaval in fact caused a deep state of shock within the parents' generation. Contributing factors included a rapid collapse of its material foundation and social structure resulting from the loss of its essential means of production—namely, the land—and the subsequent change in values and codes of conduct, which created emotional and intellectual tension.[29]

After the war had scattered Palestinian society, the resulting fragmentation transformed it into a heterogeneous society. Villages and families were broken apart, and the families that reassembled in refugee camps were, for the most part, incomplete. "Fragments of families and villages that found themselves gathered in the same camp were unable to form large societies, given that the only social ties uniting them were their shared pain."[30] Anis al-Qasim summarizes this phenomenon: "Palestinian society ceased being so. It lost the social ties that had formed over many generations of belonging to the land, the city, and the family."[31]

There was another aspect to the problem of social status: in traditional Arab society, and to a significant extent in contemporary Arab society as well, the status of the individual is guaranteed by his belonging to the extended family network, father's home, and community (or clan). For the Palestinian refugees who were scattered throughout various camps and cities, this social foundation no longer existed. For example, in 1967 one West Bank refugee camp was found to have 108 households that had come from eighteen different places and belonged to an even greater number of clans. The refugees had thus lost most of the advantages of belonging to an established social structure.[32]

In effect, all social classes within Palestinian society lost their greater framework and cohesion, and, consequently, the network of relationships among them was lost as well. While traditional Palestinian social classes disappeared, the Palestinian bourgeois class also lost any ambitions or goals of its own as well as internal ties and ties with other social classes, and it was scattered throughout the Arab countries.[33] These new circumstances reduced the opportunities for new Palestinian social classes to emerge.

The role of the father, who had been dominant in traditional Palestinian society, was now transformed. His standing and authority were undermined: his status as family provider was changed by the UNRWA, and his children's dependence on him was diminished, resulting in loss of authority over his children, a weakened ability to transmit his values to them, and the dissolution of the family. The role of the family itself also changed. Because the social frameworks of the village and clan had fragmented, the smaller framework—namely, the family nucleus—became the focus of identity or affiliation.[34]

In concluding his 1955 study of refugees' attitudes, Fred Bruhns mentions "the peculiar character of Arab society, where cohesion is derived less from economic values than from values involving personal and traditional ties." In his view, the attempt to apply Western social values to Arab society "appears to be a point where Western understanding of the Arab falls, perhaps tragically, short." In the course of his study, it became apparent to Bruhns that "refugees, as a group, feel uprooted to a much greater extent socially than they do economically.... It was found that to the refugees [social uprootedness] means mainly the severance of personal and traditional ties connected with the concepts of home, family, clan, and community." Moreover, these lost ties "constitute the main source of their psychological security and balance.... Secondary relationships, i.e., those with persons not definitely known, are infinitely less rewarding in terms of psychological security than they are in Western societies.... To an Arab, leaving his home is profoundly disturbing, even with the prospect of economic betterment."[35]

Bruhns's conclusion is illustrated by the results of a survey of the refugee camp Jelazoon. The study, conducted by the Shiloah Institute in the autumn of

1967, concluded, "The refugees are not grouped by background or village of origin. There is no such arrangement in the camp, and even [refugees] from the same village residing in the same camp do not form such groups. Rather, ties between former villagers are expressed in the fabric of individual relations that link family members and people who came from the same region."[36]

The Parents' Generation: Loss of the Land

A key factor at the heart of the Palestinian refugee's world, which contributed significantly to Palestinian social solidarity, is the land. Besides the notion of physical ownership, the concept of "the land" embodies an entire network of related values, aspirations, and longings. The land was and remains the centerpiece of collective memory for Palestinians generally and refugees specifically. Before 1948, Palestinian society was primarily agrarian, and the land was therefore virtually the entire world for the Palestinian. Hence one can appreciate the extent of the trauma for refugees, as their displacement from Filastin entailed the loss of their land. This loss and the longing to return to the land—'awda—became the strongest factor uniting Palestinian society after 1948, and portrayals of the land that the refugees had left behind acquired a degree of idealization far beyond the conditions that actually existed in 1948.

The loss of their land also resulted in the loss of social status for the parents' generation. The refugees viewed the loss of land as causing the deterioration of their social standing and separating them from their surroundings. The phrases "he who has no land has no religion or homeland" and "anyone without land is contemptible" became commonplace. Matters were further exacerbated when other Arabs accused the refugees of selling their lands to Jews and regarded them as rootless because they did not possess land. This attitude toward the refugees on the part of their neighbors was further reinforced by the refugees themselves, who shared their perspective. Even in 1967, nearly twenty years after they had ceased to earn a living from their lands, refugees still maintained the value system of an agrarian society, according to which there is no substitute for dispossession. "Refugees said that being dispossessed is like having the mark of Cain on their foreheads and that their inferior status follows them everywhere and will continue to pursue them even after a century has passed."[37]

A close link existed between the land and the myth of return ('awda). Each fed into the other, increasing its power and impact.

The Vision of the Return—'Awda

The world of the 1948 generation of refugees centered on the slogan of return to Filastin, that is, 'awda. This generation viewed the slogan in a passive rather than active sense, after it was persuaded that its chances of returning to its homeland would best be served not by active measures on its part but by the Arab states, which promised to liberate its land in the near future. Over time, the slogan of 'awda began to acquire the qualities of a vision and permeate not only the lives of the parents' generation but also those of future generations, although its content, significance, and manner of realization changed from one generation to the next.

Consequently, the perception of 'awda was relegated to a separate sphere, distinct from that of day-to-day reality. Nor was any attempt made to examine it critically. For Palestinian refugees, it symbolized redemption from the state of loss and the nadir they had reached after 1948.[38]

Arab leaders, statesmen, and writers fueled the Nakba generation's hope that the 'awda would soon take place, and the Arab media showered the refugees with promises of returning to Filastin and to their homes. Special programs for refugees on Arab radio stations would conclude with the slogan "we will return" (*innana 'a'idoon*). Radio dramas reinforced this hope. Radio Amman had a long-running operetta that began in 1955, titled "The Returnees" ("al-'A'idun"), while Radio Damascus broadcasted a special program under the heading "Talk of Return" within the framework of "The Filastin Segment" in the years after 1948. In refugee camps, schools were decorated with slogans that said "we will return" and with pictures of the cities and villages of Filastin, as were textbooks. A special oath was composed for children, pledging return, and maps and textbooks were adorned with the slogan "we will return." Arab states also issued stamps with this slogan. Parents and children were identified by their place of origin, in addition to their names. Children told stories of their villages of origin, as relayed by their parents. The streets of the Gaza Strip were filled with signs stating "we will return" and "Jaffa awaits you."[39] The Palestinian press in the Gaza Strip and the general Arab press were filled with poems of longing and glorious descriptions of all aspects of Filastin.

Palestinian literature, and especially Palestinian poetry from the years after 1948, was primarily devoted to the Nakba. Known as "literature of the Nakba" (*adab al-Nakba*) or "literature of exile" (*adab al-manfa*), this literature depicted the circumstances of the refugee in stark terms, full of despair and defeat. The generation of the refugees (parents) was therefore termed "the generation of defeat" and its poets were known as "the defeated."[40] The term was not intended as an insult but, rather, as a description of the subject matter of Palestinian poetry during this period in the eyes of its poets and writers—despair, bitterness, and lament.

The vision of return was at the heart of the poetry of Fadwa Tuqan, the most prominent poet of the early 1950s. Tuqan published numerous collections of poems describing the refugee condition, including *Wahdi ma'a al-Ayyam* (1952), *Wajadtuha* (1959), and *Nida' al-Ard*. Her poetry "described the determination of the refugee to return at any cost" as well as his dream of fulfilling his oath of returning to his land.⁴¹ Other poets also wrote poems about the return. In her collection of poems, *Al-'Awda min al-Nab' al-Halim* (1960), Salma al-Jayusi wrote that "the 'awda will only be attained by way of a long, realistic, and difficult journey." The refugee poet from Gaza, Harun Hashim Rashid, published at least six collections of poetry during the 1950s addressing the issue of return, among others. These collections include *'Awdat al-Ghuraba* (1956) and *Ardh al-Turath* (1959). His poetry expresses his belief that the 'awda would indeed be realized. Among the symbols that Harun Rashid and other poets used as an expression of return was the key to their homes, which the Palestinians would carry with them throughout their travels while in exile. Rashid even devoted a poem specifically to this issue, in which "the key is sanctified and serves as an object of praise and prayer."⁴²

Against this background and in light of the policy of Arab states to preserve the Palestinian problem as a bargaining chip, the Palestinian refugees categorically rejected any suggestion that their problem be resolved through permanent settlement in the countries where they were then located.

According to Fawaz Turki, it was in effect a private as well as collective decision on the part of the refugees to reject any assimilation within Arab societies, which in his opinion they hated. Accordingly, any initiative aimed at improving their living conditions within the camps had to come from the UNRWA rather than Arab governments:

> The UNRWA begin to plant trees along the dirt track. They begin to rebuild some of the mud houses. They begin to remove the tents. They begin to beautify the camp. That's what they say they are doing, making the place more habitable.... We don't want the sons of dogs to make the place more habitable, [the refugees] say to each other. We want to return. What they are doing is to make our stay here more permanent.... The following day ... we uproot [the trees].⁴³

Fred Bruhns, in a 1955 study of a sample group of refugees in the Gaza Strip, concluded that only about 10 percent were willing to accept a permanent solution not based on returning to their original places of residence. He found that one of the reasons for this unwillingness was that they perceived permanent resettlement as "acceptance of permanent defeat and of permanent expatriation." Furthermore, resettlement "can be accomplished only with the far-reaching cooperation of the Arab governments concerned.... But what inter-Arab cooperation exists is directed precisely the other way, namely, toward maintaining the refugees under United Nations responsibility in their present uneconomic locations and toward preventing a genuine, large-scale economic integration."⁴⁴

In 1964, the Norwegian couple Ingrid and Johan Galtung conducted an extensive study of Palestinians in the Gaza Strip. They reached the same conclusion.

In their words, "It is difficult to imagine a social group with a more homogenous perception and definition of past and present than the refugees in the Gaza Strip ... [r]egardless of age, income, educational level and the social status in general of the persons we spoke with." They note that "at the entrance to the Gaza Strip from the Egyptian side, there is an obelisk with a map of Palestine and the slogan, 'We shall return,'" adding that "everybody in the area was willing and able to repeat this if asked" and that "Palestine, like Israel for the Jews, has become the magic country, a possession they do not possess but that has possessed their minds." They found strong opposition to anything that could be interpreted as the settlement of refugees in Gaza. "Any symbol that could be seen as a capitulation to the Israelis was seen as treason." They also found that any effort to improve the refugees' living conditions, or to make arrangements that could be interpreted as permanent settlement and concrete evidence of their lack of commitment to the theme of returning to Palestine, was completely rejected. The researchers explained this perspective in terms of the refugees' sense that agreeing to such changes means relinquishing their belief in the return and admitting that it is a remote goal. The Galtungs concluded that the refugees' doubts about returning to their homes did not undermine their certainty that eventually a united military effort by the Arabs would succeed in defeating Israel. The refugees believed—on the basis of the financial and numerical superiority of Arab peoples and armies— that eventually they would return.[45] Presumably, this assessment is applicable not only to Gaza Strip refugees but also to West Bank refugees.

The Palestinian refugees' view as just presented is also reflected in annual UNRWA reports from the 1950s. For example, in its discussion of the Palestinians' desire to return to their homes in Palestine, the UNRWA report for 1959–60 states that nearly all researchers who had studied the problem emphasized the refugees' strong desire to return to their homeland and their rejection of any other solution. This feeling, which did not diminish over time, was reinforced by the people and governments of the host countries.[46]

Given the importance of the Nakba and the vision of return in the collective memory of the refugees, it is not surprising that the past, before expatriation, was depicted in ideal terms and became an important part of the refugee's daily life. Fond reminiscence became the means of dealing with harsh reality. Fawaz Turki notes that in the eyes of the first generation of refugees, the present does not exist at all, and history came to a standstill in 1948: "To them the present was insanity, not a natural continuum of what was. To relate to it, they would transform it into an arrested past. A past governed by Palestinian images, Palestinian rites.... They would look at themselves in the mirror of their past, for had they looked at the present, the mirror would have been cracked. The image of their reality blurred." Turki further observes that "a Palestinian child, whether born in Beirut, Amman, or Damascus, would be instructed to identify himself as a

Palestinian from Haifa or Lydda or any other town that had been his parents' birthplace."⁴⁷

The idealization of everything related to the land that the Palestinians had left (school, village, orchard, stream), compounded by longings, formed part of their commitment to 'awda. In his 1965 booklet *Biladuna Filastin*, Mustafa al-Dabbagh nostalgically describes Filastin as if every village had remained unchanged since 1948: "The pure land, the good land, the green valleys, the vineyards, the olive groves, the hills, and the flourishing meadows." Dabbagh asks, "When will we return and see our villages, our cities, and the gardens of our homes? When will we return to the place where we truly want to live and die? We are waiting for the moment when we return to our good land."⁴⁸

Such longings and idealistic descriptions can also be found in the Palestinian press from the 1950s in the Gaza Strip and in the Jordanian press from the same period. For example, in 1952, the Gaza-based newspaper *al-Raqib* published a letter describing Jaffa under the headline "Dreams of Reality," undoubtedly written by a refugee:

> Beyond the horizon facing me, memories surfaced as I gazed at the waves of the sea. Riding on the wings of these memories, I reached the good land, the land of my childhood, where I grew up. I recalled quiet, beloved Jaffa. I recalled the beautiful, beloved brides. I recalled the streets, where boxes of merchandise from neighboring countries would be piled up. I recalled the beautiful streets and tall buildings. I recalled all this, until I felt that my heart was melting because of these faraway, lovely memories.⁴⁹

Another letter from the same year, under the heading "Memories," was submitted to the newspaper by a Palestinian refugee who described the orchards of Filastin "that looked like gold in the light of day and silver in the dark of night."⁵⁰ Similar descriptions appeared in the monthly *Filastinuna*, which was published by Fatah starting in 1959.

In the aftermath of defeat and the founding of the state of Israel, Palestinian ideologues, poets, and writers—conscious of the weakness of their claims to a historic link between the Palestinian national movement and Filastin itself and of the absence of a historical heritage that compared to Judaism's historical ties to the land of Israel—sought to base their relationship to Filastin on emotional ties. A typical example of this approach can be found in a 1963 article by Tibawi, who asserts that "the most significant literary and artistic output has hitherto been unnoticed not only by independent students of the Palestine problem but surprisingly also by Arabs and Zionists alike. They have all been so preoccupied with manifest political matters that they have failed to assess the political power of ideas and emotions." His study aims "to call attention only to representative samples of this [Palestinian] literary and artistic output, and to point out the part it is likely to play in the course of general Arab political thought on Palestine, and in bringing up generations of Palestine Arabs to whom the aim of regaining the homeland is becoming more and more an article of faith."[51]

Tibawi concludes that "the present Arab emotion concerning 'the return' is no less intense than the sentiments expressed by the Psalmist: 'If I forget thee, o Jerusalem, let my right hand forget her cunning... if I prefer not Jerusalem above my chief joy.'" His perspective is reflected in the assertion that "there is already a striking similarity between present Arab aspirations and emotions concerning 'the return' and those from which Zionism was born. There is thus a 'new Zionism' in the making, an 'Arab Zionism' with the aim of returning to the homeland." Tibawi believes that "it is not likely that serious Arab intellectuals will take too long to recognize the significance of their own 'Psalmists' who remember Jerusalem and long for Palestine." To reinforce his views on the importance of emotions for a national awakening, he queries, "Need one remark that ideas and emotions have only too often proved more effective than armor?" and then adds, "Like the old Zionists, 'the new' [Palestinians] quite obviously intend to translate aspirations and emotions into achievement and action. They may still be vague concerning the means, but there is no doubt about the intentions. This is a phase, after all, through which the old Zionists, too, had to pass before their triumph."[52]

The vision of return became an inseparable part of daily life and of the spiritual and cultural life of the Palestinians—a social ideology of sorts. Indeed, the vision of return infused the very threads of their social fabric, until it became, in effect, a religious experience. The Nakba became a sacred national symbol of identity. The 1948 exodus from Filastin came to be defined as *hijra*, a term with religious significance that refers to the Prophet Muhammad's migration from Mecca to Medina and embodies the promise of return and further conquests.[53]

Tibawi and other Palestinian writers focus strongly on the element of longing for "the homeland of Filastin" in post-1948 Palestinian poetry as evidence of the emotional ties between Palestinians and Filastin. This literature of exile (*manfa*) is based on a sense of foreignness and deep longing.

One of the frequently cited poets of the 1950s is Mahmud al-Hut, a Jaffa native who studied at the University of Beirut. In one of his poems he describes Filastin as "paradise lost," thereby granting it the same status as the heavenly Garden of Eden.[54] Another poet, who "represents the Psalmist spirit and new Zionism," is Ahmad Fahmi, a native of Safed. He describes "the feelings of the refugee, who misses not only his city of birth but also all parts of his homeland."[55] One of his poems describes "the beautiful mountains of Safed, the enchanting Yarmuk [River], morning in the hills of Galilee." The subject matter of this poetry invites the claim that "these Palestinian writers are reiterating the emotions expressed by the first Jewish settlers in Filastin."[56]

Two additional noteworthy poets from the 1950s who expressed longing for the homeland are Salma Jayusi and Mu'ayn Bsiso. The latter also described Filastin as paradise.[57]

The same motifs that characterize 1950s Palestinian poetry appear, even more expressively, in Palestinian art, which in essence was political art comparable to the poetry of the Nakba. This art is informed by the experience of exile and uprootedness that characterized Palestinian society after the Nakba. Palestinian art from the 1950s, and to a certain extent from the 1960s as well, embodies such motifs as the return, longing for the homeland of Filastin, idealization of anything related to the homeland that was left behind, and depictions of it as "paradise lost." Like the literature of the Nakba, Palestinian art from the decade immediately following 1948 may be termed "art of the Nakba." In her book *Palestinian Art*, Gannit Ankori devotes a special chapter to this topic under the title "Exile and Memories: Art after 1948," that is, the first decade following the Nakba.[58] Ankori notes,

> The dominant features that differentiate between post-Nakba art and pre-1948 culture are a deep sense of fragmentation that is a direct result of the Nakba itself. This fragmentation impacted Palestinian art in numerous ways related to both style and content.... Also, after the Nakba a dialectic between rootedness and displacement came to dominate Palestinian art as a defining thematic focus. Finally, in several sectors of Palestinian society (particularly those close to the PLO establishment) the emphasis on Palestinian nationalism, with its urgent political agenda, replaced the slow evolutionary development that characterized art in pre-1948 Palestine, which allowed for ethnically diverse, non-nationalist and individual expressions alongside the articulation of collective identity components.[59]

Two painters from the decade immediately following the Nakba are particularly prominent among Palestinian artists from that time, and each represented a genre of Palestinian painting that complemented the other's: Ismail Shammout portrayed the "road to exile" while Ibrahim Ghannam portrayed "nostalgia for the past in Palestine." These two, alongside their counterparts in Palestinian literature and poetry, contributed to the construction of a new Palestinian identity. After the Six Day War, the genre known as "resistance literature" emerged. This literature was greatly influenced by the Palestinian fida'i organizations, which believed in armed struggle for the liberation of Filastin and represented the "new Palestinian."[60]

Gannit Ankori concludes, "The three dominant themes of mainstream Palestinian art ... the road to exile, the armed struggle, and nostalgic images of the lost homeland—played a significant role in the construction of Palestinian national identity. On a small scale, Shammout, Ghannam, and their colleagues performed tasks that were analogous to those of the Mexican mural painters, particularly Diego Rivera. . . . They constructed a visual narrative of Palestinian nationalism long before its history was written in textbooks."[61]

Social Alienation

Palestinian solidarity was also an outgrowth of the social alienation and isolation that the refugee population suffered. These factors enhanced Palestinian consciousness and galvanized Palestinian identity. According to a study of Arab social alienation by Halim Barakat,[62] Palestinian society was the most alienated of all. Despite this dynamic, or perhaps because of it, the refugee society became conscious of its shared destiny, which in turn contributed to social solidarity and rebellion among the second generation of the Nakba. Their raised consciousness helped the refugees cope with the phenomena of social alienation and isolation: "The dominant feeling among refugees was one of alienation and foreignness within Arab society: The Palestinian was consistently proved to be weak and frightened, having lost his self-respect. It was long claimed that he has atrophied, and [exists in the form of the] living dead. He has been accused of selling his homeland and has been contrasted with his brothers in Algeria, as a way of insulting the Palestinian and glorifying the Algerian."[63]

Anis al-Qasim summarized matters as follows: "What Palestinians encountered in Arab countries was not what they had expected from their brethren, and this was a bitter disappointment. Only small, powerless women's groups came to their aid. The refugees were greeted with hostility and animosity by their brothers in Arab countries. They were accused of consuming the Arab bread. . . . The Palestinian lost his way not because he emigrated, but because he lost his home and was unable, even if he wanted, to belong to the [new] place. The Palestinian was unable to escape his feeling of alienation."[64]

Palestinians were treated as second-class citizens: "In the Arab setting, Palestinians encountered political, legal, and social treatment that reinforced their sense of inferiority. They developed a sense of social alienation from local societies and an unwillingness to integrate with them. Redemption for them did not mean maintaining a certain lifestyle but, rather, release from the blows dealt by the new reality."[65]

In his book *The Disinherited*, Fawaz Turki conveys the Palestinian refugees' sense of alienation very effectively:

> If I was not a Palestinian when I left Haifa as a child, I am one now. Living in Beirut as a stateless person for most of my growing-up years, many of them in a refugee camp, I did not feel I was living among my "Arab brothers." I did not feel I was an Arab, a Lebanese, or, as some wretchedly pious writers claimed, a "southern Syrian." I was a Palestinian. And that meant I was an outsider, an alien, a refugee and a burden. To be that, for us, for my generation of Palestinians,

meant to look inward, to draw closer, to be part of a minority that had its own way of doing and seeing and feeling and reacting. To be that, for us, meant the addition of a subtler nuance to the cultural makeup of our Palestinianness.[66]

Fawaz Turki further describes how wherever he went, people would simply call him "Palestinian," not even taking the trouble to learn his name. At the candy factory where he worked as a youth, he was regarded with scorn and animosity on the part of coworkers who were natives of the place, and his employer would treat him harshly and pay him less than he paid others.

In a book chapter titled "The Palestinian," Samira ʿAzzam describes the suffering of middle-class Palestinians seeking employment, who were subjected to discrimination and humiliation. She describes the failed efforts of a Palestinian shopkeeper in Beirut to assimilate into society: "Within the neighborhood where his shop is located—a shop that does not differ from the others—he is known only as 'the Palestinian.' He is identified as 'the Palestinian,' he is pointed out as 'the Palestinian,' and he is cursed as 'the Palestinian' when the need arises. His was the same fate as that of the Armenian shoemaker who devoted 30 years of his life to repairing the shoes of his neighbors, yet no one cared or wanted to know whether his name was Hasif, Sarkis, or Artin—his full name was 'the Armenian.'"[67]

Fawaz Turki, in seeking to define the standing of the Palestinian within Arab society, actually sees a similarity to the Jews. He relates an experience he had:

> I was at the beach with a group of Lebanese I knew from Ras Beirut and spotted a Jewish friend of mine sitting on the sand by himself and asked him to come and join us. When the fellow's identity was revealed his fellow Lebanese became hostile, addressing him as if the responsibilities of Zionism were his, as if he were uncomplainingly to carry the burden of exclusion, and carry it under the chin. In a moment of incomprehension (for so it seemed to me in those days) I became a Jew, the Jew became a Palestinian, bound into a commonwealth of peoples heavily laden, heavily oppressed. My hate for the bourgeois Arab and his value structure, whether I viewed them in a political context or not, intensified further. The irony of my plight was that as I grew up my bogeyman was not the Jew (despite the incessant propaganda that Radio Cairo subjected us to), nor was he the Zionist (if indeed I recognized the distinction), nor was he for that matter the imperialist or the Western supporters and protectors of the state of Israel, but he was the Arab.[68]

The disintegration of social structure and the emotional shock resulting from the destruction of their world created a sense of apathy toward any possibility of political or social organization—such as trade unions—within refugee camps. The salient feeling within the generation of refugees was that of complete acceptance of political blows, as part of the way of the world and the will of God.[69]

Presumably, one might expect that the refugees' situation would result in their assimilation within the surrounding Arab community. In practice, the converse occurred. In fact, it actually galvanized their collective consciousness. The key to understanding this dynamic is the ability of Palestinians, particularly the refugees because of their difficult circumstances, to preserve and even reinforce their Palestinian consciousness and identity. This process encompassed all levels of Palestinian society, especially the residents of refugee camps.

In addressing this phenomenon, Fawaz Turki reaches the following conclusion: "If alienation breeds an attraction to radical ideology, then Palestinian youngsters found ample cause for incitement in their exclusion from society. They became the most left wing and revolutionary group in the Arab world, espousing progressive causes or extreme views that alarmed their parents and antagonized other Arabs. They rejected above all old political heroes, religious and class hierarchies, and the remote social, economic, and ideological values of yore."[70]

Notes

1. Yehoshafat Harkabi, "The Palestinians in the Fifties and Their Awakening as Reflected in Their Literature," in *Palestinian Arab Politics*, ed. Moshe Ma'oz (Jerusalem: Academic Press, 1975). See also the Hebrew version, *Haffalastinim Me-Tardima le-Hit'ororut* (Jerusalem: Magnes, 1975).

2. Harkabi surveyed the following writings: Mustafa al-Dabbagh, *Biladuna Filastin* (Beirut: Dar al-Tali'a , 1965–66); Niqola al-Dur, *Hakadha Da'at wa Hakadha Ta'ud* (Beirut: Dar al-Hawadith, 1963); Subhi Yasin, *Tariq al-'Awda 'Ila Filastin* (Cairo, 1961); Lutf Ghantus, "'Athar al-Tarkib al-Tabaqi fi al-Qadiyya al-Filastiniyya," *Dirasat 'Arabiyya*, November 1965, December 1965; Walid al-Qamhawi, *Al-Nakba wa al-Bina' fi al-Watan al-'Arabi*, 2nd ed. (Beirut: Dar al-'Ilm le al-Malayeen, 1962); Nasir al-Din al-Nashashibi, *Tadhkarat 'Awda* (Beirut: al-Matktab al-Tijari, 1962); Naji 'Alush, *Al-Masira 'Ila Filastin* (Beirut: Dar al-Tali'a, 1964); Anis al-Qasim, *Min al-Tih 'Ila al-Quds* (Tripoli: Dar al-Nashr, 1965).

3. Harkabi, "The Palestinians," 51, 73, 85.

4. See Ben-Gurion Archives, Ben-Gurion Research Institute for the Study of Israel and Zionism, Sede Boker, Israel: Collection of reports and surveys prepared by the IDF, Intelligence Branch, Research and Assessment Department, and other papers and documents from Israel State Archives, 1949–60.

5. The Arab League Secretariat, *Mazabit Jalasat Dawr al-Jami'a al-'adi al-Thani 'ashar li-Majlis al-Jami'a*, March 25–July 16, 1950.

6. For an extensive list of books against Israel and Zionism published in the 1950s, see Na'im Shahrabani, *Hassikhsukh ha-'Aravi Yisra'eli: Bibliografya shel Sfarim ve-Pirsumim be-'Arvit* [The Arab-Israeli conflict: Bibliography of Arabic books and publications] (Jerusalem: Truman Institute, the Hebrew University of Jerusalem, 1975). See also "Bibliography," in Yehoshafat Harkabi, *Arab Attitudes to Israel* (Jerusalem: Israel Universitities Press, 1976).

7. Jamal 'Abd al-Nasir, *Falsafat al-Thawra* (Cairo: Maslahat al-Isti'lamat).

8. Nasir, Cairo Radio, May 23, 1967.

9. For the reactions of the Arab world to Nasir's measures, see Shemesh, *Arab Politics, Palestinian Nationalism and the Six Day War*, 191–94, 218–27.

10. Nasir, Cairo Radio, November 7, 1956; *al-Ahram*, December 8, 1956.

11. Nasir, Cairo Radio, November 7, 1956, January 17, 1957, February 11, 1957, July 26, 1957, December 23, 1957, March 20, 1958, September 5, 1958, December 25, 1958, December 25, 1960.

12. Nasir, Cairo Radio, July 24, 1957, May 15, 1958, December 23, 1958, February 17, 1960, December 25, 1960.

13. On the background to the escalation of the Arab-Israeli conflict from 1957 through 1963, see Shemesh, *Arab Politics*, 1–41.

14. On the struggle over water, see Moshe Shemesh, "Prelude to the Six Day War: The Arab-Israeli Struggle over Water Resources," *Israel Studies* 9, no. 3 (2004): 1–45.

15. On the Samu' raid and its repercussions, see Moshe Shemesh, "The IDF Raid on Samu': The Turning-Point in Jordan's Relations with Israel and the West Bank Palestinians," *Israel Studies* 7, no. 1 (2002): 139–67.

16. Salah Khalaf (Abu Iyad), *Filastini Bila Hawiyya* (Kuwait), 52

17. 'Isam Sakhnini, "Tamthil al-Sha'b al-Filastini wa Munzamat al-Tahrir al-Filasiniyya," *Shu'un Filastiniyya* 15 (November 1972): 27.

18. Student Notebook, Cairo University, 1958. This notebook, in which one of Fatah's founders outlined the ideology of Fatah, was captured by IDF soldiers during the raid on Beirut in April 1973. It is presumed that the notebook was written by Yusif al-Najjar or Kamal 'Udwan, both of whom were killed in this operation.

19. Abu Iyad, *Filastini*, 57.

20. Abu Iyad, *Al-Muharrir*, January 7, 1976.

21. Zurayq, *Ma'na al-Nakba* ; Qustantin Zurayq, *Ma'na al-Nakba Mujddadan* (Beirut: Dar al-'Ilm le-al-Malayeen, 1967).

22. Al-'Alami, *'Ibrat Filastin*.

23. Tuqan, *Ba'da al-Nakba*

24. Moshe Efrat, "The Palestinian Refugees: The Dynamics of Economic Integration in Their Host Countries," discussion paper, *Israel International Institute for Applied Economic Policy Review*, September 1993, 6.

25. Janet Abu-Lughod, "The Demographic Transformation of Palestine," in *The Transformation of Palestine: Essays on the Origin and Development of the Arab-Israeli Conflict*, ed. Ibrahim Abu-Lughod, 160–61 (Evanston, IL: Northwestern University Press, 1971).

26. Clapp Mission, *Final Report of the UN Economic Survey Mission for Middle East*, Pt. 1: *The Final Report and Appendices*, December 28, 1949, UN Doc. A/AC/25/6, 22.

27. Efrat, "The Palestinian Refugees," 6.

28. On Karl Mannheim's perception of political generations, see Karl Mannheim, "The Problem of Generations," in *Essays on the Sociology of Knowledge*, ed. Paul Kecskemeti, 276–320 (London: Routledge & Kegan Paul, 1959).

29. Shehada Yusif, *Al-Waqi' al-Filastini wa al-Haraka al-Niqabiyya* (Beirut: PLO Markaz al-Abhath, 1976), 15.

30. Ghantus, "'Athar al-Tarkib," November 1965, 2–22; December 1965, 35–53.

31. Qasim, *Min al-Tih*, 33.

32. Yoram Ben Porat, 'Immanuel Marks, and Shim'on Shamir, *Mahane Plitim be-Gev ha-Har* [Refugee Camp on the Hillside] (Tel Aviv: Moshe Dayan Center, 1974). The research was conducted in the autumn of 1967 in the Jelazoon refugee camp near Ramalla.

33. Yusif, *Al-Waqi' al-Filastini*, 22.
34. Ghantus, "'Athar al-Tarkib," December 1965, 45.
35. Fred C. Bruhns, "A Study of Arab Refugee Attitudes," *Middle East Journal* 9, no. 2 (1955): 130–38.
36. Ben Porat, Marks, and Shamir, *Mahane Plitim*, 16.
37. Ibid., 113.
38. Ibid., 11.
39. Anya Francus, *Al-Filastiniyyun* (Beirut: Dar al-Nahar, 1969), 34.
40. Raja' al-Naqqash, *Mahmud Darwish—Sha'ir al-Ard al-Muhtala*, 3rd ed. (Cairo: Dar al-Hilal 1972), 71. The first edition was published in 1969.
41. Salih al-Ta'ma, "Al-Mas'ala al-Filastiniyya fi al-Adab al-'Arabi al-Hadith," *Shu'un Filastiniyya* 12 (August 1972): 111.
42. Ibid., 111–12; see also Kamil al-Sawafiri, *Al-Shi'r al-'Arabi al-Mu'asir fi Nakbat Filastin* (Cairo: Matba'at Nahdat Misr, 1964), 467–93.
43. Fawaz Turki, "To Be a Palestinian," *Journal of Palestine Studies* 2, no. 11 (1974): 8.
44. Bruhns, "A Study of Arab Refugee Attitudes," 132.
45. Ingrid Galtung and Johan Galtung, "Some Factors Affecting Local Acceptance of a UN Force: A Pilot Project from Gaza," *International Problems* (Israel) 1–2 (1966): 258, 260, 262.
46. UNRWA, *Annual Report 1959 of the Director of UNRWA (1 July 1958–30 June 1959)*, UN General Assembly, 14th sess., supp. 14, UN Doc. A/42/3.
47. Turki, "To be a Palestinian," 6; Fawaz Turki, *The Disinherited: Journal of a Palestinian Exile* (London: Monthly Review Press, 1972), 39.
48. Mustafa al-Dabbagh, *Biladuna Filastin*, vol. 1, pt. 1 (Beirut, 1965), 39.
49. *Al-Raqib* (Gaza), September 17, 1952.
50. *Al-Raqib*, February 17, 1952.
51. A. L. Tibawi, "Visions of the Return: The Palestine Arab Refugees in Arabic Poetry and Art," *Middle East Journal* 17, no. 5 (1963): 507–26.
52. Ibid.
53. See Rosemary Sayigh, "Palestinian Camp Women as Tellers of History," *Journal of Palestine Studies* 27, no. 2 (1998): 42–58.
54. Quoted in Ta'ma, "Al-Mas'ala al-Filastiniyya," 111.
55. Quoted in Tibawi, "Visions of the Return."
56. Quoted in Ta'ma, "Al-Mas'ala al-Filastiniyya," 110.
57. Ibid.; see also Tibawi, "Visions of the Return."
58. See Gannit Ankori, "Exile and Memories: Art after 1948," in *Palestinian Art* (London: Reaktion Books, 2006), 47–56; on Shamout, see also Tibawi, "Visions of the Return."
59. Ankori, "Exile and Memories," 47–48.
60. Ibid.
61. Ibid., 54.
62. See the Hebrew translation of an article by Halim Barakat, "Hannikur ve-ha-Mahpekha ba-Hayyim ha-'Arbiyim [The alienation and the revolution in the Arab life]," *Mawauf* (Beirut) 5 (July–August 1969), in *Arab ve Israel*, ed. Yehushafat Harkabi, vol. 1 (Tel Aviv: Am Oved, 1974).
63. Niqola al-Dur, *Hakadha Da'at wa Hakadha Ta'ud* (Beirut, 1963), 261.
64. Qasim, *Min al-Tih*, 17, 20, 22.
65. Yusif, *Al-Waqi' al-Filastini*, 16.
66. Turki, *The Disinherited*, 8.

67. Samira 'Azzam, "Filastini," in *Al-Sa'a wa al-'Insan* (Beirut: al-Mu'assasa al-Ahliyya), 70–79. This passage was translated from Arabic to Hebrew by Shim'on Ballas in *Hassifrut ha-'Arvit be-Sel ha-Milhama* [Arabic literature in the shadow of the war] (Tel Aviv: Am Oved, 1978), 47.
68. Turki, *The Disinherited*, 53.
69. Ben Porat, Marks, and Shamir, *Mahane Plitim*, 68.
70. Turki, *The Disinherited*, 39.

6 The "Sons of the Nakba" Generation

Emergent Leadership of the New Palestinian National Movement

THE 1948 NAKBA and all its repercussions, including refugee life within the camps, constituted the type of "historical event" that Karl Mannheim describes as a contributing factor in the creation of a new "political generation." This historical event shaped an entire generation of Palestinians who, in turn, led the sociopolitical shift from which emerged the new Palestinian national movement, visibly manifested in January 1965 with the first guerrilla action perpetuated by Fatah.[1]

It was only natural that during its formative years the second generation of refugees who experienced the living conditions of their refugee parents would be greatly influenced by these conditions and even rebel against them. The circumstances of the Nakba generation constituted the social and political context that enabled the emergence of the new Palestinian national movement, which the second generation of the Nakba led. This generation has been described as the "Sons of the Nakba" (Abna' al-Nakba) or the "Generation of Liberation" (Jeel al-Tahrir). An exception to this generational pattern was the Palestinian intelligentsia, who took an active part in the establishment of the Arab Nationalists Movement (ANM) as early as 1951.

Two seemingly contradictory processes took place during the 1950s in the Arab world and contributed significantly to the development and reinforcement of the Palestinian national awakening: On the one hand, the Arab national movement led by Nasir reached the height of its success during this time. The union between Egypt and Syria in February 1958 inspired Palestinian hopes that Arab unity would lead the way to the liberation of Filastin, as Nasir preached to the Arab world. On the other hand, after the disintegration of the UAR (United Arab Republic) in September 1961, the Palestinians, including the Sons of the Nakba generation, were greatly disappointed with the Arab world in all matters concerning the resolution of their problem. This situation contributed to the second generation's shift toward independent Palestinian activity for the liberation of Filastin and actualization of the vision of return.

Those refugees who were teenagers when they left their homes in 1948 with their parents can also be classified as belonging to the generation of leaders of the new Palestinian national movement. These youth had experienced the war, that is, they had been uprooted and turned into refugees—indisputably a traumatic experience. As a consequence, they underwent rapid social change precisely when they were in their formative years. Indeed, most leaders of the Palestinian organizations were born during the 1930s and were adolescents during the war of 1948. This generation of the Sons of the Nakba took the leadership role upon itself. Also in this group are those born in the 1940s who were already living in refugee camps when they experienced the war, or who internalized this experience from their parents. This generation, in contrast to their parents' generation, was characterized by social cohesion and a strong Palestinian consciousness, indicating a high level of social solidarity.

The founders of Fatah first became active during the conquest of the Gaza Strip in the framework of the Sinai War and its aftermath. Most leaders and founders of the organization were in their mid-twenties—or late twenties at the most—when they began their underground activities. Most first became politically active in the context of the Palestinian student union in Egypt, some were activists in other Arab countries, and some were members of Palestinian student unions in West Germany. Yasir Arafat, the oldest of this group, was born in 1929; Salah Khalaf (Abu Iyad) in 1933; Kamal 'Udwan in 1935; 'Atalla 'Atalla, a Fatah military commander, in 1936; Faruq al-Qadumi in 1935; Mahmud 'Abbas (Abu Mazen) in 1933; Rafiq al-Natsha in 1934; Hani al-Hasan in 1933; Hakam Bal'awi in 1934; Nabil Sha'ath in 1938; and Yusif al-Najar in 1931.

A study conducted by the Palestine Liberation Organization's (PLO's) Planning Center, which was aimed at collecting data about casualties among fida'i organizations in the period between January 1965 and October 1971, discovered that 12 percent of all casualties had been born during the 1930s. That is, they were in the same age group as the leaders of the Palestinian movement. Those born during the 1940s (1940–48) constituted 40.4 percent of all casualties. If we combine a portion of the figures in the latter category with those of the previous category (taking into account that they joined organizations during the early 1960s), we find that 20–25 percent of all casualties were in the same age group as the leaders and had the experience of being refugees during their formative years. This percentage is significant and indicates the transformations within the second generation of the refugee population after 1948 as well as the extent to which members of this generation identified with the leadership that emerged from it, across its political spectrum. If we do not include the age group of the founders of Fatah and other Palestinian organizations (those in their thirties), we arrive at the figure of 74 percent of casualties from the age group of the Generation of Liberation (Jeel al-Tahrir)—a high percentage and an indicative factor in the strong social cohesion of this generation.[2]

In May 1969, the Israel Defense Forces (IDF) conducted a social study of guerrillas whom it had captured after the Six Day War, with the aim of examining the "motives and morale of fida'i organizations." A partial sampling of 327 cases was examined, out of a total of 600 guerrilla cases selected for review. The conclusions of the partial study were confirmed by an assessment of the entire sample. The following are some of the important conclusions for our purposes:

- The average age of fida'iyyun was 24. The average fida'i was single with a level of education above elementary school (83 percent). His family had been uprooted from its home because of the war. The fida'iyyun were divided into youngsters (ages 16–25: 72 percent), adults (ages 26–34: 24 percent), and elderly (ages 35–42: 4 percent).
- Among the fida'iyyun, 76 percent were single, 13 percent were fathers of small families (up to two children), and 10 percent were fathers of large families.
- A total of 10 percent of the fida'iyyun lacked an education. A total of 12 percent had an education beyond the level of secondary school; 18 percent had a partial elementary-school education; 23 percent had a full elementary-school education; 18 percent had a partial secondary-school education; and 20 percent had a full secondary-school education.
- Those who had joined the armed struggle for semi-ideological reasons were primarily refugees, that is, sons of parents who had left their ancestral lands during the 1948 Arab-Israeli War and relocated to refugee camps in Jordan or sons of families who had escaped their places of residence after the Six Day War and moved to the East Bank of the Jordan River.
- Those who had joined the armed struggle for ideological reasons were, for the most part, well educated, and among the educated members many had resided in Europe for long periods of time.

The new Palestinian national movement was founded and led by well-educated university graduates, most of whom became politically active as students. Some (Fatah) operated from the outset within the framework of an independent Palestinian organization, and the remainder (the Popular Front for the Liberation of Palestine and the Democratic Front for the Liberation of Palestine) became politically active within the framework of a pan-Arab movement, and only at a later stage did they engage in independent Palestinian activity in the context of the Palestinian national movement. Some members of the Palestinian leadership underwent military training when they first became politically active (including Arafat, Ahmad Jibril, Khalil al-Wazir); this training was provided by Arab armed forces, in particular, Egyptian and Syrian, as well as military training camps in Algeria.

It is important to underscore the main difference—aside from the ideological one—between the founders of Fatah and the founders of Arab Nationalists Movement, out of which the Popular Front for the Liberation of Palestine emerged. The Fatah leadership was entirely Sunni Muslim (a large majority of the Palestinian population is Sunni), and evidently the Islamic element played an important role for Fatah's founders, who established strong ties with Saudi Arabia and Kuwait. In publications such as *Filastinuna*, Fatah does not highlight this characteristic of its founders, but the Islamic element surfaces indirectly in reading material produced for its cadres.

For example, a booklet titled *Code of Conduct for the Revolutionary Fighter*, issued by Fatah's Department of Recruitment and Administration, includes ten passages from the Quran and parables about Muhammad's conduct during war and the importance of believing in God.[3] In contrast, among the leadership of the Popular Front and the Democratic Front, the Christian element is prominent: George Habash, Wadi' Hadad, and Na'if Hawatma were Orthodox Christians (the last being an Orthodox Christian from Salt, on the East Bank of the Jordan River). The extreme violence of the Arab Nationalists Movement, from which the Popular Front under Habash's leadership emerged, was perhaps intended to demonstrate that their being Christian did not diminish their Arab or Palestinian nationalism. Habash himself underscored this point in 1969: "We try to overlook religion. Most of our nation is Muslim, but many are Christian. We do not wish to cause additional conflicts."[4]

Palestinian Political Party Activism in the Era of Pan-Arab Ideology

It is only natural that the Palestinians' new leadership would have a well-developed political consciousness, not only because of its high level of education but also because of the social and political conditions in which it was raised—in refugee camps and across various parts of the Arab world. Members of this generation were more sensitive to their surroundings than their parents had been. Thus they formed a negative attitude toward their lives and the lives of their parents, and they were fully determined to remedy the situation.

A study of the Jelazoon refugee camp undertaken by the Shiloah Institute sought to measure the political consciousness of interviewees. Out of 108 interviewees, only 74 men answered the political questions in some form. Of these, 20 interviewees—that is, 27 percent—showed a high level of political consciousness; 33 interviewees—44.5 percent—had a moderate level of political consciousness; and 21 interviewees—28.5 percent—had a low level of political consciousness. The group with a high level of political consciousness can generally be described as young and educated, having at least a secondary school education or higher. All were below the age of 41 (with one exception, age 42), and most were in the lowest age group (15–17 years old). The study suggests that a larger number of young interviewees would have been recorded as having a high level of political consciousness if their parents had not pressured them to refrain from discussing politics during their interviews. In the group with a high level of political consciousness, all the ideologies associated with political parties active in the West Bank (all of which were underground) were expressed. The most prominent were two radical, nationalist, pan-Arab movements—the Arab Nationalists Movement and the Ba'th Party.[5]

The well-developed political consciousness of the second generation of the Nakba also created a sense of awareness regarding political problems in the Arab world generally and the Palestinian problem specifically. Members of this generation were greatly influenced by the ideas of the Arab Nationalists Movement that were disseminated during the 1950s, and hence they were more nationalistic than their parents. At the same time, they were less individualistic than their parents. Their nationalist outlook (during the initial phase of their political activism) was pan-Arab. They hoped that the Palestinian problem would be resolved through inter-Arab action. In this way they differed from their parents, who refrained from any political activism.

Educated Palestinians joined the political movements that emerged in Arab countries during the 1950s—such as the Arab Nationalists Movement, the Ba'th Party, communist parties, and other pro-Nasir groups—and, consequently, they became familiar with political perspectives that were salient in both the West and the East. The movements served as political schools for these young members of the intelligentsia, at a time when the disintegrated Palestinian society lacked any body or institution capable of providing a political education. Through these political movements, educated Palestinians and political activists learned about various aspects of governance as well as the means and ways of establishing a new political movement. Evidently, these movements achieved their greatest impact on educated Palestinians through national consciousness-raising, which included the concept of a struggle for self-determination, be it through political activity or by means of violence, that is, "armed struggle."

Khalil al-Wazir, a founder and leader of Fatah, wrote in his memoirs that three currents emerged in the Palestinian arena in the aftermath of the Nakba, none of which yielded any results, in his opinion. The first current comprised those waiting for an Arab savior, a modern Salah al-Din, to arrive with his army and liberate Filastin. Those who belonged to this current were encouraged by the regime changes in several Arab states but were disappointed when these regimes began to explain that they "do not at this time have a plan for Filastin." Those of the second current saw a need to rebuild Arab society on the basis of a new foundation and infrastructure, and they turned their attention to national political action through political parties. Accordingly, various sectors of the Palestinian population aligned themselves across the political spectrum of the various parties, believing that if they take over the governments of countries surrounding Israel, they would be able to create a strong, healthy Arab society capable of withstanding the Zionist threat and pursuing the liberation of Filastin. "Our young people participated in all the campaigns of these parties, and as a result a Palestinian in one party would end up struggling against his Palestinian brother in another party. It later turned out that parties that reached ruling status in a number of Arab countries were far removed from the path to liberation, and all they did was reinforce disputes and divisions, rather than reinforce unity and solidarity." The main activity of the third current entailed waiting for an international struggle or a World War III that would enable the liberation of Filastin.[6]

The Sons of the Nakba generation aspired to belong to the political institutions of Arab countries. "In the 1950s almost every Palestinian belonged to a political party or movement, from the extreme right to the extreme left. A young man who did not belong was considered a burden on society, that is, dishonorable."[7] Fatah explained this development in greater detail, emphasizing that "during this period young Palestinians comprised the largest relative number of members [of these ideological movements]. It was rare to find a Palestinian who did not belong to one of these ideological movements."[8]

Despite the lack of Palestinian self-organization, members of the second generation were evidently neither politically inactive nor unaware. As we have seen, the level of political consciousness among the Sons of the Nakba generation was very high, but it was channeled into pan-Arab rather than Palestinian organizations and movements. While their parents had refrained from political engagement, whether for social or psychological reasons, the younger Palestinian generation tended, initially, to engage through pan-Arab parties, both because they were inspired by Nasir's pan-Arab perspective and because they believed that the Palestinian problem would be resolved by pan-Arab action. On this matter, Shafiq al-Hut observes, "Amidst the intensity of campaigns during this period of nationalism, a period characterized by revolutionary national pride, pioneering Palestinians did not see Palestinian self-organization specifically focused on efforts to liberate Filastin as necessary, because they viewed the overall national struggle as the path to their own return and liberation."[9]

This generation of national reawakening and new Palestinian leadership took on a rebellious character. It rebelled against the conditions under which it and its parents lived, against the Arab states' treatment of it, and against the apathy and lack of initiative to effect change that prevailed among its parents' generation. Abu Iyad, a founder of Fatah, effectively conveyed this dynamic in his description of the early days of Fatah: "At the time Fatah was a group of young Palestinians who were rebelling against the prevailing reality, a reality of divisiveness and, in particular, disintegration [of the Egyptian-Syrian union], a reality of failure on the part of Arab parties in matters of genuine struggle. The young men who grew out of this reality and rebelled against it are the founders of Fatah."[10]

It seems that the leaders of the new Palestinian national movement, in all its forms, were conscious, even profoundly so, of being the leaders of a generation as well as leaders of a national movement. In other words, they recognized that they were leading a national movement and—in equal measure—they felt that they were expressing the longings of a new generation of Palestinians. Khalil al-Wazir saw himself as one of the Sons of the Nakba. In his memoirs, he presents two founding documents of the organization in which he apparently had a hand. The first was written "in the mid-1950s," according to him, and signed by the Supreme Central Committee of Fatah. This document presents the organization's political plan while addressing "my brother, son of Filastin" and "my brother, Son of the Nakba"—phrases that recall the opening lines of the 1958 Ideological Notebook outlining Fatah's body of tenets, as well as evoke editorials of *Filastinuna* from 1959. The second document is from 1964, "after we established our organizational base of operations and defined our conceptual, political, and organizational options," and is titled "The Outlook in Light of Political and Legal Accusations and the Logic of the Palestinian al-'Asifa." In it the writer seeks to defend Fatah's perspectives, which do not take political or social arguments into account. For our purposes, it is significant that the document is signed by a "Son of the Nakba" and asserts, among other things, that "we, the Sons of the Nakba, have endured 17 years of exile and civil and legal oppression and an atmosphere rife with accusations.... This multitude of accusations has—for the Sons of the Nakba (and I am one of them)—given rise to a complex."[11]

In explaining the motives behind its founding, Fatah stated (in 1969), "There are a few reasons [for the founding of the movement], including the belief of a number of Palestinian pioneers that a struggle based on political parties would not lead to the liberation of Filastin, especially when most of these pioneers belonged at the time to different Arab parties or were loyal to various Arab regimes. The failure of efforts conducted though political parties led these pioneers to revisit their revolutionary modus operandi for the liberation of Filastin."[12] Abu Iyad emphasizes that the founders of Fatah were "in essence educated Palestinians. Their thinking was that it is necessary to pave the way towards a different reality, and to this end it was necessary to embark on some form of armed struggle."[13]

In concluding the discussion of this issue, it is fitting to cite a passage from an ideological essay of Fatah, composed at Cairo University in 1958 by one of the organization's founders. Under the title "My Brother," the writer addresses the "young Palestinian":

Are you a member of a political party? I am sure you chose this route only once you became convinced that it was the best way to participate in the campaign for the liberation that will return you to your homeland. But are you sure that you have achieved what you want for the hope of return?

I call upon you today to join me in translating your national passion into a more positive course . . . to play a part that awaits you in order to save the campaign . . . a better course for the leadership of the homeland, far from all these disputes . . . a clear course where our starting and ending points will be defined. . . . To state it more starkly: Here is a movement that has a past and future but no present . . . a future represented by young people in their 30s and a past represented by old people in their fifties. Between them is a gap that functions as the lost link in the political history of the Palestinian people . . . and in other words—of the Palestinian problem.[14]

The Politicization of Daily Life

The politicization of refugees' lives (and of all the Palestinians) also contributed to social cohesion. Setting "the return" (*'awda*) or "liberation of the land" as the top priority dictated what was virtually the one and only public agenda of all Palestinians in general and the refugees in particular.

The refugee society was very political. The Sons of the Nakba generation had a highly developed social consciousness, perhaps the most developed of the comparable social strata throughout the Arab world, and Palestinian society had the most developed political consciousness among Arab states. One of the contributing factors was that the generation of the Sons of the Nakba was, as noted, characterized by a high percentage of educated individuals compared with other Arab societies. Fatah asserted that "the desire to liberate the land is the glue that forces everyone to sacrifice all else for the sake of liberation of the stolen land. . . . The slogan of the liberation movement during the liberation phase is 'everything for the sake of liberation of the land' and, therefore, all ideological disputes are set aside."[15] The desire to mobilize and concentrate all Palestinian and Arab potential toward the revolution necessitated postponing any discussion of the social aspects of the Palestinian state until after the land had been fully liberated, because such a discussion could distract and scatter the revolutionary forces in their search for long-term platitudes that bear no relation to current reality. "The Palestinian people are undergoing [only] a national revolution, not a simultaneous national and social revolution. The type of struggle needed to achieve each of these two goals differs from [the type needed to achieve] the other."[16]

For these reasons, Fatah did, in fact, succeed in becoming the salient political force guiding the new Palestinian national movement. In the course of his study of refugees in Lebanon, Samir Ayyub, a Palestinian sociologist, reached the following conclusion: "The Palestinian looked only at the political aspect of his reality and neglected the day-to-day life of this reality, which he had no hope of changing except by resolution of the political problem. Consequently there was a lack of direct, clear, and defined social content in the political plans of Palestinian organizations and their popular institutions, such as workers' unions, student unions, and women's unions."[17]

Fatah praised Palestinians' contributions to strengthening the pan-Arab national movement. In August 1967, it asserted, "The truth is that the migration of the Palestinian people to most of the Arab states reinforced pan-Arab national ties and advanced the Arab national movement because the Palestinian Arab became a partner of Arab peoples in their problems and struggles. This partnership gave the pan-Arab struggle a practical, solid foundation."[18]

Education as a Contributing Factor in Social Mobility and National Awakening

Palestinian writers, researchers, and research institutes have pointed out that the educational levels among Palestinians, and refugees specifically, were higher than those in Arab states. The pioneering researcher in this field was Nabil Sha'ath, then director of the PLO's Planning Center and a professor of business management at the University of Beirut. In 1972, he published a study titled "High Level Palestinian Manpower," which included the following conclusions:

- The number of Palestinian university students compares well with the number of Israeli university students.
- The rate of growth in the number of Palestinian graduates is perhaps greater than that of the Israelis.
- The ratio of higher level manpower and the ratio of present Palestinian university students to the total Palestinian population [are] higher than the ratio for any Arab country (including Egypt and Lebanon).[19]

Sha'ath's conclusions are confirmed by the findings of censuses conducted in several Arab states. For example, the Syrian census for the years 1960, 1970, and 1981 found that the level of education among Palestinians was higher than that among Syrians. Moreover, during those years, the Palestinians in Syria made noticeable progress in the area of higher education: in 1981, they constituted 2.8 percent, compared to 1.6 percent in 1970 and 0.5 percent in 1960.[20]

(See Table 6.1.) The rising level of education among Palestinians and Syrians in Syria is also reflected in these data.[21] (See Table 6.2.)

The following observations emerge from the data presented in Table 6.2:

- The level of education in refugee camps in the Damascus area (making up a majority of the refugee camp residents in Syria) is lower at each educational stage than the average level of education of the

Table 6.1. Palestinian and Syrian populations by level of education, per national census figures for 1960, 1970, and 1981 (age 10 and above), by percent

	Palestinians			Syrians		
Level of Education	1960	1970	1981	1960	1970	1981---
Illiterate	46.2	33.4	20.2	62.6	54.2	38.8
Knowledge of reading and writing	34.7	28.6	25.6	26.3	25.3	25.9
Elementary	11.4	21.6	27.8	7.0	12.9	20.6
Junior high school	*	(7.7)	(12.4)	(1.0)	(3.9)	(7.3)
High school	*	(5.9)	(8.4)	(1.0)	(2.4)	(4.6)
Secondary (total)	6.2	14.6	23.3	2.8	6.8	13.2
Higher education	0.5	1.6	2.8	0.3	0.7	1.5
TOTAL	100	100	100	100	100	100

* No information available

Table 6.2. Level of education among Palestinian refugees and Syrians, 1981–85 (age 10 and above), by percent

	Palestinian Refugees			Syrians	
Educational Stage	Entire Population (1981 census)	Survey of 5 Camps in Damascus Area	Survey of 12 Camps and Neighborhoods (1984–85)	Al-Yarmuk Survey (1984)	Entire Syrian Population (1981 census)
Below Elementary	45.6	60.4	42.0	36.2	64.7
Elementary	27.8	25.8	30.2	30.9	20.6
Above Elementary (partial or full)	23.3	13.3	25.5	29.3	13.2
Higher Education	2.8	0.5	2.3	2.6	1.5
TOTAL	100	100	100	100	100

entire Palestinian refugee population in Syria. Despite this lower average, the level of education of Palestinian refugees in UNRWA camps in the Damascus area is higher than the countrywide average for Syrians at each educational stage, with the exception of higher education.

- The level of education in the neighborhood of al-Yarmuk is higher at each stage than both the average educational level of Palestinian refugees in Syria and the average educational level of Syrians. This figure is especially significant considering that the Palestinian refugees concentrated in this neighborhood have been economically and socially successful in terms of integration and settlement in Syria.

A special study published in 1975 by the PLO Research Center under the title *Palestinian Education: Reality and Problems* states, among other things, that "although there are no statistics about the number of Palestinian students scattered throughout the world, we know that their number ranges between 40,000 and 50,000. This means that the percentage of students was 13.3–16.6 percent (or 133–166 students per 1000 Palestinians). This percentage surpasses the figures for every Arab country and even some European countries." The study emphasizes that "the number of Palestinian students surpasses the number of Jewish students in occupied Filastin, as the number of students in Israel was 37,343 in 1969–1970." In addressing the increase in rates of elementary and secondary school pupils within the Palestinian population, the study finds that "[this] increase greatly influenced the social composition of the Palestinian people. The Palestinian people numbered 1.4 million in 1948, yet now it numbers more than 3 million. The number of [elementary and secondary school] pupils in 1948 was nearly 146,000 and now exceeds 819,000. If we add the number of university students, the total number of students reaches 865,000. That is, a total of 28.83 percent of the entire Palestinian population are receiving an education."[22]

In seeking to explain the findings of his study, Nabil Sha'ath cites the following possible explanations, among others, for the high level of education among Palestinians:

- Faced with expulsion and exile, the Palestinian had to seek a versatile education and to exercise mobile professions enabling him to acquire and hold gainful employment for himself and his large family.
- Educational and professional success brought psychological compensation to the dispossessed Palestinian.
- In an Arab world where educational attainment and academic degrees are important criteria of social and professional success, the Palestinian had to study harder to enhance his personal competitive power and overcome the disadvantages emanating from his "refugee" status.
- The Palestinians were able to acquire education through self-help and family cooperation, the opening up primarily of Egyptian universities and to a lesser extent other Arab universities for qualified

Palestinians free of charge or for very moderate fees, a small amount of UNRWA scholarship aid, and by earning scholarships for study abroad.[23]

According to Palestinian writer Lutf Ghantus, education was a crucial tool for "vertical mobility" in refugee society. The pursuit of studies was the only key that made it possible to exit the camps, and it fostered the education of a relatively large segment of the young refugee population.[24]

In addressing this issue, Fawaz Turki observes, "Education, probably seen as the only tangible investment for the future, became to a Palestinian family the most crucial and the most momentous accomplishment ever. There was nothing else a young Palestinian could hope for, cling to, touch with his being. We studied like ones possessed. To drop out of school, not to contemplate going to college, not to surpass the achievements of our Lebanese, Syrian, or Jordanian tormentors, was to us a stigma and a badge of shame."[25]

Evidently, some educated Palestinians developed a sense of superiority toward other Arab peoples. They saw themselves as a chosen group, proud not only of their educational achievements but also of their contributions to the Arab world. As a result of their abilities and skills as well as the needs they were able to meet, this arrogance sometimes reached excessive boastfulness—perhaps as a counterweight to memories of the treatment they and Palestinians generally had received during the decade immediately after the Nakba. In the words of Anis al-Qasim, for example, "There will come a day when history will recognize that Palestinians brought the Arab countries from the Dark Ages to the twentieth century."[26]

Emergence of the New Palestinian Personality

The main goal of the leaders of the new Palestinian national movement was to change the image with which Palestinians had been branded for years. This image had been reinforced during the 1950s, accompanied by such labels as "refugee," "expatriate," "parasite," and "helpless"—a people ruled by and led by others. Thus "liberation of the Palestinian person," alongside "liberation of the Palestinian land," became an objective.

In order to lead their struggle on their own, Palestinians had to enlist the entire society. During the second half of the 1950s, this meant enlisting the second generation of the Nakba for the sake of the national goal. Enlistment on this scale was proved possible because of the strong solidarity that Palestinian society had achieved: no longer was the Palestinian subservient; rather, he was a fighter, the fida'i who sacrifices himself to achieve the national goal.

The terms "new Palestinian personality" and "new Palestinian person" were the component elements of the new Palestinian nationalism, reflecting the background out of which it emerged. They express the image of the Palestinian who was reawakened after years of absence from the political arena of the Middle East, whose personality was formed in reaction to the complex of alienation and persecution, guardianship and oppression that befell the Palestinians after 1948. The "new Palestinian personality" also represented the "restoration of Palestinian dignity." Indeed, this longing to restore the dignity of the "Palestinian personality" is a salient theme of the Palestinian National Charter. Article 17 (1968 edition) states, "The liberation of Filastin, from a human point of view, will restore to the Palestinian individual his dignity, pride, and freedom."[27]

The Palestinian fida'i served as a symbol of the new Palestinian person: "Our people are not a people who wear the identity of the refugee, but rather the identity of the fida'i fighter."[28] Under the heading "Revolutionary Personality," Fatah's January 1970 magazine stated, "The Palestinian revolution asserts itself as the only alternative, presenting to the world the personality of the Palestinian fighter who returns after 20 years of oppression, cruelty, and submission, in order to fight for the right to live on his land . . . to present to the world the personality of the Palestinian fighter—tough, persistent, and uncompromising and unyielding until he brings justice, freedom, and equality back to the land of peace [Filastin]."[29]

The Myth of Armed Struggle: Expression of the New Palestinian Identity

The vision of 'awda was indeed transmitted to the Sons of the Nakba generation, which then took on the burden of the new Palestinian national struggle and provided the popular foundation for this struggle and activities on its behalf. The vision itself, however, took on a different meaning from the one it had for the Nakba generation. No longer was there an expectation that Arab states would liberate Filastin. Rather, the Palestinian people themselves were to lead the campaign for the liberation of Filastin. Thus the concept "liberation of Filastin" became a synonym for 'awda in an active sense; that is, by liberating Filastin one returns to Filastin, but with a different approach now—through armed struggle. Subsequently, armed struggle became an essential principle of the new national movement and a source of its right to exist, as manifested in the appearance of the fida'i organizations—foremost among them Fatah—that led the new Palestinian national movement to achievements through armed struggle. From their beginning in the early 1960s, these organizations spoke of "liberation" (*tahrir*) as much as they spoke of 'awda. Accordingly, the concept of "liberation" appears in the names of all the Palestinian organizations that emerged in the early 1960s, such as the Palestinian National Liberation Movement, the Popular Liberation Front, the Arab Liberation Front, the Palestine Liberation Front, and the Popular Front for the Liberation of Palestine.

The myth at the heart of the Palestinian national reawakening, which more than any other factor shaped the new Palestinian national movement, was the "struggle" or "armed struggle" or "resistance" (*al-muqawama*). The Sons of the Nakba generation united and mobilized itself for the armed struggle, bringing along their parents' generation, or its survivors, as well. Leaders of the new Palestinian national movement viewed armed struggle as the only means to attainment of their goal, namely, the establishment of the state of Filastin on the entire land of Filastin. It is no wonder, therefore, that the monthly *Filastinuna* devoted much space to this issue in all its aspects, including examples of other national movements' armed struggles and various theories of resistance. The armed struggle thus became the primary expression of the new Palestinian identity and the new Palestinian. In other words, "I struggle; therefore I am."

The myth of struggle is also an expression of competition with Jewish nationalism and the struggle undertaken by the *yishuv* (the Jewish settlement in Palestine before the establishment of Israel). The purpose of this myth was to imply that, just as the Jewish yishuv had struggled against British rule to achieve recognition of its right to statehood in this land, so too the Palestinians have undertaken a struggle entailing bloodshed. The Palestinian struggle, however, was not only against the British but also against the yishuv, that is, the rival Zionist movement. In time, the Palestinians sought to prove that the fida'i organizations' struggle, officially launched in January 1965, was, in fact, a continuation of the "armed struggle" of the Palestinian Arabs in Filastin that began in 1919; that is, there was historical continuity to the armed struggle of Palestinians in Filastin. This claim of a historically continuing armed struggle on the part of the Palestinians in Filastin in turn fueled the myth of armed struggle that became the symbol of the new Palestinian national movement.

The new leadership and heads of Palestinian organizations sought to strengthen Palestinians' national consciousness and increase their motivation to "sacrifice and be daring." Toward this end, they successfully depicted the Arab revolt of the 1930s as "the 1936–1939 revolt against the Jewish yishuv and foreign rule" and the "great revolt of 1936–1939." In so doing, they were cultivating the myth that these revolts contained the elements of "courage," "daring," "persistence," and "dying in the name of God" (*istishhad*) and that they provided a personal model for organizations' members in their struggle against Israel. Thus, for example, in his survey of the "continuing history of our struggle," Abu Jihad notes the "revolts in which our people participated in 1920, 1923, 1927, 1929, 1935, 1936, and 1939, when our people rose up and revolted against the new Zionist-imperialist invasion."[30]

At the heart of the myth of struggle stood 'Iz al-Din al-Qassam. Palestinian literature has awarded this local leader titles of honor, courage, and daring, with no basis whatsoever in historical fact. The Palestinian public needed historical models and, therefore, believed in these stories to such an extent that any new publication about him, especially if issued by fida'i organizations, would add another layer to the myth and place the image of Qassam even further beyond its true historical dimensions. Through these depictions of his image and deeds, fida'i organizations were, apparently, seeking to learn the lessons of the past and transmit these lessons while retroactively justifying their course of action.

In discussing the 1936–39 revolt and 'Iz al-Din al-Qassam's image, Abu Jihad states, "Our people took political and military action.... The rebel hero 'Iz al-Din al-Qassam fell as a martyr (*shahid*) in the Ya'bad groves.... His blood was fuel for the revolt that lasted three years, until 1939.... Our people's revolt was stopped because of the accursed call of Arab kings and presidents. Our people answered this deceitful call, and the revolt was suspended."[31]

Jibril's organization, the Popular Front—General Command, outdid itself when it published a special pamphlet titled *al-Qassamiyyun*, in which it described the deeds of 'Iz al-Din al-Qassam and his group.[32] The Democratic Front for the Liberation of Palestine (of Na'if Hawatma) describes Qassam as "a man who played an essential role in preparations for the revolt—pragmatically in terms of organization and preparation, and politically by propagating the concept of armed revolt among workers in villages."[33] Fatah material describes the events of 1936–39 thus: "The 1936 revolt was the greatest revolt in the history of our people."[34]

Another element in the myth of a continuing Palestinian struggle was the effort to highlight the role of Palestinians in the 1948 war. The monthly *Shu'un Filastiniyya*, published by the PLO Research Center, devoted much space to studies of this issue. Palestinian researchers also joined this endeavor by way of studies that included descriptions of various battles in which Palestinians had taken an active part. This phenomenon is reflected, for example, in a book by Muhammad al-Sha'ir, who devoted a special chapter to "Fida'iyyun Actions in 1947–1948." The chapter surveys the activities of the Holy Jihad Army (al-Jihad al-Muqaddas) under the command of 'Abd al-Qadir al-Husayni.[35]

The armed struggle was also seen as a revolt against the social conditions of refugees living in camps and as an expression of independent action by the new Palestinians and nondependence on Arab states. The armed struggle was intended, in their view, to enlist the Arab states in a war against Israel as a means of restoring the dignity lost in 1948.[36]

A positive contributing factor that prompted the Palestinian national awakening was the success of the Algerian revolt, which served as a model for the principle of armed struggle in action. Most Palestinian researchers and writers point to this example, as did the leaders and founders of fida'i organizations. The lesson learned from the Algerian revolt was "the ability of the people in any Arab territory to fight the enemy and liberate the homeland, relying on its own independent resources and on the aid of peoples in other territories."[37] It proved to the Palestinians that "a people that takes the initiative into its own hands to handle its problems is capable of fulfilling its national aspirations."[38] In this context Fatah also underscored that "undoubtedly the success of the Algerian revolution . . . had a great influence on the formation of the beginnings of the organization."[39]

Abu Iyad summarized the Algerian influence as follows: "It can be said that the success of the Algerian revolution played an important part in this development, because young Palestinians felt that they were not inferior to their Algerian brothers and that they could develop [their own] slogan of armed struggle and implement it."[40] Furthermore, the impact of the Algerian struggle on Palestinians is indicated in the publication of a series titled Revolutionary Studies and Endeavors, of which five out of a total of eleven pamphlets that were published after the public emergence of Fatah in 1965 and after a rise in fida'iyyun activity were dedicated to the endeavors and lessons of guerrilla wars and "popular wars" of other peoples. One pamphlet, *Revolution and Violence—The Path to Victory*, cites passages from theory posed by Frantz Fanon, who in 1956 became the ideologue and editor of the main periodical of the National Liberation Front (Front de Libération Nationale [FLN], in French) in Algeria.[41] Another pamphlet, *The Chinese Endeavor*, included passages from Mao's guerilla theory.[42] The pamphlet titled *The Vietnamese Endeavor* included passages from Giáp's book.[43] The fourth pamphlet was *The Cuban Endeavor*.[44]

* * *

In sum, the social and political living conditions of Palestinian refugees gave rise to an important, defining phenomenon: social solidarity. This solidarity steadily evolved and even intensified over time, alongside and in conjunction with the Palestinian national reawakening. The most powerful expression of this solidarity is the complete support and widespread trust that the Palestinian leadership received. Especially significant is the support it received for the notion of reviving a Palestinian entity as first floated in the Arab arena in 1959. Support for this cause grew and evolved over time into an aspiration for self-determination and the establishment of a Palestinian state.

Notes

1. Mannheim, "The Problem of Generations."
2. Basim Sirhan, "Shuhada' al-Thawra al-Filastiniyya," *Shu'un Filastiniyya* 9 (May 1972).
3. Fatah, Maktab al-Ta'bi'a wa al-Tanzim [Mobilization and Organization Bureau], *Min 'Ikhlaqiyyat al-Muqatil al-Thawri*, pamphlet no. 4 (The Young Fighter Library, n.p., n.d.).
4. George Habash, interview, *Politiken* (Copenhagen), April 20, 1969.

5. Ben Porat, Marks, and Shamir, *Mahane Plitim*, 92–94.
6. Wazir, *al-Bidayat*.
7. Abu Iyad (Salah Khalaf), *al-Tali'a* (Cairo), June 1969, 61.
8. Fatah, *Min Muntalaqatal—al-'Amal al-Fida'i*, pamphlet no. 1 in the series Dirasat wa Tajarib Thawriyya, August 1968, 39.
9. Shafiq al-Hut, *Haqa'iq 'Ala Tariq al-Tahrir* (Beirut: PLO Markaz al-Abhath, 1966).
10. Abu Iyad, *al-Tali'a*.
11. Wazir, *al-Bidayat*, 56–72.
12. Fatah, Maktab al-Ta'bi'a wa al-Tanzim [Mobilization and Organization Bureau], *Al-Thawra al-Filastiniyya wa Marahil Tatawwuriha*, internal publication no. 106 (n.p., March 31, 1969), 6–7.
13. Abu Iyad, *al-Tali'a*.
14. Fatah, Ideological Notebook.
15. Fatah, Maktab al-Ta'bi'a wa al-Tanzim Mobilization and Organization Bureau], *Al-Tala'i' al-Thawriyya*, pamphlet no. 7 of the Fatah Political Cadres' Course, Second Program (n.p., n.d.), 3.
16. *Al-Thawra al-Filastiniyya*, no. 22 (January 1970): 10; see also, Khalid al-Hasan (a Fatah leader), *Shu'un Filastiniyya*, no. 4 (September 1971): 281–82.
17. Samir Ayyub, *Al-Bina' al-Tabaqi lil-Filastiniyyin* (Beirut: Dar al-Hadatha, 1984), 275–76.
18. Fatah, *Min Muntalaqat*, 38–39.
19. Nabil Sha'ath, "High Level Palestinian Manpower," *Journal of Palestine Studies* 1, no. 2 (1972): 94.
20. Moshe Efrat, *Haplitim ha-Filastinim—Mihkar Kalkali ve Hivrati, 1947–1974*, Research Report no. 10 (Tel Aviv University, September 1976), 80–83. His conclusions are based on the official Syrian censuses of 1960 and of 1970. See also Efrat, "The Palestinian Refugees," 101, 128–29.
21. Ibid.
22. Nazih Qura, *Ta'lim al-Filastiniyyin—al-Waqi' wa al-Mushkilat* (Beirut: PLO Markaz al-Abhath, 1975), 147.
23. Sha'ath, "High Level Palestinian Manpower," 95.
24. Ghantus, "'Athar al-Tarkib," 45. See also Qasim, *Min al-Tih*, 21; Shafiq al-Hut, *Al-Filastini bayna al-Tih wa al-Dawla* (Beirut, 1977), 36.
25. Turki, *The Disinherited*, 41.
26. Qasim, *Min al-Tih*, 20.
27. Munzamat al-Tahrir al-Filastiniyya (PLO), *Al-Mithaq al-Watani al-Filastini*, official publication, (Cairo, 1964).
28. Salah al-Din al-Dabbagh, "Haq al-Sha'b al-Filastini bi-Ardihi wa al-'Awda 'Ilayha," *Shu'un Filastiniyya*, 41–42 (February 1975): 139–53.
29. *Al-Thawra al-Filastiniyya* 22 (January 1970): 11.
30. Khalil al-Wazir (Abu Jihad), Sawt al-'Asifa Radio, January 1, 1981.
31. Ibid.
32. Salah Ayyubi, *Al-Qassamiyyun, Lamahat Matwiyya 'An Tarikh al-Nidal al-Filastini* (Popular Front for the Liberation of Palestine—General Command), 3.
33. Popular Democratic Front for the Liberation of Palestine, *Malamih Tatawwur al-Nidal al-Filastinin*, 8–9.

34. *Al-Thawra al-Filastiniyya* 19 (September 15, 1969): 8; see also Ghassan Kanafani, "'Thawrat, 1936–1939, fi Filastin, Khalfiyyat wa Tafaseel wa Tahlil," *Shu'un Filastiniyya* 6 (January 1972): 45.

35. Muhammad al-Sha'ir, *Al-Harb al-Fida'iyya fi Filastin* (Beirut: PLO Markaz al-Abhath, 1967), 2, 145, 184–85, 191.

36. See Abu Iyad (Salah Khalaf), *Filastini Bila Hawiyya* (Kuwait), 68–69.

37. Adnan Badr, "'Sab' Sanawat li al-Jabha al-Sha'biyya li Tahrir Filastin'," *al-Hadaf* (Beirut, December 14, 1974).

38. Sakhnini, "Tamthil"; Francus, *Al-Filastiniyyun*, 70.

39. Fatah, *Al-Thawra al-Filastiniyya, Ab'aduha wa Qadayaha, 'Aduwun Qawiyun Lakinnahu Laysa Usturiyan*, two-part pamphlet in the series Dirasat wa Tajarib Thawriyya, 82–83.

40. Abu Iyad, *al-Tali'a*.

41. Fatah, *Al-Thawra wa al-'Unf, Tariq al-Nasr*, pamphlet no. 3 in the series *Dirasat wa Tajarib Thawriyya* (August 1967).

42. Fatah, *Al-Tajriba al-Siniyya*, pamphlet no. 4 in the series Dirasat wa Tajarib Thawriyya (August 1967), 3–4.

43. Fatah, *Al-Thawra al-Vietnamiyya*, pamphlet no. 5 in the series Dirasat wa Tajarib Thawriyya (August 1967), 7–10.

44. Fatah, *Al-Tajriba al-Kubiyya*, pamphlet no. 6 in the series Dirasat wa Tajarib Thawriyya (August 1967), 3.

7 Manifestations of the Palestinian National Awakening

The Arab Nationalists Movement, Fatah, the Ba'th Party, and the General Union of Palestinian Students

In the absence of Palestinian political parties or organizations, which disappeared in the aftermath of the 1948 Arab-Israeli War, some members of the Palestinian intelligentsia turned to political activism through pan-Arab political organizations. Although their participation in political activism was not massive in scale, the Palestinians distinctly stood out. The main manifestation of Palestinian participation was through the Arab Nationalists Movement (ANM), in whose establishment and development Palestinians played a key role. They were also active in the Ba'th Party and the Communist Party (in Jordan, after 1948).

The First Harbinger: The Arab Nationalists Movement— From a Pan-Arab Movement to a Palestinian Fida'i Organization

The core group of leaders who decided in the summer of 1951 to found the Arab Nationalists Movement comprised eight students who had nearly completed their studies at the University of Beirut. They were all active in the association al-'Urwa al-Wuthqa (the Firmest Bond), which had been founded at the University of Beirut in the early 1930s as a student cultural association. Its activists included Qustantin Zurayq, who attracted a group of intellectuals from the university, Palestinians among others.

The core founding group of the Arab Nationalists Movement comprised the following individuals: George Habash, its vital spirit, the son of a Palestinian grocer from Lydda; Hani al-Hindi, a Syrian, the son of a high-ranking officer in the Iraqi army and later the Syrian army; Ahmad al-Khatib, a Kuwaiti from a middle-class family; Wadi' Hadad, the Palestinian son of an Arabic teacher from Safed; Salih al-Shibil, a Palestinian from Acre and the son of a merchant; and Hamid al-Jaburi, an Iraqi. The first three were medical students and the others were economics and political science students. Five of the founders—with the exception of Habash, who had completed his studies—were in their senior year at the university. Habash and Hindi had also served in the Arab Salvation Army during the 1948 war, which Habash had joined as a medic.¹

George Habash fled with his family in 1948 from Lydda to Jordan, an event that proved formative for him and shaped his views. In his words,

> The Israelis came to Lydda and forced us to flee. It is a picture that does not leave my mind and that I will never forget. Thirty-thousand people walking, crying, screaming with terror . . . women carrying babies on their arms and children clinging to their [skirts], with the Israeli soldiers pointing weapons at their backs . . . some people fell by the wayside, and some did not rise again. It was terrible. If you see such things your mind and heart are altered. . . . Humans must change the world, they must do something, they must kill if needs be. To kill, even if that means that we in turn become inhuman.²

The founding of the ANM was preceded by extensive activism on the part of this group, especially the Palestinian founders. Habash and Hindi remained very bitter and frustrated after the war, primarily because of the ties they claimed existed between Arab governments and Britain as well as the Zionist movement. Consequently, they decided, it was necessary to punish every Arab leader seeking peace with Israel and to undermine all armistice agreements, including by means of attacks against Arab interests. By March 1949, Habash and Hindi were engaged in founding a clandestine Beirut-based organization named Kata'ib al-Fida' al-'Arabi, together with a small number of Syrian, Iraqi, and Egyptian activists. A senior leader of the Arab Nationalists Movement claims that the movement was an expanded version of the activism undertaken by Kata'ib's founding nucleus, which explains the latter's influence on the organizational and conceptual structure of the ANM, especially during its early years.³

Kata'ib was a fida'i organization of young nationalists who believed in the liberation of Filastin through "revenge." The official political outlook of Kata'ib was, in essence, "the destruction of Israel, which depends on Arab unity." Kata'ib spoke of assassinating Arab leaders who were seen as responsible for the loss of Filastin, foremost among them Nuri al-Sa'id, an Iraqi, and King 'Abdulla of Jordan. They agreed among themselves that Jews were not to be distinguished from Zionists, and that every Jew was considered a target for revenge.⁴

The organization's members underwent training in guerrilla activities, including the use of incendiary devices, explosives, and gunfire. By August 1949, only four months after its official establishment, Kata'ib had already launched a dozen attacks against various targets in Beirut and Damascus. The first attack took place on August 6, against a synagogue in Damascus, resulting in twelve deaths and twenty-seven injured. At the same time, the Alliance School in Beirut was attacked. The attacks were designed to sabotage the armistice agreement of July 20, 1949, between Israel and Syria. During the following year, the British and

American consulates in Damascus, as well as a foreign school and the UNRWA office, were attacked. Kata'ib failed in its attempts to strike at Arab leaders, specifically King 'Abdulla and Nuri al-Sa'id.[5]

Kata'ib's dissolution was a result of action on the part of the Egyptian group, two of whose representatives in the military leadership of the organization proposed assassinating Adib Shishakli, Syria's ruler at the time. Three members of the leadership opposed the proposal, including Habash and Hindi, asserting that Shishakli was not responsible for the Filastin Catastrophe. Yet the Egyptian group stood its ground and even made an assassination attempt against Shishakli on November 20, 1950. The failed attempt drew the attention of government security forces, who arrested the members of the group behind the operation. Subsequently, thirteen members, including leaders, were arrested, Hindi among them. George Habash was in Beirut at the same time and thus avoided arrest. Following the trial of those arrested, Kata'ib ceased being active.[6] Habash returned to action in the framework of the association al-'Urwa al-Wuthqa and was even chosen as its leader.

The core founding group of the Arab Nationalists Movement met in Beirut in the summer of 1951, in order to draw the lessons to be learned from the failed Kata'ib endeavor. It was proposed that a new, clandestine nationalist organization be established, but in actuality the group remained active in the framework of the association al-'Urwa al-Wuthqa until 1955.

In late 1951, George Habash returned to Jordan and opened a community clinic in Amman, which served the residents of the refugee camps for practically no fee. In mid-1952, Wadi' Hadad joined the clinic. Their aim was to establish themselves prominently within Jordanian political life. An Arab cultural club named al-Muntada al-'Arabi was their first station.[7] Habash and Hadad found fertile ground for their activities in Jordan amidst the intelligentsia, especially among doctors, lawyers, and engineers. Prominent among those who joined them from the West Bank were two physicians, Salah 'Anabtawi and Subhi Ghosha. During this time, the ANM was also joined by a Jordanian named Na'if Hawatma, born in 1935 in Salt, Transjordan, to a poor Christian family of Bedouin origin. Hawatma had completed his studies at Beirut Arab University in the mid-1950s and returned to Jordan.

On settling in Amman in late 1951, Habash was determined to adopt the approach of armed struggle against Israel. Indeed, shortly after Wadi' Hadad joined him, the two formed the first fida'i core group and tried to smuggle its members into Israeli territory, but the Jordanian army learned of this effort and successfully thwarted it.[8]

In late 1952, the core group founded the Association Opposing Peace with Israel (Haya'at Muqawamat al-Sulh ma'a 'Isra'il), a front that was primarily active among circles of "dispossessed Arabs" (al-nazihin al-'Arab) and the "Arabs of

Filastin." In accordance with the pan-Arab perspective, the ANM refrained from using the terms "the Filastin people" or "refugees," resolutely adhering instead to the all-inclusive nationalism of the Palestinian problem (*qawmiyyat al-qadhiyya*). As time passed, however, the ANM began to use terms that referred to the Palestinians as a people, such as "Palestinian Arab youth" (*al-shabab al-'Arabi al-Filastini*).[9]

In early 1953, the ANM began to publish a weekly eight-page newsletter titled *al-Tha'r* (*Revenge*). The Association Opposing Peace with Israel, the weekly newsletter, and other position papers helped the ANM infiltrate refugee camps and student circles and, thereby, recruit a number of young Palestinians, who were dispatched to establish clandestine cells in refugee camps in Syria, Lebanon, and Jordan. Prominent among these young Palestinians was Ahmad al-Yamani (who in time became a member of the Political Department of the Popular Front) and Abu 'Adnan Qays (later a member of the Political Department of the Democratic Front). At the time the ANM evidently succeeded in recruiting almost a hundred young Lebanese and Palestinians, who clandestinely disseminated its newsletter and trained youngsters under the cover of student, youth, and scout camps.[10] Through *al-Tha'r*, the ANM called for the enlistment of the "dispossessed" to establish "an authority [*hay'a*] among their ranks, that will represent them and lead all the dispossessed from every tent or part of the Arab world to join in the Arab convoy."[11]

During its years of publication, which began on November 20, 1952, and continued until mid-1958, *al-Tha'r* addressed the following topics: the significance of the Nakba; the Jews as the enemy—rejecting the distinction between Judaism and Zionism and arguing that the state of Israel poses a danger not only to Filastin and its people but also to the Arab nation as a whole because Israel "will by its nature seek to expand, even if we ignore Filastin"; and the solution as conveyed in one word—"revenge" (*al-tha'r*): "When we raise the flag of revenge ... our intention is to demand the return of all of Filastin to the Arabs and the expulsion of the Jewish invasion from Arab land." The newsletter also called for the establishment of a revolutionary organization that would lead the dispossessed forward "for the sake of return [*'awda*] and in order to prepare them for war."

The liberation of Filastin was the primary goal of the ANM, and this goal would not be attained unless Arab states were freed from Western colonial oppression and could then focus their resources against Israel. Wadi' Hadad was cited in this context as having told potential recruits that "the road to Tel Aviv passes through Damascus, Baghdad, Amman, and Cairo."[12]

In the meantime, in early 1954 George Habash founded the newspaper *al-Ra'i* in Jordan and served as its editor-in-chief for a year, until it was shut down by the authorities because of its extreme political stances. After the closure of the newspaper, Habash turned to underground activities and began disseminating propaganda material and organizing demonstrations that included confrontations with Jordanian security forces. Hani al-Hindi continued to publish *al-Ra'i* in Damascus, until its reappearance in Jordan in 1956 after Glubb Pasha was removed as commander-in-chief of the army and the Nabulsi government was appointed. The political atmosphere in Jordan then became more accommodating for Arab nationalists, and they even participated in the October 1956 elections in Jordan, although they lost.

With the collapse of the Nabulsi government in April 1957 and the prohibition against political party activism, the ANM's activities and standing in Jordan took a downturn. Habash and his colleagues went underground and began taking part in hostile activities against the regime. Consequently, many ANM members were arrested, including Wadi' Hadad, who remained under arrest until his release in 1960. Habash and Hawatma escaped to Damascus. Habash remained in Damascus, where he oversaw the activities of the ANM's chapters. Hawatma moved to Iraq and helped long-standing members of the Baghdad chapter, including Basil al-Kubaysi, strengthen the chapter and increase its activities. Relations between the ANM and the regime in Iraq worsened during the years 1962–63. Hawatma was arrested, released in February 1963, and expelled to Beirut.[13]

According to Habash a few weeks after the Sinai War, the core founding group of the ANM convened its first conference, on December 25, 1956, in Beirut. Habash did not consider it a true conference but rather a meeting of leaders, yet the other founders insisted that the meeting be referenced as the first conference. The conference decided to adopt the pan-Arab name "al-Shabab al-Qawmi al'-Arabi"—a name that depicts it as an independent party, distinct from other national parties. Thereafter, the ANM became known among political circles in the Arab world as both "al-Shabab al-Qawmi al'-Arabi" and "al-Qawmiyyun al-'Arab." The founding group of the ANM did not make a final decision regarding its name, and continued to use both.[14]

The first conference elected a National Executive Committee to serve as the ANM's collective national leadership. It comprised eleven members, including three Palestinians: George Habash, Wadi' Hadad, and Salih al-Shibil. All were among the leaders of al-'Urwa al-Wuthqa. Six had been part of the founding nucleus that conceived of the movement during a meeting in the summer of 1951, while the remaining five were members of the first cadre of leaders of the same core group.[15]

During the years 1956–57, the ANM increased its membership in Jordan, including in East Jerusalem and the West Bank. For the first time it reached the Gaza Strip, where it enlisted some members of the Muslim Brotherhood to join its ranks. The ANM also achieved considerable success among UNRWA schoolteachers in various refugee camps. It recruited teachers in most of the camps throughout the West Bank, Syria, and Lebanon.[16] The real momentum in terms of membership, however, came with the rise and spread of Nasirism after the Sinai War and the unification of Egypt and Syria.

The massive support for Nasir after the three-pronged attack on Egypt in October 1956, which peaked with the unification of Egypt and Syria in 1958, highlighted how weak the Arab Nationalists Movement had been until then. It also underscored the ANM's political insignificance during the 1950s and its organizational limitations. With the exception of Jordan and Kuwait, the ANM remained—at least until 1958—a clandestine organization, completely irrelevant to the dynamic political life in the Arab Mashriq. Until 1960, it never had more than fifteen members in Syria, most of whom even said that it should be disbanded and that it served no purpose after the establishment of the United Arab Republic (UAR). This situation drove George Habash, who had been in hiding in Amman, to shift his base of activity to Damascus to preserve the ANM's core group.[17]

In Iraq, the ANM had no more than twenty members on the day of its coup d'état, July 14, 1958, while in Lebanon the movement had shrunk by 1957 to a group of high school students participating in semi-military ceremonies in scout camps.[18] In Egypt, the ANM was limited to a group of students who had been expelled from the American University of Beirut during late 1954 and early 1955 because of demonstrations against the Baghdad Pact. They succeeded in taking over the Kuwaiti affiliate of the General Union of Palestinian Students (GUPS), which became a front for the ANM.[19]

After the establishment of the UAR in February 1958 and the revolution of July 1958 in Iraq, the ANM was no more than a "closed group of friends (or a group of brothers—*akhwiya*) of modest size in organizational terms and of limited political presence, with the possible exception of its chapters in Kuwait and Jordan." Habash himself used the term "student organization"[20] to describe the organizational activity during this period. It may reasonably be assumed that the ANM's alignment with Nasir's policy and Egypt's support for the ANM contributed to its expansion and to the recruitment of new members, as well as to its positioning within the Arab political arena, which included its participation in the UAR government while the union existed. In other words, the tide of Nasirism released the ANM from its state of isolation and turned it into a movement of the masses.

The Palestinization of the Arab Nationalists Movement, 1959–67

Intensive discussions within the Arab arena surrounding the concept of a Palestinian entity, compounded by Egypt's ever-increasing engagement in this issue, created a difficult dilemma for the Arab Nationalists Movement: how to balance its emphasis on Arab unity with the need to focus on Filastin, and to what extent their commitment to Nasir precluded independent military action against Israel.

Against the background of the ANM's alignment with Nasir's strategy and policy, as well as Nasir's campaign against the mufti, the Lebanese chapter launched a scathing attack against the mufti and the Arab Higher Hay'a (Authority) in late August 1959. On August 30, a group named al-Shabab al-'Arabi al-Filastini (Arab Palestinian Youth) in Lebanon—a cover name for ANM members in Lebanon—issued a strong condemnation of the mufti and the hay'a in the Lebanese press.[21]

The increased activity on the part of ANM chapters in Arab countries led Palestinian members to begin asking themselves what the Palestinian role was within a framework that requires pan-Arab action. In the opinion of 'Isa al-Shu'aybi, this question—which became acutely pertinent after the unification of Egypt and Syria—resulted in the establishment of a Filastin Committee within the ANM in 1958.[22] In contrast, Yezid Sayigh, citing Habash, notes that only in 1959 did the ANM establish its Filastin Committee, comprising members of its Palestinian cadre, as an organizational framework for its Palestinian members. The members of this committee, according to Sayigh, included Habash, Hadad, 'Usama al-Naqib (a Palestinian from Syria), Zahi Qamhawi (a Palestinian from Jordan), Ahmad al-Yamani, and 'Abd al-Karim Hamad (a Palestinian from Lebanon).[23] Habash saw this committee as the core of the future Popular Front for the Liberation of Palestine (PFLP).[24]

The committee had been established in the aftermath of the March 1959 Egyptian initiative to revive the Palestinian entity and the inter-Arab discussion that followed. The ANM regarded itself as duty-bound to take a stance on this issue in light of the questions raised by Palestinian members, especially after Nasir had unequivocally rejected the option of any independent military action for the liberation of Filastin. In his speeches, Nasir had declared that Egypt would not initiate a confrontation with Israel until it had completed the buildup of its armed forces so as to ensure a decisive victory, and that Egypt would choose the time and place for war. Nasir's speeches also conveyed clearly to his Palestinian listeners that he did not have a plan for the liberation of Filastin. According to Yezid Sayigh, this position of Nasir's is apparently what drove the Filastin Committee of the Arab Nationalists Movement to consider military options for the liberation of Filastin.[25]

The ANM's Filastin Committee did indeed discuss military options for the liberation of Filastin in the course of its lengthy debates and disputes. During these discussions, the committee formulated four courses of action: liberation of Filastin through an organized war in which states of the Arab League participate; liberation of Filastin by the Palestinians themselves; liberation of Filastin through the unified state, that is, the UAR; or liberation of Filastin by the Palestinians with the backing of the UAR.

After debating the matter, the Filastin Committee rejected the first three alternatives and opted for the fourth, which placed responsibility on the Palestinians to lead the way and assigned them a clear role, with the support of Egypt.[26] The committee established contact with the UAR, met with Nasir during one of his visits to Damascus in 1959 (in a meeting attended by 'Abd al-Hamid al-Sarraj, chairman of the Executive Council of the Northren Region of the UAR, and requested that he train the Palestinians and provide them with arms. Nasir acquiesced to these requests, which had been presented to him in the name of "the dispossessed (*nazihin*) Palestinians in Lebanon." Subsequently, a number of Palestinians received training in Syria from officers who were sympathetic to the ANM. A few days after the dissolution of the UAR in September 1961, thirty weapons were transferred to the trainees.[27]

The collapse of the Egyptian-Syrian union altered the situation. As a result of the disengagement from Syria, the ANM lost its primary training base and refuge, its secure supply routes to Lebanon and Jordan, and approximately half of its Syrian members. Habash, Hindi, and Hadad found refuge in Beirut, and the task of rebuilding the Syrian chapter fell to low-ranking cadets who remained there, among them Salah, Bilal al-Hasan, and 'Usama al-Hindi, Hani's younger brother, who was appointed to head the chapter as well as the Military Action Committee established there. These cadets faced a difficult problem, as Syrian membership in the ANM had declined significantly. Most of them were Palestinian students, and only fifteen were Syrian.[28]

The disengagement was also a blessing for the ANM, enabling it to establish direct ties with Egypt. Muhammad Nasim of Egypt's general intelligence service was dispatched to Beirut to revive the ANM's chapter in Lebanon, where he met with ANM leaders Muhsin Ibrahim and Mustafa Baydun. The two sides entered a period of close relations. The Egyptian contact was Sami Sharaf, director of the Office of the President for Nasir. Salah Nasr, chief of the general intelligence service, and Sha'rawi Juma'a of the general intelligence service were responsible for coordination at the operational level. The closer ties with Egypt also brought promises of direct military aid and training for ANM members on the part of 'Abd al-Hakim 'Amir, commander-in-chief of the Egyptian army.[29]

The discourse within the Arab Nationalists Movement regarding an independent Palestinian entity intensified in 1962, after Algeria's declaration of independence. Many Palestinian members of the ANM were inspired by the Algerian revolt, as well as by the September 1962 takeover of Yemen's government by republican officers. Nasir's admission in June 1962 before the legislative council in Gaza—that neither he nor the other Arab states have a plan for the liberation of Filastin—generated tension within the ANM and intensified Palestinian members' demands for Palestinian self-organization within the movement. Against this background, serious efforts commenced, with the aim of establishing a separate Palestinian chapter (a Palestinian section, in effect) within the ANM, and rank-and-file Palestinians even took preliminary steps toward the establishment of an autonomous entity for their particular region and initiated armed action against Israel. They had grown weary of ideological discussions, and particularly of ideological debates launched by "leftist" leaders of the ANM, none of whom had Palestinian roots. Indeed, because five members of the Executive Committee in 1963 were Lebanese and one—Hawatma—was a Jordanian residing in Lebanon, they were able to oppose military activity, fearing repression by the Syrian Deuxième Bureau (intelligence service), and they avoided direct contact with ANM members in the refugee camps. The 1963 announcement by the state of Israel of a plan to divert the waters of the Jordan River intensified anger and frustration on the part of rank-and-file Palestinians in the ANM, who interpreted this move as a sign of Arab weakness and apathy regarding their fate.

Against the background of these developments, a core group of Palestinian members met in Beirut, probably in October 1963, and decided to establish a separate section for Palestinians within the Arab Nationalists Movement. Wadi' Hadad and Amin al-Hindi were still in hiding, but Hadad evidently knew about the meeting and approved of its outcome, given that he was a dynamic, action-oriented man with no patience for theory or ideology of any sort, particularly not the Marxist outlook of the ANM's "leftist" members. The decision taken in Beirut inspired Palestinian members of the ANM in all other Arab countries to set up separate Palestinian sections, while remaining subordinate to the local leadership in the region (*qiyadat iqlim*) and maintaining ties to "the leadership of the new Palestinian action" in Beirut.

Shortly after these developments, in early 1964, George Habash managed to escape from Syria and reach Egypt, where he met with Nasir. His aim was to neutralize the tension that had formed between ANM members there and the Egyptian intelligence as a result of differences of opinion regarding the policy on 'Aden (and because of which ANM members in Cairo had been arrested and briefly imprisoned). On returning to Beirut, Habash established contact with Hadad and Hindi. He secured the agreement of the ANM's Executive Committee to permit an autonomous Palestinian section within the framework of the movement. The position of the Executive Committee was affirmed at the ANM national conference in May 1964, although Habash and other members of the old guard, who were considered "nonleftists," were in no hurry to adopt the call for independent armed action and thereby defy Nasir, who at the time was opposed to such action.[30]

Throughout this period, discussions within the Arab Nationalists Movement regarding a Palestinian entity were limited in scope, but the emergence by then of nearly thirty-six organizations in the Palestinian arena compelled the movement to give pragmatic consideration to some form of Palestinian action as an expression of the new Palestinian awakening. Therefore, the ANM decided to act quickly in setting up chapters of the Palestinian section in Lebanon, Kuwait, and Syria. These chapters were subordinate to the regional leadership, which in turn was subordinate to the Leadership Committee for Palestinian Action of the Movement (al-Lajna al-Qiyadiyya lil-'Amal al-Filastini fi al-Haraka), established in 1964.[31]

Certain resolutions of the first Arab Summit in January 1964 fundamentally changed the situation for the Arab Nationalists Movement as well. These resolutions, supported and promoted by Egypt, addressed the establishment of a Palestinian entity, the appointment of Ahmad al-Shuqayri as head of the first Palestinian Congress, and his subsequent election as head of this entity, the PLO. The ANM then decided to merge with the PLO and operate within its framework, thereby shaping its very structure from the outset in a manner that accorded with its own outlook.[32] The Arab Nationalists Movement underwent two additional phases before the Six Day War on the way to its full Palestinization: the establishment of the Leadership of Palestinian Action (Qiyadat al-'Amal al-Filastini) alongside the movement's leadership, in effect replacing the Filastin Committee, and the establishment of a Palestinian section within every chapter of the ANM in all countries where it was based.

These organizational changes gave rise to two Palestinian mechanisms within the ANM: a Filastin section in every country-based chapter and a Palestinian leadership body at the level of the ANM's leadership. The Filastin sections were subordinate to the Leadership of Palestinian Action as well as the chapter leadership. The Leadership of Palestinian Action was responsible for "Palestinian action, preparation for armed struggle in the Palestinian arena, and the preparation and training of fighters." Wadi' Hadad oversaw preparations for fida'i operations. Indeed, already by 1964, the ANM's Leadership of Palestinian Action had succeeded in infiltrating its first fida'i cell into Israel, an action that resulted in the death of someone known as Khalid, who has come to be regarded as the first *shahid* (martyr) of the ANM's Filastin section.[33]

The Palestinization of the Arab Nationalists Movement reached its fruition after the Six Day War with the establishment in December 1967 of the Popular Front for the Liberation of Palestine. The Arab Nationalists Movement had, in essence, arrived at the end of the road when Palestinianness overrode its national pan-Arab character, and it became a Palestinian organization in the full sense of the word.

The Palestinian National Liberation Movement—Fatah

In the annals of the new Palestinian national movement, Fatah (Harakat al-Tahrir al-Watani al-Filastini) is regarded as the first Palestinian movement since 1948 in every sense. The name "Fatah" first surfaced in the Middle East arena after January 12, 1965, when Israel issued a public announcement about an action undertaken by the organization's military arm, al-'Asifa, on the night of January 1, 1965. The action, directed against the national water carrier near 'Ilabun in northern Israel, entailed the planting of explosives but did not inflict any damage. Israeli intelligence had learned about the existence of this organization and its plans to carry out actions in Israel approximately two to three weeks before the first operation. At the time, however, security authorities did not ascribe it any importance, even though the organization's name had appeared in its magazine, *Filastinuna*, much earlier.

Internal Fatah publications and remarks by the organization's founders attribute the idea of establishing an "armed Palestinian movement" to the period of Israel's occupation of the Gaza Strip between October 1956 and March 1957. According to one publication, after Israel's conquest, a number of young, educated Palestinians came together and decided to join efforts. Most of them were members of the Palestinian student union in Cairo, and they shared the outlook of "a new path for the campaign [against Israel]." According to this source, the nucleus of the organization took shape over the course of about two and a half years: "During 1958 more and more milestones were set for this group of young people, who called themselves 'Harkat Tahrir Filastin.' They took the initials of the organization's name, Hataf [HTF], and reversed their order [to FTH, or Fatah]." Within two years, "Fatah pioneers were working to disseminate their ideas among the scattered masses of the Palestinian people, while recruiting supporters, training them, arming them, and preparing them for the revolution."[34] Also in 1958, the core ideas of the movement crystallized and began to appear in the pages of its monthly, *Filastinuna*.[35] According to Abu Iyad, "the organizational structure of Fatah was established in October 1959, during a meeting of Fatah's founders in Kuwait,"[36] but only toward the end of 1962 and during 1963 did clandestine chapters begin to be founded in Lebanon, Kuwait, and to a lesser extent in the Gaza Strip. In 1963, Fatah also established its first office in Algeria, where a number of its members underwent military training.

Writing retrospectively about the early days of activity, Abu Jihad, one of Fatah's founders, stated that "during the second half of 1957, the first meeting of the Fatah movement took place, a meeting of a group of activists." They numbered no more than five activists from various regions of Filastin, each one of whom brought with him his experience of struggle in one of these regions. Like Abu Iyad, Abu Jihad also recounts that Kuwait was the site of the first meeting.[37] Indeed, Fatah publications emphasize that the movement began its organizational activities in the Gaza Strip one year after Israel's occupation ended.

One can discern several characteristics of Fatah's organizational activities during the 1950s: the organization actually originated from the merger of a few Palestinian organizations that were active in a number of Arab states, primarily

Lebanon, Syria, the Gaza Strip, Jordan, and Persian Gulf states. Some operated as part of existing Arab political parties or organizations. Most Fatah founders (with few exceptions) grew up in refugee camps, especially in the Gaza Strip, where they had arrived during the course of 1948. The organization's core founding group included activists from Arab political parties that existed during the early 1950s, most of whom were members of or indeed activists in the Muslim Brotherhood. In this connection, we see the Islamic underpinnings of the organization's ideology, which solidified during the second half of the 1950s and throughout the 1960s. In contrast to the process that the Arab Nationalists Movement underwent, Fatah's founders refrained from discussing social matters or adopting a stance toward one or another Arab regime. They limited themselves to focusing on the prime objective of massive recruitment for the cause of Filastin's liberation, deferring discussion of social issues until after liberation.

The process of Fatah's consolidation was relatively slow, lasting a number of years before it shifted to the operational phase in January 1965. Enlistment was not massive, and Palestinian public interest was very limited, apparently because of universal or near-universal identification with Nasir and his approach and because of a lack of faith in the organization's ability to achieve the liberation of Filastin. Indeed, when the name "Fatah" first surfaced in 1959 in *Filastinuna*, Nasir was at the peak of his popularity, having become the sole source of hope in the eyes of the Palestinian masses. Fatah's ideas and call for an armed struggle contradicted the Arab strategy espoused by Nasir at the time. During its early years, therefore, Fatah did not enjoy substantial support among the Palestinian public. This situation is the likely explanation for its slow rate of growth over the course of several years and for its near-total isolation among Palestinians.[38]

A few of Fatah's founders, including Yusif al-Najar, Salim Za'nun, and Fathi Bal'awi, had joined the Muslim Brotherhood during the 1948 war, when they were in their late teens or early twenties. Other founders were even younger. Khalil al-Wazir, Salah Khalaf, Kamal 'Udwan, and Yahya 'Ashur were high school students in Gaza. What brought them together was their school and their membership in the Muslim Brotherhood, which was active in the Gaza Strip during the 1950s.

Yasir Arafat, who became Fatah's leader, had joined the Muslim Brotherhood in 1948, at the age of twenty, while an engineering student at Cairo University. According to reports, he fought under the command of 'Abd al-Qadir al-Husayni and later with the Muslim Brotherhood unit in Gaza and Jerusalem. On returning to Cairo, he joined a volunteer reserve officers' course for university students. He also participated in attacks organized by the Muslim Brotherhood against British forces in the Suez Canal during 1950 through 1954 as well as in the training of students during 1953 and 1954. In addition, he was active in the General Union of Palestinian Students and even served as its president in 1952, where he met his future coleaders of Fatah.[39]

Khalil al-Wazir (Abu Jihad) is regarded as Fatah's true founder. He escaped with his parents from Ramalla at age thirteen, and in 1951, as a teenager, he joined the Muslim Brotherhood. At age sixteen, he was already the leader of a group of two hundred youths, most of whom were two years younger than he was. He also established a clandestine network for independent military action. When the Muslim Brotherhood was declared illegal in Egypt in 1954, Wazir and his colleagues officially left the organization.[40] The Sinai War was the real impetus for the establishment of Fatah. Khalil al-Wazir later recounted, "When the three-pronged attack was launched and the enemy conquered the Gaza Strip, the first question that came to our minds was how to engage a large number of Palestinians from the strip in our military action and how to focus support on popular resistance movements in Gaza."[41]

Khalil al-Wazir highlights three schools of thought that emerged among Palestinians at the time: one originated amidst a group of young people in Cairo and called for gathering Palestinian leaders together and urging them to establish a clearly defined framework for leadership of the Palestinian people. This approach was attempted several times, but because of the leaders' ineffectiveness and internal strife within the group, these efforts reached a deadlock. A second school of thought held that it was necessary to declare a government in exile, to be established on the ruins of the All-Palestine Government, with the aim of representing the Palestinian people and leading the struggle for the reinstatement of Palestinian rights. This concept was thwarted both by Arab rejection and by obstacles posed by Arab leaders. The third school of thought held that the existing Arab reality would not permit the establishment of a Palestinian organization; therefore, Palestinians should go underground and work in a completely clandestine manner, until they are able to impose themselves on reality and make it recognize them. "The last school of thought was the true expression of the aspirations and experience of the vast majority of the Palestinian public.... Thus the conditions became ripe for the birth and announcement of Fatah."[42]

In mid-July 1957, some of Fatah's future founders completed their university studies or migrated to the oil-producing states of the Persian Gulf in search of employment. Five of them, including Yasir Arafat and Khalil al-Wazir, met in Kuwait late that year and decided to found a clandestine organization.[43] They were joined by a few Palestinian activists from Syria and Gaza. The group's first cell was established during 1957 (although some Fatah sources cite 1958 as the year of its founding).[44] According to Wazir, the founders who gathered together in Kuwait formulated two documents—"Haykal al-Bina'a al-Thawri" (Outline of the revolutionary structure) and "Bayan al-Haraka" (Announcement of the movement)—and agreed on "Fatah" as the name of the organization. The former document represented what became one of the clearest and most representative expressions of Fatah's perspective and of the roots of its organizational structure, including its view that "freedom is taken, not granted."[45]

A Cairo University notebook, bearing the handwritten date of 1958, includes a sketch outlining the ideological principles of Fatah, which later appeared in the monthly *Filastinuna* and in other publications of the organization in 1968. This notebook constitutes clear proof of Wazir's argument regarding the timing of the consolidation of the organization's ideology.[46]

New members joined the core founding group in Kuwait during 1959, the most important of whom was Salah Khalaf (Abu Iyad). Khalid al-Hasan, who worked in Kuwait's Department of Public Works, became an enthusiastic supporter and took advantage of his position in the municipality to secure entry visas to the Emirates for Fatah members. At this point, the movement's founding group began to seek a public stage for itself. Such a stage was provided by a former member of the Lebanese chapter of the Muslim Brotherhood, Tawfiq Khouri, who had a license for a periodical named *al-Nida'*. He changed its name to *Nida' al-Hayat-Filastinuna* and began publishing it in October 1959 in Beirut, as the official magazine of Fatah.[47]

Filastinuna played an important part in making potential members and like-minded groups aware of Fatah and served as an address for the organization. In his memoirs, Khalil al-Wazir mentions the importance of the monthly publication in enlisting the support of Palestinian groups and establishing contact with the Palestinian diaspora. Through this publication, Fatah forged links with some forty other groups. Wazir himself, who in 1957 had worked as a teacher in the southern district of Saudi Arabia, helped increase Fatah's contacts and spread word of its existence among six hundred Palestinian teachers who worked in various districts of the kingdom, including Jeddah and Mecca.[48]

Among Fatah's new recruits were additional former Muslim Brotherhood members, including 'Abd al-Fatah al-Hamud, Majid Abu Shrara, and Ahmad Quray' (all three of whom later became members of Fatah's Central Committee). Syria's disengagement from the union with Egypt encouraged new members to join the movement, including Ba'th activists such as Faruq al-Qadumi, who left the party to join Fatah. Mahmud 'Abbas moved to Qatar, where he found work as a director of human resources in public service, a position that enabled him to find employment for many Palestinians as teachers and office clerks. While in Qatar he met former members of the Muslim Brotherhood, such as Yusif al-Najar, Kamal 'Udwan, and 'Abd al-Fatah al-Hamud. 'Abbas also visited the Gaza Strip under guise of seeking workers, and thus established contact with Fatah founders located there. Hani al-Hasan registered at a German university, where he filled a key position in the Palestinian student union and increased its influence among thousands of Palestinian students and workers in West Germany. Ha'il 'Abd al-Hamid joined Hani al-Hasan and together they produced a pamphlet titled *Al-Kifah al-Musallah—Tariq al-'Awda* (The armed struggle—The road to return). In the meantime, Khalil al-Wazir reestablished ties with his friend from Gaza, Yahya 'Ashur, who had established a Palestinian student union in Austria, where he was studying, and with a student leader in Spain, Salih al-Ka'kabani.[49]

Fatah's membership grew as embittered Ba'th Party members joined the movement following the dissolution of the Syrian-Egyptian union. At the same time, however, Nasir's increasing popularity prevented massive enlistment in Fatah. It remained, at most, a network of separate organizations and associations until a 1962 meeting in Kuwait consolidated them, gave them a sense of common goal, and produced a new set of leaders. During the latter half of 1963 or early 1964, Ha'il 'Abd al-Hamid and Hani al-Hasan joined this group of leaders. Thus the movement's leadership took shape, with its members congregated around Yasir Arafat: Salah Khalaf, Khalil al-Wazir, Mahmud 'Abbas, Faruq al-Qadumi, and 'Adil 'Abd al-Karim. Other key figures included Khalid al-Hasan, Munir Sweid, and Salim Za'nun in Kuwait, and Mahmud al-Khalidi, Husam al-Khatib, and Mahmud Falaha in Syria. Aside from Qadumi, who came from the West Bank, all were refugees.[50]

Regarding Fatah's activities in Jordan—or more specifically in the West Bank—Khalil al-Wazir notes,

> In 1961 or 1962 I moved from Kuwait to Amman, which was in the midst of a revolt in the context of party politics. . . . Upon my arrival, political contacts with all groups were initiated, and thus we went from city to city in the West Bank. Our communications officer in Tulkarm was Hilmi al-Sabrini, who had set up the most important communications center in that region. In 1962 I returned to the West Bank, and we then successfully established a consolidated organization in the Hebron region, which included nearly 40 members. During this time Arafat frequently visited the West Bank, and he then began reorganizing the skeletal structure of the organization and reinforcing it.[51]

Jordan's security authorities were well aware of these activities on the part of Fatah (as well as other Palestinian organizations that emerged during this period), and they associated them with the Palestinian National Liberation Front (Jabhat al-Tahrir al-Watani al-Filastini).[52] Fatah's hostile attitude toward the Hashemite regime was reflected in various issues of *Filastinuna*.

An important development in relation to Fatah's standing in the Arab arena, and thus also to the communist bloc, was the opening of a Fatah chapter in Algiers and the appointment of Khalil al-Wazir as its head. In his memoirs, Wazir highlights the opening of this chapter and its activities. He describes the chapter's role and undertakings as "a concrete historical role."[53]

As an independent state, Algeria embraced Fatah politically and militarily, and increasingly so as the years passed. Even before Algeria's 1962 declaration of independence, ties were forged between Fatah and the FLN. Arafat, in fact, attended Algeria's independence celebrations, and during this visit it was agreed that a "bureau" for Palestinians would be opened in Algiers under the authority of Fatah. On Arafat's return to Kuwait, it was decided that Khalil al-Wazir would resign his teaching position and travel to Algiers to assume responsibility for overseeing the Fatah office there. A directive on behalf of the Algerian president regarding the "Filastin bureau" in the capital city was issued on September 23, 1963. It defined the bureau as being in "general service of the Palestinian cause," and its objectives as being in the spirit of Fatah's perspective and the Algerian revolt.[54]

In his memoirs, Khalil al-Wazir relates that when he began his activities in Algeria there were only fourteen Palestinians, who were teachers by profession. Therefore, the first mission of the local Fatah office was to increase the size of the Palestinian community in Algeria by encouraging hundreds of students to enlist in Algerian universities and by employing Palestinian teachers in the country. During the office's first two years of operation, the number of Palestinian teachers in Algeria reached four hundred. It later rose to one thousand.

Fatah's office in Algeria began publishing bulletins and magazines that served as a stage for publicizing its own activities and those of Fatah generally. These included *Filastinuna* and *Sarkhat Filastin* (Cry of Filastin) as well as the 1964 pamphlet *This Is Our Plan—Revolution until Victory*. At times, Fatah's magazine *Filastinuna* also reproduced articles or columns from those publications.

Fatah's office in Algeria also set up a training camp and organized special military training courses at the military academy Chercell, whose graduates received the rank of officers. Many of those who completed these training camps later took part in Fatah operations that included attacks against Israelis as well as confrontations with the Jordanian army.

The Fatah office in Algeria played an important part in forging ties between Fatah and a number of communist bloc countries that had relations with Algeria and whose leaders would visit the country. Thus Fatah succeeded in establishing relations with the People's Republic of China, North Korea, North Vietnam, Albania, and East Germany. The salient and most significant achievement of the office in Algeria was the historic visit of a Fatah delegation, headed by Yasir Arafat and Khalil al-Wazir, to the People's Republic of China during March 15–18, 1964. The delegation arrived as guests of the Committee for Afro-Asian Solidarity, and its visit led to the opening of a "Filastin office" in the Chinese capital and to the start of a close relationship. In the course of this relationship, China would later provide equipment and weapons to Fatah, most of which arrived by way of Syria. After the visit to China, Khalil al-Wazir traveled to North Korea for a visit.[55]

Filastinuna

The first issue of *Filastinuna* was published in October 1959, and the magazine continued to appear as a monthly publication until the eve of Fatah's first operation, in November 1964. The publication was launched after the pivotal meeting in Beirut and adoption of the organization's name. This move was, indisputably, a bold and brilliant one on the part of Fatah's founders, who did not shy away from openly issuing a publication in their own name even though they were part of an underground organization. Without a doubt, *Filastinuna* was successful in bringing together various Palestinian groups and encouraging them to unite and take action, as well as in attracting new members to join Fatah.

Forty issues of *Filastinuna* were published in all. Khalil al-Wazir was the main contributor, although many articles carried the initials of Arafat and others were written by Tawfiq Khouri, the editor-in-chief and licensed publisher of the magazine. The topics covered in *Filastinuna* focused primarily on war and the armed struggle against Israel. Likewise, the magazine called for the rejection of any plan that enabled the continued existence of the state of Israel and of any attempts by Arab states to assert hegemony or patronage over the Palestinians and the Palestinian cause. Above all, *Filastinuna* focused on the obligation of the Palestinian people to take its fate into its own hands and on the need to consolidate all Arab resources for the armed struggle against Israel. Special, prominent attention was given to the matter of recognition of an independent Palestinian entity and to the call for independent Palestinian action in the framework of the overall Arab struggle for Filastin. The magazine also carried ideological articles as well as writings of Palestinian historians. The editors' religious background was reflected in their frequent references to stereotypical images of Jews and Judaism.

The main aspects and themes of *Filastinuna* can be summarized as follows: its target audience was the Sons of the Nakba or the Nakba youth, on whom it called to lead the Palestinian people toward liberation and social solidarity. It frequently featured chapters from Filastin's history, including the story of the Palestinian people's struggle against the Zionists, with emphasis on the 1936–39 revolt. These were peppered with stories of bravery, foremost among them the story of 'Iz al-Din al-Qassam, as well as stories of cities and villages in Filastin. It called for the establishment of national, revolutionary Palestinian governance over the Arab parts of Filastin. It rejected all proposed solutions to the Palestinian problem and all plans for the settlement of refugees. Likewise, it rejected all partition plans. It called for the establishment of a new fida'i movement that would be purely Palestinian and would annihilate the state of Israel.

The Socialist Arab Ba'th Party

From 1949 until September 1961, when Syria disengaged from Egypt, no special framework for Palestinian members was established within the pan-Arab party. The Ba'th Party preferred that its Palestinian members remain scattered throughout Arab countries and that their political activism be conducted within the framework of the local chapters of the party.[56]

Until mid-1960, the Ba'th Party's position regarding the Palestinian issue avoided any concrete consideration of a Palestinian entity. At the same time, however, it emphasized that the manifestation of this entity must be grounded in the party's pan-Arab ideological principles and that the Palestinians must act within the party framework rather than the framework of a separate entity.

When the Syrian chapter of the Ba'th Party closed, after the Egyptian-Syrian unification in February 1958, the party's Lebanese chapter became its focal point for activities relating to the Palestinian issue and the Arab-Israeli conflict. Palestinian members of this chapter were very active on behalf of the Palestinian entity and in pursuit of a special status to be granted to Palestinian members of the party. They were greatly influenced by the intensive activism of Fatah members in Lebanon and of Arab Nationalists Movement members. Undoubtedly, they were also influenced by the appearance of the monthly *Filastinuna* in Beirut and by the call it issued for independent Palestinian action. Indeed, in 1959 they began to put pressure on the National Command of the Ba'th Party to grant them a separate political framework. The Palestinian Ba'thists in Lebanon were the most vocal of the Palestinian members of the party, perhaps because they were the most marginalized. They even succeeded in acquiring some military experience during the Lebanese civil war in 1958, and, eventually, in the absence of strong party supervision after the closure of its Syrian chapter, they also succeeded in achieving some measure of autonomy.

The Lebanese chapter of the Ba'th Party devoted special attention to the Palestinian problem, at times even criticizing the stance and activities of the National Command (national leadership) with respect to the Palestinian issue. At the same time, the chapter leaders did not actually defy the general position of the National Command.

On the eleventh anniversary of the Nakba, the Ba'th Party for the first time addressed the role of Palestinians in the general Arab campaign against imperialism and division. On May 15, 1959, the Lebanese chapter of the party published a statement demanding that Arab organizations and governments "increase their efforts for the liberation of Filastin by ensuring proper conditions for the dispossessed (*nazihun*) and maintaining a constant state of preparedness for the Arab national struggle to reclaim our land."[57]

During a December 1959 regional congress of the Lebanese chapter of the Ba'th Party, the political report submitted to the conference by the Lebanese chapter's leadership was criticized for "not addressing the Filastin problem." Conference resolutions, accordingly, requested the Lebanese leadership "to pay more attention to the problems of Palestinians alongside other residents of Lebanon, in light of the overall influence of the Palestinians on Lebanon generally and on the party mechanism in particular." The conference also called on the newspaper *al-Sahafa*, the mouthpiece of the party in Lebanon, "to take an interest in the Filastin problem in general and in the problems of Palestinians and reports about their conditions in particular, and to devote special attention to the voice of the returnees [*'a'idun*]."[58]

At the fourth national congress of the Ba'th Party, in late August 1960, a change was evident in the party's position on the issue of the Palestinian entity and, by implication, in its stance on the question of Palestinian party members organizing separately. This congress was the first one at which the "Palestinian entity" became a central issue in discussions and inter-Arab propaganda. The Ba'th National Command was no longer able to avoid taking a stance on this issue, especially in light of the discussion of the Palestinian issue expected to take place at the Arab foreign ministers' conference scheduled for January 1961. Nor could the National Command ignore the criticism leveled against it regarding this matter. The starting point for the stance adopted by the party was "adoption of the Algerian revolution as the first political mission assigned to the National Command."[59]

In explaining the background to the shift in the Ba'th Party's stance during the fourth national congress, Faysal al-Hurani, a Palestinian writer-journalist and a Ba'th activist, states,

> During the era of the Egyptian-Syrian union, a significant development took place within the Arab and socialist Ba'th Party. The Palestinian constituents within the party were among the most active of the party members in Syria, Jordan, Lebanon, the Gaza Strip, and elsewhere. Because of their special interests in and engagement with Palestinians circles, these constituents were influenced by the calls for attention to the issue of a Palestinian entity and by the proposals of national Palestinian organizations with leanings toward independence. Activism on the part of these constituents within the party succeeded in compelling the leadership to give attention to the question of a Palestinian entity, despite the difficulty of doing so in light of the party's inter-Arab principles, which reject any separate entity that does not correspond with the perspective of a united, pan-Arab entity. Eventually, groups within the party began organizing separately as Palestinians. This development and the successful effort to establish the Algerian National Liberation Front swayed the [fourth] national congress, and it adopted resolutions [regarding a Palestinian entity].[60]

The resolutions of the fourth national congress, especially "A Memorandum from the Ba'th Party to the Arab Foreign Ministers Conference Regarding the Problems of Filastin and Algeria" (January 31, 1961), conveyed the revised position of the party on the issue of a Palestinian entity. It held that an entity uniting the sons of Filastin should be established, and that the proper way to establish "this entity for the struggle of the Palestinian people" was by forming a "popular liberation front for the liberation of Filastin." (Around this time the party also began using the term "a Palestinian political entity.") The party rejected "any initiative by an Arab state or group of Arab states to establish their own Palestinian mechanisms" that would serve as a tool in their own propaganda machinery or a tool for promoting their own Arab policy.[61]

The National Command of the Ba'th Party, headed by Michel 'Aflaq and Salah al-Bitar and supported by the Jordanian-born prominent ideologue Munif al-Razzaz, strongly objected to calls for the establishment of a separate Palestinian section (*shu'ba*) within the party. They viewed it as conflicting with their principle of a unitary pan-Arab ideology. Their position did not change even after Syria's disengagement from Egypt. Nor did it shift following the internal split within the party on the question of Filastin, when Akram Hurani, one of its founders, and the regional leadership voiced support for the establishment of a Palestinian section. Refusing to change their position, 'Aflaq and Bitar took refuge in Beirut.

After the UAR's dissolution, calls increased for more attention to be given to the Palestinian national character, and Palestinian Ba'th members intensified their calls for special organizational Palestinian representation within the party. The Ba'th leadership, headed by Michel 'Aflaq, initially denounced these calls but ultimately acquiesced in light of overwhelming support in the party for promotion of the Palestinian national character, as well as the persistence of numerous Palestinian members of the party on this matter. Against this background, a clandestine meeting took place in Lebanon, with the participation of Palestinian representatives of the party from Lebanon, Syria, Jordan, and the Gaza Strip alongside representatives of the party's (pan-Arab) National Command. This meeting addressed the question of a separate Palestinian organization within the party, but it did not yield immediate, concrete results. The only outcome related to the Palestinian issue was the establishment—under the National Command— of a special committee, named the Palestinian Pan-Arab National Committee (Lajnat Filastin al-Qawmiyya), which was composed of Palestinians and citizens of other Arab countries.[62]

Yezid Sayigh relates that Palestinian members of the Ba'th Party in Lebanon had already established a separate shu'ba within the Lebanese chapter of the party in 1960. This section was headed by National Command members 'Abd al-Wahab al-Kayali and Khalid al-Yashruti, among others. Yashruti was later described by the party as someone who established a guerrilla group named the "Palestinian Liberation Front" (Jabhat al-Tahrir al-Filastiniyya), which conducted a reconnaissance operation in Israeli territory in 1961. Another example of the activities of the Ba'th Party's Palestinian section, according to Sayigh, was the participation of its members in the wording of a memorandum presented to Arab foreign ministers in Baghdad in January 1961 in the name of the Ba'th Party. This memorandum described a shift in the party's policy on the Palestinian issue. According to Sayigh, the Lebanese chapter of the party, which met in mid-November 1962, recommended that a Palestinian section be established within the party, but the National Command again rejected this concept in a meeting held shortly after the 1963 coup d'état that restored the party to power in Damascus. Following this coup, pressure by Palestinian members of the Ba'th Party in Syria began to manifest in the form of a separate Palestinian representation within the party. The Palestinians were aware that Fatah, the Arab Nationalists Movement, and Ahmad Jibril's Palestine Liberation Front "were busily recruiting in the refugee camps" in Syria. Consequently, the National Command relented slightly, allowing the Palestinians to gather in the *shu'ba* of Damascus University, which quickly became the nucleus of a Palestinian grouping consisting of about eighty members.[63]

The sixth national congress of the Ba'th Party convened during October 23–25, 1963, against the background of the rise to power of the party in Iraq and Syria. The congress adhered to its basic position regarding a Palestinian entity, with a slight shift compared to the resolutions of the fourth national congress. This change was the outcome of discussions held in the Arab League Council in September 1963 regarding the question of a Palestinian entity. The policy statement that was issued on conclusion of the congress devoted a section to the Palestinian problem. It declared, among other things, that the congress "decided to implement the concept of a 'Filastin Liberation Front' (Jabhat Tahrir Filastin). It calls on Arab countries generally and the revolutionary governments in Syria and Iraq specifically to provide all the means necessary for the formation and organization of this front."[64]

The resolutions of the sixth national congress reflected ongoing changes in the position of the Ba'th Party regarding the manner of Palestinian self-organization. They also reflected the National Command's recognition that the party needed to accommodate developments relating to the issue of a Palestinian entity and Palestinian organizations. The National Command's objective during the congress was to engage Palestinians in activism within the framework of the party, or more specifically, the framework of the Filastin section of the party, and to prevent losing Palestinian members of the party to autonomous activism outside of the party framework. Ba'th leaders, especially those based in Lebanon, were well aware of the existence of clandestine Palestinian organizations in Arab countries. Their answer to this phenomenon was to be found in the conception of a Filastin Liberation Front as an organization subordinate to the Ba'th National Command, which would include the Palestinian members of the party as well as others recruited from beyond the party.

The General Union of Palestinian Students

Another important expression of the Palestinian reawakening of the 1950s and a reflection of its formative character was the political and organizational activity of the General Union of Palestinian Students. It included activism on the part of Palestinian students concentrated in places such as West Germany, Austria, and even the United States.

The political activism of Palestinian students during the early 1950s, and even more so during the latter half of this decade, merged seamlessly with the Palestinian national reawakening. These students were at the vanguard, raising the flag of struggle on behalf of an independent Palestinian entity and an independent Palestinian struggle. It is no wonder, therefore, that the Palestinian student union provided a framework for struggles among the various political currents operating therein, foremost among them the Baʻth Party, the Arab Nationalists Movement, and, above all, the members of Fatah. In fact, Fatah's founders emerged within the Palestinian student union, and the founders of the Arab Nationalists Movement were students at or graduates of the University of Beirut.

Palestinian student activism entailed not only activities of a strictly professional union; it also served as a framework for political activism. Some of Fatah's early activists from universities in the West were familiar with the governments in those countries and, in particular, with the evolution of the countries' respective national movements. The activists spent time in those places with the aim of recruiting sympathizers to their organization from the Palestinian student body.

The General Union of Palestinian Students was founded in November 1959 in Cairo. The date is not coincidental. During this time, Arab nationalism under the leadership of Nasir reached its peak, culminating in the union between Egypt and Syria. The unification was a source of inspiration for Palestinians, who saw it as a milestone on the path to Filastin's liberation. It was only natural, therefore, that educated circles of Palestinians would be among the first to respond to this unification, especially after the idea of reviving the Palestinian entity was raised by Egypt in March of that year. Nor is it surprising that Cairo, specifically Cairo University, was the center of university student activism because most of Fatah's founders and future leaders studied there. The same was true for the General Union of Palestinian Students, which was founded in Cairo.

The establishment of the General Union of Palestinian Students was preceded by the establishment of various Palestinian student associations. A key development during this phase took place in 1952, when the leadership of the Palestinian student association in Cairo, which had been established in 1944, was overtaken by "revolutionaries" and Yasir Arafat was elected as its president, a position he held until 1956. During this time, Palestinian student associations existed in various Arab capitals as well, but the association in Cairo was the oldest and largest of them. Initially, the association focused mainly on cultural and social issues, and after the Nakba it took a strong interest in the Palestinians' situation.

During the period of Arafat's presidency, the association expanded its activities and was even recognized by the Arab League and other official Arab authorities as the largest elected popular Palestinian body. In 1955, it was accepted to the International Student Congress as an observer. The delegates to this congress were Yasir Arafat, Salah Khalaf (Abu Iyad), and Zuhayr al-ʿAlami—future founders of Fatah. In 1958, the association became a full member of the International Union of Students and participated in this capacity in the International Student Congress in Peking that year.

The emergence of the Palestinian cause in the Arab arena, its centrality in Arab discourse, and the national enthusiasm inspired throughout the Arab world by the Egyptian-Syrian union combined to motivate the leaders of the association in Cairo, with encouragement from the UAR, to found the General Union of Palestinian Students. The mission of the GUPS, as later defined, was "to serve as a nucleus for students to organize and to prepare themselves for a campaign aimed at reclaiming Filastin through strengthened ties between Palestinian students and other international and Arab student organizations, and in particular through coordinated efforts with the Arab student movement on behalf of Filastin and a fateful collective campaign."[65]

The first congress of the General Union of Palestinian Students opened on November 29, 1959 (marking the anniversary of the 1947 UN resolution adopting the partition plan). Four delegations—from Cairo, Alexandria, Damascus, and Beirut—participated in the congress, and representatives of Palestinian students from Asyut, Egypt, attended as observers. Representatives of Arab student unions in non-Arab countries also attended.

The congress addressed organizational matters for the most part. The preamble to the GUPS charter asserted that Palestinian students "believe in the strong relationship between general Arab unity and the liberation of Filastin, and in the pioneering role that the Palestinian student must take in leading his people. Therefore, they announce the establishment of a national union for the students of Filastin, to serve as a nucleus for popular Palestinian organizing and take action in order to return to the stolen homeland, using all means permitted by the articles of this charter."[66]

The GUPS demonstrated that it was a true political body as much as it was a professional body, possibly even more so. In the first phase of its existence, during the period of Egyptian-Syrian unification, the GUPS was governed by Baʿth Party members and its policy reflected the disagreement between Nasir and Baʿth leaders (who in December 1959 resigned from the UAR government). The GUPS Executive Committee—the body responsible for its continuous administration—supported the Baʿth, maintained a policy in conflict with Egypt's policy, and even suspended its activities in the Arab student union headquartered in Cairo. These measures created tension between the Executive Committee and chapters of the

GUPS, some of which even attempted to topple the GUPS leadership. Although the latter received assistance from the Arab Nationalists Movement, they did not succeed in removing the Ba'th delegates during the second GUPS congress, which convened in Gaza from October 25 until November 2, 1962. Moreover, Ba'th delegates managed to secure a majority in the GUPS Administrative Council (the highest authority between congresses) and Executive Committee.

Despite division within its leadership, the second congress adopted historic resolutions. Under the influence of discussions within inter-Arab forums on the revival of a Palestinian entity and the dispute between Egypt and Iraq on this issue, the congress called for the establishment of a Palestinian entity, a Palestinian liberation army, and an organization for the liberation of Filastin.[67]

The struggle within the GUPS leadership and between it and GUPS chapters intensified in light of the success of the Ba'th Party during the second congress. Members of the Arab Nationalists Movement within the Administrative Council, who were in Cairo at the time, succeeded, with Egyptian backing, in removing a number of Ba'th Party members from the Executive Committee (which elected the Administrative Council) and formed a provisional Executive Committee composed of independents and ANM members. Egyptian authorities provided assistance, among other means by deporting students who were Ba'th Party members and by preventing several Ba'th Party members on the Administrative Council from entering Egypt. The Ba'th students who were removed from the Administrative Council or deported to Damascus declared themselves the true representatives of the GUPS and established their own Administrative Council. Thus the union was, in actuality, divided. GUPS chapters, which numbered 26, tipped the balance by declaring support for the provisional Executive Committee in Cairo. As a consequence of these developments, the GUPS policy and the composition of its leadership went from being an internal issue to an inter-Arab—and primarily Syrian-Egyptian—issue, which was not resolved until the third GUPS congress.[68]

The third congress of the General Union of Palestinian Students convened in Gaza from February 17 to March 5, 1964, and marked a new phase of activity. Control of the union shifted to the Arab Nationalists Movement, whose political outlook was decisively pro-Nasir. ANM members were successful in this respect because they joined forces with representatives of Fatah in the union, which had strong bases in the West Germany and Austria chapters, and with independent representatives, who had strong bases in the Alexandria and Port Sa'id chapters.

The official number of attendees at the congress was 107, but, in fact, only 95 members, representing twenty-five chapters, were present. No delegates from the Ba'th Party (or Syria) attended the congress. Eight Syrian delegates arrived clandestinely at the congress, bearing affidavits empowering them to represent many of the Syrian chapter's members. They were officially received only as observers because no elections had been held in the Syrian chapter.

In light of Ahmad al-Shuqayri's efforts to establish a Palestinian entity after the Arab League resolutions of September 1963, the third congress represented, in some sense, the materialization of this entity whose establishment had been a topic of discussion since March 1959. Indeed, at the time—two months before the Jerusalem Congress at which the PLO was founded—the GUPS was the only Palestinian political body in the Arab and Palestinian arena. This explains the special interest that both the Egyptians and the Syrians had in the student union.

The resolutions of the third congress of the General Union of Palestinian Students were primarily political in nature. They addressed the Palestinian problem generally and the issue of a Palestinian entity specifically. The resolutions' preamble stated, "The Union has expressed its opinion regarding: (1) the ongoing struggle of Filastin's Arabs to organize themselves in order to participate in the campaign [against Israel] for the return; (2) the call for a summit meeting to form the Palestinian entity; [and] (3) the need to establish a single Palestinian organization on a proper revolutionary foundation, given that having a multiplicity of Palestinian organizations threatens the integrity of revolutionary action on behalf of Filastin."[69]

Among other matters, the conference passed resolutions affirming the following:

- A leadership that properly represents the Arabs of Filastin is to be established. Towards this end, a general conference should be convened, with representatives elected by all Palestinian unions and organizations. This conference will elect a National Council from its own ranks, which will serve as its supreme authority and represent the Arabs of Filastin, and this council will elect the Palestinian leadership from within its own ranks.
- The General Union of Palestinian Students has a pioneering role in establishing the Palestinian entity, in addition to the other obligations that the union must take upon itself.
- The Administrative Council should elect five of its members to form a committee, to be named the "Committee for the Palestinian Entity." This committee will function in cooperation with the other sectors of Filastin's Arabs in order to form the unions proposed in plans for the entity.[70]

Another noteworthy resolution of the conference relates to Palestinian student activity in Jordan. Jordan did not permit the establishment of a separate student union for Palestinians, who were considered Jordanian citizens, and discussions toward this end between the GUPS Executive Committee and the Jordanian government were not fruitful. The conference, therefore, decided to establish clandestine chapters in Jordan.[71]

* * *

After the PLO was established in June 1964 and, by its very nature, became the manifestation of the Palestinian entity, the resolutions of the third congress were no longer practicable. Nevertheless, they should be seen as an expression not only of the prevailing mood at the conference, but primarily of the role of the General Union of Palestinian Students in the Palestinian national reawakening.

Notes

1. On the group that founded the Arab Nationalists Movement, see Muhammad Gamal Barout, *Harakat al-Qawmiyyin al-'Arab* (Damascus: al-Markaz al-'Arabi le al-Dirasat al-'Istiratijiyya, 1997), 34–39; Yezid Sayigh, *Armed Struggle and the Search for State—The Palestinian National Movement, 1949–1993* (Oxford: Clarendon Press, 1997), 71–73.
2. See 'Isa al-Shu'aybi, *Al-Kiyaniyya al-Filastiniyya, 1947–1977* (Beirut: PLO Markaz al-Abhath, 1979), 84; Fu'ad Matar, *Hakim al-Thawra* (London: Highlight Publications, 1984), 18–20.
3. Sayigh, *Armed Struggle*, 72; Barout, *Harakat al-Qawmiyyin al-'Arab*, 29.
4. Barout, *Harakat al-Qawmiyyin al-'Arab*, 29.
5. Ibid., 42; Sayigh, *Armed Struggle*, 72; see also Basil al-Kubaisi, *The Arab Nationalists Movement, 1951–1971: From Pressure Group to Socialist Party* (Washington, DC: ProQuest Dissertations, 1971), 33–36, 44–47.
6. Kubaisi, *The Arab Nationalists Movement*, 68–90; Barout, *Harakat al-Qawmiyyin al-'Arab*, 42; Sayigh, *Armed Struggle*, 72.
7. Matar, *Hakim*, 32–34; Barout, *Harakat al-Qawmiyyin al-'Arab*, 47–48; Kubaisi, *The Arab Nationalists Movement*, 45–49.
8. Matar, *Hakim*, 84.
9. Barout, interview with Habash on March 11, 1996, *Harakat al-Qawmiyyin al-'Arab*, 300.
10. Ibid.; Sayigh, *Armed Struggle*, 79.
11. Barout, *Harakat al-Qawmiyyin al-'Arab*, citing Faysal Khalul, "Harakat al-Qawmiyyin al-'Arab, Qira'a Jadida li-Tajriba fi Dhimmat al-Tarikh," *al-Fikr al-'Arabi* 28 (July–August 1982): 184.
12. Wadi' Hadad cited by 'Isam Sakhnini, "Nashrat al-Tha'r-Qira'a fi Muqaddimat al-Fikr al-Muqawim," *Shu'un Filastiniyya* 21 (May 1973): 119–27.
13. 'Imad Naddaf, ed., *Na'if Hawatma Yatahaddath* (Damascus: Dar al-Katib, 1997), 47–50.
14. Matar, *Hakim*, 42; Barout, *Harakat al-Qawmiyyin al-'Arab*, 68–69.
15. Barout, *Harakat al-Qawmiyyin al-'Arab*, 69–70.
16. Ibid., 69.
17. Barout, interview with Habash on March 11, 1996, *Harakat al-Qawmiyyin al-'Arab*, 103; Matar, *Hakim*, 66.

18. Muhsin Ibrahim, *Harakat al-Qawmiyyin al-'Arab min al-Fashiyya 'Ila al-Nasiriyya* (Beirut: Dar al-Ṭali'a, 1970), 24, as cited in Barout, *Harakat al-Qawmiyyin al-'Arab*, 103.
19. Barout, *Harakat al-Qawmiyyin al-'Arab*, 103–4.
20. Habash, in Matar, *Hakim*, as cited by Barout, *Harakat al-Qawmiyyin al-'Arab*, 104.
21. *Al-Kifah* (Beirut), August 30, 1959.
22. Shu'aybi, *Al-Kiyaniyya*, 85–86.
23. Ibid., 86; Sayigh, *Armed Struggle*, 78.
24. Habash, in Matar, *Hakim*, 61.
25. Sayigh, *Armed Struggle*, 78.
26. Shu'aybi, *Al-Kiyaniyya*, 86.
27. Sayigh, *Armed Struggle*, 79n52; Habash, in Matar, *Hakim*, 87–98.
28. Sayigh, *Armed Struggle*, 76.
29. Matar, *Hakim*, 87.
30. Barout, *Harakat al-Qawmiyyin al-'Arab*, 299–301; Sayigh, *Armed Struggle*, 77, 80.
31. Barout, *Harakat al-Qawmiyyin al-'Arab*.
32. On the ANM's attitude toward Shuqayri, see Shemesh, *The Palestinian Entity*, 49–50.
33. Habash, in Matar, *Hakim*, 116.
34. Fatah, *Nabdha Tarikhiyya 'an Harakat Fatah*, pamphlet no. 2 for the Cadres' Course, 1968; Fatah, *Al-Thawra al-Filastiniyya al-Musallaha wa Marahil Tatawwuriha*, internal publication no. 106, December 31, 1971.
35. Fatah, Ideological Notebook. See also the first issue of *Filastinuna*, October 1959.
36. Abu Iyad, *Filastini*, 61.
37. Khalil al-Wazir (Abu Jihad), interview in the biweekly *Sawt al-'Asifa* (mouthpiece of Fatah), no. 25, January 25, 1979, 10, cited by Shu'aybi, *Al-Kiyaniyya*, 51–52.
38. On Egypt's attitude toward Fatah and its actions, see Shemesh, *Arab Politics*, 94–105.
39. Sayigh, *Armed Struggle*, 81.
40. Wazir, *al-Bidayat*, 17.
41. Khalil al-Wazir (Abu Jihad), *al-Safir* (Beirut), April 25, 1988.
42. Wazir, *Al-Bidayat*, 21–22.
43. Khalil al-Wazir (Abu Jihad), *Sawt al-'Asifa*, November 1, 1979; see also Wazir, *al-Bidayat*, 24.
44. Wazir, *al-Bidayat*, 24.
45. Ibid., 24–25.
46. Fatah, Ideological Notebook.
47. Sayigh, *Armed Struggle*, 84.
48. Wazir, *al-Bidayat*, 25–26, 74–76.
49. Sayigh, *Armed Struggle*, 87.
50. Ibid.
51. Wazir, *al-Bidayat*, 79–80.
52. Ben-Gurion Archives, Ben-Gurion Research Institute for the Studay of Israel and Zionism, Sede Boker, Israel: Private collection of documents from the Jordanian government's Security Services files (1962–64), captured by the IDF in the Six Day War.
53. Wazir, *al-Bidayat*, 29.
54. Ibid., 35–36.
55. Ibid., 27–28, 47.
56. Faysal al-Hurani, *Al-Fikr al-Siyasi al-Filastini, 1964–1974* (Beirut: PLO Markaz al-Abhath, 1980), 60.

57. *Al-Sahafa* (mouthpiece of the Ba'th party in Lebanon), May 15, 1959.

58. Report on the 4th Regional Congress, a secret internal circular distributed by the party in Lebanon, December 1959, 199–211, in Nidal al-Ba'th, *Al-Qutr al-Lubnani, 1951–1961*, vol. 8 (Beirut, March 1972).

59. Hurani, *Al-Fikr al-Siyasi*, 19.

60. Ibid.

61. Nidal al-Ba'th, *Al-Qiyada al-Qawmiyya 1955–1961*, vol. 4 (Beirut, 1964), political resolutions of the fourth National Congress, September 1960, 228–38; Memorandum to the Arab Foreign Ministers from the Conference in Baghdad, January 31, 1961. See also "The Filastin Liberation Front Is the Road to Return (to Filastin)," *al-'Ishtiraki* (mouthpiece of the Ba'th Party), March 11, 1961.

62. Hurani, *Al-Fikr al-Siyasi*, 19.

63. Sayigh, *Armed Struggle*, 68, 93–94.

64. Discussions of the sixth national congress, article titled "Jabhat Tahrir Filastin," October 1963, 167, in Nidal Hizb al-Ba'th al-Ishtiraki, *'Abr Mu'tamaratihi al-Qawmiyya, 1947–1964* (Beirut, June 1971).

65. On the establishment of the GUPS, see Shihada Musa, "Hawl Tajribat al-Ittihad al-'am li-Talabat Filastin," *Shu'un Filaastiniyya* 5 (November 1971): 178–93. See also *Al-Mawsu'a al-Filastiniyya*, pt. 1 (Damascus, 1984), 63–69.

66. Musa, "Hawl Tajribat," 180.

67. Laurie A. Brand, *Palestinians in the Arab World: Institution Building and the Search for State* (New York: Columbia University Press, 1988), 84.

68. Ibid.; Musa, "Hawl Tajribat," 189.

69. Musa, "Hawl Tajribat," 186.

70. Ibid.

71. Ben-Gurion Archives, Ben-Gurion Research Institute for the Study of Israel and Zionism, Sede Boker, Israel: Private collection of documents and files of the PLO offices in Gaza, captured by the IDF in the Six Day War, special report on the debate that took place in Cairo on December 22–31, 1965, prepared by the PLO Popular Organization Department and submitted to the PLO Executive Committee, February 5, 1966.

8 The Palestinians of the Gaza Strip under the Egyptian Government

GAZA STRIP RESIDENTS had a relatively high degree of political consciousness. Consequently they underwent a much more intensive process of Palestinization than did Palestinians anywhere else in the diaspora, with the possible exception of those in refugee camps in Lebanon. The Gaza Strip Palestinians maintained some measure of autonomy in their daily life, including their political life.

The part of Filastin that was captured by Egyptian forces in the 1948 Arab-Israeli War was not annexed to Egypt. It was named "the Gaza Strip" or, as officially defined by Egypt in 1949, "The Area under the Supervision of Egyptian Forces in Filastin" ("al-Mintaqa al-Khadi'a Liraqabat al-Quwwat al-Misriyya bi-Filastin"). In line with its status as occupied territory, the Gaza Strip came under the jurisdiction of the Egyptian Ministry of War. The administrative authority responsible for Gaza was headed by a military governor appointed by the minister of war, and later by an administrative governor or general governor appointed by the president of the republic.

In legal terms, the Gaza Strip's autonomous status was reflected in rules and regulations issued by its governor, which were published in an official newspaper produced specifically for the Gaza Strip, titled *al-Waqa'i' al-Filastiniyya*. The regulations issued by the military governor and, later, by the administrative governor of the Gaza Strip applied to all aspects of the daily lives of Gaza's residents.

The first edict was issued on June 1, 1948, by General Ahmad Salim, under his full title of "Administrator of the Royal Border Guard, Military Governor of the Eastern Desert, and Administrative Governor of the Areas under the Supervision of the Egyptian Forces in Filastin." In this edict, he appointed his deputy governor.

Among the important edicts issued on the commencement of Egyptian rule are the following: Edict No. 4 of September 1, 1948, establishing a nighttime curfew between the hours of 9 p.m. and 5 a.m. the following morning (subsequently, the hours of the curfew were occasionally changed); a special order on September 30, 1948, delineating the fishing zones along Gaza's coastline; an edict prohibiting demonstrations and large gatherings, and an edict establishing censorship over all publications in Gaza, both of which were issued on June 21, 1948; an edict issued on November 24, 1951, regarding prohibitions on entering and exiting the

Gaza Strip, including by sea, without the written permission of the governor or his representative in Cairo; and an edict imposing tariffs on exports from the Gaza Strip, including fruits and vegetables. In 1957, the first volume of edicts was published, which contained all the governors' edicts issued during the years 1948–56.[1]

The Egyptians regarded the Gaza Strip as occupied territory in every aspect and placed restrictions on entry and exit, requiring the permission of the central government in Cairo or its representative in Gaza. Furthermore, they imposed a long-lasting nighttime curfew as well as restrictions on fishing in the coastal waters of Gaza. These restrictions gave rise to attacks against the government by the Egyptian opposition. For example, the Cairo weekly *Akhbar al-Yawm* (an anti-Wafd Party newspaper) published an article in May 1951 under the headline "Imperialist Egyptian Invaders and the End of the Exploitative Egyptian Occupation" in which it described the Egyptian authorities' treatment of Gaza Strip residents in negative terms.[2] In response, the newspaper *al-Ahram* published two articles in 1951, authored by the editor-in-chief, describing his impressions of what was happening in the Gaza Strip. He praised the Egyptian government while listing complaints of the strip's residents regarding their economic conditions.

Al-Ahram's editor told his readers that in conversations with Gaza's elders (Rushdi al-Shawwa, mayor of Gaza; Musa al-Surani, representative of the mufti in Gaza; and Qasim al-Fara, municipal secretary for Khan Yunis), they demanded, in the name of the residents, that the Gaza Strip be annexed to Egypt. Another demand of the residents was that they be permitted to enlist in the Egyptian army, to fight unemployment in Gaza and to protect it from Israeli attack. According to the newspaper, a third demand frequently voiced by Gaza residents was to revoke the high customs tariffs between Egypt and Gaza, or at least reduce them significantly. A bank manager in Gaza described the import and export policies and the tax policies of the Egyptian authorities to the editor of *al-Ahram*, explaining that they deplete Gaza's resources, given the high taxes on essential goods and the fact that Egyptian authorities do not encourage imports from Gaza. *Al-Ahram*'s editor expressed Gaza residents' demand that they be granted some form of legal status that will make it easier for them to leave Gaza, as well as the option of temporary Egyptian passports. He added that the residents feel as if they are in prison because the lack of any official documents prevents travel. (When the All-Palestine Government was established, it issued passports of its own to Palestinian residents of the Gaza Strip. With these passports residents could travel outside of Gaza if they had the permission of the Egyptian military governor. Entry into Gaza required permission from the governor's representative in Cairo.)[3]

The calls for Egypt to annex the Gaza Strip were reiterated a number of times after *al-Ahram* published these articles, but Egyptian authorities rejected them.

In April and July 1949 and again in November 1950, Rushdi al-Shawwa requested that Gaza be annexed to Egypt. The Egyptians rejected his request each time, explaining that they were thereby protecting "the independence of Filastin."

In actuality, Egypt's rejection of the calls for Gaza's annexation stemmed from a number of other factors. Egypt was adhering to the Arab League Council's resolution that Gaza not be annexed, and it even claimed that Jordan had violated this resolution by annexing the Arab parts of Filastin. (Egypt, in fact, led the initiative that threatened to expel Jordan from the league because of this violation.) In addition, Egypt sought to avoid the financial burden involved in annexing Gaza, while maintaining its position as chief military liaison in Filastin. Moreover, the Egyptians were evidently concerned that Gaza's annexation would give rise to a wave of refugees seeking employment in Egypt, thus creating a social and security problem.

Egyptian policy changed only slightly after the 1952 military coup of the "Free Officers." The changes related mostly to security restrictions and entry and exit restrictions for the Gaza Strip. From time to time, Egypt's policy continued to generate social and political unrest among Gaza's residents, who demanded better economic conditions and, in particular, freedom of transit to and from Gaza.

The Egyptian government in Gaza, as in Egypt itself, had a security system that included the investigation as well as strict monitoring of all political party activity, such as that of the Muslim Brotherhood, the communists, and even the Arab Nationalists Movement. Reports about their activities and movements, especially travel from Gaza to Egypt, were submitted by the investigative division of the government in Gaza to the general investigative division in Cairo.

After Egypt resumed control over the Gaza Strip—following a brief period of Israeli rule in the aftermath of the Sinai War—the Egyptian authorities arrested Rushdi al-Shawwa in May 1957. Shawwa, who had served as mayor of Gaza under Israeli rule as well, was accused of cooperating with Israel. Before his arrest, the security division of military intelligence in Cairo had requested information about him and his activities from the investigative division in Gaza. Along with Shawwa, some twenty to thirty other individuals were arrested and transferred to Cairo. They were charged with sending threatening letters to a number of figures in Gaza and with disseminating anti-Egyptian propaganda in the strip. At the same time, the governor of Gaza asked the city's mukhtars to circulate a petition for signature by Gaza residents, expressing support for continued Egyptian rule.

The Gaza Strip provided a good laboratory for implementation of the Egyptian perspective on a Palestinian entity. The government's starting point was the constitutional status of the Gaza Strip, which as noted was defined in 1949 as "The Area under the Supervision of Egyptian Forces in Filastin." This status was reiterated in a constitution granted to the Gaza Strip in 1955 as a gesture toward the residents, in response to internal unrest.⁴ To emphasize the Gaza Strip's special status as autonomous and separate from Egypt, during a September 1960 discussion of Gaza's constitutional status, the Egyptian Council of State held that it was "an autonomous entity in the international sense, and the government mechanisms in Gaza are those of a state that is an independent entity (*kiyan mustaqil*) and do not depend on the political entity of the UAR." The council further held that

> the most explicit expression of the strip's independence is the fact that the 1955 constitution for the area under the supervision of Egyptian forces in the strip has ruled that the executive entity is subordinate to the general administrative governor of the strip, alongside the Executive Council, while the judicial authority [is to be found] in the Supreme Court and other courts. The fact that the UAR appointed some members of the legislative authority, the executive authority, and the judicial authority does not undermine the independence of the strip in the international sense. Rather, it is an expression of the right of the supervising state, including its mechanisms and forces, to actualize this goal.⁵

At some point in early 1962 (the precise date is unclear), the official in charge of passports, travel, and identity cards in the Egyptian government in Gaza, Salah 'Isa, issued "Guidelines in Relation to Laws and Rules regarding Palestinians." The substance of some of these guidelines is as follows:

- The vast majority of Palestinians in the Gaza Strip are to use Palestinian refugee travel documents, whose use was authorized by the Arab League on January 17, 1954.
- The All-Palestine Government in Cairo issued passports for Palestinian use, but Egyptian authorities discovered irregularities in the production of these passports and has issued orders not to recognize any passport granted by that government after January 1, 1962.
- Gaza Palestinians are to travel to Egypt or elsewhere using Palestinian refugee travel documents and permits issued by the passport authority in Gaza, on the condition that there is nothing that would pose an obstacle to the request for travel and that [such travel] does not constitute any violation (in terms of nationality or in terms of smuggling laws and so forth).
- Palestinian residents of Gaza must obtain entry permits for any state to which they wish to travel, including Arab states. Citizens of Arab League states are not required to obtain entry permits for Arab states, or may receive them free of charge.
- If Palestinians who relinquished their Palestinian identity and acquired another citizenship wish to visit the Gaza Strip, they will be permitted to reside there temporarily on the condition that they later resettle permanently in their state of residence. If they were

originally from the Gaza Strip, or arrived there after the Palestinian Nakba, and they wish to reside permanently in the Gaza Strip, then they must relinquish the non-Palestinian citizenship they had acquired and reassume their original Palestinian identity.[6]

In his book about the Palestinian entity, 'Isa al-Shu'aybi notes that as a result of political unrest in Gaza after Israel's withdrawal in 1957, political life in the strip was transformed with the establishment of a Legislative Council and an Executive Council in 1958. The members of these two councils were appointed by the Egyptian government, and each was headed by the governor general. Most of the members were officers in the Egyptian government of Gaza. At the same time, a political organization of the people was established in Gaza, the Palestinian Arab National Union.[7]

During 1958, the Egyptian government took initial steps to set up the institutional bodies of the Palestinian National Union, but as efforts commenced toward Egyptian-Syrian unification, Egypt stopped focusing on those institutional bodies. Once the UAR was founded, it became the only Arab state to actualize the representational aspect of the Palestinian entity, by establishing "independent" representative bodies for Palestinians. It did so, however, not on a democratic basis but, rather, in a manner that served the voting patterns of the UAR. The practical manifestation of these institutions was the establishment of the Palestinian National Union (the counterpart of the National Union—the UAR's ruling party). The Palestinian National Union was first established in Gaza in 1959, with its leaders appointed by the Egyptians. Specifically, on March 2, 1959, the administrative governor of the Gaza Strip announced the appointment of the Supreme Executive Committee of the Palestinian National Union, headed by Munir al-Rayis, the mayor of Gaza. In July 1960, the first elections were held for the institutional bodies of the Palestinian National Union, beginning with Syria, which was part of the Egyptian-Syrian union at the time. Elections were held in the Gaza Strip only in January 1961. The elections to the Palestinian National Union's institutions were conducted in the two regions of the UAR under strict supervision of the authorities, through elections to local committees, regional committees, and a general conference that elected the Supreme Executive Council. Voting rights were granted to every Palestinian over the age of eighteen.

The first general conference of the Palestinian National Union in Egypt took place in January 1961, with the participation of 360 delegates. Egypt took a step to further highlight the principle of Palestinian representation by including a declaration—which lacked any operative significance—in the provisional constitution of the Gaza Strip (March 1962). The declaration asserted that "the Palestinians in the Gaza Strip constitute a national union that includes all Palestinians everywhere" and that "the governor general will publish laws in the name of the Palestinian people." The Legislative Council of the Gaza Strip, which included twenty-two members elected from the Palestinian National Union, was described as "representing the Palestinian people."[8]

The new constitution granted to the Gaza Strip by the Egyptian authorities in March 1962 was described as "provisional, until a permanent constitution for the state of Filastin is approved." It claimed that "the Gaza Strip is an integral part of the land of Filastin" and is expected to become part of the future Palestinian state. In explanatory remarks contextualizing the constitution, the Egyptian president asserted, among other things, that "Filastin is a valuable and inseparable part of the glorious Arab homeland."[9]

In practice, Egypt's policy toward the Gaza Strip differed from its declared position regarding the need to establish the Palestinian entity's institutions, which presented Gaza as part of the Palestinian territory and as a "laboratory" for implementing the various ideas relating to this entity. In actuality, the Egyptian governor ruled the Gaza Strip as if it were an Egyptian territory in every sense. Although the three authorities of the state (judicial, legislative, and executive) were established in accordance with the constitution as an expression of Palestinian autonomy, in practice the constitution enabled Egypt to continue governing Gaza as if it were Egyptian territory, with the residents having minimal governmental participation and no real authority.

The source of authority for the government in Gaza was and remained the Egyptian government and its various branches. The 1962 constitution was granted to Gaza in an effort to prove that Egypt was implementing its ideas regarding the revival of a Palestinian entity, but, in fact, it did so without consulting with the Palestinian residents. Egypt's interests, primarily its security interests, were what guided it in formulating this constitution: Gaza's governor was indeed called a "governor general," but in practice he was a military governor in every sense. The executive authority was subordinate to him. Of the forty-four Legislative Council members, a total of twenty-two, including the deputy governor, ensured complete Egyptian control over this council. The heads of the Executive Council's administrative body (its various departments) were typically officers appointed by the Egyptian minister of war, and, in fact, the entire executive authority was appointed by the minister of war (excluding the chairman).

The Egyptian media portrayed the constitution as an expression of Egypt's concern for the Filastin problem and the Palestinian people: "With the granting of this constitution the Palestinians regain a sense of the power of their special entity, and Gaza is turned into a nucleus for the state of Filastin and a symbol of its existence, mission, and future. From now on, laws will be issued in Gaza in the name of the Arab nation of Filastin, and the people themselves will rule over this part of the region of Filastin, while benefiting from their rights and laws." Contrasting their situation with that of the Palestinians in Jordan, it was stressed that "the Gaza Strip represents the only Palestinian land on which lives a people that preserves its Palestinian identity."[10]

The new constitution of the Gaza Strip was also a response to the internal political unrest that had surfaced in the strip between December 1961 and February 1962. This was the most intense state of unrest since Egypt had resumed control over the strip in 1957. It encompassed Gaza's permanent residents as well as the refugees. The unrest resulted from the harsh economic conditions that prevailed and the restrictions that the Egyptian government imposed on residents. The financial laws issued by Egypt in 1961, including the nationalization of assets, were implemented in Gaza as well, and they caused residents to fear for their economic future, especially after the arrest of property owners in Sinai and al-Arish.

With the dissolution of the UAR, many Palestinian teachers returned from Syria to Gaza. Obstacles were also imposed that made it difficult for teachers to relocate to Arab oil-producing states, to the extent that some were forced to take part in operations involving infiltration into Israel as a condition for receipt of a permit to exit Gaza. The unrest was also fueled by strident propaganda against Egypt on the part of Jordan, which took advantage of the refugee problem to attack the government in Cairo. This ongoing unrest caused the Egyptian regime to conclude that there existed both an internal and an external conspiracy aimed at undermining the Egyptian government in Gaza. Their assessment was based on the following information and indications:

- Reports that reached Egypt about increasing Jordanian activities in the Gaza Strip, which included the smuggling of weapons, ammunition, and money through Israel, and the infiltration of 150 Jordanian agents for the purpose of inciting a revolt against the Egyptian government
- The dissemination of material opposing the Egyptian government in Gaza, whether by Jordanians who had infiltrated Gaza or by locals
- Tension along the border with Israel in light of IDF operations, and the Egyptian assessment that these operations were part of an "imperialist conspiracy"; that is, operations intended to hurt Egypt by means of an Israeli attack aimed at severing the Gaza Strip from Sinai[11]

Because of the ongoing unrest, the Egyptian government took a number of measures, most notably the aforementioned announcement of a new constitution for the Gaza Strip, and, at a later stage, it took steps to establish a Filastin Liberation Front (Jabhat Tahrir Filastin). The latter initiative was, of course, another Egyptian attempt to calm the mood in Gaza and was, in fact, driven mainly by developments in the Arab arena.

Among the specific measures taken by the Egyptian government, certain economic, political, security measures stand out. Among the economic measures were the following:

- A presidential decree (of February 1, 1962) regarding the "immediate" employment in Egypt of about three thousand high school graduates, most of whom were unemployed
- Widespread publicity surrounding the decision that employment conditions for Palestinians from Gaza in the government administration and public institutions would be identical to those of Egyptian citizens
- The replacement of Egyptian teachers in the Gaza Strip—whose numbers had reached two hundred and whose employment was a source of bitterness among residents—with teachers who were residents of Gaza[12]

Concerned about the deteriorating security situation in Gaza, the Egyptian government also took a number of harsh measures in February and March 1962. Foremost among these were the following:

- The formation of special cells comprising members of fida'iyyun units, with the aim of conducting searches in homes and other locations to arrest suspected Israeli and Jordanian agents or individuals distributing anti-Egyptian material
- Increasing the duration of the curfew imposed on the Gaza Strip to cover the hours of 6 p.m. through 6 a.m. the following morning
- Placement of the Palestinian brigade and the security forces in Gaza on alert; and, likewise, placement of units along the Egyptian-Israeli border in a higher state of readiness to prevent infiltration from Jordan to Gaza
- Shaykhs in Sinai being ordered to report on anyone planning to infiltrate Gaza
- Collection of all weapons in the possession of Gaza residents holding civil defense positions
- A visit by the Egyptian director of military intelligence to Gaza in February 1962 to assess its state of security[13]

Other measures were aimed at highlighting "Palestinian representation" and made use of the Egyptian media. "The Filastin Segment" during the "Sawt al-'Arab" radio broadcasts was expanded, for example, and on October 29, 1962, it was renamed "The Voice of Filastin Broadcast" (Sawt Filastin). In March 1962, the weekly *Akhbar Filastin* was launched, under the auspices of the weekly *Akhbar al-Yawm*. Beginning in March 1963, this weekly was edited and printed in Gaza, and in 1964 it became the official mouthpiece of the PLO.

The crowning glory of Egyptian measures to establish representative bodies for the Palestinians was to be the idea that took shape during 1962 regarding the establishment of a Filastin Liberation Front (Jabhat Tahrir Filastin). It was modeled on the Algerian Liberation Front but modified to suit the Palestinian cause. The concept was first raised in late 1961, but only in August 1962 did the Egyptians begin to implement it. They held meetings with Palestinian politicos in Jordan and Lebanon with the aim of convening a founding conference for "the Front," proposing that it be composed of three bodies—political, military, and financial—and that it be based in Beirut. Egypt's aim was that this front be a political movement that serves as an umbrella group for all existing Palestinian organizations, including trade unions. The political organization of the front would be based on a "general congress" elected by Palestinians everywhere. Toward this end, activists on behalf of this front in Gaza held meetings with Palestinian activists in Arab countries.

The establishment of a Filastin Liberation Front was a topic of discussion in Gaza's Legislative Council over the course of several sessions. On conclusion, on September 23, 1962, the council decided to establish a Filastin Liberation Front that would take action "towards actualizing the concept of return and the restoration of stolen rights."[14] During an earlier meeting of the Legislative Council, on September 3, its chairman, Haydar 'Abd al-Shafi, had announced that "preparations are under way to establish a Palestinian national front that will operate in all territories for the restoration of stolen rights."[15] A month later, 'Abd al-Shafi added that "it is a practical necessity that Palestinian efforts be consolidated in one front and under one leadership. Historical responsibility obligates the sons of the Gaza Strip, because they are on Palestinian land and inside a free Arab country, to unite and prepare a strong national regime, in order to serve as a center for all Palestinians."[16] By April 1963, his approach had changed. He now voiced implied criticism of the action being taken regarding a Palestinian entity, primarily by Palestinian politicos, and he called for initiative and activism on the part of young, activist, educated Palestinians. Presumably, 'Abd al-Shafi knew about the activities of Fatah members, at least in the Gaza Strip, and other clandestine Palestinian initiatives already under way in a number of Arab countries.

In a telegram Haydar 'Abd al-Shafi sent to the program "The Filastin Segment" (in the spoken Palestinian dialect on Cairo Radio), which was read aloud during the program, he stated, among other things,

> The Palestinian people in its current geographical circumstances has become an unstable body and therefore needs social "rehabilitation." The responsibility for this "rehabilitation" falls on the shoulders of the Palestinian intelligentsia. We sense that there is an urgent need for active Palestinian leadership,

which makes it necessary to take immediate and proactive action and call upon the Palestinians in Gaza, Syria, Iraq, Egypt, Lebanon, and Kuwait to elect representatives who will form a core group that will consolidate all the Palestinian potential. In this way the nucleus of a Palestinian leadership will be established and be able to develop over time.[17]

The host of the radio program, who evidently understood Shafi's implied criticism of Egypt's policy on the Palestinian issue, added a comment after broadcasting the telegram: "Up to this point Haydar's remarks are correct, yet we are certain that as long as Gaza continues to serve as a base, the nucleus should be established within the Legislative Council and the Palestinian National Union. This nucleus will establish contact with Palestinian communities in every single country and ask them to send representatives to the nucleus, which will take the leadership role upon itself."[18]

* * *

Egyptian efforts to establish a Filastin Liberation Front continued through 1963, until Egypt abandoned the idea because of difficulties in actualizing it. The main obstacles were the September 1963 resolutions of the Arab League on a Palestinian entity, the appointment of Ahmad al-Shuqayri as the representative of Filastin to the league, and the January 1964 resolution of the first Arab Summit on the revival of a Palestinian entity. The underlying principles regarding the establishment of a Filastin Liberation Front, however, served as a model for the structure and composition of the PLO as founded by Shuqayri in 1964.

Notes

1. *Al-Waqa'i' al-Filastiniyya, al-Jarida al-Rasmiyya li-Qita' Ghazza*, vol. 1, 1948–56 (Cairo, 1957).
2. *Akhbar al-Yawm* (Cairo), June 25, 1951.
3. *Al-Ahram*, June 11, 1951, June 19, 1951.
4. "Al-Qanun al-Asasi lil-Mintaqa al-Waqi'a Tahta Raqabat al-Quwwat al-Misriyya," *al-Jarida al-Rasmiyya*, statute no. 225, 1955.
5. Judicial decision of Majlis al-Dawla, *al-Ahram*, September 6, 1960.
6. Ben-Gurion Archives, Ben-Gurion Research Institute for the Study of Israel and Zionism, Sede Boker, Israel: Private collection of documents and files of the Egyptian government in Gaza, captured by the IDF in the Six Day War.
7. Shu'aybi, *Al-Kiyaniyya al-Filastiniyya*, 71.
8. *Al-Ahram*, March 9, 1959, May 16, 1959, May 27, 1959, May 20, 1960, March 10, 1962; *Akhir Sa'a*, May 23, 1962; *al-Sha'b* (Cairo), February 17, 1959; *al-Hayat*, February 18, 1959.
9. For the text of the constitution, see "Al-Nizam al-Dusturi li-Qita' Ghazza," *al-Jarida al-Rasmiyya*, no. 75, March 29, 1962. See also note 8.

10. Muhammad Fawzi and 'Umar Rushdi, in *Al-Sihyoniyya wa Rabibatiha'Isra'il* (Cairo, June 1962), 387–388. See also "Commentaries," Sawt al-'Arab Radio, March 7, 1962, March 11, 1962; *al-Ahram* and *al-Jumhuriyya*, March 10, 1962.

11. Summary of Intelligence Information, Ben-Gurion Archives, Report of the IDF Intelligence Branch.

12. *Al-Ahram*, February 1, 1962, March 8, 1962.

13. The details of these security measures are based on Ben-Gurion Archives, Ben-Gurion Research Institute, Sede Boker, Israel: Private collection of documents and files of the Egyptian government in Gaza, captured by the IDF in the Six Day War.

14. As early as November 1961 the pro-Egyptian newspaper in Lebanon had mentioned the concept of a "Filastin Liberation Front," see *Kul Shay'*, Novement 11, 1961. On Palestinian and Arab activities, see *al-Akhbar* (Cairo), November 5, 1962, May 15, 1963; *al-Jumhuriyya*, November 5, 1962; Interview with Haydar 'Abd al-Shafi, *Nida' al-'Awda* (Gaza), October 1962; *Roz al-Yusif*, November 5, 1962, August 12, 1963; *al-Sayyad*, May 3, 1962, August 16, 1962; *al-Hawadith*, November 29, 1962.

15. Haydar 'Abd al-Shafi, Cairo Radio, September 4, 1962.

16. Haydar 'Abd al-Shafi, *Nida' al-'Awda* (Gaza), October 1962.

17. Haydar 'Abd al-Shafi, "Filastin Segment," Cairo Radio, April 13, 1963.

18. "Filastin Segment," Cairo Radio, April 13, 1963.

Part III
The West Bank Palestinians under Hashemite Rule

The "Palestinization" Process in the Shadow of Egyptian Subversion and Influence

9 The Palestinians under the Hashemite Regime

EVER SINCE THE establishment of the Emirate of Transjordan in 1921 and the appointment of 'Abdulla as emir by British secretary of state for the colonies Winston Churchill, the Hashemite family has been struggling with the question of Jordan's identity as a nation-state. Indeed, Jordan actually lacks some of the basic requirements of a nation-state that are present in other Arab states, such as Egypt, Iraq, and Syria. Over the years, Jordan lacked a national Jordanian identity that would be unequivocally recognized by the Arab states. Moreover, in times of crisis affecting Jordan's relations with other Arab countries—particularly Egypt, Syria, and even the Palestine Liberation Organization (PLO) under Ahmad al-Shuqayri—the latter would publicly cast doubt on Jordan's right to exist as a nation-state, describing it as an artificial state created by the British. The only element of the past that served as a legitimate historical foundation for the Hashemite family was the Great Arab Revolt (1916–18) led by the Sherif Husayn, patriarch of the Hashemite dynasty. To this day, that revolt is celebrated in Jordan as a national holiday and an expression of the "struggle for Arab national liberation."[1]

Over the years, residents of the emirate, especially among its Bedouin population, steadily developed a sense of national identity and of belonging to a nation-state with a unique identity of its own. In time the Arab Legion became one of the symbols of the new Jordanian entity, and the establishment of the Hashemite Kingdom of Jordan in 1946 gave additional impetus to the construction of a separate Jordanian identity.

The annexation of the West Bank by Jordan was expected to contribute, at least partially, to resolving the problem of Jordanian identity. Annexation provided Jordan with an important basis for its right to exist and to define its own national identity: Jordan was bearing responsibility for the Palestinian problem and serving as the sole representative of the Palestinians. Hashemite patronage over Jerusalem was another factor, one with religious significance that contributed to the formation of this new Jordanian-Palestinian identity. In other words, once Filastin had been wiped off the region's geopolitical map, Jordan replaced it as representative of the Palestinians—as reflected in the slogan "Jordan is Filastin and Filastin is Jordan." For the first time, King 'Abdulla and, later, King Husayn could confer a national identity on their kingdom, one that would be recognized by the Arab world and justify its national, including territorial, existence. But there was a catch: over time, it became apparent that, paradoxically, the addition of a Palestinian majority to the kingdom was more destructive than constructive as regards the creation of a national Jordanian identity along the lines to which King 'Abdulla aspired.

Given our perspective of more than sixty years, it would be banal to point out that the annexation of the West Bank to the Hashemite Kingdom of Jordan in April 1950 fundamentally changed the history of the kingdom. The most significant change to leave its mark on the entire system of governance and life in Jordan was the change in composition of the kingdom's population. According to realistic assessments, the population in the Kingdom of Jordan in June 1949 comprised 522,000 residents, of whom 65,000 were Palestinian refugees (including those in camps). After annexation of the West Bank, Jordan's population reached 1,182,000 residents, of whom 725,000 were Palestinians.[2] The kingdom of Jordan lost its homogeneity and tranquility, and Transjordanians became a minority in their own state, which ruled over a Palestinian majority.

King 'Abdulla and, later, King Husayn refrained from using the term "annexation," preferring the term "unity of the two riverbanks" (*wahdat al-diffatein*). With our perspective of several decades, and taking into account the political and social disengagement of the West Bank from Jordan after the Six Day War, we may conclude that the "unity of the two riverbanks" never came into being in the true sense of the phrase. Indeed, it was not even a possibility given the major disparities—cultural, political, historical, and to a certain extent economic—between the two population groups of the two respective riverbanks.

In any event, after its annexation the West Bank became part of the territorial and national element of the Palestinian problem, which in turn became a theme in the domestic policy, foreign policy, and inter-Arab policy of the kingdom. From King Husayn's perspective, the Palestinian issue was "fateful"—a "matter of life or death" for Jordan and a decisive factor in its national security.

The Policy of the Hashemite Regime

On March 14, 1949, the "independent" status of the West Bank came to an end. On that day, it was decreed by law that the military government was terminated and that government officials in the West Bank were subordinate to the central government in Amman. The Jordanian regime's policy toward West Bank Palestinians can be explained in terms of several characteristics.

First, the process of "Jordanization" that was imposed on the Palestinian population during the 1950s aimed to turn Palestinians into fully fledged citizens of Jordan, with affinity and political loyalty to the Hashemite kingdom. That is, it was aimed at assimilation of the Palestinian majority into the Transjordanian minority. In this context, all West Bank residents and refugees who arrived in the kingdom were granted Jordanian citizenship. Likewise, West Bank residents were seemingly granted appropriate representation, as it was ruled that they would have equal representation in government bodies: half of the members of government, half of the members of the House of Representatives (twenty out of forty), and half of the members of the Senate (ten out of twenty). Yet key positions of authority, including important government posts—such as the defense and interior affairs portfolios as well as senior military positions—remained in the hands of the Transjordanians, of course. West Bank representatives were given less sensitive portfolios, such as social and economic ones. The most important portfolio granted to a West Bank representative was foreign affairs, but the foreign minister did not actually carry much weight in setting foreign policy; his position consisted primarily of diplomatic representation and the representation of Jordan in inter-Arab forums.

Second, an inherent and ever-increasing tension was created between the central government in Amman and the Palestinian population of the West Bank. Lingering historical animosity from the mandate era, the imposed annexation of the West Bank, and the appearance in the West Bank of political forces opposed to the government combined to form the backdrop to this tension. During the 1950s and even during the early 1960s, the government had to cope not only with problems arising from the annexation of a large number of Palestinians but also with problems stemming from unceasing subversive efforts on the part of Nasir's Egypt and Syria aimed at undermining the kingdom's domestic stability. The Egyptian and Syrian media were used to incite Palestinian residents of the kingdom, who in turn played a key role in the implementation of Egyptian and Syrian policy—whether by undertaking attempted coups or by fomenting popular revolt.

Third, the Jordanian regime established a security and intelligence network, which steadily expanded over time, to strictly monitor any oppositionist political activity. The regime relied on the loyalty of its armed forces and the loyalty and efficacy of security and intelligence mechanisms, and with their support it managed to survive despite attempts to undermine it and despite the hostility of many Palestinians.

All the important dignitaries of the West Bank, especially those suspected of acting against the regime, were subjected to strict surveillance and monitoring. These dignitaries were primarily concentrated in Nablus, and prominent among them were Hikmat al-Masri, Walid al-Shak'a, Ma'zuz al-Masri, Salah al-'Anabtawi, and Akram Zu'aytir. The regime imposed strict censorship over mail and placed wiretaps on the telephone conversations of political activists in the West Bank, and sometimes even on those of senior government officials.

Publications critical of the regime that were sent to Jordan were confiscated before they could reach their destination.

Fourth, the regime's relations with the Palestinians and the former's policy toward the latter were influenced and challenged by Egypt's March 1959 proposal to the Arab League regarding the revival of a Palestinian entity. This concept was received with great enthusiasm by Palestinian West Bank residents, but it was sidelined by the Jordanian regime because of the threat it posed to the integrity and stability of the kingdom. Nonetheless, once the idea had surfaced, the Palestinians of the West Bank became a source of incitement and a threat to Jordan's domestic politics.

The Palestinians of the West Bank

From a historical perspective, it becomes evident that most West Bank Palestinians refused to accept the status imposed on them by the Jordanian government, for fear that their national Palestinian identity would be lost and their hopes of returning to Filastin dashed. Given the vast divide between the two population groups in the Hashemite Kingdom of Jordan, the "unification of the two riverbanks" continued to exist only in official Jordanian documents (such as the weekly political reports of West Bank regional or district commanders). For most West Bank residents, the "unification of the two riverbanks" remained an empty slogan, and at times they even continued to regard the West Bank as part of the territory of Filastin.

The Palestinian public in the West Bank was primarily pro-Egyptian, anti-Western, and especially anti-British. The Palestinians adopted Nasir's pan-Arab nationalism with practically no reservations, and they pinned their hopes for a solution to their problem on him. They also adopted his slogan that "unity is the way to liberate Filastin," and they were therefore greatly disappointed when the Egyptian-Syrian union collapsed in September 1961.

During the 1950s and early 1960s, the Palestinian intelligentsia had leanings toward pan-Arab and pro-Nasir movements. The West Bank was the popular base for the ideological political parties that were established and developed in Jordan. Indeed, the parties that emerged in the kingdom were of an inclusive statewide character, but most of their members and their center of activity were in the West Bank. The Ba'th Party, the Communist Party, and the Arab Nationalists Movement had strong roots in the West Bank. Of the four daily newspapers published in Jordan, three were edited by Palestinians: *Filastin*, *al-Difa'*, and *al-Jihad*.

From the very outset, annexation of the West Bank generated feelings of discrimination and deprivation among Palestinians. These feelings resurfaced from time to time during periods of domestic crisis or nationalist upsurge, such as the crises of December 1955 and April 1963 as well as the severe crisis that followed Israel's raid on the village Samu' in November 1966. The feelings of deprivation steadily intensified. According to a January 28, 1966, report of the Saudi consul in Jerusalem, they centered on the following issues:

- Inequality between Palestinians and Jordanians in the allocation of government posts, both high- and low-ranking positions
- Inequitable representation of the two sides of the Jordan River in the House of Representatives in relation to the percentage of Palestinians within the population, who actually constitute a majority
- A prohibition on Palestinians bearing arms or undergoing military training to bolster the defense of villages and the areas near the frontline
- The absence of Palestinian officers in Jordanian military units—including units on the West Bank, units serving along the border, and units on the East Bank
- Efforts to assimilate the Palestinian identity into the Hashemite kingdom, that is, the attempted Jordanization imposed on the Palestinian population
- Government objection to the establishment of industrial enterprises on the West Bank despite recurrent Palestinian demands and the concentration of all development and construction plans on the East Bank at the expense of the West Bank.[3]

Relations between the Jordanian regime and Ahmad al-Shuqayri worsened as a result of Jordanian measures to restrain PLO activity inside Jordan. This prompted the Saudi consul in Jerusalem to send a report to the Saudi foreign minister describing the views of Jerusalem Mayor Ruhi al-Khatib. According to the consul, the mayor was regarded as "among those who believe in the need to find some form of expression for the Palestinian personality in the framework of the Jordanian crown and the unification of the two riverbanks, taking into account the latest Arab and international circumstances." Among other findings, the consul's report of November 1, 1965, which was based on conversations with Ruhi al-Khatib and other local Palestinian leaders, concluded as follows:

> The first area in which the Palestinians would like to make progress is the holding of untainted elections to establish a Palestinian National Council on the West Bank. Their underlying aim in this regard is to convey indirectly to the Jordanian government that they are not satisfied with the current Jordanian House of Representatives, that it does not represent Palestinian interests as much as it represents the interests of a group of merchants and tribal leaders from the East Bank, and that its legislative capacity and its authority are limited. It [the House of Representatives] does not address political issues in

a manner that accommodates the feelings of Palestinians. Palestinians from all groups claim that the Jordanian government's system of elections does not address citizens in an equitable manner. It grants residents of the East Bank the same proportion of votes, but the ratio between them and West Bank Palestinians is 1:4. Therefore, they aspire to have a House [of Representatives] in which Palestinians would constitute a substantially larger majority, accurately representing their numbers, where they could discuss problems of state, the economy, and various other issues, as well as the establishment of a government and equality in governmental positions and projects, in a manner that would be just for the Palestinians, taking into account that they are a substantially large majority. Otherwise, they will continue to feel that they are discriminated against and that their rights are being undermined, and that every government thus established does not represent their interests. . . . In fact, all of this is true, and from my many conversations I have gathered that on this point there is a large gap [that prevents] merging the two riverbanks. As a result, King Husayn is losing a great deal of sympathy among moderates and those interested in reinforcing the unity of the two riverbanks.[4]

In contrast to these aspirations and demands of the West Bank Palestinians, the most that the government was willing to grant them in terms of rights, without endangering its supremacy or rule over the Transjordanians, was full equality in the government in line with its own particular perception. The Jordanian regime never admitted that a Palestinian majority existed within its own population, typically describing the Palestinian population—or those of Palestinian descent—as half of the kingdom's residents. At times, it even claimed that the original Transjordanian population constituted a majority. Moreover, all West Bank representatives within the House of Representatives (excluding those elected in October 1956) and the Senate, mayors, and commanders of districts and regions in the West Bank in practice served as representatives of the government to the residents, rather than the reverse. The loyalty of governors and commanders of districts and regions was very important to the regime given the extensive authority they were granted in all matters relating to the preservation of order.

The Palestinians' self-segregation, opposition to Jordanization, preservation of Palestinian identity, and bitterness over discrimination were manifested among West Bank and refugee camp residents, both directly and indirectly, in a number of spheres. The first sphere comprised sometimes violent protest demonstrations, popular gatherings, and dissemination of leaflets on the occasion of historical or local political events, or in response to retaliatory actions by Israel in the context of growing tension along the border. Examples include the aftermath of the Qibya operation in October 1953, the government's interest in joining the Baghdad Pact in December 1955, the signing of a tripartite pact by Iraq, Egypt, and Syria in April 1963, and, in particular, the events that transpired in the aftermath of the Samu' operation in November 1966. Positions opposing the policies of the regime were also expressed in this manner around election time (in 1951, 1954, and 1956), when candidates' or political parties' platforms were formulated and publicized.

Another sphere of protest entailed issuing petitions by dignitaries and political activists, sometimes also signed by officials such as members of municipal councils or the House of Representatives. The demands voiced in these petitions and leaflets addressed matters of foreign and domestic policies. Examples of the former include a call not to sign a peace agreement with Israel, and a call for termination of the Anglo-Jordanian Treaty and the establishment of diplomatic relations with the Soviet Union. Matters of domestic policy addressed in these petitions and leaflets included freedom of expression and elimination of the British influence in the Arab Legion, that is, the expulsion of British officers. Qadri Tuqan, for example, an opposition leader and member of the House of Representatives, harshly criticized the Anglo-Jordanian Treaty of 1948 in the pages of the Lebanese newspaper *al-Hayat* on November 21, 1953.[5]

The House of Representatives also served as a platform for views against the regime, which were often a source of discomfort for the Jordanian government. These included demands for liberalization, democratization, and the armament of villages on the frontline. The House of Representatives had no qualms about causing the government to resign by threatening not to approve the budget, as exemplified by an argument that took place in the House of Representatives in April 1953 regarding the 1953–54 state budget. During this argument, nearly all West Bank representatives harshly criticized the government for its plan to balance the budget by taking a loan from the British. They demanded that the government strengthen its ties with sister Arab states and seek material assistance from them. They also demanded that the government "permit researchers, intellectuals, delegates, and citizens to express their views and have their say."[6]

Disagreement with the regime was concretely manifested, above all, by participation in opposition parties, just as Palestinian intellectuals in other Arab countries joined these parties (the Arab Nationalists Movement and the Ba'th Party, and to some extent the Muslim Brotherhood). An interesting and unusual phenomenon, compared with other Arab countries, was the emergence of ideological parties in Jordan, most of whose members and supporters were West Bank Palestinians. One may view the year 1952 as the beginning of activity by these parties, after the new Jordanian constitution came into force on January 3 of that year, permitting the establishment of political parties, albeit with some reservations.[7]

Acts of infiltration from Jordan into the territory of Israel exacerbated the security situation along the border, which in turn increased tensions between the regime and the Palestinian population in villages along this border. The Palestinian population of the West Bank was generally sympathetic to acts of infiltration.

Local government and security officials on the West Bank were similarly sympathetic to these acts, which is why they were rather lax about carrying out the legion's orders to use all possible means to prevent infiltration. The acts of infiltration served economic objectives as well as guerrilla objectives. They included killing and sabotage instigated by Egyptian and Syrian intelligence or initiated by local Palestinians with the aim of striking against Israel or aggravating relations between Israel and Jordan. IDF retaliatory actions in response to these acts of infiltration and sabotage steadily intensified, culminating in the Samuʻ operation in November 1966.

Egypt's attempts at subversion among Palestinian residents of the West Bank during the years 1955–56 and during the years after the Sinai War served to fuel hostility and tension between the Hashemite regime and the Palestinian population. The situation reached the point that, in the aftermath of the Samuʻ operation, members of the senior Jordanian echelon began to contemplate the possibility of structurally changing the kingdom's governance system by granting some form of autonomy to the West Bank.

It is no wonder that as the years passed, West Bank residents increasingly lost confidence in the regime, and their confidence continued to decline in parallel with the reciprocal process of increasing "Palestinization," that is, the reinforcement of Palestinian identity among Palestinian residents. The Palestinization process gained momentum, in particular, after the idea of reviving the Palestinian entity surfaced and the new Palestinian national movement emerged, as symbolized by the appearance of the PLO and fidaʼi organizations under Fatah leadership. The underlying tension that developed between the regime and the Palestinian population of the West Bank intensified over the years. The Palestinian political activists who had taken an active part in establishing political parties found that this population provided fertile ground for their activities and protestations regarding discrimination against Palestinians and the government's Jordanization policy. Of particular salience in this regard were the Baʻth Party, Arab Nationalists Movement, Muslim Brotherhood, and Communist Party.

A series of frequent crises and confrontations erupted between the regime and West Bank residents between April 1950 and the Six Day War. Indeed, this period can be depicted as a *single, ongoing crisis* with occasional intermissions. It was a crisis focused on the kingdom's foreign policy more than on its domestic policy. Most of these crises were related to Nasir's pan-Arab policy, the worsening of the Arab-Israeli conflict in the aftermath of the Sinai War, and the emergence of fidaʼi organizations. Every crisis (or minicrisis) deepened the division between the two riverbanks and made their unification less feasible and practicable.

The first confrontation erupted as early as July 1951, when a Palestinian assassinated King ʻAbdulla. Although the assassination did not cause severe instability in the kingdom, it reflected the deep hostility of Palestinians toward the Hashemite monarchy, which in their view had betrayed the Palestinian cause.

An early and foretelling expression of the unrest, bitterness, and sense of discrimination among Palestinians can be found in the conference organized by fifteen West Bank delegates of the House of Representatives on July 26, 1952. At the conference, it was decided to send a memorandum to the prime minister, signed by the "Palestinian delegates" and issuing the following demands for reform: (1) Jerusalem's development and the preservation of its economic standing should be pursued; (2) effective defense of the border should be pursued, and Israel should be prevented from shelling Arab villages within its territory and from fortifying its own outlying areas (Hadassah); (3) emergency martial law regulations (entailing the denial of liberties, detention of citizens without trial in camps and prisons, and repression of the freedoms of speech, press, assembly, and political gatherings) should cease to be used excessively, and prisoners should be released; (4) resettlement of refugees beyond the territory of the Hashemite kingdom should cease; (5) the kingdom's development plans, most of which are implemented in the East Bank, should be applied more equitably; (6) refugees must be permitted to enlist in the military, the police force, and the National Guard; (7) government efforts to combat official corruption should be more effective, and government discrimination against West Bank residents should cease; and (8) the current citizenship law, which is overly burdensome for Palestinians who are beyond Jordanian territory and wish to return to their homeland, must be changed.

Jordan's censorship authorities prohibited the publication of this memorandum, but Prime Minister Tawfiq Abu al-Huda responded to it indirectly at a press conference on August 23, 1952. According to him, every delegate, in addition to being a representative of the entire nation, must represent his constituents' interests, and this memorandum reflected the responsibility of these delegates toward their constituents. He added that it was not the appropriate time politically or economically to create a separate, independent state on the West Bank and that rumors regarding this matter should not be taken seriously.

* * *

The events discussed in this chapter demonstrate that the opposition enjoyed widespread popular support in the West Bank, but this support had not yet been consolidated in terms of organization, goals, and leadership.

Notes

Part III is based primarily on two sources: (1) Ben-Gurion Archives, Ben-Gurion Research Institute for the Study of Israel and Zionism, Sede Boker, Israel: Collection of reports and surveys prepared by the IDF, Intelligence Branch, Research and Assessment Department, and other papers and documents from Israel State Archives, 1949–60; and (2) Ben-Gurion Archives, Ben-Gurion Research Institute for the Study of Israel and Zionism, Sede Boker,

Israel: Private collection of documents and files from Jordanian government in the West Bank (DJG), including Security and Intelligence Services files, 1962–64, captured by the IDF in the Six Day War.

    1. See "The Unity Pact between Jordan and Iraq," Amman Radio, February 14, 1958. For a thorough study of Jordan's tackling of this issue during a later period, see Iris Frochter-Ronen, "Yarden ve ha-'Etgar ha-Falastini: Hitmodedut shel Yarden 'im ha-Sugiya ha-Falastinit Kekhelek mi-Tahalikh Gibush Zehuta ha-Le'umit u-Kfi she-ha-Nose Mishtakef be-Sifrei Limud Yardeni'im, 1964–1994" [Jordan and the Palestinian challenge: Jordan's handling of the Palestinian issue as part of the consolidation of its own national identity and as reflected in Jordanian textbooks, 1964–1994] (PhD diss., University of Haifa, July 2003).

    2. Efrat, "The Palestinian Refugees," 6.

    3. DJG, Report by the Saudi Consul in Jerusalem to Saudi Foreign Ministry, January 28, 1966.

    4. DJG, Report by the Saudi Consul in Jerusalem to Saudi Foreign Ministry, November 1, 1965.

    5. Qadri Tuqan, *al-Hayat* (Beirut), November 21, 1953.

    6. DJG.

    7. For an extensive review of the political parties in the West Bank, see Amnon Cohen, *Political Parties in the West Bank under the Jordanian Regime, 1949–1967* (Ithaca, NY: Cornell University Press, 1982).

10 First Crisis
Aftermath of the Israel Defense Forces Raid on Qibya

THE ISRAEL DEFENSE Forces (IDF) raid on Qibya on the night of October 14–15, 1953, took place during a time of already heightened concerns that Israel intended to renew the war against Jordan. The attack did not come as a surprise to the Jordanians, as all the villages in this sector had been placed on alert—in anticipation of a retaliatory attack—immediately after an assault in Yehud, Israel. The raid on Qibya came in the aftermath of a long series of assaults in Israel that had been carried out from across the Jordanian border. Between January and October 15, 1953, a total of forty-nine Israeli civilians were killed and seventy-nine were injured as a result of these cross-border actions. On the night of October 13, 1953, specifically, infiltrators from Jordan threw a grenade into a house in Yehud that was located ten kilometers from the border with Jordan. The explosion caused the death of a mother, a baby of one and a half years, and a toddler of three and a half years. Another child and a seventy-year-old woman were seriously injured. The infiltrators had crossed the armistice line near the village of Qibya, and their tracks led to a house near the police station in Rantis. The Jordanians felt that the perpetrators of the murder in Yehud had gone too far, and they tried to dissociate themselves from it. The British chief of staff, General Glubb, turned to General Bennike, chief of staff of the UN observers, requesting that he convey to the Israeli General Command his promise to identify the perpetrators.

A later report by Israeli intelligence determined that during the Qibya raid sixty-seven Jordanians were killed, including fifty-six civilians, primarily women and children, and fifteen were injured. A total of forty-one buildings where shelled, including a school, a pumping station, and a police station. Most of the villagers and the National Guard refused to return to Qibya after the raid and even objected to the restoration of the ruins. The National Guard personnel who did return to the village refused to accept the weapons and ammunition provided to them. Only after pressure from the authorities did the residents return to the village, and calm was restored.

For the government of Jordan, the raid on Qibya posed the most difficult test of its relations with the Palestinian population since the annexation of the West Bank.

It took immediate measures to ease conditions for the village, including speedy restoration of the ruins and punishment of those legion members who were guilty of not providing timely support. In particular, it fired the commander of the third infantry brigade (responsible for the West Bank), Brigadier-General Nigel Ashton.

After the raid, the overall feeling within the Palestinian public was bitterness and anger at the Arab legion for not providing timely reinforcements for the village—a failing that was interpreted as a lack of concern for frontline villages. Accordingly, after the raid the legion responded to residents' demands for increased defense of these villages, although this measure did not completely calm the tempers among the Palestinian public, which pointed an accusatory finger at the government, the legion, and the British.

Immediately after the IDF raid, riots broke out in the West Bank, lasting from October 17 until October 25. These included demonstrations in most cities, partial or full strikes in several cities, petitions to governors and the prime minister demanding removal of the British influence in the army and of Glubb, armament of the frontline villages, Arab financial support, and more. Dignitaries and political party activists and leaders took an active part in these happenings, seeking also to coordinate activities across the West Bank, but without much success. The riots were accompanied by propaganda and incitement on the part of Egyptian and Syrian media outlets.

The following calendar entries summarize official reports on the West Bank residents' reactions to the raid on Qibya.

> *October 17, 1953*: The regional commander for Jenin, in his summary of the day's events in his region, noted that the public was in a hysterical mood, and that there was a rumor circulating widely in the region according to which the Arab Jordanian Army had not rushed to provide assistance, even though it had the capacity to do so. On Saturday, October 17, schoolchildren set out to demonstrate in Jenin, and they were joined by extremists who called for a strike. The number of demonstrators reached three thousand. They shouted, "Out with the British" and "Get rid of Glubb." The speakers at the demonstration placed responsibility on the British commanders of the Jordanian army, demanding that command be transferred to Arab officers, that the National Guard be reinforced, and that frontline villages be provided with arms. Moreover, a preparatory committee was established to convene a popular conference, with Qadri Tuqan appointed secretary.
>
> On the same day, a demonstration also took place in Tulkarm, in which a hundred young people participated. In Ramalla, twenty House of Representatives delegates gathered (half the House, equal to the number of Palestinians in it) and decided to demand that the government act urgently to arm the National Guard and fortify frontline villages.[1]
>
> *October 18, 1953*: Ramalla Radio reported on Glubb's reaction to the raid on Qibya as follows: "The bitterness in Jordan in response to the IDF operation is

stronger than it was upon conclusion of the Filastin war.... The residents are demanding speedy retaliation ... although the government feels obligated to respect the armistice agreement and the Jordanian forces are taking measures to prevent infiltration."[2] Expressions of Palestinian fury continued that day. Tulkarm dignitaries presented a petition demanding that the Jordanian army be released from British command.

Jenin's regional commander reported that the entire city had gone on strike that day, and that some four hundred children had participated in a demonstration throughout the city streets. The demonstration was then joined by schoolgirls and others, thus reaching a total of about one thousand. The mayor, Mufti Jenin, and a House of Representatives member, Najib al-Mustafa, presented a petition to the regional commander, demanding the armament of the National Guard and reinforcement of frontline villages.

October 19, 1953: The regional commander for Nablus reported on a meeting of the following members of the House of Representatives: Qadri Tuqan, 'Abdulla al-Rimawi, 'Abd al-Rahim Jarar, Hafiz Hamdalla, Rashad Maswada, and Walid al-Shak'a. They decided to release a joint statement calling on the (Palestinian) people to, among other things, support the following demands: the commencement of action to respond to Israeli assaults, the liberation and cleansing of the army from foreign command and influence, the armament of the National Guard so that it could provide supplementary assistance to the armed forces, the reinforcement of frontline villages, assurance that there would be no agreement on peace with Israel, and resistance to any proposal for the resettlement of Palestinians.

October 20, 1953: A partial strike was reported in Qalqilya. It lasted for a few hours, during the course of which the strikers presented a petition addressed to the prime minister demanding, among other things, the armament of the National Guard, reinforcement of the frontline, and military training for refugees. On the same day, prime minister promised that "there is no peace with the Jews and no solution to the question of Filastin other than on the basis of the UN resolutions and in the framework of the Arab League resolutions.... Any talk of refugee resettlement is utter nonsense."[3]

October 21, 1953: On October 24, the governor of Nablus summarized the events of October 21 in his city. According to his report, on that day a demonstration took place in the streets of Nablus, with nearly four thousand participants, mostly young, led by a number of the city's dignitaries and leading figures. Fa'iq al-'Anabtawi and Qadri Tuqan promised to bring the demonstrators' demands to government attention. Foremost among these were the traditional demands not to make peace with Israel, to release the military command from foreign influence, and to reject all plans for the resettlement of refugees.

On October 21, demonstrations also took place in Qalqilya and Salfit, where demonstrators reiterated the demands raised in Nablus. On the same day, a strike took place in Jenin as well, and Near East Radio (al-Sharq al-Adna) reported on a demonstration in Jerusalem that drew ten thousand participants.[4]

October 22, 1953: On this day the preparatory committee representing popular organizations in Nablus decided to hold a public conference in the city on October 29. The main objective of this conference would be "to address the critical problems arising from the Filastin Catastrophe [*Karithat Filastin*] and to unite the fronts of struggle in this state." Among the decision makers behind this initiative were Fa'iq al-'Anabtawi, 'Adil al-Shak'a, Shawkat Kamal, 'Abd al-Majid Abu Hijla, Husayn al-Khafish, Muhammad al-'Amad, and Qadri Tuqan. [It is not known whether the conference eventually took place, but it is reasonable to assume that it did not.]

* * *

The raid on Qibya was the first time that young King Husayn, who had only recently risen to the throne, was put to the test of dealing with the Palestinians in his kingdom. Conceivably one could view the events after Israel's raid—during which Palestinian residents demonstrated, conducted strikes, and were injured—as the first uprising (*intifada*) of Palestinian residents of the West Bank against the Jordanian authorities. In any event, King Husayn managed to pass this test successfully and maintain public sympathy, despite complaints regarding the legion. At the same time, he had not yet succeeded in making his mark on developments in domestic and foreign policy, a failing that would be strongly felt during later crises between the Palestinian population and the Hashemite regime in Jordan.

The Jordanian government came through the Qibya crisis with relative success. It managed to contain public condemnation of the authorities within reasonable bounds, while preserving the balance between its own pro-British stance and the nationalist position.

As the 1953 confrontation was first of its kind and scope, the Palestinian responses that it triggered were restrained compared with confrontations yet to come: the demands of opposition leaders and West Bank dignitaries focused on the event itself and its outcome; they did not extend to matters related to Palestinian life under Hashemite rule. Nonetheless, they did reflect a dissent and bitterness that would intensify in later confrontations.

Notes

1. Al-Sharq al-Adna Radio (Near East Radio, British radio station in Arabic transmitted from Cyprus), October 18, 1953.
2. Ramalla Radio, October 18, 1953; DJG.
3. Ramalla Radio, October 20, 1953; DJG.
4. Al-Sharq al-Adna Radio, October 21, 1953.

11 Second Crisis

In the Shadow of Egyptian Subversion, December 1955–April 1957

Integration of West Bank Palestinians into Egypt's Subversive Activities

Egypt's campaign of political and military subversion in Jordan and its integration of the Palestinian population into these efforts, with the involvement and assistance of Syrian intelligence services, is an inseparable part of any discussion of Jordan's domestic situation during the period preceding and after the Sinai War and of the Palestinization that the kingdom's Palestinian population underwent at the time. One cannot understand the developments that took place among the Palestinians of Jordan without analyzing Egypt's extensive effort to enlist their participation in promoting its own policy regarding the Hashemite regime. The two processes were interrelated and mutually influential. The Jordanian regime recognized and understood this mutual influence and made every effort to neutralize it, with occasional, temporary—but never lasting—success. In this regard, time was definitely not on the side of the regime in Amman.

One of the manifestations of opposition to the Hashemite regime and its policy on the Arab-Israeli conflict was the phenomenon of infiltration and cross-border acts of sabotage and murder in Israel. The Egyptians and Syrians took an active part in these activities over the two years preceding the Sinai War, and West Bank residents were recruited as members of the fida'i organizations that emerged during the late 1950s. These activities exacerbated the security situation along Jordan's border with Israel, eventually deteriorating to the state of affairs that sparked the Sinai War and—a decade later—the Six Day War and Jordan's participation in the war effort alongside Egypt.

The West Bank Palestinians served as a convenient platform for the pursuit of Nasir's policies in the Arab arena generally and in Jordan specifically. The Egyptians used all the tools of subversion—political and military means as well as media—to achieve their objectives. Egypt sought, in particular, to destabilize Jordan and undermine the regime to the point of collapse or the formation of a "national" government that would adopt Egyptian foreign policy. Egypt's subversive efforts in Jordan were an integral and inseparable part of its campaign to undermine other Arab states, and in the course of conducting this campaign it fully exploited the Palestinian factor.

Egyptian subversive activities began in mid-1955 and continued until 1957. They were sparked, evidently, by IDF retaliatory action in Gaza on February 28, 1955. In the context of its subversive efforts, Egypt employed two mechanisms against the Jordanian regime, each reinforcing the other while exploiting the Palestinian factor. The first mechanism aimed to undermine the regime politically, in particular by influencing Jordanian foreign policy and preventing Jordan from joining the Baghdad Pact. The second mechanism was based on the fida'i cells that operated against Israel from the Gaza Strip, Jordan, Syria, and Lebanon. This integration of political and military campaigns ensured Egypt a number of important successes in its struggle against Jordan's foreign policy and, to a certain extent, against its domestic policy as well.

Egypt's political and military efforts to undermine Jordan (and other Arab countries), especially its efforts in the West Bank, were directed by the Office of the Prime Minister. The prime minister at the time was Nasir, before his election to the presidency in 1956. Operational orders came from the prime minister himself, by way of the "director for political affairs" in the Office of the Prime Minister, Wing Commander 'Ali Sabri. Sabri handled political subversion and strategic intelligence. Working alongside him in the Office of the Prime Minister was Major Kamal Rif'at, an intelligence officer responsible for operations of the fida'i network and related and organizational issues. A third participant in this system was police officer 'Abd al-Rahman Makhyun (of Egypt's internal security services), who took an active part in political subversion in Jordan. These personalities were responsible for coordinating intelligence operations in Arab countries (Jordan, Syria, and Lebanon), and they closely supervised these operations.

The Palestinian unit of fida'iyyun was established in the Gaza Strip in April 1955 by the Egyptian army, at the initiative of the intelligence officer responsible for the strip, Lieutenant Colonel Mustafa Hafiz. It was deployed for the first time during the latter half of 1955 to retaliate for Israeli actions along the border between Israel and Egypt. Egypt's moves in deploying the fida'iyyun were as follows: In response to an incident on the Egyptian border on August 22, 1955, fida'iyyun from the Gaza Strip were deployed directly from the strip toward the end of the month. In addition, fida'i cells from Jordan and Lebanon were deployed as secondary forces; the goal was to increase Israel's insecurity and distract its security forces, as well as to embroil Jordan and Lebanon in clashes with Israel while highlighting Egypt's role as the initiator in the campaign against Israel. After the IDF campaign in Khan Yunis (August 31, 1955)[1] and after the ceasefire agreements, Egyptian authorities issued an order to suspend acts of violence but to continue reconnaissance and intelligence activities; the same order also held that the reorganization and expansion of fida'i groups in Jordan should commence immediately. On October 24, 1955, Egypt dispatched a notice alerting fida'i groups in Jordan that they should be ready for action within a week. This notice was apparently linked to the decision of Egypt's General Command to capture the Sabha military posts in the demilitarized zone between Egypt and Israel, including posts on the Israeli side of the zone, as it was clear to the Egyptians that this action could result in clashes with Israel. The posts were indeed captured two days later.

On November 5 and 6, 1955, fida'i operations resumed, but they were temporarily suspended a few days later. On November 23, an order was issued to terminate them completely, underscoring that this was an "order of the prime minister" (namely, Nasir himself). The termination came a day after General E. L. Burns, the chief of staff of the UN Truce Supervision Organization, had issued a warning to 'Abd al-Hakim 'Amir, Egypt's minister of war and chief of staff, saying that Egypt would face grave danger if it continued supporting fida'i operations from the territory of other Arab countries. His warning was based on talks he had held with Israeli security personnel and the impression he had formed from Israel's public relations efforts regarding fida'i operations.

Even after fida'i operations ceased, fida'i groups in Jordan continued to organize. The fida'i organization that was established and conducted activities in Jordan, under Egyptian command and operation from mid-1955, was of a clandestine nature and, in addition to taking action against Israel, served Egypt's subversive intentions in Jordan. In fact, from mid-September 1955, Jordan became a primary target of Egyptian military and political subversion.

The Egyptian military attaché in Amman, Colonel Salah Mustafa, had full authority over fida'i activities in and from Jordan, including the responsibility for recruiting, training, and deploying fida'iyyun. He provided them with funding, weapons, and equipment. When special envoys were dispatched from Egypt for related activities, they were subordinate to the military attaché. Salah Mustafa oversaw designated commanders of squads, who in turn commanded a number of cells with four to six members. In mid-1956, Mustafa had five to seven cells at his command. These were concentrated in bases in Irbid, Shuni, Ramalla, Jenin, Tulkarm, Qalqilya, and Dahariya.

Some of Salah Mustafa's recruits had previously had ties to Egyptian intelligence and were transferred from espionage to fida'i service. During September 1955, Mustafa changed his recruiting practices to make them partially visible to the public, opening recruitment offices in Amman and West Bank cities. During October and November 1955, five groups were readied for action: in Dahariya, Qalqilya, Tulkarm, Jenin, and the Latroun region. The aim was to cover the entire length of the Jordanian border area, enabling the operatives to speedily shift their center of operations from one sector to another.

In early December 1955, the IDF captured a member of the Jenin group. In response to a report by the military attaché, Cairo ordered that the existing group be disbanded and a new one formed, to be composed of different members. This step reflected the Egyptian objective of keeping the fida'iyyun in a state of readiness during times of cease-fire as well, and it demonstrates how easily Egypt could recruit operatives.

In addition to its known methods of subversion, such as the use of Egyptian media for propaganda purposes and the purchase of newspapers (for which Egypt also used Saudi funds), Egypt used influential Palestinian dignitaries with ties to the Egyptian embassy in Amman. Prominent among these were Walid Salah, former foreign minister, whose pro-Egyptian position was starkly evident during his term in office; Walid al-Shak'a from Nablus, a delegate in the Jordanian House of Representatives; Hikmat al-Masri, a House of Representatives delegate from Nablus; and 'Abdulla al-Rimawi from Ramalla. Salah and Shak'a visited Cairo in mid-October 1955, and Salah was even received by Nasir. In December 1955, he was compelled to leave Jordan, and he relocated to Syria. At times fida'i operations and subversive political activities overlapped, when Palestinian political activists were used for fida'i purposes.

The Palestinian population's sympathy toward Egypt and its willingness to enlist in Egypt's service, as well as the freedom of action that the Egyptian military attaché and his aides enjoyed in Jordan, are evidenced by the near-public manner in which political activists and fida'iyyun were enlisted. Recruitment offices operated in several West Bank cities: Hebron, Jerusalem, Nablus, and Ramalla. Volunteers underwent physical exams and were then sent to the main office in Amman, where they were interviewed by one of the Egyptian officers. Volunteers who were accepted were then sent to training camps in Jordan. A few individuals were also sent for training in Egypt. Volunteers received a monthly stipend as well as financial support for their families. Likewise, financial support was promised in the event of their death.

Jordanian security and intelligence personnel, as well as Glubb Pasha and the security and intelligence divisions subordinate to him, were aware of this extensive Egyptian activity. For example, on June 8, 1955, Glubb sent a confidential letter to the regional commanders for Nablus and for Jerusalem, warning of Egyptian activities aimed at forming cells in Syria and Jordan that would infiltrate Israel for purposes of sabotage and terrorism. Given the importance of and strong interest in this notice, its main points are in the following:

> We have received reports from various parties according to which the Egyptian authorities are seeking to form gangs in Syria and Jordan that will infiltrate Israel and carry out acts of sabotage and terrorism, thereby causing a confrontation between other Arab states and Israel, with the aim of easing pressure on the Gaza Strip. The UN observers [Central Command] informed

us that the Jews had informed UN authorities that they had arrested an infiltrator between the region of Hebron and the Gaza Strip. He carried documents proving that the Egyptian authorities had contacted people in the Jordanian kingdom to persuade them to carry out acts of sabotage in Jewish territory and then to enter the Jordanian kingdom—acts that would probably result in the Jews retaliating against Jordan.[2]

Similarly, on September 10, 1955, the Central Command of the Jordanian Legion sent a dispatch detailing Egyptian activities to commanders of various regions:

> We have received confidential messages according to which armed infiltration into the occupied region has resumed, alongside incidents between Egypt and the Jewish authorities. Undesirable elements have been propagandizing among refugees, urging them to join the infiltration movement. . . . As this activity causes tension and fighting among peaceful residents on the frontline along the armistice line, you are requested to pay diligent attention to this matter and take measures regarding those who are threatening overall security, and to inform us of the results.[3]

The regime was aware that fida'i actions received a great deal of support among West Bank Palestinians and the Arab public in general. Against this background, Jordan's response was tentative. It included close monitoring of known activists and lobbying and public relations—aimed at the Egyptians as well—which drew on concerns regarding Israeli retaliation. Matters reached such a degree of activity that in December 1955 the Jordanian chief of staff personally asked the Egyptians to stop carrying out fida'i activities in Jordan.

Notably, in mid-January 1956, the commander of the Jordanian Legion's Jerusalem brigade undertook to transmit a message to Israel regarding the "renewed activity of Egyptian agents on Mount Hebron." Presumably the message, conveyed by a British diplomat, was approved by legion headquarters. In his message the brigade commander added that weapons had been stolen from a Jordanian National Guard depot in the village of Yatta and that "there is a likelihood that fida'i activities will be resumed, but it is not clear if these will be directed towards the [Jordanian] regime or towards Israel."[4]

In addition, the fida'iyyun were used in order to incite Palestinians in Jordan and try to turn them into a force that would undermine the Jordanian regime. Fida'i operatives were also used for political purposes such as organizing demonstrations and disturbances. Activities along these lines were carried out, for example, when the Turkish president visited Jordan, with the aim of making his visit a failure. Palestinian dignitaries from the West Bank, with whom the Egyptians cultivated close ties, were also turned into political propagandists for Egypt. Prominent among these was Walid Salah, who after being forced to flee Jordan because of his role in fida'i activities, engaged in political incitement in line with the Egyptian outlook. The Egyptians also tried to attract embittered soldiers from the Jordanian Legion and forge ties with them.

Egypt's efforts to establish its influence among the Palestinian population in Jordan were highly successful. The Egyptians took advantage of the refugees' generally favorable inclination toward Nasir's policy in the conflict and their hostile stance toward the Hashemite regime in Jordan in order to enlist them in Egypt's subversive efforts. The Egyptians systematically portrayed Jordan's arrest or detention of Palestinian refugees for fida'i activities as Jordanian persecution of the refugees.

The Palestinian Role in the Upheavals surrounding Jordan's Accession to the Baghdad Pact

On December 6, 1955, General Gerald Templer, chief of the Imperial General Staff, arrived in Amman with the aim of persuading Jordan to declare that it intends to join the Baghdad Pact. Toward this end, he proposed incentives in the form of military and financial assistance for the Jordanian Legion and termination of the 1948 Anglo-Jordanian Treaty. A week later (on December 13), Templer received Jordanian counteroffers formulated by a ministerial committee. These stated that Jordan was willing to join the pact on the condition that it not entail any obligations beyond its borders and that financial assistance for the legion be paid to Jordan's treasury rather than deposited in the legion's bank account in London. Egypt intervened to prevent Jordan from agreeing, thereby thwarting the British effort and generating the worst crisis to befall the kingdom since the assassination of King 'Abdulla.[5]

Nasir was determined to derail this British effort and was prepared to use all available means to do so. He made full use of the political and military subversion network that Egypt had established in Jordan during 1955, while exploiting the nationalist Palestinian factor within the kingdom. Egypt launched a brutal, unprecedented campaign of propaganda against Jordan and the Baghdad Pact, arguing that Jordan's accession to the pact would be a step toward signing a peace agreement with Israel.

Egypt's propaganda campaign was successful in preventing Sa'id al-Mufti's government from continuing to support Jordan's accession to the Baghdad Pact. Four Palestinian government ministers—Minister of Public Works Na'im 'Abd al-Hadi, Minister of Trade and Development Sam'an Da'ud, Minister of Postal Services 'Azmi al-Nashashibi, and Minister of Justice 'Ali Hasana—demanded as precondition, receiving Egypt's acceptance of Templer's proposals, but their demand was rejected. Consequently, they resigned and, following them, the entire government resigned on December 13, 1955. As a result, Templer failed in his mission, even though he had been certain when he left Jordan that it would join the pact.

On December 15, 1955, King Husayn appointed Minister of the Interior Hazzaʿ al-Majali prime minister. Majali was determined to have Jordan join the pact, but on his second day in office, after having declared his intentions of pursuing talks about accession, demonstrations and disturbances of unprecedented intensity erupted in West Bank cities and refugee camps. In Jerusalem, Western consulates were attacked and the Turkish and French consuls were injured; in Amman, a general strike was declared, and the opposition convened a "national congress" that issued nationalistic demands. Egypt again made clear that it would not tolerate Jordan's accession to the Baghdad Pact, and on December 19 the king informed the British ambassador to Jordan that it would be impossible for Jordan to join the pact in the indefinite future.[6]

On December 20, after four days of violent uprisings throughout the kingdom, Majali resigned. On the same day, King Husayn dissolved the parliament and called for new elections. The question of joining the Baghdad Pact was postponed until after elections, and the demonstrations ceased. As a result, the question of Jordan's accession to the pact actually fell off the agenda. It appears that King Husayn was startled by the pressure Egypt was applying and by the passions of Palestinian West Bank residents, and he sacrificed the government and agreed-on policy in the hope of restoring calm, even if only temporarily. His retraction of declared policy on this issue was the first time that the street, as the conduit of anti-Western inclinations in the kingdom, had forced the ruling government—with its traditionally distinctly pro-British policy—to bow to popular sentiment. In hindsight, General Templer's failure to secure Jordan's participation in the Baghdad Pact is undoubtedly attributable to the Palestinian West Bank residents.

The progression of uprisings opposing Jordanian accession to the Baghdad Pact, as outlined in the following summary of events, clearly illustrates the role of the Palestinians in Jordan during this severe crisis.[7]

December 13, 1955: Meetings and consultations took place among dignitaries in West Bank cities, and the Baʿth and Communist parties distributed flyers opposing Jordan's accession to the pact. In response, the legion's units surrounding Amman were placed on alert and the police took preparatory measures to close the roads of the West Bank.

December 14, 1955: Palestinian political activists supportive of Egypt increased their propaganda against the Jordanian government. They depicted its possible accession to the Baghdad Pact as binding the kingdom to Western aspirations and weakening the bargaining power and independent maneuverability of the Arab world. On that day, the mufti's government resigned, following the resignation of four of its Palestinian ministers.

December 15, 1955: Hazzaʿ al-Majali formed a new government and warned that he would crush uprisings with an iron fist. The domestic situation in the Kingdom worsened when massive demonstrations broke out in Nablus, Ramalla, and Jenin. In Nablus, women and children pelted legion soldiers with stones and empty bottles. In Amman, a peaceful demonstration took place and a strike broke out. House of Representatives delegate Walid al-Shak'a took it on himself to organize the protests in Nablus, and eleven of the city's dignitaries informed the king of their objection to Jordan joining the Baghdad Pact. The police showed exceptional restraint in handling the demonstrations and did not disrupt the protesters. Anwar al-Khatib and 'Abdulla Na' was were arrested and released.

December 16, 1955: The situation in the kingdom worsened when the army opened fire on demonstrators in Amman. Two brigades were deployed to the West Bank as military reinforcement, and the cities therein were blockaded with barbed wire fences. These measures did not prevent thousands of protesters in Nablus and Amman—schoolchildren and refugees in particular—from taking to the streets. Walid al-Shak'a and 'Abd al-Qadir Salih were arrested in Nablus. All the stores in Nablus and Amman were shut down, and threats were issued that any open stores would be burned. Stores were shut down in Jenin as well, and those that did not close were looted by protesters. The demonstrations resulted in violent confrontations with the police and army, and rumors circulated about fatalities, injuries, and detainees. In Jerusalem, thousands demonstrated after the afternoon prayers at the Dome of the Rock, shouting insults against Majali and the West. The National-Socialist Party condemned the government of Jordan and called for fierce opposition to Jordan's accession to the Baghdad Pact. In light of the deteriorating situation and military intervention, a curfew was imposed on West Bank cities and Amman. In Amman, the police also used live fire, and in Jenin armored vehicles were dispatched to the streets, where they drove straight into the crowds, and soldiers used batons to beat protesters. A policeman in Amman was seriously injured and died three days later. There were reports of dozens of injuries among security forces.

December 17, 1955: Angry demonstrations continued throughout Jordan's cities, accompanied by a general strike, massive popular gatherings, and school closures. The minister of education issued an order shutting down all the schools in the kingdom. Military vehicles were pelted with stones in Jerusalem, Nablus, and Hebron. Violent confrontations with the army took place in the region of around Jericho and among refugees from the camps of 'Ayn Sultan and Nu'eima. Vehicles of Western consulates and the UN were attacked. Demonstrations also took place in the East Bank—Amman, Irbid, Karak, and 'Aqaba. British military vehicles were pelted with stones in 'Aqaba, and an attempt was made to set the city's fuel depots on fire. Post offices in West Bank cities were set on fire. At a massive gathering in the Nuzha Cinema in Jerusalem, protesters called for the disengagement of the West Bank from Jordan and decided to send a delegation to King Husayn. Delegation member 'Abdulla Na'was, a Ba'th Party leader, told the masses that if the delegation's demands were not met, an armed revolt would break out in Jordan. On the same day, a meeting of Nablus dignitaries threatened revolt if the government of Majali did not resign. The Jordanian army continued to surround West Bank cities as well as Jordan's capital city of Amman. Efforts to disperse the demonstrations without resort to arms failed. The Jordanian prime minister informed a reporter from the Reuters news agency that Jordan still needed to discuss its accession to the Baghdad Pact with Britain and that a final decision on this matter had not yet been reached.

December 18, 1955: Turbulent demonstrations continued throughout the kingdom's cities, resulting in dozens of injuries. Government offices, postal services, and police stations in the areas around Hebron, Bethlehem, and Nablus were attacked. Demonstrators attacked UN and UNRWA offices in Hebron, damaging them severely. Telephone lines were cut. Refugees from the region of Jericho broke into Musa al-'Alami's Arab Development Society, vandalized and looted it, and fled only when the army arrived. In Nablus, at least one vehicle belonging to the legion was blown up and destroyed, the office of the British deputy consul was attacked, and the British flag was torn. In Jerusalem, UN vehicles, including that of General Burns, were destroyed. In Amman, protesters demonstrated at foreign embassies and threw stones at the US embassy. Peaceful demonstrations took place in Irbid and the districts of Karak and Ma'an. Delegations from the West Bank (including a Nablus delegation headed by Anwar al-Khatib) met with King Husayn. Given the deteriorating situation, the king addressed his subjects through Ramalla Radio, calling for quiet and national unity in light of the danger posed to Jordan by Israel. The king also called for calm to be maintained and asserted that Jordan's policy was based on the understanding that no Arab state would act on its own regarding the Filastin issue.

December 19, 1955: In the evening, it was announced that the House of Representatives had been dissolved and that a transition government had been formed, which would serve until the next elections. Hazza' al-Majali declared that the question of Jordan's accession to the Baghdad Pact would be determined by these elections. At the same time, disturbances in West Bank cities and Amman continued, with massive rioting in Nablus, Jenin, and Ramalla. In Amman, an angry demonstration took place, with schoolchildren, government officials, and Arab Bank officers participating. The demonstrators marched through the area where foreign missions were located, shouting words of support in front of the Egyptian and Saudi legations and words of condemnation at Iraq, Turkey, and Britain. A car belonging to the American ambassador was attacked while transporting the embassy's first secretary and was rescued by the army. Refugees demonstrated in front of the Office of the Prime Minister. In Jerusalem, an assembly was held with the participation of city council members, dignitaries, ministers, and former delegates, and the Department of Trade decided to demand that protesters who had been arrested or detained be released and that Jordan not join the Baghdad Pact. The consulates of France and Turkey in Jerusalem were attacked. At the Turkish consulate, three hundred people rioted over the course of two hours and the consul sustained a minor injury to his hand. The director of the French hospital and the French consul were also injured. A large demonstration took place near the Dome of the Rock. The army showed reluctance in scattering the demonstrators. Explicit orders issued by Jerusalem's governor, Hasan al-Katib, to defend the consulates were obeyed only partially, and control over the rioting at the Turkish consulate was lackadaisical: only after an hour and a half did a company of soldiers arrive to scatter the crowds by firing a few bullets into the air. The fire at the consulate burned for a long time before it was extinguished because the firefighters were slow to arrive. In Bethlehem, demonstrators took over the police station and government offices. The city's governor imposed a curfew on the city during the hours of 4 p.m. through 6 a.m. In other West Bank cities, peaceful strikes took place, with the participation of all government officials. Representatives of various cities and the Department of Trade in the West Bank convened in al-Bira to discuss an all-Jordan conference before December 23. A delegation representing the West Bank was appointed to meet with the king in Ramalla. It was also decided to declare a general strike. Two dignitaries—Sulayman al-Nabulsi and Shafiq Rsheidat—were arrested, and simultaneously the National Guard was ordered to be on alert, for fear that Israel would exploit the disturbances to its advantage.

December 20, 1955: Prime Minister Majali officially resigned, and the king instructed Ibrahim Hashim to form a transition government. At the same time, demonstrations continued in Jerusalem, including demonstrations of support for Egypt. Protesters attacked the French and US consulates, but this time they inflicted little damage. Protesters also broke into the Qishle compound and released the previous day's detainees. Jerusalem newspapers went on strike for the day to show support for the demonstrators, while schools were reopened. In Bethlehem and Hebron, angry protests took place, and in Hebron UNRWA depots were set on fire. Protests also took place in Nablus. Ramalla and the Jericho region were quiet.

December 21, 1955: Life began to return to normal. The government took measures to placate the public, making various promises, releasing detainees, and reopening schools in Nablus.

These events amounted to an impressive victory for opposition leaders and West Bank Palestinians, and naturally for Egypt and its leader, Nasir, as well. The Palestinian press in Jordan carried headlines highlighting "the will of the people" and asserted that "the people are not dead; they are strong," emphasizing that "these events serve as a warning to the rulers of Jordan that pacts contrary to the will of the people cannot be imposed on the people." Egyptian propaganda engaged in a full frontal assault on the British influence in Jordan, offering to provide financial support in place of British support. Young and inexperienced, the twenty-one-year-old King Husayn was shocked by the powerful impact that West Bank residents and Egypt had had on Jordan's domestic and foreign policy.[8]

The newspaper *Filastin* reported on December 23 that "united political organizations" in Jordan had issued a communiqué to the Jordanian people on conclusion of their conference in Amman. The conference produced the following demands, among others: opposition to the Turkish-Iraqi pact, the promise of free elections, no military intervention in political life, transparent vote counting for the House of Representatives, release of political prisoners, and the prosecution of those responsible for opening fire. Evidently, this conference comprised a delegation from West Bank cities as well as the active participation of the National-Socialist Party headed by Nabulsi (the delegation itself arrived in Amman on December 21, 1955, and met with the prime minister).[9]

Life began to return to normal but not for long. On January 5, 1956, Jordan's minister of the interior issued the following announcement: "After carefully reviewing the request to convene a popular assembly in Amman in order to discuss general problems, I have found that this matter . . . conflicts with the general aspiration to preserve the calm. Accordingly, I ordered that the assembly not be convened."[10] Two days later, protests were renewed in a number of Jordanian cities, including Amman, Nablus, and Jerusalem. During the course of these protests, demonstrators burned cars and broke the windows of the US embassy in the capital. Consequently, a curfew was then imposed on Amman, Jerusalem, and Nablus. The protests continued on January 8 as well, and demonstrations on a smaller scale took place in the days that followed, until they died down completely. The curfews continued until January 14.

On January 9, Samir al-Rifa'i, deputy prime minister and foreign minister in the government of Ibrahim Hashim, formed a new government to replace the one that had resigned on January 7. Rifa'i declared that Jordan would not join the Baghdad Pact, and he was successful in stabilizing Jordan's rule, containing nationalist outbursts, and adopting a neutral policy in the Arab world, as well as maintaining good relations with Britain. On January 31, 1956, Rifa'i's government received the House of Representatives' vote of confidence by a majority of 34–3, with one abstention (one delegate was missing). Rifa'i reiterated his government's position that it would not sign separate pacts: "I hereby announce once again that we will not join the Baghdad Pact."[11]

In the aftermath of the events of December 1955 through January 1956, IDF intelligence analysts became concerned about Jordan's fate. Evidently, their concerns were shared by other Arab states and in particular by Britain, whose standing in Jordan was among the most recognized and accepted and whose concerns were no less understandable than those of Israel.

On February 2, 1956, IDF intelligence circulated an assessment of the situation under the heading "Possible Developments in Jordan—The Division of the Kingdom," which concluded that the events of the preceding months indicated that the future disintegration of Jordan was a reasonable possibility "for the first time since the 1920s." The next day this formulation was revised as follows: "Following recent events in Jordan, the possibility of the kingdom's disintegration has been raised as an issue for internal consideration among interested states for the first time since the 1920s. Accordingly, interested states—whether [they view this matter] positively or negatively—have taken steps to advance any development and even to direct its course in a way that serves the special interests of each particular state." Ultimately, the Jordanian regime successfully managed to emerge from the crisis of late 1955 through early 1956, and the threat it represented was, for now, deferred. However, the crisis would soon resume and enter a new phase with the formation of a national, pro-Egyptian government following the October 1956 elections in the kingdom.

The December 1955 crisis in Jordan was the first phase of an ongoing crisis that lasted until April 1957. This crisis embodied all the elements that would repeatedly resurface during the crises that erupted in the kingdom over the years to come, such as in April 1963 and November 1966. The common denominators in these crises were the Palestinian national reawakening and Egyptian intervention and subversion. In each crisis situation, the West Bank Palestinians and political activist members of the opposition parties played an active role.

The second phase of the ongoing crisis was a natural outcome of the first—the removal of General Glubb from the position of legion commander-in-chief (on March 1, 1956) and of a large number of senior British officers. Removal of the British influence from the legion had been a consistent demand of the opposition for years, as well as one of the national demands put to the Hashemite regime. The objection to British influence was steadily fueled by the Egyptian propaganda.

The third phase of this lengthy, ongoing crisis was the appointment of 'Ali Abu Nuwar as chief of staff of the Arab Jordanian Army on May 24, 1956, and his promotion to the rank of *amir-liwa'* (major general) less than three months after having been appointed commander of the infantry brigade and only two months after having been appointed head of the operations branch of general staff headquarters for the Arab Jordanian Army. Before his meteoric rise, he had had no combat or staff experience beyond the position of brigade intelligence officer and brigade administrative officer. At the time of Glubb's dismissal, he served as an aide for King Husayn and apparently had a hand in the dismissal. Abu Nuwar was the leader of a group of nationalist pro-Nasir officers who called themselves the "Free Officers." He was an anti-Western nationalist who viewed the integration of the Arab Jordanian Army into the Egyptian system both as a political and military solution and as a key to personal advancement. Indeed, as expected, in his new position he increased military cooperation with Egypt and Syria, and the Arab Jordanian Army was joined to the joint Egyptian-Syrian military command, a branch of which was opened in Amman.

This phase of Jordan's domestic crisis also entailed continuing acts of subversion by Egypt, including the activation of fida'i cells from Jordan, the Gaza

Strip, and Lebanon. After the deterioration of the situation on the Gaza border in March 1956, the Egyptians started planning to mobilize fida'iyyun as a form of retaliation. An explicit Egyptian order to deploy them was issued immediately after Israel's artillery shelling of Gaza City on April 5. This shelling, in turn, had followed on the heels of various acts of sabotage, including the laying of mines along the borderline with Gaza, which injured twelve Israelis, and near-daily instances of Palestinians infiltrating from Gaza, striking at Israelis, and retreating under Egyptian cover.

The Egyptian response was not late in coming. As they had during the previous outbreak of hostilies in August 1955, the Egyptians again employed the weapon of the fida'iyyun who were on alert and at their disposal. The duration of the fida'i operation was limited by the president's office to three days, April 7–10, both to reduce the risk of an IDF response and to conclude the operation on the eve of the UN secretary general's visit, on April 11 (in practice, the fida'i actions continued a few days longer).

Because of shortcomings in organization and preparation, Egypt's use of the fida'iyyun did not successfully achieve its objectives. In fact, operations were conducted only from the Gaza Strip, and a significant number of fida'iyyun actually retreated to Jordan. During the three nights of this operation, sixty assaults or acts of confrontation took place—roughly twenty per night. Assessments in Israel were that at least three cells infiltrated the northern Negev from Mount Hebron. In all, twenty cells were identified, each one comprising five individuals on average.

The operational objectives were to ambush transportation routes and boobytrap the roads, sabotage agricultural facilities (primarily waterworks), and blow up houses in unprotected settlements. In addition, the fida'i cells that were expected to be dispatched from other Arab countries were ordered to sabotage military facilities, including airbases, and to take action in Israel's major cities. Israeli intelligence estimated that some 150 fida'iyyun were on Israeli territory. During these actions, the fida'iyyun suffered eleven deaths, five prisoners, and several injuries.

The wave of fida'i operations sparked a great deal of enthusiasm among Palestinians generally and those in the Gaza Strip and West Bank specifically. They saw these actions as the beginning of a war under Egypt's leadership for the liberation of Filastin. The fida'iyyun who retreated to Jordan were received as heroes: a fida'i group that reached Mount Hebron was enthusiastically received with celebrations organized by the local authorities, and, in another instance, dozens of fida'iyyun were received as guests of Jordanian army bases.

The October 1956 Elections and April 1957 Crisis

The fourth phase of crisis was preceded by the king's June 26, 1956, dissolution of the Jordanian House of Representatives (which had been elected on October 1954) on the grounds of "cessation of cooperation between it and the government." The king took this step after the House of Representatives delegates had begun adopting pro-Egyptian, oppositionist stances and it became evident to the government that it would not secure the vote of confidence scheduled for June 27. Most delegates demanded that the Anglo-Jordanian Treaty be revoked, not merely amended as the government requested. The government therefore advised that the king dissolve the House of Representatives, and on June 30 Prime Minister Saʿid al-Mufti resigned as well. Ibrahim Hashim was appointed to replace him the following day, and his government called for elections to the fourth House of Representatives.[12]

The elections of October 21, 1956, took place without government intervention. These were the freest elections in Jordan to date. They were conducted within the atmosphere of nationalism that prevailed throughout the Arab world at the time, including Jordan and, in particular, the West Bank. The background factors contributing to this atmosphere included Nasir's nationalization of the Suez Canal in July 1956 and the resulting Suez crisis, and in particular the deteriorating situation along the Jordanian-Israeli border, which stemmed from fida'i operations and retaliatory IDF action. Other contributing factors were the talks that had been taking place between Jordan and Iraq and the publicity surrounding Iraqi forces dispatched to Jordan. Chief of Staff Abu Nuwar undoubtedly took measures to ensure that the Arab Jordanian Army not intervene in these elections as it had routinely interfered in previous elections. Indeed, King Husayn was personally interested in having freely held elections this time. The outcome of the elections did not come as a surprise to anyone following the developments in the West Bank or in Jordan generally since the crisis surrounding the Baghdad Pact.

The election results did in fact mirror the mood of the people in the kingdom generally and in the West Bank specifically. The opposition secured a decisive majority in the House of Representatives—twenty-two out of forty delegates. The National-Socialist Party, headed by Sulayman al-Nabulsi, received twelve mandates—a substantial number—while supporters of the regime numbered sixteen. A total of thirteen out of twenty elected West Bank representatives were leaders or activists from opposition parties.

On October 27, 1956, the king instructed Sulayman al-Nabulsi to form a government. A day earlier, Hikmat al-Masri, a National-Socialist, had been selected as chairman of the House of Representatives. The new nationalist government revoked the Anglo-Jordanian Treaty, granted legitimacy to the Communist Party, and in April 1957 decided to establish diplomatic relations with the Soviet Union.

As such, the Sinai War and the Suez campaign broke out at a time when the political atmosphere in Jordan, and particularly in the West Bank, was nationalist, pro-Egyptian, and anti-Western. Egypt's influence reached its peak when the Egyptian military command made plans, in January 1957, to dispatch six military delegations to Amman to discuss Egyptian military assistance to the Arab Jordanian Army in the areas of air defense, armored forces instruction and training, and intelligence on Israel. Toward this end, the director of Egyptian intelligence personally arrived in Amman in late January 1957.

These political and military developments threatened King Husayn's rule, and it appeared that he was losing control of the government. For the first time in Jordan's history, the collapse of the kingdom seemed possible, and the question being asked in the corridors of Israel's and Britain's foreign ministries and the US State Department was the following: "Where is the kingdom headed?"

At the last moment, King Husayn took a series of bold, dramatic steps that were intended to suppress the opposition. On April 19, 1957, he fired Prime Minister Nabulsi, after having earlier fired Chief of Staff Abu Nuwar on April 13. In firing Abu Nuwar, Husayn took advantage of the 'Alya Brigade's suspicious movement around the region of Zarqa, where confrontations had taken place between units loyal to the king and units subject to the influence of Abu Nuwar and his cousin Ma'an Abu Nuwar, the brigade commander appointed by Abu Nuwar himself. The king also disbanded the political parties and the National Steering Committee and had their leaders arrested. The diplomatic immunity of Communist Party delegates in the House of Representatives was rescinded, and they too were arrested. Likewise, all trade unions were disbanded. Those members of the Nabulsi government who had not managed to escape to Syria were placed under house arrest.

Husayn's April 1957 "counter-coup" put an end to Egypt's efforts (which had been ongoing since 1956) to gradually gain control over Jordan through Palestinian leaders and Transjordanian leaders and officers.

The changes that had been instituted in the Arab Jordanian Army and the composition of the Jordanian government did not prevent Egypt from continuing its subversive efforts in Jordan and taking advantage of the nationalist political atmosphere in the country. Fida'i cells at the disposal of the Egyptian military attaché remained in the kingdom, and some were deployed from there to conduct reconnaissance missions in Israeli territory. In early March 1957, in light of information gathered by Egyptian intelligence, the Egyptian military attaché in Amman deployed fida'i cells in the Tulkarm sector to carry out reconnaissance missions in Israeli territory. Earlier, in mid-February, Egypt's intelligence services had received information about concentrations of Israeli forces, partial mobilization in Israel, and a possible launch by Israel of a localized attack to wipe out fida'i centers. A similar deployment of cells took place in early May 1957 as well.

Thus, Egypt and Syria acted unceasingly to undermine the domestic stability of Husayn's regime and bring about its collapse, both before the Egyptian-Syrian unification in February 1958 and for the duration of the union itself. Without a doubt, these acts of subversion found fertile ground amidst the West Bank

Palestinian population and members of the opposition within this population's leadership. Egypt and Syria's motivation to topple Husayn grew even stronger after his attempted "counter-coup" in April 1957, which in practical terms put an end to Egyptian efforts to take over Jordan.

Egypt and Syria's plans and attempts to incite a popular revolt in Jordan—by smuggling in large amounts of weapons, ammunition, and explosives for use by opponents of the regime—came to the attention of Jordan's security authorities, who then placed the opposition's leaders under house arrest and arrested other coconspirators. An attempt to carry out a military coup between July 17 and 19, 1957, was thwarted by the preemptive arrest of the plot's leaders, thanks to credible information that originated in Israel and reached the hands of Jordan's security authorities. Among those arrested were leaders of the Free Officers—foremost among them Colonel Mahmud al-Rusan and Colonel Radi al-'Abdulla. Another attempted military coup, scheduled for the night of March 15–16, 1959, was thwarted when the leader of the plot was arrested on March 14.

Egypt's acts of subversion in Jordan peaked on August 29, 1960, when Syrian intelligence, in cooperation with Jordanian exiles and their supporters in Jordan, sought to assassinate the ruling elite of the Hashemite regime. The plan achieved partial success: Prime Minister Hazza' al-Majali was killed by a time bomb that had been planted in his office building. In addition to Majali, the director of the Office of the Prime Minister, the head of the Department of Tourism, the head of the Majali tribe, and six other individuals were killed, and nearly 50 people were injured. The conspirators had also hoped to strike at King Husayn, who was expected to moderate the government meeting. When they failed, they tried to target him in other ways, including by smuggling a bomb into his palace. They tried, in addition, to blow up the building of the Jordanian broadcasting authority. These efforts failed. Undoubtedly, this plot had originated with the Jordanian exiles, headed by 'Abdulla al-Rimawi and 'Ali Abu Nuwar, who had been trying since April 1957, from Damascus, to topple Husayn's regime. Presumably, Egyptian ammunition and explosives had been transferred to Damascus for use in this plot.

The coup in Syria on September 28, 1961, which led to the disintegration of the UAR, freed Jordan from the threat posed by Egypt's base for subversive action in Damascus. Although this base was reestablished in Lebanon, the operational possibilities in Jordan were reduced. Moreover, Jordanian (and Lebanese) intelligence personnel in Lebanon were able to monitor these activities regularly. The Jordanians, for their part, sought to retaliate against the Egyptians for their continuing subversion efforts by way of agents whom they smuggled into Gaza in 1961, who then disseminated anti-Egyptian pamphlets in the strip.

Beginning in September 1962, Egypt eased its pressure on Jordan, primarily because the Egyptian army was heavily engaged in Yemen. In the meantime, a new problem had arisen in the Arab arena, which had a major impact on the Palestinians of the West Bank, on their relations with Jordan, and on relations between Jordan and Egypt—namely, the revival of a Palestinian entity and, subsequently, the practical measures taken to establish a representative Palestinian organization, resulting in the formation of the PLO by Ahmad al-Shuqayri.

Notes

1. The Khan Yunis Operation was a reprisal operation following fida'i actions, which included an IDF raid on the city of Khan Yunis.
2. DJG.
3. Ibid.
4. Ibid.
5. See Templer's final report on his mission to Jordan and his conclusions, the National Archives of the United Kingdom, FO, 371, 1051/127; see also Hazza' al-Majali, *Qissat Muhadathat Templer*; see also Uriel Dann, "The Foreign Office, the Baghdad Pact and Jordan," *Asian and African Studies* 21 (November 1987): 247–61.
6. For a summary of the December 1955 events in Jordan surrounding the Baghdad Pact, see Uriel Dann, *King Hussein and the Challenge of Arab Radicalism* (Oxford: Oxford University Press, 1989), 21–30.
7. DJG and IDF Intelligence Reports.
8. Dann, *Hussein and the Challenge*, 130.
9. *Filastin*, December 23, 1955.
10. Ramalla Radio, January 5, 1955.
11. Rifa'i, Ramalla Radio, January 31, 1957.
12. *Hamizrah he-Hadash* 7, no. 4 (1957): 292–93; *Hamizrah he-Hadash* 8, no. 1 (1957): 54–55. The first House of Representatives was elected in 1950 and dissolved in 1951 by the king; the second was elected in 1952 and dissolved in 1954; the third was elected in 1954 and dissolved in 1956.

12 The Crisis of April 1963
West Bank Palestinians and the Revival of a Palestinian Entity

THE APPEARANCE IN March 1959 of the item "revival of a Palestinian entity" on the agenda of the Arab League Council heralded a new era in the history of the Hashemite Kingdom of Jordan and its Palestinian residents. Nasir's objective in raising this issue was to turn the Palestinians into a major and separate party in the Arab-Israeli conflict by forming a Palestinian entity, the most important element of which would be the election of institutions to represent the Palestinians. Nasir aspired to see national Palestinian rule over the Palestinian territories, that is, the West Bank and the Gaza Strip.

King Husayn and the ruling elite in Jordan fully understood the significance of the Egyptian proposal, which further received the backing of the Iraqi leader, Qasim, in December 1959. Qasim proposed that the "eternal Palestinian republic" be established initially on the land of the West Bank and Gaza Strip, and later on all of Mandatory Palestine. The significance from Jordan's perspective was that such a step would undermine its territorial integrity, and indeed its very existence, given that two-thirds of its residents were Palestinians, or "Jordanians of Palestinian descent," as the regime preferred to call them. Husayn perceived resistance to this notion as an element of the struggle for the survival of his kingdom.

In opposing the idea of a Palestinian entity, the king tried to persuade the Arab world that the Palestinians within his kingdom supported his stance; thus he reinforced his claims that "Jordan is Filastin and Filastin is Jordan" and that Jordan represents the Palestinians. During the years 1959–63, he took measures to prove that the Palestinian population in his country backed his policy on this matter. These measures included, among others: arranging for statements of endorsement; organizing supportive gatherings and other activities on the part of the House of Representatives and the Senate aimed at the adoption of resolutions supporting his policy and condemning Nasir and Qasim's plans; dispatching messages from Palestinian political activists on the West Bank to meetings of the Arab League reviewing this issue; conducting tours—including by the king himself—of West Bank villages; and launching large-scale public relations campaigns to recruit "spontaneous" support for himself and his policy. The king was aiming to prove to the Arab world that Palestinian residents of the West Bank supported preservation of the "unity of the two riverbanks" and Jordan's continued representation of the Palestinians.

The regime's efforts to prove that West Bank Palestinians "supported" its policy were starkly evident in intelligence and political reports prepared by West Bank district and regional investigation and security officers, who depicted the regime's stances as the supposedly dominant outlook in Palestinian public opinion. Yet, even in these reports, one can find evidence of attitudes that differed from the perspective of the Palestinian public as the regime sought to portray it and, in fact, reflected viewpoints that opposed the government and supported both a separate Palestinian entity and Nasir's policy. For example, in the September 7, 1959, mid-monthly political report of the Nablus regional commander (and in other political reports of district and regional commanders during the same period), one can find indications of opinions among West Bank residents that support the establishment of a Palestinian entity, as well as other expressions of Palestinian identity, and of the regional commanders' measures to address these viewpoints and to curry favor with the regime in Amman.

Among other findings, the April 24, 1960, report of the Nablus regional commander stated as follows:

> According to credible sources, on the night between March 2 and 3, 1960, Nash'at al-Masri, Haj Ma'zuz al-Masri, Walid al-Shak'a, and Rashid al-Nimr met in the home of Nash'at al-Masri in Nablus. Their talks focused on the establishment of what was termed a Palestinian government. After a lengthy discussion, they decided [the following]:
>
> 1. Nash'at al-Masri would spread the word about the [Palestinian] government among official circles to secure their support for the establishment of a Palestinian government.
> 2. Walid al-Shak'a would work to secure villagers' support for the same goal, as he had business relations with them and many supporters in the villages.
> 3. Ma'zuz al-Masri would be responsible for securing the support of VIPs and senior officials in Nablus.
> 4. Rashid al-Nimr, with the cooperation of Ma'zuz al-Masri, would work to secure the support of prominent businessmen and the residents of Nablus.

In April 1960, the division responsible for investigations in Jordan received information that "efforts are under way on the part of some West Bank political activists to persuade West Bank ministers and dignitaries not to cooperate with the government and not to rejoin the government in the event that Hazza' al-Majali's government resigns."[1]

The visit of political activist Ahmad al-Shuqayri in the West Bank, which began on April 25, 1962, was warmly received by the residents and sparked discussions among local political activists about the issue of a Palestinian entity and the need to "let the Palestinians decide their fate, as the Algerians did." According to Jordanian sources, "Shuqayri's visit drew a great deal of attention in the Nablus region and became the talk of the town." It was also reported that at Shuqayri's meeting with the "national bloc" in Jordan (including Sulayman al-Nabulsi, Hikmat al-Masri, and Walid al-Shak'a), they asserted that they would not work for the liberation of Filastin "before Jordan is liberated from the regime imposed on them."

In sum, the Palestinian public in West Bank was aware of developments relating to the issue of a Palestinian entity—including the plans of Nasir and Qasim, which became the topic of the day—and it followed the resolutions of Arab League meetings on this matter with interest. Political activists held meetings to discuss the establishment of a Palestinian government and promotion of the concept of a Palestinian entity throughout various sectors of society. At one of the meetings, Hikmat al-Masri urged people not to give up on the UAR as regards the issue of a Palestinian entity in all its aspects. Indeed, an April 11, 1960, report of the Jordanian intelligence that was unusual in its content and assessment stated that "most residents of Jerusalem have leanings toward the UAR: 70 percent of West Bank residents supported the concept of the entity, in contrast to open expressions of support for the king and his policy." This report appears to be fairly accurate about the actual mood among Palestinians. It was also reported that attention to the question of a Palestinian entity was reigniting concern among West Bank residents regarding discrimination against refugees as compared with the treatment of East Bank residents, and that Palestinians were asserting that "the establishment of a Palestinian republic will preserve our dignity and rights, in light of the still ongoing discrimination between Jordanians and Palestinians in terms of military appointments, in the government apparatus, in distribution of food, and in the issuing of business licenses."

The Crisis of April 1963

On April 17, 1963, a domestic crisis broke out, the worst Jordan had known since April 1957.[2] The background to this crisis was an announcement regarding the tripartite unification of Egypt, Syria, and Iraq on April 16, 1963. The announcement incited nationalistic fervor within the Palestinian population in Jordan, which was encouraged and inflamed by these three states in the hopes of upsetting the stability of the regime in Jordan. Once again, the fate of the Hashemite regime was up in the air. The Ba'th coups in Iraq (February 8, 1963) and Syria (March 8, 1963) were a blow to the regime in Jordan, which rightly feared their impact on the kingdom's internal stability. Among nationalistic circles and within the opposition in the West Bank, hopes increased that the kingdom too would soon experience a coup or at least establish a nationalist government. The Jordanian regime was aware of the situation and worked hard to repress any indication of activity hostile to it, and even took measures to preempt the possibility of subversion on the part of Syria and Egypt, which indeed was not late in coming. The regime also reinforced its intelligence and security networks, preemptively detained hostile oppositionists and nationalists, and made use of the Arab Jordanian Army's mechanized brigade, which comprised only Bedouins and was designated for the defense of government nerve centers and institutions.

On March 27, 1963, Wasfi al-Tal submitted the resignation of his government to enable King Husayn to address the new situation in the Arab world. The king appointed Samir al-Rifaʻi as his replacement. On matters of foreign policy, Rifaʻi took steps to demonstrate Jordan's identification with the Arab federation and its integration into unification-related developments while preserving its independence. On the domestic front, he implemented a liberal policy aimed at placating public opinion and the opposition while expanding the popular foundations of his government, and he released most of the political prisoners. Through this policy, Rifaʻi indirectly paved the way for the crisis that erupted on April 17.

Indicators of the crisis to come were evident by April 13, when schoolchildren in Nablus and other cities tried to carry out demonstrations, which were immediately suppressed. On April 15, the security services issued an assessment that the following day's joint announcement regarding unification was expected to trigger "demonstrations of joy, especially among schoolchildren" and that "the instigators will be Baʻth Party activists, Arab Nationalists, and Nasirists." On the basis of lessons learned from similar events in the past, and in order to defend the regime's stability effectively, on April 14 the General Security Services established the following policy guidelines, which were transmitted the next day to units in the field:

> Any attempted demonstration by schoolchildren should be forcibly suppressed. When dispersing demonstrations, batons should be used first and then water hoses; if they have not dispersed, then tear gas grenades should be used; if this measure is not successful and the situation cannot be controlled, the matter should be referred to the administrative governor to determine the appropriate response. It is absolutely prohibited to use live fire; gunfire is permitted, if necessary, only upon receipt of *written* permission from the district governor. In the event of loss of control by the security forces [police], military units will be called upon to fulfill their duty, but only upon the orders of the district governors. The use of gunfire by the armed forces [Arab Jordanian Army] to disperse the demonstrators will be a measure of last resort, and only after receipt of written permission from the district governor.

The first phase of the crisis continued from April 17 to April 19, 1963. The assessment of Jordan's security services proved to be accurate. On the day after the tripartite union was announced, a wave of demonstrations erupted throughout the West Bank, the likes of which had not been seen since December 1955. Hundreds of individuals, mostly schoolchildren, demonstrated in support of Nasir and the union, calling out "Come on, Amman," "We want unification," "King, we want unity," and "Long live the three-starred flag." During these demonstrations, UAR flags and posters of Nasir were raised, and flyers were distributed at demonstration focal points calling for Jordan to join the federation and become "the fourth star in the Arab world of eternity." In major cities demonstrations were organized by opposition leaders and activists (in Nablus by House of Representatives delegate Hatim Abu Ghazala, who delivered a speech to the demonstrators and called on the authorities to refrain from disrupting the broadcasts of Sawt al-Arab Radio, and in Tulkarm by ʿAwad Mahmud ʿAwad).

On April 18, the government decided to prevent preparations for demonstrations of any sort, beginning that morning, and assigned the responsibility for implementing this decision to the General Security Services. Simultaneously, by request of the district governors, the army was placed in a state of readiness to intervene, in case the situation deteriorated and the police lost control. A brigade was assigned to each district. The commander of the al-Amira ʿAlya Brigade, for example, assigned a battalion to ensure the security of Nablus, Jenin, and Tulkarm, having ascertained that demonstrations were likely in each of these cities and their surroundings. Brigade commanders issued operational orders on April 18, in accordance with the government decision and the previously mentioned instructions issued by the General Security Services on April 14.

The demonstrations continued on April 18 and 19 as well, although on a smaller scale, and the police were able to disperse them and control the situation. In a few cities shots were fired into the air but there were no injuries.

The second phase of the crisis lasted approximately one week (April 20–26). On April 20, the intensity of the demonstrations escalated, with about four thousand participants in some of the cities, compared with a few hundred during the first phase. Hot spots included the cities of Jerusalem, Hebron, Nablus, Jenin, Tulkarm, and, to a certain extent, Irbid as well. The demonstrators' goal was to influence the vote of confidence in the Rifaʿi government, which was scheduled to take place that day.

The police were completely unable to control the demonstrations (especially in Jerusalem). Demonstrators used live fire. In Jerusalem, an attempt was made to take over the broadcasting authority building, and demonstrators set fire to tires and Jordanian flags. The police headquarters in Jenin was pelted with stones by demonstrators who climbed on it and ripped the Jordanian flag while also shooting at the army.

At the request of district governors, the army was mobilized to suppress the demonstrations by force. They opened fire on demonstrators, causing deaths and injuries. There were prolonged exchanges of fire between demonstrators and the military, especially in Jerusalem, Nablus, Jenin, and Tulkarm. Following these events, the military imposed a curfew on the hot spots of protest and succeeded in exerting control over West Bank cities.

On April 20, Jordan's House of Representatives held a meeting to discuss the situation in the kingdom and the government's policy. In opening this discussion, Prime Minister Rifa'i delivered a message that stated, inter alia,

> The demonstrators opened fire and hit one of the security personnel. In order to prevent the situation from deteriorating and to protect life and property, orders were issued for the army to enter the city of Jenin immediately and disperse the demonstrations. In Jerusalem . . . the demonstrations reached the Old City, with shots being fired from windows and balconies. When the governor of Jerusalem informed me of this development, which posed a threat to the security of citizens and property, I instructed him to impose a curfew, and the army would restore order.[3]

According to the official district reports, the casualty figures resulting from the demonstrations of April 20-21 were as follows: the Nablus district (covering Nablus, Tulkarm, and Jenin)—six dead and twenty-six injured; the Jerusalem district—three dead (within the city itself) and thirty-one injured (twenty-one in the city); Ramalla—thirty-one injured; Hebron—two dead and eight injured; 'Ajloun—two dead and eighteen injured; Balqa—eight injured; Amman—three injured. The ages of the casualties varied between seventeen and twenty generally, although there were a few older ones. Among security forces, fourteen military personnel were injured during the demonstrations.

On April 21, widespread arrests of demonstrators took place. Arrestees included members of the House of Representatives (seventeen were arrested, including Hatim Abu Ghazala from Nablus, Najib al-Ahmad from Jenin, and 'Awad from Tulkarm). Two days later, opposition leader Sulayman al-Nabulsi was placed under house arrest.[4] In addition, refugee camps in the regions of Amman and Jericho were watched more closely than before. On April 25, the number of arrests in the Nablus district reached 138, with another 62 suspects not yet caught. Surveillance was increased over individuals identified as dangerous. On April 22, the Nablus regional commander presented the General Security Services with a list of 103 individuals from Nablus, 14 from Tulkarm and 32 from Jenin, all of whom had been identified as Nasirists and inciters of strikes, demonstrations, and disturbances. Half of these were arrested, including opposition activists and leaders from the Ba'th Party, the ANM, and the Communist Party.

Given the deteriorating situation, on April 22 a curfew was imposed on Jordan's major cities, including West Bank cities. Middle schools and high schools were closed, and the two riverbanks of the Jordan River were, in effect, disconnected from one another. In light of the worsening domestic situation, King Husayn delivered a harsh speech that afternoon, in which he asserted, among other things, "I will carry forth as a soldier rather than a king, as a rebel Hashemite Arab rather than a ruler. Woe to anyone who seeks to block this convoy. I fear no one but God. We reached out to our [Arab] brothers, with a clean, honest, strong hand, not out of weakness or fear or supplication. I warn [Jordan's neighbors] against planting fear [through] slogans of unification."[5]

The intensity of the demonstrations diminished immediately on implementation of the regime's measures on April 22, although they did continue sporadically and on a smaller scale until April 26. By April 25, a state of calm was essentially restored throughout the kingdom, and on April 26, life returned to nearly normal. The curfew was partially lifted, though it was maintained during the nighttime in a few centers of unrest. On this day the regime started taking steps to alleviate tension: in addition to the gradual lifting of the curfew, most detainees were released, and schools reopened on May 9. On May 11, the army was released from domestic security missions, responsibility for which was returned to internal security forces. The army was, however, kept on reserve in a state of readiness in case the situation deteriorated. The doubts that had surfaced in public opinion regarding the future of the tripartite union, alongside Egypt's renewed propaganda campaign against the regime in Syria, almost certainly contributed to the restoration of calm.

The demonstrations of April 20 achieved their political objective: thirty-two of sixty Jordanian House of Representatives members voiced opposition to the Rifa'i government and only eleven expressed support for it. Rifa'i saw the writing on the wall and announced his resignation even before the vote of confidence in his government took place.[6] In his place the king appointed his own uncle, Sherif Husayn Nasir bin Jamil, but given the latter's weak personality, the king continued to rule in practice and to consult with Samir al-Rifa'i.

On conclusion of the new government's first meeting, on April 21, the prime minister stated that the government would "use an iron fist to subdue anyone who tries to disrupt the state of clam and incite riots. It will in no way whatsoever permit the incitement of riots and manipulation of emotions for the sake of personal interests."[7]

In evaluating the background to the crisis and its consequences, it is important to emphasize that the events of April 1963 in Jordan, including the West Bank, were not the outcome of planned Nasirist subversion, that is, subversion by Nasirist agents or their envoys in Jordan. Nasir was partly right when he argued before Western diplomats in late April 1963 that he "had no part in the turbulent events that occurred in Jordan, and they were all the product of the Jordanian people's initiative and will."[8] In actuality, it was a spontaneous outburst on the part of Palestinian West Bank residents driven by the fervor of national sentiment and long-term effects, which generated cumulative power of the sort that can erupt in times of crisis. The major demonstrations were organized by a number of opposition members from the House of Representatives and by local opposition activists, and they reflected feelings of hostility toward the regime and pro-Nasir leanings among Palestinians.

In summarizing the events of April 1963, the British consul in Jerusalem wrote, "Too many bridges have been destroyed between the East and West Banks for there to be any genuine prospect of any enduring national reconciliation. Republican sentiments are being more widely and more boldly expressed here; and even amongst the more moderate elements, whose Royalism rested on the illusion that a Hashemite chieftain could ever become so domesticated as to be capable of conversion into constitutional monarch, Hussein's future role is tending to be seen in terms of a life Presidency in a Jordanian Republic."[9]

Notes

1. All the Jordanian commanders' reports and intelligence and security reports are from DJG.
2. Details of the April crisis, its background, its repercussions, and the reactions of the Palestinian population and the opposition are based on DJG, unless otherwise noted.
3. Rifa'i, Amman Radio, April 21, 1963.
4. Nabulsi was released on August 7, 1963, alongside other opposition activists such as Hatim Abu Ghazala, Najib al-Ahmad, and Hamid Farhan, all of whom participated in the demonstrations.
5. Husayn, Amman Radio, April 22, 1963.
6. Samir al-Rifa'i, Amman Radio, April 20, 1963.
7. Husayn Nasir Bin-Jamil, Amman Radio, April 21, 1963.
8. See the report from Israel's foreign ministry to the Israeli embassy in Washington, DC, May 3, 1963, Israel State Archives, 3377/5.
9. National Archives of the United Kingdom, FO, Jerusalem to FO, FO 371/170268, xc11526, April 24, 1963.

13 The Palestinians of Jordan, 1965–66

Between Shuqayri, Husayn, and the Emergence of Fatah

JORDAN'S ASSIMILATION OF the prevalent outlook at the Arab League Summit, and especially the positive turn its relations with Egypt took when it joined the endeavor to establish the PLO, yielded a relatively long period of internal calm (1964–65). During this time, the regime was able to alleviate the tension created by internal security measures and make conciliatory gestures, including releasing security-based prisoners and arrestees or detainees and pardoning political exiles. This domestic state of calm did not, however, earn King Husayn the support of Palestinians in his kingdom but, rather, significantly increased the nationalist mood among Palestinian West Bank residents. During this period, Nasir's prestige further increased, and pictures of him openly reappeared in Jordan's cities, including in the West Bank. Wasfi al-Tal, prime minister during the decisive period between February 1965 and March 1967, was the key figure in helping King Husayn formulate and consolidate his domestic policy and inter-Arab policy generally and his policy toward the PLO and Shuqayri specifically. From Jordan's perspective, Tal was the right man to handle Egypt and Syria's subversion efforts as well as Shuqayri's efforts to use the Palestinian population in Jordan to undermine internal stability.

Shuqayri (who established the PLO in June 1964) demanded freedom of action for himself among the West Bank Palestinians—that is, the option of recruiting them in support of the PLO and of Egyptian policy on the Palestinian entity. In practice this option meant undermining the kingdom's sovereignty and creating dual political affinities among its Palestinian population. The opposing positions held by Husayn and Shuqayri as well as their strong difference of opinion regarding the PLO's modus operandi in Jordan exacerbated the conflict between the PLO and Jordan over the hearts and minds of West Bank Palestinians, to the point that confrontation became inevitable. This period marked the beginning of a process in which this political—at times armed and violent—struggle was transformed into an existential struggle between the Palestinian entity and the Jordanian entity. Indirectly, this struggle reinforced the sense of a Palestinian identity among Palestinian residents of Jordan and made the threat to the regime's stability more concrete. After its founding, the PLO posed a dilemma to Palestinians in Jordan for the first time since 1950: Was their political loyalty to the Hashemite regime, which had annexed the West Bank in 1950, or to the Palestinian organization that had been established to represent them?

King Husayn's fundamental position regarding the composition and purpose of the PLO were clear and well defined from the outset. In contrast, Shuqayri's official position regarding the purpose of the PLO was intentionally vague at first. It became clearer only toward the end of 1965 and during 1966, as Shuqayri's relations with Jordan worsened and his stated views became more vehement. Both Husayn and Shuqayri invoked the slogan "Jordan is Filastin and Filastin is Jordan" but with opposing interpretations.

In the near term, Shuqayri sought to achieve "personal autonomy" for the West Bank population loyal to the PLO. In Shuqayri's view, the Palestinians had to be allowed to "freely actualize their national undertaking, as had other Arab peoples during their struggles." Toward this end, it was necessary to establish independent Palestinian political and military structures on behalf of West Bank residents and to integrate these into the activities of PLO political structures such as the Palestinian National Council, the "Palestinian popular organization," and the Palestinian army. Shuqayri believed that if this goal could be achieved in the short term, then the Palestinian entity would outweigh the Jordanian entity in the long term, both because the Palestinian population was a majority in Jordan and because the Palestinians surpassed the Jordanians in various areas (such as education). In his view, territorial sovereignty would be attained after "personal autonomy" was achieved. Shuqayri's mottos—"the Palestinian is a Jordanian and the Jordanian is a Palestinian" and "unity of the two riverbanks"—should be understood in this context.

In early 1965, Shuqayri began to address the central problem relating to PLO activities among the Palestinian population of the West Bank. He engaged in negotiations with Jordan, which continued until February 1966. Building on the Palestinian population's support for the PLO, Shuqayri presented the Jordanian government with a number of demands relating to the organization's activities in Jordan—some within the military sphere, others about the activities of PLO bodies and their standing in Jordan. Implementation of these demands would have meant duplicate governance and the creation of a population group with autonomous rights within the Jordanian kingdom. Under such circumstances, the PLO would be another executive arm in Jordan, responsible for the Palestinian sector, most of which was located within a delineated territory—the West Bank. That area thus become an autonomous territory of sorts, where the PLO would enjoy special rights denied to the Jordanian government, such as representation of two-thirds of the kingdom's residents. Palestinians in Jordan would then be loyal to an independent Palestinian body outside of Jordan, and the Palestinian national consciousness would continue to increase and grow stronger. In time, a stronger national consciousness could result in more expansive national demands—such as autonomous Palestinian rule separate from Jordan or a confederate Jordanian kingdom. Moreover, as the Palestinians constituted a majority of the population, meeting Shuqayri's demands would turn the kingdom of Jordan into a Palestinian state with Jordanians as a minority—essentially an "alternative homeland" (*al-watan al-badil*).

Jordan's leadership, headed by King Husayn and Prime Minister Wasfi al-Tal, fully understood the significance of Shuqayri's demands. Unsurprisingly, therefore, they completely rejected most of them, even though they reached a tactical agreement with Shuqayri (on March 1, 1966) regarding some of the less important demands. The articles of this agreement delineated the PLO's modus operandi among Palestinians in Jordan. Under the agreement, Shuqayri's undertaking in the West Bank was granted independent standing, thereby circumventing the law with respect to the 1957 abolition of political parties. It was clear that government signed this agreement with no intention of implementing it in practice. The Jordanian elite was aware of the negative impact that even partial implementation of Shuqayri's demands would have for the regime's standing among West Bank Palestinians. Indeed, a March 5, 1966, memorandum from Wasfi al-Tal—which was classified as "top secret" and circulated to government ministers, the chief of staff, district governors, the head of general intelligence, and the head of the General Security Services—clearly outlined the regime's policy regarding the activities of Shuqayri and the PLO in Jordan. The key points of this policy left no doubt about Jordan's position regarding Shuqayri's demands, particularly those that could have a negative impact on the regime's standing in and full sovereignty over the West Bank.

Wasfi al-Tal, architect of this policy, proceeded to implement it in practice, in both spirit and letter. As a result there erupted the worst confrontation ever to take place between Husayn and Shuqayri, in the course of which Shuqayri launched a series of relentless attacks aimed at undermining the kingdom's right to exist. He even called for Jordan to be turned into a provisional alternative homeland for Palestinians.

The principles underlying Jordan's perspective on the PLO and its activities among Palestinians in Jordan, as formulated and implemented by Wasfi al-Tal, were the following:

- "The PLO is the Arab branch of Jordan and Filastin," and its activities must accord with "the mandate of the Jordanian entity and its political and social beliefs, which are detailed in its laws."
- "Full responsibility is placed on the state to direct, organize, and guide the citizens in accordance with the law. Any activity in any

context ... shall be conducted by means of state institutions or their approval." This provision meant that any measure or statement relating to PLO activities among West Bank Palestinians must be based on "(1) The integrity of the entity of the Kingdom of Jordan, its interests, and its internal unity; (2) The constitution and rules of the state; and (3) The sovereignty of the state and consideration of its security and foreign and domestic policy."
- Jordan is the sole representative of the Palestinians, as most of its residents are Palestinian. Therefore, no "Palestinian bodies" other than the kingdom's Jordanian bodies are to be established. Jordan's interpretation of the phrase "Jordan is Filastin and Filastin is Jordan" was the opposite of Shuqayri's, as Jordan emphasized "Jordan" rather than "Filastin." The Palestinians of Jordan, accordingly, were "Jordanians of Palestinian descent,"—that is, the Palestinians of the West Bank were assimilated among Jordanian citizens, with no separate representation of their "Palestinianness" or the Palestinian entity.
- The Palestinian entity is first and foremost a diplomatic necessity. "The PLO was founded with the aim of advancing the Palestinian cause and organizing and mobilizing the Palestinian potential outside of Jordan."
- There is no place in Jordan for any military unit, no matter how small, that is not subordinate to the command of the Arab Jordanian Army and does not bear its emblem.[1]

These principles essentially speak for themselves. Their terms prohibited any PLO activity, especially given that most of the organization's personnel and activists in Jordan, especially in the West Bank, came from a political party or could be classified as such. If he wanted to undertake activities within the kingdom, Shuqayri had no alternative but to turn the PLO into an organization under Jordanian auspices.

A few weeks after the Cairo agreement between Jordan and the PLO was signed (on March 1, 1966), as the two were cooperatively preparing for elections to the Palestinian National Council, the Jordanian regime began to implement measures in the spirit of Wasfi al-Tal's memorandum of March 5. In early April, a series of detentions took place, which continued intermittently during May and June, in the course of which about three hundred opposition party activists and leaders were detained (from the Ba'th Party, Communist Party, and ANM), most of whom were from the West Bank. This measure was, in fact, a deliberate, preventative step against the core group of PLO activists and "popular organization" that Shuqayri had begun to establish, as well as their leaders. The detentions served a dual purpose: removing activist instigators, lest the "popular organization" turn into a nationalist source of incitement, and thwarting plans for "Filastin Day" demonstrations in the West Bank that were expected to take place on May 15, 1966, and mark the start of "Filastin Support Week" declared by the PLO. The authorities feared the eruption of riots, as had occurred on that day one year earlier, and, indeed, they successfully prevented the intended events of this week. The ongoing wave of detentions was also aimed at weakening Shuqayri's control over West Bank activities in advance of the Palestinian National Council's third conference.

It is instructive in this context to note the remarks of the Saudi consul in Jerusalem, in his report to the director general of Saudi Arabia's Foreign Ministry, on May 10, 1966:

> Tal's comments about destructive leftist parties were the starkest and harshest of any Arab prime minister, especially in recent years. This is a result of the power and threat potential that leftist parties held in the past, which prevented many from speaking about [these parties]. Despite the sensitive situation in Jordan, Tal's remarks clearly demonstrate his determination to strike a decisive blow against these parties and their supporters, and to prevent their continued activity. Tal was clear and upfront regarding all aspects of his government's stance towards leftist parties and their activities, especially in defining the concept of the left [by which he means] the Ba'th Party, the Arab Nationalists Movement, and the Communist Party.[2]

King Husayn's speech of June 14, 1966, in 'Ajloun marked a turning point for both sides. During this important speech, which, in fact, was an announcement that relations with the PLO were being terminated, King Husayn outlined Jordan's policy toward Shuqayri's activities among West Bank Palestinians. In addition, the king underscored the regime's grave view of PLO activity in the West Bank and the impact of this activity on the residents' political loyalty and the regime's stability.

The key points of Husayn's speech that relate to our discussion are the following:

- "The Palestinian problem is ... *a question of life or death, a question of survival or obliteration.*"(Emphasis added.)
- "Those who trade in the problem [of Filastin], the demagogues and saboteurs [who work] in the service of international communism have taken over the organization [PLO]. They have denied the right of the majority within their organization [Palestinian residents of Jordan] and they tried to grant themselves the status of custodians over us, over Filastin, and over the people of Filastin."
- "The unity of the two riverbanks is a unity that has received God's blessing, and the people support it. Any call for duplication or

partial division of this unity is a call not directed towards God [that is, it is impure]. Any effort by any organization that espouses the goal of liberation must integrate itself into our effort. *We will sever any hand raised with malicious intent against the unity of this country and cut out any eye that looks upon us with hatred.*"[3] (Emphasis added.)

The Emergence of Fatah

Undoubtedly, the emergence of Fatah in January 1965 was a new and significant factor in relations between the Jordanian regime and the Palestinian population in Jordan. The activities of Fatah and other fida'i organizations that emerged later (such as the Palestine Liberation Front [Jabhat al-Tahrir al-Filastiniyya]) gave rise to internal problems related to the Palestinian population and the extent of its sympathy and support for these organizations and to external problems related to the worsening situation along the border with Israel as a result of the activities of these organizations and Israel's retaliatory actions. Indeed, already by 1964, Jordanian intelligence was well aware of the recruitment of fida'iyyun, but the timing of Fatah's commencement of guerrilla activities came as a surprise.

In addressing Fatah activities, the regime faced a difficult dilemma, among other reasons because of the implications for Palestinian West Bank residents, especially the residents of frontline villages. On the one hand, Fatah actions were likely to worsen the situation along the Jordanian-Israeli border and provoke Israeli retaliatory action. This concern was the reason that many of the orders issued by the Arab Jordanian Army's General Command and the commander of the western front, as well as the orders of brigade and battalion commanders, held that Fatah actions along the border should be prevented and infiltrators should be arrested. On the other hand, in light of the strong sympathy Palestinians in Jordan had for Fatah actions, Jordan could not publicly express fierce opposition to these actions and could not appear to be derailing the struggle against Israel.

Accordingly, Jordan's handling of Fatah in 1965 was generally cautious. The authorities in Jordan did not devote special efforts to repressing Fatah, primarily to avoid opening another front in its struggle with Palestinians besides the front represented by its struggle with the PLO. During this year, Jordanian intelligence services developed an effective network for intelligence and information gathering, monitoring, and surveillance of the organizational activity of Fatah and other fida'i organizations in the West Bank, which had become a major source for recruiting, organizing, and mobilizing fida'iyyun for guerrilla action in Israel. The main participants in this organizational activity were the villages along the borderline, some of which served as bases for launching fida'i guerrilla strikes in Israel. In 1965, Fatah activities were concentrated, for the most part, on operations within Israel and efforts to recruit guerrilla fighters to the organization. In terms of Jordan's domestic security, these activities were less dangerous than PLO activities.

Nevertheless, the Jordanians did increase their internal security services' surveillance and monitoring of Fatah cells, especially in the regions of Qalqilya, Tulkarm, and Nablus, with the aim of learning about planned operations in advance. Orders were also issued to military and police units in the region of Nablus to increase reconnaissance missions and oversight taskforces. Thus, for example, the Jordanians were able to arrest the fida'iyyun who had carried out an operation in Kfar Hess, Israel, on February 28, 1965. On their way back through Jordan, they were arrested near Tulkarm, where they were imprisoned for two months. Later they were brought to trial before the governor of the Nablus district, who postponed their trial indefinitely.

It is significant that a broad cross section of the West Bank Palestinian population felt sympathy for Fatah. These included politicians and political activists, among them PLO activists who expressed their support for the organization not only in word but also in deed, thus further exacerbating the growing tension between the regime and the Palestinian population. Jordanian security authorities knew full well who were the politicians and influential actors from the West Bank with sympathy for Fatah and its activities. They included, among others, House of Representatives member Muhammad Hijja from the Hebron region, who even provided assistance to the organization's members, for example, by securing their release from arrest or detention. In this context, on August 4, 1965, the director of General Security Services, Radi 'Abdulla, informed the commander of the Hebron region, that "we know that House of Representatives member Muhammad Hijja is assisting the organization Fatah and infiltrators in reaching the occupied area. I am surprised that to date you have not informed us of the details of this man's activities, even though he is well known to you given that he is the representative from Hebron. You should undertake a clandestine investigation and provide us with the details."[4] The director of security's argument was valid: the activities of Hijja and others were almost certainly known in the region, but because of Hijja's status and influence, the regional commander and governor refrained from reporting on him (it should be noted that Hijja's activities were also known to the Israeli intelligence).

The involvement of Palestinian West Bank politicians in Fatah activities is also exemplified by the movement "Fatah Supporters." It was founded by political activists from the region of Jerusalem, Jericho, and Hebron, most of whom were influential and had close ties to the regime. An announcement regarding the movement's founding in Jerusalem and a transcript of its first statement appeared in the Lebanese newspaper *al-Hayat* in August 1965.[5] The Jordanian censorship authorities removed this notice from the newspaper's version in the kingdom.

In December 1965, Jordanian authorities seized a car that was loaded with weapons and registered to Jerusalem resident 'Umar al-Khatib, whose sister was married to the mayor of Jerusalem, Ruhi al-Khatib. The plan had been to transfer the weapons from Jerusalem to Hebron. More arms and money were found in 'Umar al-Khatib's home. In his interrogation, he identified Fatah in Kuwait as the source of the weapons. He also relayed what he knew about the Fatah Supporters movement and its members—Rasim al-Khalidi, 'Is-haq al-Dazdar, Yasir Abu al-Su'ud, Tawfiq Abu al-Su'ud, Subhi al-Tamimi, 'Abd al-Khaliq al-Kaylani, Fathi al-Kalouthi, and Fu'ad al-Kalouthi—all of whom were arrested and transferred to Amman. They admitted belonging to the movement, yet claimed that they had not engaged in acts against the Jordanian regime but, rather, against Israel. With the exception of the car's owner and Subhi al-Tamimi, they were later released.[6] The regime's treatment of these political activists accorded with its cautious policy toward influential individuals who supported Fatah.

The regime's policy regarding Fatah and its activities in the West Bank changed during 1966 and continued to change until the Six Day War broke out. This change, reflected in increased efforts on the part of security authorities to repress the organization's activities, was the result of two interrelated developments: increased Fatah activities both within Jordan itself and within Israel originating from Jordan, and the regime's harsher measures against the organization, especially near the border, as a consequence of Fatah's increased activities and Israel's acts of retaliation. Additional contributing factors included reports about Fatah members training in Syria in preparation for guerilla action against the regime in Jordan; US pressure on Jordan to increase preventive measures against the fida'iyyun and block their infiltration into Israel to prevent the situation along the border from worsening; and warnings and messages from Israel, conveyed to Husayn through the UN and the US, calling on Jordan to intensify efforts aimed at preventing Fatah members from infiltrating into Israel and to arrest them in Jordan.[7]

This shift in Jordan's policy resulted in widespread arrests of dozens of Fatah members in the West Bank who were being monitored by Jordanian security services, and of individuals suspected of belonging to the organization. During the course of these arrests, large quantities of weapons and explosives were discovered and seized. Simultaneously, harsh orders were issued—including directly by the king—instructing military commanders to prevent the fida'iyyun from crossing the borders.

In 1966, the reports of Jordanian security services regarding arrests of Fatah members and seizures of weapons and explosives increased. Between May 1 and

10, 1966, for example, there were reports of arrests of approximately thirty individuals suspected of belonging to Fatah and engaging in prohibited political party activities. On October 1, it was reported that the minister of the interior had decided to place thirty-nine Fatah members, mainly from the Irbid refugee camp and northern Shune, under house arrest, and to arrest twenty-six individuals suspected of infiltrating into Israel.

From early 1967 until the Six Day War, Jordanian security authorities continued monitoring Fatah activities in Jordan, especially after learning about the recruitment of new members into the organization from among West Bank residents, the dissemination of pamphlets, and the smuggling of funds into Jordan. They continued to arrest Fatah members, but for the most part did not put them on trial.

The regime's severe measures against PLO and Fatah activists prevented the domestic situation from deteriorating to the point of potential destabilization. These measures did not eliminate the threat of possible future destabilization, but they did at least slow down the process. Yet there was a catch: the Jordanian regime could not prevent the Palestinization of West Bank residents. Indeed, the measures it adopted actually accelerated this process, galvanized the Palestinian West Bank residents' sense of Palestinian identity, and weakened their political affinity with the Hashemite kingdom, to the point that their loyalty shifted to the representative Palestinian institutions that emerged—the PLO and fida'i organizations.

Notes

1. Tal memorandum, March 5, 1966, DJG; for details of the March 1, 1966, agreement, see Shemesh, *Arab Politics*, 82–85.
2. DJG.
3. Husayn, Amman Radio, June 14, 1966.
4. DJG.
5. *Al-Hayat*, August 5, 1965.
6. PLO Radio, December 29, 1965; see also *al-Ahram*, January 16, 1966; *al-Muharrir*, January 7, 1966.
7. Moshe Zak, *Husayn 'Ose Shalom* [Husayn makes peace] (Ramat Gan: Bar-Ilan University Press, 1996), 80–82.

14 The Crisis of November 1966

The Aftermath of the Israel Defense Forces Raid on Samuʿ

THE REACTIONS OF the Palestinian population in Jordan to the November 13, 1966, IDF raid on the village of Samuʿ indicated that the Palestinization of this population was intensifying. Some of the events that followed on the heels of the raid deserve attention, as they reflect the culmination of the Palestinization process and the failure of the Jordanization process among this population. Other contributing factors included inter-Arab discussions about reviving the Palestinian entity, Ahmad al-Shuqayri's activities in this context, the founding of the Palestine Liberation Organization (PLO), and in particular the emergence of Fatah and other fidaʾi organizations, as well as harsh confrontations between Shuqayri and the Jordanian regime over the activities of the PLO chairman in the West Bank. The unrest that erupted in the West Bank resembled the earlier unrest of April 1963 in form, but was more vehement and violent this time, lasting from November 15 to 29, 1966.[1]

The simultaneous outburst of demonstrations in several main localities and in refugee camps across the West Bank, in combination with credible intelligence that Jordan had acquired, indicates a certain degree of planning. Undoubtedly, in contrast to the April 1963, this time the demonstrations and disturbances were backed by members and activists of the West Bank's "national leadership," which included leaders of the long-standing opposition and members of the ANM and the Baʿth and Communist parties. The unrest was also fomented by activists and agents in Jordan who had been enlisted by Shuqayri in Jordan and participated in inciting the population when the opportunity arose. Members of the national leadership—especially those based in Nablus and Jerusalem—were fully coordinated in organizing protests against the regime and its policy toward Shuqayri, the PLO, and Fatah. As in April 1963, schoolchildren, refugees, and the rank and file were prominent among the demonstrators. There is truth in the claims of Jordan's leadership that the instigators were PLO and Communist activists with funding from sources outside of Jordan.

After the Samuʿ raid, the national leadership convened two meetings: the first on November 21 by leadership members in Nablus, and the second on November

22 by leadership members in Jerusalem. Each leadership published its own protest pamphlets following its meeting. The content of the Nablus pamphlet was broadcast that very night on PLO Radio. The content of the two pamphlets was identical and therefore reflected the stance of the national leadership of all West Bank residents. Among the signatories were members of the House of Representatives and Senate, members of the municipalities of Jerusalem and Nablus, and members of the Nablus Chamber of Commerce.

The two pamphlets called for a "popular conference to discuss the fateful problems of the homeland," to be organized by committees from Jordan's various districts. They also raised a number of demands, including the following: provision of arms to residents of the frontline villages and fortification of the frontlines in accordance with decisions of the military experts of the United Arab Command (UAC); mandatory conscription (including Palestinian residents of Jordan); cooperation with the other Arab states bordering Israel, including permission for Arab military units to enter Jordan and provide reinforcement to the Jordanian armed forces, as well as Jordan's accession to the mutual defense pact between Egypt and Syria; full cooperation with the PLO, enabling it to establish direct contact with the populace in Jordan and undertake action in Jordan in furtherance of its mission; no obstruction of Palestinian fida'iyyun; and no interference in the people's discussion of fateful issues.

The leadership's demands exhibit a high degree of nationalism, as manifested in support for PLO activities in Jordan and the former's demands of the latter, support for the position of the UAC regarding the entry of Arab forces into Jordan, and in particular support for Fatah activities in the kingdom and for Fatah operations from Jordan into Israel. The leadership's demands also implied that the opposition should be permitted to engage in political and party activities in the West Bank.

The most significant aspect of the pamphlets and their content was that they reflected the first occasion on which the entire West Bank, under an all-inclusive leadership comprising representatives of all public institutions and political parties in the West Bank, had successfully organized itself to coordinate the positions it presented to the Jordanian regime. This leadership identified almost entirely with Shuqayri's demands of Jordan and his efforts on behalf of the Palestinian entity, especially the organization of Fatah, which the leadership viewed as the manifestation of the forthcoming Palestinian national governance.

The positions of the national leadership of Palestinians in Jordan were a source of discomfort for the regime and even of surprise in terms of their intensity and extremism. The shock they caused the regime led King Husayn to seek an appropriate response that would reflect his sense of this moment as a turning point in relations between the Palestinians and the Hashemite regime.

The decisions of the national leadership in Nablus and Jerusalem (with which leaders of the other West Bank cities agreed) to convene a popular conference led to the establishment of preparatory committees for a popular convention scheduled for Jerusalem on December 5, when a "national covenant" of West Bank leaders would be announced. More than 150 representatives from West Bank and East Bank cities and villages were invited. On November 27, a meeting was held at the Nablus mayor's office, with the participation of dignitaries from Nablus and delegations from Jerusalem and Ramalla. At this meeting, the text of a covenant (concluding statement) was formulated, to be approved at the conference on December 5.

Jordanian security authorities, who had advance notice of the plans to convene a popular conference in Jerusalem, sought to block it at all costs. Some conference organizers were arrested, and documents relating to the conference in their possession were confiscated. In addition, the conference itself was prohibited from taking place. On December 5, Jordan's director of General Security Services issued the following statement to all police district commanders:

> After the authorities decided to prohibit the conference scheduled for December 5, 1966, there was [nevertheless] an intention to convene this conference and thereby defy the order. The preparatory committee [for the conference], which met on Friday [December 2, 1966] and considered every possibility, including that it would not be possible to convene the conference, prepared a draft statement that would serve as a covenant of sorts, to be disseminated after Monday, December 5, 1966. There is a general consensus to declare a strike on Monday, December 5, 1966, throughout the state, especially in Nablus. Al-Najah College decided to strike if the schools in Nablus are opened that day, suspending studies until the arrested teachers have been released. The other high schools intend to strike as an act of solidarity, and this would lead to officials going on strike. *I request that the necessary steps be taken to prevent these actions and [that you] strike with an iron fist against anyone who takes it upon himself to carry out these acts or participate in them.*[2] (Emphasis added.)

This order was also conveyed to lower ranks within the police. In the end, the conference did not take place, although a statement on behalf of the conference was issued.

On November 27, the pro-Egyptian Lebanese newspaper *al-Muharrir* published the key points of the covenant that was intended to be adopted at the December 5 conference. The statement was also broadcast on Cairo Radio that same day, on the basis of the *al-Muharrir* report. On December 2, the national leadership approved the covenant after it realized that it would not be possible to convene a conference, and its text was published in Jordan and beyond on December 5. On the same day, the covenant was also announced on PLO Radio, and on the following day, the text of the conference resolutions were published in the Cairo newspaper *al-Jumhuriyya*.

The following are the key points of the covenant, or "The Statement of the Popular Conference That Took Place in Jerusalem on Monday, December 5, 1966," as expected to be approved by the conference had it taken place, and as published in a pamphlet disseminated throughout the West Bank and broadcast via Arab media outlets:

1. This conference is being convened in light of the emergent popular anger ... that reflects the people's will, which holds this people is the source of (government) authority and has the right to determine the policy of its homeland. We call for cooperation with the states of the world on the basis of equality and mutual respect, in the spirit of the principles of positive neutrality and nonalignment and on the basis of the liberation of Filastin and the pan-Arab national (*qawmi*) interest.
2. The conference believes in the unity of the Arab people in Jordan in terms of struggle and fate.
3. [The conference] demands that the constitution and sovereignty of law be honored, that general liberties be permitted, that the dignity of citizens be protected, and that the use of state-of-emergency regulations restricting general liberties be abolished.
4. [The conference] believes that the Arab armed struggle, grounded in the policy of Arab liberation, is the only way to destroy the Zionist-imperialist foundation and reclaim the stolen homeland.
5. [The conference] demands that units of Arab armed forces be brought into Jordan, to reinforce the courageous Arab Jordanian Army, as a way of implementing the plans of the United Arab Command.
6. The conference supports the PLO *as the sole representative of the will of the Palestinian people*. [Emphasis added.] The conference demands that the government of Jordan permit the organization [PLO] to carry out its sacred pan-Arab national [*qawmiyya*] duties and grant it the necessary freedom to implement its military, financial, and organizational plans, including relations with the Palestinian people for the sake of recruitment, organization, and military preparation, on the basis of the national Palestinian covenant and [in accordance with] UAC resolutions.
7. The conference recognizes the importance of fida'i operations as part of the campaign for the liberation of Filastin, and therefore demands that all Arab states bordering the occupied region not obstruct the fida'iyyun.
8. [The conference] emphasizes the necessity of arming and fortifying the frontlines, in accordance with the plan formulated with the agreement of the Arab Jordanian Army command, the PLO, and the UAC.
9. The conference demands the release of detainees and arrestees.

The Cairo newspaper *al-Jumhuriyya*, which published the key points of the covenant on December 6, as noted, also listed its signatories, the members of the preparatory committee—presumably because the conference had not taken place and the text of the covenant published in the West Bank was unsigned.[3] According to the newspaper, the signatories included the following prominent members of the national leadership: Sulayman al-Nabulsi, Ahmad al-Farhan, Ja'far al-Shami, Najib Rsheidat, Hazim Nusayba, Bashir Bustami, Nadim al-Zaru, Musa Abu Ghosh, 'Izzat Qarman, Ibrahim Bakr, Falah al-Madi, Ruhi al-Khatib, Bahjat Abu Gharbiyya, 'Is-haq al-Dazdar, 'Ali al-Taziz, Fahmi al-'Abushi, Fa'iq Barakat, Yusif 'Abda, Husni al-Suqi, Hilmi Hanun, Husayn Sabri, Yasri Sha'ur, 'Isam 'Abd al-Hadi, Zlikha al-Shihabi, Hikmat al-Masri, Salah al-'Anabtawi, Qadri Tuqan, Ahmad Kan'an, Muhammad Tawfiq al-Yahya, 'Abd al-Khaliq Yaghmur, Sidqi al-Ja'bri, Yusif al-Takruri, Rashad al-Khatib, Hafiz 'Abd al-Nabi, Ramadan Hijja, and Isma'il Abu 'Alan.

Notably, among the signatories were prominent Transjordanian traditional opposition leaders from the 1950s, such as Sulayman al-Nabulsi and Najib Rsheidat, whose inclusion was intended to give the document a collective Jordanian character rather than only a West Bank Palestinian character.

For the most part, the list of Palestinians published by *al-Jumhuriyya* represented the salient political leaders in the West Bank during this period. The names on this list, alongside the signatories of the Jerusalem and Nablus pamphlets—members of the liaison committee of the Jerusalem leadership, most of whom participated in the conference's preparatory committee—represented the core nucleus of the national leadership that directed the riots in the West Bank after the raid on Samu'. These individuals also emerged as the prominent national leadership after the Six Day War.

The content of the conference's concluding statement represented the culmination of the Palestinization and radicalization processes that West Bank residents had been undergoing since the issue of reviving a Palestinian entity arose in the Arab and Palestinian arenas, and especially since the PLO was founded and Shuqayri became active in this area. Most of the points contained in the statement reiterated points that had been raised in the pamphlets of the Nablus and Jerusalem leaderships, and some were even more extreme, tending toward the Egyptian-PLO position and even that of Fatah. It is worth noting the demand for a policy of positive neutrality and nonalignment, that is, relations with the European Eastern Bloc. Recognition of the PLO as the "sole representative of the will of Palestinians," the call for freedom of action for Shuqayri in Jordan, recognition of "the importance of fida'i operations," and support for the "armed struggle" (advocated by Fatah)—all served as unprecedented, open incitement against the regime in Jordan, suggesting that the PLO was indeed the true representative of Palestinian aspirations in the kingdom. Also noteworthy are the demands of the national leadership in all aspects of democratization of the regime, such as equality of representation, political freedom of action, and recognition of "the people as the source of government" as an expression of full partnership in the Jordanian opposition movement. These points imply a demand for democratic representation of the Palestinians in electoral institutions and government, in proportion to their percentage in the population (that is, two-thirds). The demand that the Jordanian regime adopt the articles of the covenant would, in fact, have constituted the conversion of Jordan into the "state of Filastin," its alignment with the nationalist stance of the Egyptian camp (Egypt-Syria), and its transformation into an Egyptian puppet state.

On November 25, the Saudi consul in Jerusalem summarized the situation in the West Bank following the raid on Samu':

> West Bank residents will absolutely not accept the current situation, as long as they adhere to their well-defined and well-known demands: limited constitutional monarchy; free elections in accordance with the population census, on the basis of which a good [fully representative] House of Representatives will be established; the establishment of a parliamentary government based on the parliamentary majority, which will work for fair [standing] of Palestinians in the armed forces and various government positions; the formulation of clear Arab-Palestinian policy with the objective of and a plan for the liberation of Filastin; the adoption of a neutral stance with respect to the inter-Arab dispute; and, when necessary, standing alongside anyone working for the liberation of Filastin.[4]

The Saudi diplomat reached what he regarded as the "definitive" conclusion that "unless these demands are met, the satisfaction and stability that the West Bank needs will not be attained. In such circumstances the government will be in a difficult situation and constant state of alert, especially under current conditions, with the media outlets of Egypt, Syria, and the PLO intensifying their harsh attacks against Jordan, attacks that undoubtedly always find a sympathetic ear." According to the Saudi consul, "Jordan lives, if you will, under two identities—the Jordanian identity with its demands, and the Palestinian identity with its demands. As long as [the regime] prefers to operate under its Jordanian identity and sidelines the demands of its Palestinian identity, stability and calm will only be relative and temporary, and will be disrupted at every opportunity.[5]"

In addressing the stance of the "very moderate"—presumably the Palestinians close to government or holding government positions—the Saudi diplomat wrote, "They are not satisfied with Wasfi al-Tal's government, idiosyncrasies, and harsh treatment of West Bank residents, or with its lack of response to their measured advice that some demands should be met in order to calm the prevailing mood, and that provocative speeches and declarations against the public and harsh treatment should be avoided."[6]

For the Jordanian regime, the Samu' crisis was another recurrence of the struggle for survival, which it successfully endured once again without damage, although from the regime's perspective, the struggle did leave some undesirable impressions. It marked another confrontation between the Hashemite government and the Palestinian population of the West Bank, which, if not suppressed, could spread to the East Bank. The preexisting crisis of faith between the regime and the Palestinian population grew even more severe following the events of November 1966. Indeed, a rift formed between the regime and the moderate Palestinian leadership, which played a key part in the government.

The Palestinian writer 'Isa al-Shu'aybi proposed that the Samu' events be called a "Palestinian intifada." According to him, "The uprising after Samu' was characteristically part of the Palestinian identity revolution." Shu'aybi added that "by comparing the demands raised during the Samu' demonstrations, which were termed 'Palestinian demands,' with the demands that drove the demonstration in 1956 [after Qibya, presumably] and in 1963, it would appear that the 1966 intifada was the most prominent indicator of the increased Palestinian [internal awareness] to date."[7]

In summarizing the events in the West Bank after the raid on Samu', Samir Mutawi presents information from "a knowledgeable source who prefers to stay anonymous," according to whom "so intense was Palestinian feeling that leading figures on the West Bank decided to declare the creation of an independent Palestinian state on the West Bank. They believed that Egypt and Syria would not hesitate to recognize it and that in such circumstances the Jordanian government would find it difficult to resist such a movement. This was one of the reasons why Prime Minister Tal swiftly moved to dissolve Parliament and impose martial law." Mutawi adds, "[Hazim] Nussaibah describes how 'leaders of the West Bank were called to the Royal Palace where they were given a stiff reprimand' by the King and Tal for their alleged support of Shukairy [Shuqayri] and their threat to break away from Jordan." Mutawi concluded, "Thus, the Israeli attack on Samu created a deep rift between the Government and the Palestinians, including some of those in positions of influence."[8]

The most significant consequence of the Samu' raid was the shock to the Jordanian elite resulting from their understanding of the developments that West Bank Palestinians had undergone and the national awakening they were expressing. This shock led the Jordanian elite, especially King Husayn, to consider the need for change in the kingdom's ruling structure by granting a certain measure of "autonomy" to the West Bank.

In his book *Jordan and Filastin: An Arab Perspective*, Sa'id al-Tal addresses this issue:

> As a matter of truth and history, the foundations of this plan [of March 1972 for a united Arab kingdom] were laid in 1966 [after Samu']. At the time King Husayn agreed in theory to these foundations and principles, but the reservation of some others regarding this plan and the objection of still others delayed the translation of this plan into fact. Thus [its implementation] was postponed, until the June [Six Day] War broke out, which changed matters. . . .

Implementation of many organizational reforms that Jordan was on the verge of carrying out [at the time], naturally including the plan for a united Arab kingdom, was delayed.[9]

After the Six Day War, in November 1968, King Husayn was already considering ideas about granting autonomy to the West Bank. Interestingly, during the period under review, the oppositionist activities of the Palestinian population in Jordan did not translate into an irredentist Palestinian movement to overturn the regime in Jordan or to secure genuinely equal rights in this context.

Notes

1. For details of the IDF Samu' raid, see Shemesh, *Arab Politics*, 85–89; Moshe Shemesh, "The IDF Raid on Samu': The Turning Point in Jordan's Relations with Israel and the West Bank Palestinians," *Israel Studies* 7, no. 1 (2002).
2. DJG.
3. *Al-Jumhuriyya*, December 6, 1966.
4. DJG.
5. Ibid.
6. Ibid.
7. Shu'aybi, *Al-Kiyaniyya*, 125–26; see also Sakhnini, "Al-Kiyan al-Filastini," 62.
8. Samir Mutawi, *Jordan in the 1967 War* (Cambridge: Cambridge University Press, 1987), 81.
9. Sa'id al-Tal, *Al-Urdun wa Filastin: Wajhat Nazar 'Arabiyya* (Amman: Dar al-Liwa' le al-Sahafa wa al-Nashr, 1984), 128–30.

Part IV
Ahmad al-Shuqayri: Between the Arab Hammer and Palestinian Anvil, 1964–67

A Predictable Failure of Leadership and the Peak of a Leadership Crisis

15 Ahmad al-Shuqayri's Path to PLO Leadership

A Role Awaiting a Hero versus a Leader Imposed from Above

AHMAD AL-SHUQAYRI WAS born in Tibnin, Lebanon, in 1908. His father, As'ad al-Shuqayri, had been among the dignitaries of Filastin during the Ottoman and British Mandate eras. In 1916, Ahmad al-Shuqayri moved from Lebanon to the city of Acre, where he spent most of his youth. He attended Sahyoun High School in Jerusalem and graduated in 1926. In 1928, he entered the Faculty of Law in Jerusalem, and in 1933, he received a license to practice law. He moved to Cairo when World War II broke out but returned to Filastin in 1940. On the founding of the Arab League in 1945, he served as the representative of Shukri al-Quwatli, the president of Syria. During July through November 1945, Shuqayri was stationed in Washington, DC, on behalf of Musa al-'Alami, for the purpose of setting up an Arab public relations office. In late 1945, he returned to Filastin.

In 1950, Shuqayri joined the Syrian Foreign Ministry staff and was dispatched as Syria's representative to the United Nations (UN). In February 1951, he was appointed as deputy secretary general of the Arab League, while continuing to serve in the Syrian mission to the UN. The Syrian portion of his career came to an end in 1957, when he transferred to the post of Saudi Arabia's representative to the UN. He filled this post until August 1963, when he was dismissed for refusing to carry out the instructions of the Saudi government.

A new phase of Ahmad al-Shuqayri's political career commenced in September 1963, when, at Egypt's initiative and with its guidance, he was elected by the Arab League Council as the representative of Filastin to the Arab League after the death of the previous representative, Ahmad Hilmi 'Abd al-Baqi. During the first Arab Summit, which convened on January 16, 1964, in response to the call issued by President Nasir of Egypt, Shuqayri participated as the representative of Filastin.[1]

Ahmad al-Shuqayri's political activism on behalf of the Palestinian cause in both the Arab and international arenas drew special attention to him as a skilled representative of the cause in international forums and an expert on its details and history. All these achievements, alongside the Egyptian view of Shuqayri as the most qualified representative of Palestinians, essentially made him the natural choice as Filastin's delegate to the Arab League.

On the basis of his service as deputy secretary general of the Arab League and his longtime posting to the UN, Shuqayri developed a reputation as an experienced statesman and faithful representative of Arab and especially Palestinian interests. Given these qualifications, Shuqayri's integration into developments in the Arab world surrounding the idea of reviving the Palestinian entity was a natural and speedy process.[2]

The fortieth session of the Arab League Council (in September 1963) was a milestone in the course of events leading to Shuqayri's positioning as the head of the Palestinian institution that would soon be established with Egypt's support. On September 19, 1963, the Arab League Council approved the recommendations of the Political Committee regarding the Palestinian entity, including proposals "to appoint Shuqayri as the representative of Filastin to the Arab League Council" and "to task Shuqayri with the assembly of a Filastin mission, under his leadership, to the UN General Assembly."

The head of the Jordanian delegation to the Arab League Council objected to Shuqayri's appointment and requested that the following reservation be recorded in the minutes of the meeting: "My government does not agree with this recommendation." The Saudi representative also voiced reservation regarding this appointment and requested that the minutes indicate that "he does not agree with the principle on which the resolution was based," that is, he objected to the appointment of Shuqayri the person, but not to the need for the appointment of a Filastin representative to the Arab League.[3]

The resolution adopted by the Arab League had a significant bearing on Shuqayri's status in a number of aspects: Arab states recognized Shuqayri as the official representative of the Palestinian people and of the Palestinian cause in the Arab and international arenas, thereby fulfilling Shuqayri's long-standing aspiration of playing a leadership role in the furtherance of this cause. In addition, Shuqayri received Egyptian backing for his new position, thus providing one of the most solid foundations possible to buttress his standing in the Palestinian arena.[4]

The next step in Ahmad al-Shuqayri's path to PLO leadership was a resolution of the first Arab Summit, which convened on January 16, 1964, at the initiative of Egypt's president. The first Arab Summit resolved that "Ahmad al-Shuqayri, Filastin's delegate to the Arab League, will continue meeting with member states [of the Arab League] and the Palestinian people, with the aim of organizing the Palestinian people so that it can fulfill its role in the liberation of its homeland and its self-determination."[5] According to Shuqayri's memoirs, this resolution, which paved the way for him to found the PLO, was also "a struggle in and of itself" because King Husayn had insisted that the resolution not mention the words "Palestinian entity" and that the mention of "its self-determination" (*taqrir masirihi*) appear only after "liberation of its homeland," as he feared that some would insist on self-determination "at the present time." Shuqayri explains, "I eventually agreed to this weak formulation because I wanted to embark on the path . . . and so that the Palestinian entity would be prominent as an existing fact." He added that, as the Filastin delegate, he was afraid of leaving the summit with no mention whatsoever of the Palestinian entity.[6]

Shuqayri admits in his memoirs that he made use of "the advantages of a white lie . . . which became a national duty . . . [in order] to extort Husayn's agreement regarding a Palestinian entity," by hinting that all the kings and presidents had agreed to the proposal. He added that later, "I met with the kings and presidents and explained the issue of a Palestinian entity to them, informing them that King Husayn had agreed to a Palestinian entity and that none of them would wish to oppose him on something that should be viewed as an 'internal' matter of the Jordanian kingdom."[7]

Shuqayri's anecdotes might seem trivial, but under the circumstances in which he was operating, they served as an indication of his status and of the somewhat scornful attitude toward his leadership, an attitude that created many hardships for him in the course of convening the Jerusalem Congress and founding the PLO. These anecdotes also reflect Shuqayri's near-total dependence on the positions of Arab states generally and Egypt specifically. At the same time, Shuqayri did have the advantage not only of Egypt's support but also of the absence of any rival among Palestinian political activists who might compete with his standing and efforts on the Palestinian issue. In this sense, Shuqayri was irreplaceable. Nasir trusted him, and King Husayn believed he could manage to deal with him. Undoubtedly, Shuqayri's obsessive aspiration to succeed in his role, in order to improve the negative image ascribed to him, also worked to his advantage.

Shuqayri's leadership and maneuverability skills within the Arab and Palestinian arenas were also manifested in the way he actualized the idea of reviving the Palestinian entity at the 1964 Jerusalem Congress—in particular his success in persuading King Husayn not only to agree to his plan and actions but even to participate as the senior-ranking, dominant figure in its discussions and resolutions. Indeed, the Jerusalem Congress and the announcement at this congress of the founding of the PLO were the most impressive and perhaps greatest achievements of his political career. He succeeded in creating a Palestinian institution out of nothing while demonstrating a remarkable ability to overcome the obstacles placed before him in the Palestinian and Arab arenas.

The first gathering of the Palestinian National Council (PNC)—or as Shuqayri called it the "Jerusalem Congress"—took place at the Inter-Continental Hotel in

East Jerusalem on May 28 through June 2, 1964, with the participation of King Husayn and the secretary general of the Arab League. King Husayn delivered the opening address, and Shuqayri spoke next. The king contributed significantly to the success of the congress. Shuqayri's speech was programmatic in focus, explaining the significance of the Palestinian entity, its essence and components, as he saw them. In addition to expanding on the significance of the entity, Shuqayri sought to reassure King Husayn regarding the intentions of the Palestinian entity with respect to Jordan.[8]

At the second session of the PNC, on the afternoon of May 28, 1964, Shuqayri was elected chairman of the Jerusalem Congress as well as chairman of its Executive Committee. The congress also approved the text of the Palestinian National Charter and the founding document of the PLO. The most important outcome of the Jerusalem Congress was, undoubtedly, Shuqayri's May 28, 1964, announcement regarding the founding of the Palestine Liberation Organization (Munazamat al-Tahrir al-Filastiniyya)—the PLO.[9]

From Political Activist to Palestinian Leader

Shuqayri's transition from the status of a political activist in the service of one or another Arab state to a leadership position, especially the mission with which he was tasked by the first Arab Summit, constituted the fulfillment of his life's dream. He accepted this mission with great satisfaction, worked tirelessly to fulfill it, and succeeded beyond his own expectations.

Several salient factors affected the manner in which Shuqayri led the PLO, reinforced his own leadership status, shaped his political perspective, informed his relations with Arab states, and determined the composition of the Jerusalem Congress and the PLO Executive Committee.

The first factor was that Shuqayri had not actually been elected as the Filastin representative to the Arab League and as the PLO founder by Palestinian bodies or the Palestinian public. In fact, he was imposed on the Palestinians by Arab states, primarily Egypt.

The second factor was the deep trauma that afflicted Shuqayri as a consequence of the fact—as he depicted it—that the PLO "was born in the bed of the Arab Summit" and was bound by the conditions of the Arab arena. In his memoirs he voices regret: "I am sorry for what was my biggest mistake in 40 years of public service, that is, that the four years during which I went along with kings and presidents culminated in the Six Day War." He also admitted that, in convening the Jerusalem Congress, he invested most of his efforts "in securing the support of as many Palestinians and Arab governments as possible."[10]

Another key factor was Shuqayri's dependence on Nasir, to whom he was umbilically tied. He sought the Egyptian president's approval before he took any significant step, such as the plan for a Palestinian entity, the Palestinian National Charter, and the policy toward Jordan. Shuqayri later admitted that after the first Arab Summit—in order to implement its resolutions regarding the Palestinian entity—he met with Nasir to receive his blessing for the task ahead.[11]

Shuqayri greatly valued Egypt's support for himself and for the PLO, especially Egypt's help in fortifying his status and leadership position. In fact, there was no better alternative. Nasir's support and Shuqayri's alignment with his policies helped Shuqayri overcome the obstacles he encountered in the course of founding the PLO and helped him remain a leader until the Six Day War. These factors also assisted him in his struggle with Jordan. In addition, Nasir's support was important for Shuqayri's leadership status and image in the eyes of Palestinians, which was why Shuqayri highlighted and underscored the support he received from Nasir for himself personally and for his plans.

Moreover, Shuqayri was practically operating in a vacuum in the Palestinian arena: there were no popular Palestinian organizations or institutions on which the PLO could base itself. Shuqayri had neither a defined Palestinian territory nor a defined Palestinian population—except perhaps for the Gaza Strip—two essential components in the creation of an independent Palestinian political entity. Organizations such as Fatah or the Palestine Liberation Front operated in the underground at the time, and their political perspective conflicted with that of Shuqayri and Egypt. The only organization that supported him, albeit with some reservations, was the Arab Nationalists Movement, which at the time viewed itself as more pan-Arab than Palestinian and as aligned with Nasir's policy.

Another key factor affecting Shuqayri's leadership was his relations with Jordan. His activities on behalf of the Jerusalem Congress, his efforts to consolidate a public basis of support for the PLO, and his attempts to establish a popular organization all required Shuqayri to operate amid the Palestinian population of Jordan, especially in the West Bank. Accordingly, he had to carefully weigh the measures he took with respect to the Jordanian regime to secure King Husayn's support.

At a personal level, Shuqayri was strongly motivated to succeed in his position and thereby improve the negative image that had attached to him before his appointment as Filastin's representative to the Arab League. Yet he was unable to shed the attributes that had generated his negative image, even after he convened the Jerusalem Congress and founded the PLO. As noted, even then he was willing to resort to any means available to succeed, promote the standing of the PLO, and maintain his own status as its leader, including the use of "the white lie, which became a national duty."[12] In the inter-Arab dynamics of 1964, Shuqayri was the best-suited man for the job, but his personal characteristics and leadership style were not points in his favor.

Unquestionably, Shuqayri demonstrated remarkable organizational skills in successfully convening a national congress with the participation of more than

490 representatives from the entire Palestinian diaspora at a time when the Arab and Palestinian political arenas were in a difficult, complicated situation. Particularly noteworthy was his extraordinary success in enlisting King Husayn and even placing him center stage in the congress. Shuqayri thereby achieved a level of popularity that was unprecedented for him, although, as we shall see, it was not sustainable in the long term.

In planning the Jerusalem Congress and its composition, Shuqayri opted for a system of appointments. No Arab state would have permitted elections to a Palestinian institution in its own country, except possibly Egypt in the Gaza Strip (along the lines of elections to "national union" institutions as conducted in the past). This system of appointments was also convenient for Jordan because it granted King Husayn veto rights, which served his interest in ensuring that he would have influence over the congress. And the system of appointments was also convenient for Shuqayri, as it allowed him to supervise and control the composition of Palestinian institutions and thus guarantee maximal support for himself.

To reinforce his new leadership position, Shuqayri devoted a great deal of energy to the representative status of the institutions of the Palestinian entity he was establishing. In the final report on the first PNC, Shuqayri described its members' occupations:

> Senators, members of the House of Representative, ministers, former senators and House of Representatives members, mayors and heads of village councils in the Hashemite Kingdom of Jordan, clergymen, attorneys, physicians, pharmacists, engineers, university lecturers, student union representatives, members of the legislative council in Gaza, Chamber of Commerce leaders, merchants, members of the diaspora, representatives of women's unions, [representatives of] returnees ['a'idun] who live in tents, shaykhs from Be'er Sheva tribes, trade unions and representatives of labor unions and associations, farmers, heads of institutions and companies, bank directors and officers, and others.[13]

A close examination of the composition of the PNC reveals that Jordan was promised 65 percent of all council delegates. The geographic majority of Jordan as presented by Shuqayri did not accord with reality. Shuqayri tried several maneuvers to minimize as much as possible the impression of a large Jordanian majority and to soften severe criticism against himself in this context. The total number of representatives from Jordan reached nearly 255 and included the following individuals with the following occupations and positions: 25 members of city councils in the West Bank, 39 members of the Senate and House of Representatives, 16 former members of the Jordanian House of Representatives, 6 clergymen (two of them Christian), and media and municipality representatives. Nearly 100 PNC members from Jordan (that is, some 25 percent of the total) served at the time or had served in the past in official positions within the Jordanian government. Thus,

PNC membership overlapped with the Jordanian establishment, with Jordan's representatives promoting the Jordanian interest over the Palestinian interest or, in the best-case scenario, having dual loyalty. Undoubtedly, this composition was very convenient for King Husayn.

The 46 PNC delegates from the Gaza Strip included at least 26 Gaza government officials.[14] The Egyptians and Shuqayri were thereby able to ensure that most Gazan delegates would not deviate from Egyptian policy or from Egypt's support for Shuqayri. The Lebanese delegation was expected to have 22 delegates, but in fact 4 of these did not appear. The delegation comprised 3 representatives of the Palestine Liberation Front (Jabhat al-Tahrir al-Filastiniyya), 2 representatives of the Palestine Liberation Movement (Harakat Tahrir Filastin), 1 representative of the Arab Youth (al-Shabab al-'Arabi), and supporters of the mufti.[15] These delegates naturally had leanings toward the Syrian Ba'th position, and they presented the Jerusalem Congress with Syria's plans for the establishment of a Palestinian entity. Additional attendees of the PNC gathering, who participated as private individuals, included Fatah representatives on the Kuwaiti and Qatari delegations as well as ANM representatives on the Jordanian and Lebanese delegations.

In light of the criticism voiced within Palestinian circles regarding the pro-Jordanian composition of the PNC and Shuqayri's clear leanings toward Jordan, he established an Executive Committee that was "balanced" in membership with a tendency toward "independence," although it was still largely supportive of him. Shuqayri's efforts to include Fatah representatives in the Executive Committee failed. In addition, well-known figures from academia and the world of finance rejected his offer to join the Executive Committee. Yet he did succeed in enlisting representatives from the ANM. On August 9, Shuqayri announced the names of the fourteen members of the Executive Committee, under his chairmanship. Seven were from Jordan: Bahjat Abu Gharbiyya, 'Abd al-Khaliq Yaghmur, 'Abd al-Rahman al-Saksak, 'Abd al-Majid Shuman, Falah al-Madi, Qasim al-Rimawi, and Walid al-Qamhawi; four were from Gaza: Hamid Abu Sitta, Haydar 'Abd al-Shafi, Faruq al-Husayni, and Qusay 'Abadla; one was from Syria: Khalid al-Fahum; and one was from Lebanon: Niqola al-Dur. Shuqayri added a fifteenth delegate, Commander of the Palestinian Liberation Army (PLA) Wajih al-Madani, to the Executive Committee after the second Arab Summit approved the establishment of the PLA.

The new Executive Committee included seven known supporters of Shuqayri (thus ensuring he had a majority) and four or five who were known as independents, of whom two were ANM members and one was from Syria. Seven of the Executive Committee members had advanced academic degrees.

The Jerusalem Congress constituted a success for Shuqayri, thanks to his ability to establish a common interest between himself and King Husayn and thanks to Nasir's support. The congress thus achieved the objective of its three directors: the president of Egypt, the king of Jordan, and the new chairman of the Executive Committee of the Palestine Liberation Organization.

The successful course and outcome of the congress was due in no small part to the stance adopted by King Husayn, to his support for the congress, and to his presence at the opening session. These, in turn, resulted from the shift in his position regarding the establishment of a Palestinian entity, which amounted to a reversal of what had been his stance since the idea was first raised in March 1959. Husayn now believed that he had the ability and means to turn the PLO into an organization representing the interests of the Jordanian regime. He was swayed by Nasir and Shuqayri's promises that the Palestinian entity would not undermine the "unity of the kingdom" and its sovereignty over the two riverbanks, and he also believed that he would be able to handle a personality such as Shuqayri.

Egypt took measures to secure support for Shuqayri on the part of prominent political activists in the West Bank. Egypt viewed the activists' support as essential for the success of the PNC and the founding of the PLO and therefore advised them to support Shuqayri. For their part, these political activists attributed great importance to Nasir's views and backed them. In February 1964, two of Nablus's leading figures, Hikmat al-Masri and Walid al-Shak'a, and two pro-Egyptian Jordanian statesmen, 'Akif al-Fa'iz and Sulayman al-Nabulsi, traveled to Beirut to meet with the Egyptian ambassador based there, with the aim of discussing Shuqayri's plan and affirming Egypt's stance on the matter. Hikmat al-Masri and Qadri Tuqan traveled to Cairo in March 1964 for the same purpose. The Egyptian press, which had returned to Jordan after the first Arab Summit and the improvement in Egyptian-Jordanian relations, helped spread the Egyptian position among the Palestinian population of the West Bank, which then joined in the effort to promote Shuqayri's plans.[16]

The Ba'th Party strongly criticized Shuqayri, his plan, and the "nonpopulist" and "nondemocratic" manner in which the PNC was composed and the PLO was established. The Ba'th argued that "the PLO is a product of the reconciliation among Arab heads of state" and that its establishment was intended "to placate Cairo and Amman and suppress the demands of the Palestinian people to establish a revolutionary entity." The Ba'th position was expressed in a series of articles published in the party newspaper, al-Ba'th, in February and March 1964 and in the "Statement of the Pan-Arab National Leadership [al-Qiyada al-Qawmiyya] regarding the Palestinian Entity" of March 5, 1964.[17]

Palestinian Responses

Compared with the euphoria surrounding the Jerusalem Congress and Nasir's support for Shuqayri, the responses of Palestinian organizations were relatively restrained. There was even a certain measure of criticism regarding the composition of the conference and manner by which its attendees were appointed, and in particular the dominant influence of Jordan. These organizations, which operated underground at the time, did not yet pose any threat to Shuqayri's leadership. They only started to pose a threat in 1965, when their activities became openly visible and acknowledged by the Palestinian public.

The Jerusalem Congress presented a dilemma for Fatah. On the one hand, the composition of the congress, Shuqayri's goal for the congress, and its particular Arab state (specifically Jordanian) sponsorship necessitated its boycott. On the other hand, there were reasons that obligated attendance, such as the need not to be absent from Palestinian political life and the even more essential need to insert itself into a powerful and well-funded organization to take advantage of its resources. In the end, Fatah cast its lot in favor of participating in the congress, with the aim of "giving the PLO a powerful jump-start, a position that provoked hostility and strong criticism of Fatah." Seven Fatah delegates attended the Jerusalem Congress: Yasir Arafat, Khalid al-Hasan, Hani al-Qadumi (delegate from Kuwait), Rafiq al-Natsha, Kamal 'Udwan (delegate from Qatar), Khalil al-Wazir (delegate from Libya), and Zuhayr al-'Alami (delegate from Lebanon). They took advantage of the congress to overcome their anonymity and promote the concept of "armed struggle" and the fact of Fatah's existence. At the same time, they refrained from providing precise details about their organization to foster the impression that it was larger than it actually was. Khalid al-Hasan (Abu al-Sa'id) took an active part in the subcommittee discussions on a PNC covenant, which reviewed the drafts of a Palestinian National Charter and a constitution that Shuqayri submitted for approval by the congress. Khalil al-Wazir (Abu Jihad) served as a member of the Political Committee, and Kamal 'Udwan, Hani al-Qadumi, and Zuhayr al-'Alami served on the Committee for Popular Organization. At the time, Fatah refrained from taking part in PLO institutions, and two of its founders—Khalid al-Hasan and Hani-al-Qadumi—even rejected Shuqayri's invitation to participate in the PLO Executive Committee.[18]

The ANM had welcomed the resolutions of the first Arab Summit regarding the founding of a Palestinian entity, although it also posed a number of demands regarding their elements and content in line with its own ideological approach. In addition, it supported Shuqayri's efforts to found the PLO and participated in staffing its institutions, such as the Jerusalem Congress and the Executive Committee that Shuqayri established after the congress.

In later summarizing the June 1964 PNC and its lessons learned, the ANM criticized the Arab Summit resolutions on the issue of a Palestinian entity, saying that the summit had "not generally defined the manner in which the entity would be established, thereby widely opening the door to reactionary and opportunistic forces to take advantage [of the situation] as they saw fit." The ANM found that "the appointment of Shuqayri was in this sense the starting point, which was simultaneously accompanied by concerns and hopes." Alongside its critiques, the ANM expressed its belief that it would be possible to "urge the entity and the Palestinian organization to serve as the starting point for serious action aimed at organizing the Palestinian people and preparing it for a campaign of revenge and return."[19]

The ANM essentially viewed the founding of the PLO as a platform to expand its own activities among Palestinians and the newly established Palestinian establishment. Although Shuqayri rejected its demands, it called on its members to participate in activities to promote the PLO's founding, as it had an interest in infusing revolutionary elements into the leadership. Accordingly, it instructed its members in Jordan to "take action, alongside Shuqayri, against elements hostile to the entity, such as the Arab Higher Hay'a [al-Hay'a al-'Arabiyya al-'Ulya, headed by the mufti]." Activities on behalf of Shuqayri's efforts were particularly evident among educated ANM supporters, including students, physicians, and pharmacists. ANM leaders in the West Bank with medical training, such as Walid al-Qamhawi and Salah al-'Anabtawi, cooperated with political activists such as Hikmat al-Masri and Walid al-Shak'a in promoting PLO interests.

ANM delegates participated actively in the discussions of the Jerusalem Congress (first PNC) and in its subcommittees, and they managed to achieve a certain degree of success when they joined forces with representatives of Fatah and the Syrian Ba'th Party. During 1964–65, ANM delegates participated in administering PLO institutions, including its first Executive Committee, where Walid al-Qamhawi represented the movement. One may safely assert that for the ANM the inclusion of its representatives in PLO institutions was a source of both "hope and concern."

An important question that arises in every discussion of Shuqayri's leadership is the extent to which the Palestinian public in general and that of the West Bank in particular recognized his leadership. Not surprisingly, the Palestinian population on the whole supported Shuqayri's efforts to revive the Palestinian entity, especially when these efforts drew the support not only of the leader of the Arab world at the time, Nasir, but also of King Husayn, who ruled over the greatest concentration of Palestinians. Their support earned Shuqayri credit as a leader in the eyes of Palestinians, at least during the years 1964 and 1965, when he was at the height of his popularity.

The resolutions of the first Arab Summit regarding a Palestinian entity, Shuqayri's activities in its aftermath, the convening of the first PNC, and the resolution of the second Arab Summit approving the establishment of the PLO and PLA—all combined to inspire a great deal of enthusiasm among Palestinians. The founding of the PLO, as a concept, represented the answer to their hopes, particularly among refugee camp residents and the youngsters among them. The military aspect of a Palestinian entity, especially the notion of enlisting in a future Palestinian army, appealed to and inspired young Palestinians. Shuqayri was enthusiastically received in all the Palestinian-populated places he visited, and his negative image of the past was ignored. This dynamic was especially evident in the West Bank, across all sectors. According to reports of intelligence officers and district commanders in the West Bank, during 1964, the peak year of his activity, support for Shuqayri reached 80–90 percent among the local Palestinian population.

The Palestinians viewed the establishment of the PLO's representative institutions as the start of their journey toward self-determination. Their enthusiasm was compounded by the fact that Nasir, Husayn, and Shuqayri were cooperating in this context. This spared West Bank political activists any dual-loyalty dilemma and encouraged them to express support for Shuqayri openly at gatherings and meetings on behalf of the Palestinian entity and the PLO. Consequently, a broad, nearly all-inclusive vanguard of support emerged for Shuqayri and his activities throughout 1964 and in 1965—until the harsh dispute between him and Jordan erupted. The mufti supporters, Ba'th activists, and the Islamic Liberation Party operated against Shuqayri.

Because Shuqayri coordinated his efforts with Jordan's senior ruling officials and acted with their acquiescence, he was able to conduct his activities in the West Bank during 1964 through 1965 with almost no government intervention, although the latter did watch him closely. Various district commanders were even instructed to provide full assistance to Shuqayri.

In February 1964, Shuqayri visited the West Bank cities of Nablus, Jenin, Qalqilya, and Tulkarm. He was accompanied by the most prominent dignitaries of Nablus, including Hikmat al-Masri, Walid al-Shak'a, Da'ud Ghazala, Qadri Tuqan, Walid al-Qamhawi, and Salah al-'Anabtawi. Hikmat al-Masri and Walid Salah even traveled to Amman to meet Shuqayri on the day he arrived in Jordan. District and regional commanders and intelligence officers in the West Bank continuously reported to their superiors (in the general intelligence service) on Shuqayri's activities during his tour of the area. Among other matters, they reported on the meetings he held, the participants at these meetings, popular assemblies convened on his behalf, and the speeches he delivered during these assemblies.[20]

A few points are worth noting regarding Shuqayri's February 1964 tour of the West Bank, the authorities' treatment of him, and the reactions of West Bank Palestinians to him and to his remarks. First, Shuqayri was well aware that his remarks would reach the ears of government officials who viewed his tour as a test of his intentions. Therefore, he adhered to a tactic that he had developed jointly with Nasir, as an approach to Husayn: he heaped praise on the king and especially on the king's agreement to the founding of a Palestinian entity, among other reasons, to calm the concerns of his listeners regarding the regime's stance on this point. At the same time, he also heaped praise on Nasir. In addition, while emphasizing that there was no difference between a Jordanian and a Palestinian or between an Eastern Jordanian and a Western Jordanian, Shuqayri refrained from underscoring the most important condition for Husayn, that is, that he (Shuqayri) had no intention of severing the West Bank from the Hashemite kingdom.

Second, the Jordanian regime assigned the mayor of Jerusalem to monitor Shuqayri and accompany him throughout his visit to Jordan. Additionally, subdistrict and regional commanders reported on the visit comprehensively and immediately. Their reports accorded with government expectations. Consequently, not only was the visit not disrupted, it even received the support of the authorities. In his memoirs Shuqayri wrote that at the end of his tour, "I felt, when I entered Amman, that I was entering as conquerors enter, but without arrogance or superiority."[21]

Third, Shuqayri outdid himself in seeking to create a positive self-image in the eyes of Palestinians. He did so by presenting his past struggles and pointing to the shift in the conduct of his activities since being appointed the Filastin delegate to the Arab League and participating in the Summit alongside Arab monarchs and presidents. The emphasis he placed in his remarks on supporting Nasir was intended, among other things, to reinforce his status and image. His emphasis on the military aspect of the Palestinian entity and his negative attitude toward an all-Filastin government were his response to the Supreme Arab Hay'a and its claim of representing the Palestinian people.

Fourth, Shuqayri's tour, his speeches, and the celebrations surrounding his visit generated a remarkable degree of enthusiasm among Palestinian West Bank residents. That enthusiasm was shared by Palestinians everywhere and compounded by enthusiasm over Shuqayri's own efforts and inter-Arab efforts to revive the Palestinian entity. The fact that Nasir was a fervent supporter of the Palestinian entity and of Shuqayri made it easier for Palestinian West Bank residents to express their emotions and excitement openly—including calling for weapons to be given to them—without fearing the authorities. Shuqayri's report to the second Arab Summit and his memoirs reflected—albeit exaggeratedly—this enthusiasm on the part of West Bank Palestinians.

Notes

1. For more biographic details on Shuqayri, see the entry "Ahmad al-Shuqayri" in *Al-Mawsu'a al-Filastiniyya*, pt. II, vol. 3 (Beirut: al-Hay'a al-Mawsu'a al-Filastiniyya, 1990), 802–14. See also Shuqayri's memoirs: *Arba'un 'Amman fi al-Hayat al-'Arabiyya wa al-Duwaliyya* (Beirut: Dar Al-Nahar, 1969); *Hiwar wa Asrar ma'a al-Muluk wa al-Ru'asa'* (Beirut: Dar

al-'Awda, 1970); *Min al-Qimma 'Ila al-Hazima, Ma'a al-Muluk wa al-Ru'asa'* (Beirut: Dar al-'Awda, 1971; hereinafter *Min al-Qimma*); *'Ala Tariq al-Hazima, Ma'a al-Muluk wa al-Ru'asa'* (Beirut: Dar al-'Awda, 1972; hereinafter *'Ala Tariq*); *Al-Hazima al-Kubra Ma'a al-Muluk wa al-Ru'asa'*, vols. 1 and 2 (Beirut: Dar al-'Awda, 1973; hereinafter *Al-Hazima*). See also Arie Bo'az, "Biografia Politit shel Ahmad al-Shuqayri" [Political biography of Ahmad al-Shuqayri] (MA thesis, Tel Aviv University, March 1987).

2. Bo'az, "Political Biography," 28.

3. Ahmad al-Shuqayri, *Al-Kiyan al-Filastini*, internal report submitted to the second Arab Summit, September 1964 (hereinafter Shuqayri's Report), 10, 11, 13–14, 17.

4. Shuqayri, *Min al-Qimma*, 9–10; *al-Usbu' al-'Arabi*, August 30, 1963.

5. Shuqayri, *Min al-Qimma*, 50; *al-Ahram*, January 18, 1964.

6. Shuqayri, *Min al-Qimma*, 50.

7. Ibid., 34–44.

8. *Filastin*, May 29, 1964; PLO, *Al-Mu'tamar al-Filastini al-'Awwal*, Cairo, May 28–June 2, 1964, official brochure of the first congress (aka Jerusalem Congress; hereinafter PLO, *The First Congress*), June 3, 1964, 23–34.

9. PLO, *The First Congress*.

10. Shuqayri, *Min al-Qimma*, 20–23, 76–77; Shuqayri, *'Ala Tariq*, 3, 10, 74–77; Shuqayri, as quoted in Josef Abu Khatir, *Liqa'at Ma'a Jamal 'Abd al-Nasir* (Beirut: Dar al-Nahar, 1971), 143.

11. Shuqayri, *Min al-Qimma*, 63, 272; Shuqayri's Report, 12; *al-Ahram*, October 9, 1963.

12. Shuqayri, *Min al-Qimma*, 183.

13. PLO, *The First Congress*.

14. Shuqayri's Report.

15. *Al-Difa'*, May 6, 1964; *Kul Shay'*, May 30, 1964; Shuqari's Report.

16. DJG, documents, January–February 1964.

17. "Al-Kiyan al-Filastini Bayna al-Fikr wa al-Tatbiq" (series of articles), *al-Ba'th*, February 26, 27, March 14, 1964; 'Abd al-Wahab al-Kayali, *Al-Qadiyya al-Filastiniyya, 'Ara' wa Mawaqif, 1944–1967* (Beirut, 1973), 21–27; Declaration by the Ba'th National Command on the Palestinian Entity, in the series Al-Ba'th wa Qadiyyat Filastin, 1959–1964 (Beirut, 1974), 156–60.

18. Abu Iyad, *Filastini*, 77–79; Fatah, *Al-Milad wa al-Masira* (n.p., n.d.), 32–33; Fatah, *Mafahim Asasiyya*, 2; *al-Thawra* (magazine of the Fatah organization in Lebanon, for members only) October 21, 1976; Hurani, *Al-Fikr al-Siyasi*, 33; Kamal 'Udwan, *Muhadara* (brochure for members only), in the first course for cadres, August 16, 1972.

19. DJG, "'Adwa' 'Ala al-Mu'tamar al-Qawmi al-Filastini," *al-Wahda*, June 1964.

20. DJG, Reports of the West Bank Sub-District Commanders, documents for 1964; Shuqayri, *Min al-Qimma*, 65–70; Shuqayri's Report, 5.

21. Shuqayri, *Min al-Qimma*, 64.

16 The Struggle over Leadership of the PLO

Emergence of Fatah and Decline in Shuqayri's Status, 1965–66

The Decline of Shuqayri's Status

The year 1964 marked Shuqayri's glory days. His popularity reached its peak during this period. As euphoria in the Palestinian arena subsequently subsided, signs of an internal division began to surface within the Palestinian establishment regarding Shuqayri's approach. A struggle between Shuqayri and the opposition for leadership of the PLO began to take shape in 1965 and to challenge the manner in which the organization was being managed. The second Palestinian National Council (PNC), convened from May 31 to June 4, 1965, was the first serious test for Shuqayri as leader of the PLO.

Over time, Shuqayri's strengths, which contributed to his rise and helped him succeed in convening the Jerusalem Congress and founding the PLO, had a boomerang effect and contributed directly to his decline, ultimately resulting in his resignation from the PLO chairmanship.

The convening of the Jerusalem Congress and the founding of the PLO created great expectations among Palestinians, who hoped that the Palestinian entity would be revived and their own standing in the Arab-Israeli conflict recognized. These expectations, alongside concerns about continuing to follow Shuqayri's approach, are reflected in an article by Shafiq al-Hut, the PLO's representative in Beirut and editor of the pro-Egyptian Lebanese weekly, *al-Hawadith*. Two weeks after the Jerusalem Congress, he wrote an article under the heading "A Balance of Profits and Losses," closely examining Shuqayri's achievement, on the one hand, as well as concerns that Shuqayri would lead the PLO to failure and thus hurt the cause of the Palestinian people, on the other hand. Shafiq al-Hut knew Shuqayri well and therefore was able to pinpoint the aspects "that could cause losses to the PLO and the Palestinian people in general," but being a member of the Palestinian establishment, he chose his words cautiously. The bulk of Hut's article highlighted the profitability of the Jerusalem Congress as reinforced by Shuqayri's achievements.[1]

Shafiq al-Hut was very familiar with the Palestinian map. His observations reflected the expectations of nationalist intellectuals and activists who supported Shuqayri and his efforts to revive the Palestinian entity and establish the PLO. But the higher the expectations were, the greater the disappointment with Shuqayri would be in the near future. Hut's initial concerns were indeed validated in 1965, and in time he became one of Shuqayri's harshest critics. As a member of the Palestinian leadership, he contributed to Shuqayri's departure from the Palestinian political stage.

Shuqayri's leadership during the years 1965–67 was characterized by two principal phases:

- *Early 1965 through late 1966*: Shuqayri's one-man rule reached its peak, and he struggled to maintain his leadership in face of the strong opposition that took shape within the PLO, especially after the emergence of Fatah. Shuqayri's crisis of leadership was manifested in his conduct and efforts to justify his course of action—that of dependence on Arab states and adherence to Egyptian policy.
- *January 1967 through December 1967*: Shuqayri's crisis of leadership became more severe. He continued to struggle for survival but also made every possible mistake. Ultimately, the outcome of the Six Day War and the rise of fida'i organizations determined his political fate and led to his resignation. As a final act in his political career, however, he did succeed in forcing the Arab Summit in Khartoum to accept the three famous "no's": no recognition of Israel, no negotiations, and no peace with Israel.

Shuqayri did not understand that the manner by which he had succeeded in convening the Jerusalem Congress and founding the PLO in 1964 was not conducive to his continued leadership of the organization. He did not take into account or give attention to the changes that took place in the Palestinian arena after the founding of the PLO and the emergence of Fatah and other Palestinian organizations, which saw themselves as leaders of the new Palestinian national movement. In the eyes of many Palestinians, Shuqayri quickly came to symbolize a generation of Palestinian leaders whose time had passed. His successful accomplishments of 1964 did not bolster his position in this intergenerational struggle. Various events and developments led to a decline in his standing during the years 1965–67 and ultimately resulted in the most severe leadership crisis since the PLO was founded.

Concentration of Powers alongside Flawed Decisions

Shuqayri concentrated all forms of operational authority in his own hands. He acted not only as a prime minister and foreign minister but also as a state president who concentrated all operational powers in his own hands. In justifying his dictatorial style of management of the PLO, Shuqayri claimed that he was "thereby fulfilling the operational responsibilities in accordance with revolutionary custom" and that "the imposition of a dictatorship over the Palestinian people" was not just the "only way" available to him but also was "acceptable to the Arab and Palestinian masses alike."[2]

One of Shuqayri's salient characteristics was his desire to rule alone. He fought to maintain the exclusive authority to appoint Executive Committee members, and even to determine the number of members. Indeed, the second PNC approved his claim to these two prerogatives. Shuqayri also concentrated many other forms of authority in his own hands, and he made decisions and issued instructions on major and minor issues alike without consulting the PLO Executive Committee. He appointed Jordanians as Executive Committee members and PLO department heads without consultation. In addition, Shuqayri dismissed his opponents in the Executive Committee and PLO establishment and appointed supporters at his own convenience. He unilaterally announced the creation of new bodies within the organization as he saw fit and later declared their dissolution. The impression that emerges is that Shuqayri enjoyed his status and was blinded by the powers he had and by the position he held alongside heads of Arab states.

Shuqayri justified the concentration of powers in his hands as well as his personal decisions and style of management: "I take action on all matters relating to my operational responsibilities that cannot be delayed. I receive world press and television delegations and I speak with them about the Palestinian cause without turning to the Executive Committee. Every prime minister or foreign minister works this way, and so do I. In this manner I am fulfilling my operational responsibilities."[3]

This context is the one in which to understand the appointment of second-tier, untalented political activists to various positions in PLO institutions, which in turn made the management of these institutions extremely chaotic and dysfunctional. Shuqayri himself occupied the key positions in the Palestinian apparatus: chairman of the Executive Committee, chairman of the PNC, Filastin delegate to the Arab League, and at times head of the PLO Military Committee. He would often appear in military uniform. He also headed the delegations representing the PLO at various Arab conferences, including meetings with first- and second-ranked Arab statesmen. As early as December 30, 1964, Samir 'Abd al-Rahim, a PNC delegate from Lebanon, published an open letter in a Lebanese newspaper to the head of the PLO criticizing Shuqayri for the two positions he had taken as chairman of the PLO Executive Committee and chairman of the PNC. Shuqayri was also criticized in a memorandum he received from Nafid 'Abd al-Majid al-Hurani, a PNC delegate from Syria. At the time Hurani belonged to a Syrian-founded organization named the Revolutionary Front for the Liberation of Palestine (al-Jabha al-Thawriyya li-Tahrir Filastin). In his memorandum, which was not published at the time, Hurani complained about the prevalent atmosphere at the Jerusalem Congress, where PNC delegates "were forced to close their eyes . . . for the sake of the congress's success and the birth of the entity." The memorandum also criticized Shuqayri and in particular "his rule of one and his system of appointments based on indebtedness and his deviation from the articles of the [Palestinian National] Charter."[4]

One example of Shuqayri's unsuccessful personal decisions was the appointment on June 20, 1965, of two Jordanians to key positions in the PLO: Najib Rsheidat, secretary general of Jordan's Bar Association, as a member of the PLO Executive Committee; and 'Ali al-Hiyari (a native of Salt), as head of the PLO Military Department.[5] Shuqayri explained the appointment of Rsheidat as follows: "Jordan is the homeland of the PLO, and the people of Jordan are the people of the PLO." He added, "The government and the PLO in Jordan constitute two independent mechanisms. While the government operates at the official level, the PLO operates at the popular level. In Israel, the government and the Jewish Agency operate alongside one another, with no contradiction or clash."[6]

Shuqayri took this unprecedented step without the approval of the Executive Committee or any consultation with its members. He was harshly criticized for this action by Palestinian activists, including Executive Committee members as well as the Jordanian leadership.[7] As a consequence, Rsheidat was forced to resign from his position on the Executive Committee. After discussing this matter, on July 7, 1965, the Executive Committee accepted his resignation. Hiyari also submitted his resignation (on July 6, 1965).[8]

While the episode of Jordanian appointments was still ongoing, Shuqayri also received severe criticism from Executive Committee members and Palestinian journalists at a press conference he convened on July 3, 1965, a day before the first meeting of the new Executive Committee in Jerusalem. During the press conference, Shuqayri issued a statement with ten principles on which PLO policy and activity would be based.[9] Ghassan Kanafani reported that although the new Executive Committee had been expected to meet on July 3, Shuqayri requested it be postponed to July 4. Notification of the postponed meeting reached Executive Committee members at the same time that they learned about Shuqayri's press conference in Amman. The content of his announcement came to them as a surprise, and "some of the principles outlined by Shuqayri were not acceptable to Executive Committee members, and in their opinions conflicted with articles of the [Palestinian National] Charter."[10]

A consistent theme throughout Shuqayri's memoirs is his effort to address the criticism leveled against him for his management style in the PLO and his failings in the Palestinian and Arab arena. Toward this end, he describes the challenges, difficulties, and suffering that he endured in order to stand the PLO on its feet, secure better conditions for Palestinians, and improve their status in the Arab world. As part of his apologia, Shuqayri confesses the sin of following after Arab leaders, but argues that he had no alternative.

Fatah Joins the Struggle over Leadership—A Dilemma for Shuqayri

In setting his policy toward Fatah and its actions, Shuqayri faced a dilemma: on the one hand, Fatah's actions did not accord with Egypt's strategy at the time regarding the Arab-Israeli conflict; moreover, Egypt had doubts regarding the group and those behind it. On the other hand, as the leader of a Palestinian organization that was expected to represent the will of the Palestinian people, Shuqayri found it hard to oppose a Palestinian group that emerged on the ground at the initiative of Palestinians, a group that was conducting an "armed struggle" using Palestinian tools for the sake of "liberating Filastin."

This dilemma intensified as it became increasingly clear that the Palestinian public in general supported Fatah activities, and as in 1965–66, sympathy for the group increased among PNC members as well. Yet even then, Shuqayri opted to adhere to Egyptian policy on this matter, preferring the position he enjoyed as a consequence of supporting Nasir and his policy over appropriate representation of the PLO and his own personal popularity. Thus, on the issue of Fatah and fida'i activities, Shuqayri led the PLO as if implementing Egyptian policy, in contrast to the dominant mood at the time among Palestinians and especially the Palestinian intelligentsia, which was sympathetic to Fatah. When, in mid-1966, he changed his position regarding Fatah in favor of fida'i actions, it was already too late to earn their sympathy. By then they were fully supportive of fida'i organizations, foremost among them Fatah.

On January 2, 1965, only two days after Fatah's first action, the PLO office in Beirut denied any link between the PLO and Fatah actions in Israel. It issued a statement saying that "the PLO office in Lebanon denies having anything to do with the announcement published in the name of the 'General Command of the al-'Asifa Forces.'" The statement added that "some of the 'Command' forces began certain operations in occupied Filastin" and that "at this time the office of the Palestinian organization stresses that any military Palestinian operation against Israel comes under the authority of the Palestinian Liberation Army, which is the sole entity responsible for military recruitment among the Palestinian people for the liberation of occupied Filastin."[11]

During the course of 1965, as Shuqayri started to become aware of the importance of taking a positive stance regarding Fatah and its guerrilla operations, he formed a more detailed and cautious outlook, with the aim of taking into account Palestinian public opinion toward the organization. His stated position toward Fatah up to mid-1966 was therefore characterized by the following themes: *praise for Fatah*: "This is an organization with noble and honorable goals" (and similar statements); *adherence to the position of Egypt, while highlighting the limitations of Fatah and the risks of its approach*: "Fatah operations will drag the Arabs into a war at the wrong time for them" or "The limited operations of individuals, as carried out by Fatah, do not benefit the Palestinian cause" or "Residents of frontline villages will need protection" as a consequence of Fatah operations; and *support for the PLO*: "the only framework capable of operating at the revolutionary Palestinian level."[12] (Emphases added.)

Shuqayri's arguments were supported by the Arab Nationalists Movement, which also aided him in establishing the PLO. Being a movement aligned with Nasir's policy, its spokesmen also disapproved of the timing of Fatah operations. Shafiq al-Hut expresses this sentiment effectively: "At the time we did not identify with Fatah's outlook and did not agree with it about launching an armed struggle. We feared becoming embroiled in a war at the wrong time, and Nasir, who did not want a war at the time, provided a compass and litmus test for us."[13]

In response to such statements by Shuqayri and the Arab Nationalists, Fatah launched a public relations campaign to explain its political perspective and enhance its popularity among Palestinians. Its leaders held intensive talks with members of the first PNC and again on the eve of and during the second PNC. Because its declarations and political outlook resonated well within the PNC and among Palestinians, Fatah also issued many military announcements in which it reported on operations against Israel during this period.

The statement Fatah conveyed to the second PNC (May 1965), which it disseminated widely, included the following points:

- Criticism of the PLO and Shuqayri as its head, arguing that "armed struggle is the only way to regain the occupied homeland" and is "a strategy, not a tactic"
- Objection to "the principle of democracy as one of the characteristics of PLO activity"
- Criticism of the PLO for "trying to work within the limits of the possible": The PLO "takes but does not give"
- Criticism of the composition of the PLO Executive Committee "which did not present any achievements during the sensitive phase that our cause underwent in the past year, because of individuals within the Executive Committee itself" and because of the inter-Arab atmosphere in which it operates[14]

Fatah's statement represented the start of an aggressive public relations campaign launched by its leadership with the aim of placing the organization on the

Palestinian political map and portraying it as the main and leading Palestinian organization. The statement was intended to serve as an entry permit into the Palestinian arena, after Fatah leaders were encouraged by the positive reactions of the Palestinian public to their military operations. The PNC was the main venue for this public relations campaign, which was also the reason that Fatah's statement presented an antithesis to Shuqayri the individual, to his views, and to his management of the PLO. Although in its statement Fatah did not entirely dismiss the PLO, it did seek to introduce changes in its composition that would transform it into an armed, war-fighting fida'i organization, as opposed to a political entity as Shuqayri perceived it. Fatah was already calling for independence in Palestinian decision making. Fatah's statement reflects the remarkable determination of its leadership, already at that time, to take control of and guide the Palestinian national movement and the Palestinian establishment.

To assuage Fatah's criticism of his leadership and management of the PLO, Shuqayri had no choice but to establish direct contact with the movement's leaders. Shuqayri and Fatah's leaders were already acquainted from the Jerusalem Congress, where a few of Fatah's founders had participated. In late February 1965, a PLO delegation visiting Kuwait met with Fatah leaders in an effort to persuade them to suspend operations in Israel until PLO training of fida'iyyun was completed and to have Fatah members join the PLO. Fatah's leaders rejected their request. On March 8, 1965, Shuqayri met with the heads of Fatah in the Gaza Strip, Muhammad al-Ifranji and his deputies Abu Mu'in al-Qishawi and Musa al-Qudwa. Ifranji told Shuqayri that the authorities had confiscated Fatah weapons in the strip and that the movement intended to undertake operations in Israel from Gaza. Shuqayri promised that on his return from China, he would discuss the matter with Nasir.

Shuqayri sought to persuade Fatah leaders to suspend their guerrilla actions and to join forces with the PLO's political and military institutions. Fatah rejected this request, insisted on maintaining its militaristic character, and asserted that it would continue operating under the name of al-'Asifa. At the same time, it expressed a willingness to cooperate with the PLO in planning and executing fida'i operations by dividing and assigning missions between itself and the PLO and by including fida'iyyun from Fatah in PLO cells.[15] Fatah leaders already viewed themselves as an alternative to the PLO in the event of the latter's failure. Simultaneously, and despite its harsh criticism of Shuqayri's leadership, Fatah did ascribe importance to this official and familiar framework and to acting within this framework. Fatah did not at the time dismiss the notion of the PLO's existence, but did dispute its objectives, its composition, and its leader.

In June 1965, Shuqayri renewed his efforts to establish a close working relationship with Fatah, in the hopes of addressing and tempering criticism leveled against him because of his position on Fatah. In meetings with the movement's leaders, he reiterated his willingness to integrate many of its personnel in the PLO's political and military framework, on the condition that Fatah suspend its activities. Fatah, for its part, posed a number of conditions: continuing to operate under the name "al-'Asifa" (the storm); forming a joint Fatah-PLO independent military "government" for the planning of guerrilla activities; maintaining secrecy regarding the identity of al-'Asifa members; and maintaining links between the PLO and Fatah at the management level. The divergent positions of the two sides prevented these talks from bearing fruit.

In his memoirs, Abu Iyad (Salah Khalaf) describes the first meeting between several Fatah leaders and Shuqayri in Cairo (he does not name the date but presumably it was 1964), at which they tried to persuade him to cooperate with them:

> I tried to explain to him [Shuqayri] why we think that an organization established "from the top down" would be ineffective unless it has the support of an effective foundation. I proposed clandestine coordination between his visible activities and our clandestine activities, so that the PLO would serve as a Jewish Agency of sorts, presenting the legitimate side of the armed struggle carried out by our members. The relations between us and the PLO would be maintained through a few of our activists, whom Shuqayri could appoint to the PLO Executive Committee. Shuqayri, who knew nothing about Fatah at the time, listened with attention and interest. He asked for time to think. He later responded negatively, claiming that his role and relations with Arab regimes and his obligation not to undermine the [Arab] League's strategy—which was centered on preventing Israel from diverting the waters of the Jordan River—prevented him from forging such an alliance with us.[16]

On September 7, 1965, despite the constraints imposed on it by Arab states or perhaps, indeed, because of them, Fatah took the unprecedented step of sending a memorandum to the third Arab Summit. The memorandum presented Arab presidents and monarchs with an overview of the principles underpinning its strategy and the starting point for its activities.[17]

Fatah's public relations activities in the Arab arena continued. On March 12, 1966, in advance of a March 14 Arab prime ministers' meeting in Cairo, Fatah dispatched a memorandum in which it reiterated the principles of its operational strategy as presented in previous memoranda to inter-Arab meetings.

The shift in Egypt's stance in favor of fida'i operations led to a shift in Shuqayri's approach as well, in mid-1966. Shuqayri revised his position not only at the declaratory level but also at the practical level, albeit within the constraints of the Egyptian position. However, it was too late by then: Fatah had continued to garner sympathy and support among Palestinians and throughout the Arab world, whereas Shuqayri's standing steadily declined.

Shuqayri's efforts to establish a broad base of popular support—and thereby justify his claim that the PLO represents all Palestinians—failed. The fate of the

"Popular Palestinian Organization" was similar to that of the Palestinian National Union in Gaza during 1959 to 1961. Shuqayri's perspective of the essence of the Popular Palestinian Organization and the manner by which it should be established remained on paper, a dead letter. All the Palestinian organizations and associations, including student unions, remained outside the PLO.

The Consolidation of an Opposition to Shuqayri

Shuqayri's conduct, his style of leadership and management of the PLO, his failings, and the rise of Fatah in the Palestinian arena resulted in the consolidation of a strong opposition to Shuqayri within his own organization. This opposition included representatives of the ANM, who were actually its guiding spirit, as well as representatives of the Ba'th Party, Fatah, and other Palestinian organizations that had since emerged. By the time the second PNC was due to convene (May 31 to June 4, 1965), the opposition had already become very active. Its activities increased in reaction to steps taken by Shuqayri with the aim of removing oppositionist elements from key positions in the PLO.

The Political Bureau of Palestinian Revolutionary Forces (al-Maktab al-Siyasi li-al-Quwat al-Thawriyya al-Filastiniyya) disseminated a memorandum at the second PNC in which it reiterated the demand to transform the PLO into "the revolutionary front of the fida'iyyun." The bureau included representatives of the following organizations: the Arab Palestinian Liberation Front (Jabhat al-Tahrir al-'Arabiyya al-Filastiniyya), the Revolutionary Front for the Liberation of Palestine (al-Jabha al-Thawriyya li-Tahrir Filastin), the Front for Sacrificial Operation (Jabhat al-'Amal al-Fida'i), the Popular Front for the Liberation of Palestine (Jabhat al-Tahrir al-Sha'biyya al-Filastiniyya), the Palestine Liberation Front (Jabhat al-Tahrir al-Filastiniyya), the Palestinian National Liberation Front (Jabhat al-Tahrir al-Watani al-Filastiniyya), the National Front for Liberation (al-Jabha al-Wataniyya lil-Tahrir), and the Union of Palestinian Fida'iyyun (Itihad al-Fida'iyyun al-Filastiniyyun).[18]

An oppositionist "revolutionary wing" influenced by Fatah and its activities emerged within the second PNC. This group called for "adopting armed struggle as the path to the liberation of Filastin" and "collective leadership" of the PLO. It referred to Shuqayri's appointment of Jordanians to key PLO positions as the Jordanization of the organization and claimed that "the policy of the [Arab] Summit [regarding Jordan] is likely to result in the organization's loss of independence and the weakening of the Palestinian entity." Shuqayri was accused of implementing a one-man rule and of failing to establish a popular organization within the PLO. The oppositionist revolutionary wing grew stronger in the months preceding the Six Day War. It then accused Shuqayri of "working less on the cause of liberation and more on a bloated managerial apparatus, frequent trips by him and PLO officials, and multitudes of speeches." Leaders of the revolutionary wing included Bahjat Abu Gharbiyya, Walid al-Qamhawi, 'Is-haq al-Dazdar, 'Abd al-Khaliq Yaghmur, Burhan al-Dajani, Walid al-Khalidi, and Haydar 'Abd al-Shafi.[19]

One expression of the opposition to Shuqayri and the prevailing bitterness toward him and his management style was the wave of resignations that took place throughout the Palestinian establishment during the second PNC and especially in its aftermath—when Shuqayri emerged stronger. Even before the second PNC convened, Walid al-Qamhawi (an active ANM member) had submitted his resignation from the Executive Committee, but his oppositionist colleagues persuaded him to rescind it so that they could all resign en masse as a group. The group surmised that Qamhawi's resignation would give Shuqayri an opportunity to dismiss the rest of them and replace them with his own followers. Likewise, 'Abd al-Majid Shuman, chairman of the Palestinian National Fund, submitted his resignation to the second PNC, complaining that Shuqayri was not following the fund's regulations when withdrawing funds. Shuman too rescinded his resignation in response to pressure from PNC members.

In advance of the second PNC and in order to maintain calm, Shuqayri promised the leaders of the revolutionary wing—'Is-haq al-Dazdar and Burhan al-Dajani—that the PLO leadership and Executive Committee would work collectively, that the number of Executive Committee members would remain fourteen, and that he would work to ensure PNC elections within a year. His failure to fulfill these promises contributed to increased opposition activity against him.

Activists of the revolutionary wing followed two major currents: those who demanded that Shuqayri be replaced, and those who demanded that the Executive Committee be elected directly by the PNC, thereby lessening Shuqayri's power. In addition to revolutionary wing activists, a large number of PNC members discussed the possibility of Shuqayri's removal and even suggested candidates, such as Burhan al-Dajani, to replace him. In contrast, the ANM refrained from working for Shuqayri's removal because of their ties to Nasir, but they too aspired to change his management style in the PLO. All were of the opinion that it was necessary to change the PLO perspective, making it "revolutionary" and having it adopt the "revolutionary course of action." Under their influence, the second PNC eventually reached an unwritten decision to ask Shuqayri to hold talks with Palestinian organizations, the clandestine ones as well as those operating openly, with a view to uniting Palestinian activity.

In response to these developments, after the second PNC concluded and he was re-elected chairman of the PLO, Shuqayri began to remove opposition representatives from the organization, and in particular from the Executive Committee. On June 20, 1965, he assembled the second Executive Committee, in which he did not include ANM representatives. Moreover, he transferred ANM representatives from key positions to secondary posts within the PLO. Consequently the

ANM decided in August 1965 to have its members resign from PLO institutions and to launch an aggressive public relations campaign against Shuqayri.

The wave of resignations following the second PNC included, among others, Mundhir al-'Anabtawi, director of the Palestinian National Fund (and an ANM member), after Shuqayri decided to transfer him to the position of head of the PLO office in Indonesia; Sami Sha'ban, head of the PLO office in Khartoum; Basil 'Aql (an ANM member), PLO representative in Cairo, after it was decided to transfer him to India because he disagreed with Shuqayri's approach; and Rif'at 'Ude, head of the PLO office in Algeria.[20]

According to an ANM statement issued on September 1, 1965, "In our opinion, it is now essential to open the eyes of the Palestinian people in light of the obstacles facing the PLO." In attacking the PLO policy, the ANM claimed that "armed struggle is the only way to liberate Filastin, yet the organization in its present state is not a revolutionary tool capable of engaging in armed struggle. The lack of collective leadership is among the causes of the PLO's weakness; the experience of an entire year with the person most responsible for the organization proves that it is very far from being revolutionary."[21]

Not to be outdone, Shuqayri went on the counteroffensive. He claimed that the difference of opinion between himself and the ANM stemmed from their demand that four of their members be appointed to the PLO Executive Committee "in a clear and obvious attempt to take over the organization and subject it to the authority [of the movement]." He noted that he had "taken all measures to thwart this effort, so that the PLO would not be bound to a single Palestinian group. This sparked the ire of this movement and then [its members] submitted their resignations, as publicized." According to him, he offered Mundhir al-'Anabtawi a monthly salary of 500 Egyptian pounds to serve as head of the PLO office in Indonesia, and 400 Egyptian pounds to Basil 'Aql for the post in India, but both declined the offers. Cynically and disingenuously, Shuqayri added, "What more do you want me to do for them?"[22]

The Arab Nationalists did not take this situation lying down. In early September 1965 (with the support of the revolutionary wing, including Ba'th and Communist party members), they sent a memorandum to the PLO management and many PNC members in which they accused the organization's managers (namely, Shuqayri) of committing fundamental transgressions that could not be overlooked because they "threaten the existence of the organization."[23]

The second Palestinian National Council met in Cairo between May 31 and June 4, 1965. Its composition did not differ significantly from that of the first PNC (Jerusalem Congress). Nearly 450 members were present. Shuqayri was well aware of the harsh criticism against him, including from Fatah, in the Palestinian arena, and of announcements in the Arab media regarding potential candidates to replace him. Therefore, he took a number of steps to reinforce his popularity and forestall questions about his standing during the second PNC.[24] He made sure that Nasir would be present during the opening session of the PNC, and he skillfully and fully exploited Nasir's presence and speech, which conveyed full support for Shuqayri.

Indeed, during the opening session of the PNC, Nasir praised Shuqayri, adding, "Possibly there is room to criticize the PLO, but what the PLO must do first of all is to prove the capability of the Palestinian people to take responsibility for overcoming events and challenges." He called on PNC members to "consolidate the forces of the Palestinian people." Nasir dismissed the importance of minorities, party politics, blocs, and struggles within the PLO. In his opinion, "this is natural. It is the nature of people, when they are [together] that they struggle and clash, and everyone criticizes and demands the ideal, but all I ask of you is not to despair." In summarizing his remarks about the PLO, Nasir said, "The attack on the PLO is agenda-oriented. Even if I am critical of your deeds, I will not address them. We too have problems, and it is doubtful that all issues are soluble."[25]

PNC members fully understood Nasir's message, which was intended to neutralize the opposition and thereby support Shuqayri's reelection as chairman of the PLO, this time with greater stability than before. Thus Nasir was also indirectly rejecting the approach of Fatah. Undoubtedly, Nasir's speech softened the sting of criticism leveled against Shuqayri and helped him survive the second PNC unscathed. It is no wonder, therefore, that Shuqayri included the entire text of Nasir's speech in a pamphlet disseminated by the PLO summarizing the discussions and resolutions of the second PNC.[26]

Speaking after Nasir, Shuqayri adopted a similar stance, while also ignoring the criticism leveled against him. Unsurprisingly, he emphasized Nasir's support for the PLO and contribution to its founding and to the revival of the Palestinian entity.[27]

Another maneuver Shuqayri employed was resignation. During the first PNC meeting, he submitted his resignation from the position of PLO chairman.[28] Discussion of his resignation was postponed until after the debate over items on the agenda.[29] Ultimately, the PNC decided to accept Shuqayri's resignation but renewed his appointment as chairman of the PLO Executive Committee and granted him the authority to assemble it once again, including the right to choose the number and identity of its members. After his reelection, Shuqayri gave a speech expressing gratitude for the trust placed in him. It was an impressive accomplishment for him: not only was he reelected, but his authority to determine the number and identity of Executive Committee members was affirmed as well. He could now claim that he had been chosen by the PNC and was working under its authority.[30]

On June 20, 1965, Shuqayri announced the appointment of six members to the PLO Executive Committee as well as the chairman of the Palestinian National

Fund's board of directors. On June 23, Shuqayri announced the appointment of three additional Executive Committee members from the Gaza Strip. With these appointments, as with the previous Executive Committee, Shuqayri placed an emphasis on geographic representation. On July 4, the Executive Committee held its first session, in which it delegated responsibilities as follows: Ahmad al-Shuqayri, chairman; Ahmad al-Sururi from Nablus, vice-chairman and head of the Political Department of Arab Affairs; Sayyid Bakr from Gaza, head of the Department of Elections and General Affairs; Ibrahim Abu Sitta from Gaza, head of the Department of Popular Organization; Jamal al-Surani from Gaza, secretary of the Executive Committee and overseer of the Palestinian National Fund; Da'ud al-Husayni from Jerusalem, head of the Political Department of Foreign Affairs; Fa'iz al-Sayigh from Beirut, head of the Department of Public Relations and National Guidance; Sa'id al-'Azzi from Cairo, the department of Popular Organization; Najib Rsheidat from Jordan, for Public Relations and Elections; 'Abd al-Hamid Yasin from Jerusalem, head of delegation to the Arab League and head of the PLO office in Cairo; and 'Abd al-Majid Shuman from Amman, head of the board of directors of the Palestinian National Fund. In his capacity as PLA commander, Wajih al-Madani was added to the Executive Committee. Shuqayri also announced the appointment of 'Ali al-Hiyari, who had served as commander of the Arab Jordanian Army, as head of the Military Department of the PLO.[31]

The new Executive Committee did not include anyone from the previous Executive Committee, especially not oppositionists such as Bahjat Abu Gharbiyya or Walid al-Qamhawi. An announcement issued by the Executive Committee following its meeting of July 7, 1965, stated that it "approved the principle of collective leadership in planning and individual responsibility in execution." The announcement came on the heels of a promise Shuqayri had made to opposition members during PNC meetings—that the PLO and the Executive Committee would be subject to collective leadership.[32] This remained the composition of the Executive Committee until the third PNC was convened, in May 1966, with the exception of Najib Rsheidat, who resigned on July 7, 1965, and Sayyid Bakr, who resigned in mid-November 1965.[33]

Despite the large-scale opposition within the PNC and despite his personal failings, Shuqayri managed to retain his position. It was evident that his status was declining, and consequently the PLO as founded and shaped by Shuqayri no longer represented the Palestinians in actual fact. Yet a number of factors contributed to Shuqayri's survival, foremost among them the lack of an alternative. Jordan, which had enjoyed a majority in the first and second PNC, still viewed Shuqayri as the least of all possible evils. Opposition to Shuqayri was neither strong nor widespread enough to defeat him; nor could the opposition agree on a replacement candidate. Shuqayri's opponents understood that anyone they chose must receive Nasir's approval, yet in his speech before the PNC, Nasir had left no room for doubt that he supported Shuqayri. As there was no alternative to Shuqayri, his resignation ploy at the opening of the PNC remained just that—a ploy. Shuqayri's objective in this maneuver was to prove to his critics that no one could replace him and, thus, to secure complete and renewed trust in himself, including the authority to appoint an Executive Committee as he pleased. Once he achieved this objective, he could claim that he had been chosen by the Palestinian people rather than the Arab Summit. In practical terms, Shuqayri received a year's extension in his current position, until the third PNC. His reelection and the resurrection of his self-confidence also allowed him to ignore the promises he had made to his detractors—that he would shift to a collective style of management in governing the PLO and appointing Executive Committee members—and even to remove oppositionists from key positions in the PLO.

Shuqayri as a "Revolutionary"

Shuqayri approached the third PNC, held in Gaza from May 20 to 24, 1966, with a heightened sense of confidence, as reflected in his management of the convention and its resolutions. These resolutions had a "revolutionary" character compared with those of the second PNC. The council itself convened against a completely different background and in a completely different atmosphere from those of the second PNC, with leanings toward Shuqayri this time. For his part, Shuqayri had the courage to admit the PLO's mistakes before the council and expressed a willingness to learn the necessary lessons and address the mistakes.

The third PNC convened against the following background:

- The salient question throughout the PNC meeting and discussions was, "Where is the PLO headed?" This question arose in light of the crises that had been plaguing the organization and the political crisis in the Arab arena that resulted from the dissipation of the summit atmosphere and subsequent relapse to division between "revolutionary and progressive" states, foremost among them Egypt and Syria, and the "reactionary-conservative" camp centered around Saudi Arabia and Jordan.
- The tactical shift in Shuqayri's stance, seemingly responding to the political and ideological demands of the opposition and to fida'i organizations and their activities (following Egypt's shift toward greater tolerance), had assuaged the opposition's criticism of him.
- A severe crisis in Shuqayri's relations with Jordan had erupted following the third Arab Summit, and relations between the PLO and Jordan deteriorated after the agreement of March 1, 1966, was signed. This crisis enabled Shuqayri to adopt an extreme nationalistic stance toward Jordan.

There were 467 official members of the third PNC according to an appendix to the PLO publication summarizing the resolutions. In fact, the council sessions had far fewer members: according to a report compiled by Jordanian intelligence (or the Jordanian delegation to the Council), between seventy and eighty representatives from Jordan were absent. The Jordanian authorities preemptively arrested about twenty-five PNC members and prevented others, such as Walid al-Qamhawi, from attending. Likewise, delegates from Saudi Arabia were absent, as the Saudi authorities prohibited them from traveling to the meeting. Shuqayri, for his part, added new members to the council in order to minimize Jordan's influence on the discussions. The Jordanian majority that had existed during the first and second PNCs did not exist this time, which naturally influenced the course of discussions and the resolutions of the various subcommittees and the PNC general assembly.

The opening session of the third PNC took place on the evening of May 20, 1965. In his speech, Shuqayri made the following points, among others:

- "The PLO is facing a difficult and decisive year. The PLO was born out of the Arab Summit. But if the summit is terminated, will the PLO disappear? Never."
- Admittedly, there are irregularities and flaws within the PLO and in its management, and "we must repair them."
- "The previous phase has ended; today we have entered the phase of revolutionary national unity, which brings together all our fighters and all our revolutionary forces."[34]

This speech had the power to appease all PNC members, including members of Palestinian organizations and the opposition, with the exception, of course, of most members of the Jordanian delegation.

Two salient camps were evident in the discussions of the third PNC and its Political Committee: the camp of Jordan's supporters, which encompassed the vast majority of the Jordanian delegation and supported maintaining the PLO's traditional stances as formulated during the first and second PNC meetings (where the Jordanian delegates had, as noted, constituted a majority); and the "nationalist-revolutionary" camp, which supported maintaining the PLO framework but believed that revolutionary changes should be made to its perspective and policies. The core group of the second camp was composed of the opposition to Shuqayri that had already become noticeable during the second PNC. The activists of this camp included Shafiq al-Hut and the writer Khayri Hamad. Shuqayri saw himself as—and made a concerted effort to appear as—part of the latter camp.

Among the resolutions passed at the third PNC, those that touched on the "unity of the revolutionary Palestinian endeavor" included the following point: "The PNC demands that a collective revolutionary leadership be assembled from this united revolutionary endeavor, in accordance with the nature of the new phase into which the Palestinian cause has entered."[35]

In his concluding speech, Shuqayri emphasized these "revolutionary resolutions adopted by the PNC in all areas." He embellished his remarks with passages from the Quran, and in the rhetorical style characteristic of his speeches, he said, "There was a revolutionary consensus. Our financial resolutions are revolutionary, the military resolutions are revolutionary, [and] the organizational resolutions are revolutionary. Revolution does not end with arms. Our political resolutions are revolutionary. Our entire people is [in a state of] all-inclusive revolution. We do not tremble from or fear revolution. Our resolutions were characterized by revolution. There will be no liberation of Filastin without revolutionary stances and a revolutionary plan and revolutionary execution. That is the course of revolution."[36]

The resolutions of the third PNC, adopted under Shuqayri's direction, sought to address some of the opposition's demands while adhering to the Arab position regarding a solution to the conflict with Israel, as affirmed at Arab League Summit meetings, and indirectly avoiding the plan and operations of Fatah. The PNC resolutions were characterized by an extreme stance toward Jordan and included a secret resolution regarding the kingdom, which held that "clandestine movements will be established in every state to prevent the establishment of PLA units."[37] Shuqayri also made a gesture toward the opposition by cooperating with oppositionists in the PLO's new Executive Committee.

Shuqayri passed the test of the third PNC with relative success, which was more than even he had expected. A prevailing hope during the PNC was that Shuqayri would change direction, and he was granted an extension to remain in his position. The Palestinian organizations (with the exception of Fatah) described the outcome of the PNC as a "great success," to wit: "The PNC achieved a great victory for the [Palestinian] cause," and "representatives of the Palestinian people succeeded in reaching a consensus regarding the need to maintain the PLO, and thus they overcome the crisis of the summit and all the problems that plagued the Palestinian people."[38] The shift in Shuqayri's position in favor of fida'i activities and his extreme views on Jordan were helpful in this respect. The crisis in PLO-Jordanian relations and the fear over the fate of the PLO if the summit atmosphere were to dissipate prevented the opposition from fomenting a crisis surrounding Shuqayri personally, particularly when he promised again that he would operate in the framework of a "collective revolutionary leadership" and devote efforts to "unity of the revolutionary forces."

These hopes were soon dashed. The events that followed the third PNC "dealt a blow to all the hopes that rested on the outcome of a united Palestinian endeavor." The supposedly united activity began to die down and eventually ceased. The basic principles underpinning united Palestinian activity as approved by delegates on the eve of the PNC remained in the form of "a tombstone over a grave."[39]

Notes

1. Shafiq al-Hut, *al-Hawadith*, June 12, 1964.
2. Shuqayri, *Min al-Qimma*, 62; Shuqayri, *al-Anwar*, February 13, 1967.
3. Shuqayri, *al-Anwar*, February 13, 1967.
4. Samir 'Abd al-Rahim, *al-Kifah*, December 30, 1964; Hurani, *Al-Fikr al-Siyasi*, 123.
5. *Al-Jihad* (Amman), June 21, 1965.
6. Shuqayri, *al-Jihad*, July 4, 1965.
7. *Al-Huriyya*, August 30, 1965; Ghassan Kanafani, *Filastin* (Beirut), July 15, 1965.
8. *Al-Difa'* (Amman), September 8, 1965.
9. *Al-Yawmiyyat al-Filastiniyya*, vol. 2 (Beirut, December 1966), 12–13.
10. Ghassan Kanafani, *Filastin* (Beirut), July 15, 1965.
11. *Al-Hayat*, January 3, 1965; *al-Anwar*, January 3, 1965.
12. Shuqayri, PLO Radio, December 27, 1965; *Akhbar Filastin*, March 15, 1965; *al-Ahad* (Beirut), June 13, 1965; *al-Kifah*, June 9, 1965; *al-Ahram*, July 22, 1965; Shafiq al-Hut, *Filastin* (Beirut), December 30, 1965; *al-Sayyad*, June 3, 1965; *al-Thawra al-'Arabiyya* (Baghdad), May 15, 1966.
13. Shafiq al-Hut, *Al-Filastini Bayna al-Tih*, 65; see also Shafiq al-Hut, *al-Sayyad*, June 16, 1965.
14. See Fatah, al-Qiyada al-'Amma li-Quwwat al-'Asifa, *Al-Mudhakira al-Marfu'a min al-Qiyada al-'Amma li-Quwwat al-'Asifa 'Ila Ra'is wa 'A'da' al-Majlis al-Watani al-Filastioni fi al-Qahira fi Dawratihi al-Thaniya*, May 28, 1965 (n.p., n.d.); Fatah, *Watha'iq 'Askariyya*, pt. 1 (Beirut, 1968), 20–53; Fatah, *Wahdat al-Thawra al-Filastiniyya*, no. 9 in the series Dirasat wa Tajarib Thawriyya (n.p., n.d.); *al-'Ahhad* (Beirut), no. 6, June 20, 1965; *al-'Awda*, no. 3, October 1965; *Filastin* (Beirut), March 24, 1966.
15. *Al-'Awda*, no. 3, October 1965; Shuqayri, *al-'Ahhad*, August 15, 1965; Baghdad Radio, July 15, 1965; *al-Hayat*, May 28, 1965, February 8, 1966; *al-Kifah*, June 16, 1965.
16. Abu Iyad, *Filastini*, 77–78.
17. Fatah, *Mawaqif wa Muntalaqat Thawriyya* (n.p., n.d.); Fatah, *Al-Mudhakira 'ila Muluk wa Ru'asa' al-Duwal al-'Arabiyya*, September 7, 1965, in the series Dirasat wa Tajarib Thawriyya; Fatah, *Mudhakira 'ila Mu'tamar Ru'asa' al-Hukumat al-'Arabiyya*, June 4, 1966, in the series Dirasat wa Tajarib Thawriyya.
18. *Al-Jarida* (Beirut), June 2, 1965.
19. *Al-Huriyya* (Beirut), August 30, 1965.
20. On the activities of the opposition to Shuqayri and on the resignations and dismissals of opposition activists, see Shuqayri, *al-Jarida*, June 11, 1965; *al-Hayat* (supported financially by Saudi Arabia and Jordan, it emphasized the opposition to Shuqayri within the PLO), August 7, 9, 26, 31, 1965, and September 2, 4, 9, 1965; *al-Jihad*, August 9, 1965; *Filastin*, June 3, 1965; *Filastin* (Beirut), July 11, 1965; *al-Ahrar* (Beirut), June 30, 1965, December 22, 1965; *al-Nahar*, August 9, 1965; *al-Kifah*, September 2, 1965; *al-Anwar*, June 2, 1965, May 13, 1967; *al-Jumhuriyya*, July 7, 1965; Ben-Gurion Archives, Ben-Gurion Research Institute for the Study of Israel and Zionism, Sede Boker, Israel: Private collection of documents from Egyptian government files in Gaza and from the PLO departments in Gaza, captured by the IDF in the Six Day War, PLO Office in Gaza; DJG, files of March–May and September–October 1965.
21. *Al-Kifah*, September 2, 1965.

22. Shuqayri, *al-Hayat*, September 2, 1965.
23. *Al-Hayat*, September 4, 1965.
24. Among the names proposed as a replacement for Shuqayri were Burhan al-Dajani and 'Abd al-Rahman al-Saksak; see *Filastin* (East Jerusalem), May 30, 1965.
25. Nasir, *al-Ahram*, June 1, 1965.
26. PLO, *The Second PNC*, 66.
27. See Shuqayri's speech in Jamal al-Shuqayri, *Al-Kiyan al-Filastini* (n.d., n.p.), 38–60.
28. Shuqayri, *Min al-Qimma*, 211; *Filastin* (East Jerusalem), June 2, 1965.
29. PLO, *The Second PNC*.
30. On the PNC resolutions, see PLO, *The Second PNC*.
31. *Al-Jihad*, June 21, 1965, July 5, 1965.
32. *Al-Jihad*, July 8, 1965.
33. On the resignations, see *Yawmiyyat Filastiniyya*, vol. 2 (Beirut, December 1966), 18; *Filastin*, November 20, 1965; *al-Hayat*, November 30, 1965.
34. PLO, *Al-dawra al-Thalitha lil-Majlis al-Watani al-Filastini,* Gaza, May 31–June 4, 1966, official brochure of the Third PNC (hereinafter PLO, *The Third PNC*), 16–18, 20–47.
35. Ibid.
36. Ibid., 97–102.
37. *Al-Ahram*, July 16, 1966; DJG, Special Report on the Third PNC, supposedly written by Jordanian intelligence or by a member of the Jordanian delegation to the Third PNC.
38. *Al-Huriyya*, June 6, 1966.
39. Ghassan Kanafani, *Filastin* (Beirut), October 29, 1966.

17 The Leadership Crisis Escalates, June 1966–May 1967

Shuqayri's Challenge: Growing Support for Fatah and Changes in the Positions of the ANM and the Palestine Liberation Front

Shuqayri's status and the status of Palestinians generally were influenced by the following developments during the period between the third PNC and the Six Day War:

- Arab states, especially Egypt and Syria, reached a stalemate in all matters related to the struggle with Israel and progress toward a solution to the Palestinian problem.
- Shuqayri failed in his struggle with the Jordanian regime, and especially in his efforts to destabilize it after the IDF raid on Samu' (November 13, 1966). King Husayn emerged from this crisis with the upper hand.
- The PLO under Shuqayri's leadership—which represented practically the only achievement to emerge from the atmosphere generated by the Arab Summit—proved that it had staying power despite the doubts that had surfaced about its fate. Shuqayri's status remained dependent on Nasir's support and conditions in the Arab arena.
- The increased popularity of Fatah and other fida'i organizations that appeared during this time, such as the Palestine Liberation Front (Jabhat al-Tahrir al-Filastiniyya), reinforced the belief among Palestinians—as advocated by Fatah—that armed struggle and fida'i operations were "the only way to vitalize and advance the Palestinian cause."[1] Israel's response to Fatah's and other fida'i groups' operations, whether by statement or by retaliatory action, increased Palestinian and Arab public support for Fatah and its activities. Egypt's support for fida'i activities should also be noted in this context, although it remained limited and qualified.
- The ANM position on fida'i operations underwent a significant change. The movement began to support these activities and at a later stage even contributed to them, albeit to a limited extent.

- Fida'i operations became an integral part of the "popular war of liberation" outlook of the Ba'th Party, which rose to power in Syria in February 1966.

During this period, fida'i guerrilla actions became a salient topic in Arab discourse generally and Palestinian discourse specifically. The extensive media coverage of Fatah and its actions against Israel at the time reflected the Arab and Palestinian public's longing for the idea of the "new Palestinian" who rose up to rebel against his social conditions and negative image, an image that had attached to him since the Nakba. Arab media sources, including radio and newspaper, eagerly covered anything related to fida'i activities, Fatah, and other fida'i organizations, as well as Israel's response, of course. The Lebanese newspapers outdid themselves in this context, specifically the pro-Egyptian newspapers and those with leanings toward the ANM and the Ba'th Party. These included *al-Huriyya*, *al-Muharrir* (and its bi-weekly *Filastin*), and *al-Hawadith*, as well as other important Lebanese newspapers such as *al-Hayat*, *al-Jarida*, and *al-Nahar*. The extensive coverage of these operations by Syrian media outlets should also be noted in this context. The Egyptian press, despite its reserved official stance, also joined this media campaign. Many articles and reviews were published in support of the fida'iyyun and their activities, as were interviews with Fatah commanders and leaders of the organization. Consequently, during this period a significant shift occurred in the manner in which the Palestinian cause was presented in the Arab media and in the overall Arab approach to Palestinians.

In December 1966, Fatah launched a public relations campaign to exploit its success through the Arab media, in order to make an imprint on Arab public opinion and establish itself as leader of the new Palestinian national movement. It was aiming for victory in its struggle with the PLO and other Palestinian organizations for the hearts and minds of Palestinians. In a political statement it issued in December 1966, Fatah proudly summarized its achievements during the second half of the year, conveying a sense of success. Likewise, it emphasized the public support of the PLO for Palestinian fida'i action, for the first time ever.[2] Indeed, during the first half of 1967 and up to the Six Day War, a significant rise in Fatah recruits and in the number of individuals who wanted to volunteer for Fatah and new Palestinian organizations took place, as well as an increase in the scope and intensity of fida'i guerrilla actions.

During the second half of 1966, the position of the ANM toward fida'i operations began to shift—from disapproval to support and then to active participation on an independent basis or in cooperation with the PLO. In this context the movement began, with Egyptian assistance, to train fida'iyyun and prepare them for guerrilla operations. Consequently, the movement's priorities changed as well. In July 1966, it still viewed eradication of the Jordanian regime as a primary goal and regarded fida'i activities as ineffective as long as this regime had not been toppled, but toward the end of 1966, it was already calling for all efforts to be concentrated on fida'i operations inside Israel.[3] Thus, the movement drew closer to the position of Fatah.

The emergence of Fatah and the popularity it garnered inspired the establishment, solidification, and visible appearance of additional Palestinian organizations during 1966 and 1967. As noted, the Ba'th and ANM leaders decided to create Palestinian sections within their own organizations, which served as the political nucleus for the fida'i organizations they founded: Youth of Revenge (Shabab al-Tha'r), founded by the Syrian Ba'th Party, and Heroes of the Return (Abtal al-'Awda), founded by the ANM. In this context we should also mention the activities of the Palestine Liberation Front (Jabhat al-Tahrir al-Filastiniyya, PLF), founded by the PLO representative in Beirut, Shafiq al-Hut. The importance of the PLF stems from Hut's status as the editor of the pro-Egyptian *al-Hawadith* and as someone with very close ties to Nasir. His writings reflected the outlook and policies of the Egyptian president on the Palestinian issue generally and toward fida'i actions specifically.

In his memoirs, Shafiq al-Hut describes the establishment and formation of the PLF.[4] According to him, the idea to found such a Palestinian organization first arose in early 1961 in Beirut, that is, before the dissolution of the United Arab Republic (UAR). Supporters of this idea included Ba'th Party members, ANM members, and Nasirists. They saw no contradiction between their efforts to establish a Palestinian organization and their political party affiliation, especially when their parties had established Palestinian sections. The first core group behind this organization included Khalid al-Yashruti, 'Abd al-Muhsin Abu Mayzar (both Ba'thists), Niqola al-Dur, and Shafiq al-Hut (independents). The weekly *al-Hawadith* served as a platform for dissemination of their ideas. In 1963 the PLF's magazine *Tariq al-'Awda* first appeared, and the PLF opened new chapters in refugee camps in Lebanon and elsewhere—in the Gaza Strip, Syria, Kuwait, Egypt, Algeria, and the West Bank.[5] The first PLF conference took place during late July through mid-August 1964, when it approved its political platform. In October 1964, the PLF approved the resolution of the PLO Executive Committee to appoint Shafiq al-Hut as representative of the PLO in Beirut.[6]

In November 1966, Shafiq al-Hut issued a pamphlet, published by the PLO Research Center and titled *Facts about the Path to Liberation* (*Haqa'iq 'Ala Tariq al-Tahrir*), in which he summarized his perspective of the organization's status. This publication is especially instructive given Hut's position. After detailing the positions of the various groups within the PLO that had emerged since its founding in 1964 (seventeen Palestinian organizations), Hut arrived at the key question: "Is the PLO merely a framework within which the Palestinian entity will materialize, or is it both a framework and a leadership?" In his view, "the organization

[PLO] in its objective form represents the united Palestinian struggle as a whole, not merely as part of it. Fundamentally, the organization was established not as a new organization or group but, rather, to serve as an umbrella organization and framework for all groups, with one flag and one leadership."[7]

Hut's point is that reservations about Shuqayri's leadership need not serve to undermine the PLO as an organizational framework representing the existence of a Palestinian entity. This organizational framework should, in his view, also serve as an official framework encompassing the clandestine fida'i groups.

Shuqayri's success in passing the test of the third PNC was not long-lasting. His status as PLO chairman and leader of the Palestinian cause steadily declined because of developments in the Arab—and especially the Palestinian—arenas. As PLO leader, after the third PNC he faced two possible courses of action, both uncomfortable:

- To join the radical Palestinian stream that was challenging Arab policy regarding the Arab-Israeli conflict and PLO policy, and to turn the PLO into another fida'i organization, that is, to accept Fatah's proposal of cooperation and thus lose his "independence" and principal basis of support—Egypt. This move would result in the dissolution of the PLO, which he had built by the sweat of his brow; or
- To change his position on fida'i operations, that is, to align himself with the Egyptian policy of limited support and aid for other Palestinian organizations, and to participate minimally in carrying out fida'i actions without declaring so or claiming full responsibility. This choice would be a way of proving that the PLO was also a "revolutionary" organization that was integrated into the armed struggle.

Shuqayri opted for the second alternative, having concluded that this approach would not only avoid the risk of a confrontation with Nasir but would also accord well with the shift that Egyptian policy was undergoing. Moreover, in his thinking, he would thereby meet his obligation of addressing changes that were under way in the Palestinian arena—changes that were leading in the direction of Palestinian revolution and armed struggle.

Thus, on July 15, 1966, Shuqayri announced the new Executive Committee, which included the following individuals: Ahmad al-Shuqayri as chairman; Sa'id al-'Azzi, former Executive Committee member and close colleague of Shuqayri, as director of the PLO office in Libya; Ibrahim Abu Sitta, former Executive Committee member aligned with Shuqayri, an attorney from Gaza, as overseer of "popular organizing" activities; Jamal al-Surani, former secretary of the Executive Committee aligned with Shuqayri, an attorney from Gaza, as secretary; Raji Sahyun from Lebanon, a first-time appointee, as director of the Department of

Public Relations and National Guidance of the PLO; Nimr al-Masri, a first-time appointee, as director of the Political Department of Arab Affairs; 'Abd al-Fattah Yunis, a first-time appointee; Shafiq al-Hut, a first-time appointee, as director of the PLO office in Beirut; Ahmad al-Sa'di, a first-time appointee; 'Usama al-Naqib from Syria, a first-time appointee; Ahmad Sidqi al-Dajani, a first-time appointee, as director general of the Popular Organization Department; 'Abd al-Majid Shuman in his capacity as chairman of the Board of Directors of the Palestinian National Fund; and Wajih al-Madani, in his capacity as commander of the PLA.[8] It was a bold gamble on Shuqayri's part to assign at least five (of thirteen) positions on the PLO Executive Committee to individuals who were known for their nationalistic stance and criticism of him—Hut, Sa'di, Dajani, Yunis, and Naqib. They continued to level criticism against him throughout late 1966 and early 1967. Indeed, Shuqayri would later regret this move.

The change in Shuqayri's position in favor of support for fida'i actions was evident in two spheres: declared support and material support (including active participation).[9] Shuqayri even went so far as to declare, in September 1966, that "we believe in the popular war for the liberation of Filastin.... The PLO is a revolutionary fighting organization, which is looking forward to its first opportunity to embark on fida'i activities according to its grand plans."[10] From early 1967, Shuqayri's statements regarding fida'i operations became more extreme: "The Palestinian fida'iyyun are liberating heroes and they have the right to enter Filastin," according to PLO radio.[11]

Simultaneously, Shuqayri began planning for the possibility of a PLO transition to direct action against Israel. It appears that in August 1966 he decided, with the approval of the Executive Committee, to begin establishing fida'i cells with recruits from among Palestinians in Lebanon. The meetings at which these cells were planned took place in Lebanon under great secrecy to prevent their discovery by Lebanese intelligence services. In this respect, Shuqayri found a loyal partner in the PLF (Jabhat al-Tahrir al-Filastiniyya). Together they established Heroes of the Return (Abtal al-'Awda), a fida'i organization, in cooperation with the ANM, which was represented by Ahmad al-Yamani, one of the movement's leaders in Lebanon.[12] Shafiq al-Hut was responsible for recruiting, training, and mobilizing cells on behalf of the PLO, and Yamani was in charge of operations on behalf of the ANM, in light of his experience in this area on behalf of the Egyptians since the 1950s. Most meetings of the organization's activists took place at Hut's office in Beirut, and PLO Radio served as the main mouthpiece of the group.[13] The PLO also provided assistance through funding, weapons, and training.

In his memoirs, George Habash, one of the founders of the ANM, describes the relationship between the movement and the PLO in establishing Abtal al-'Awda: "I would like to say something about the organization Abtal al-'Awda, with which we had ties. The PLO was at that time considering establishing an armed organization in addition to the PLA. The PLO made contact with a group of young members and friends of the ANM. At the time we told these young people to work together with the PLO. The group Abtal al-'Awda commenced its armed struggle before 1967, and some of its warriors fell in battle, including Muhammad al-Yamani, the brother of our comrade Abu Mahir [Ahmad al-Yamani]."[14]

The objective for which Abtal al-'Awda was founded was infiltration into Israel to carry out intelligence and guerrilla missions without the PLO officially claiming responsibility. The first action by the group was on October 19, 1966, when an armed cell infiltrated Israeli territory through the border with Lebanon for a reconnaissance and intelligence mission, with no intention of carrying out an attack. The dispatch of a reconnaissance cell rather than a guerrilla cell reflects the dilemma Shuqayri faced: on the one hand, he wanted to prove his participation in fida'i activities, and on the other hand, he wanted to abide by the Egyptian policy of refraining from guerrilla action. This dilemma is also evidenced by Shuqayri and Hut having deliberately refrained from taking any measure that would identify the October 19 cell with the PLO or its chapter in Beirut. For this reason, Hut also deliberately refrained from eulogizing the fallen cell members and did not demand that Israel return their bodies. Shuqayri told the Lebanese security authorities that the cell had no ties with the PLO and that the organization (including its Beirut chapter) adhered to the United Arab Command (UAC) position and coordinated its military activities with the UAC. Shuqayri adopted this position despite the pressure exerted by Shafiq al-Hut and ANM activists within the organization to officially publicize the link between Abtal al-'Awda and the PLO because of its propaganda value. Presumably, Shuqayri was also concerned about the measures that Lebanese security authorities might take against PLO activists, along the lines of measures they were taking against Fatah activists at the time. Despite Shuqayri's efforts, however, the link between Abtal al-'Awda and the PLO was reported in the Lebanese press.[15]

Shuqayri was indeed successful in his efforts to create the impression of a revolutionary transformation in his position, but this was a short-lived success. Soon a dispute erupted again between him and Executive Committee members regarding his activities and conduct. At the same time, the group Abtal al-'Awda reverted to the sole patronage of the ANM and in this capacity it joined efforts in December 1967 with the Palestinian section of the movement (Shabab al-Tha'r), the Palestine Liberation Front (Jabhat al-Tahrir al-Filastiniyya), and Ahmad Jibril's group, to establish the Popular Front for the Liberation of Palestine (PFLP; al-Jabha al-Sha'biyya li-Tahrir Filastin) under the leadership of George Habash.

The shift in Shuqayri's position on fida'i actions drew a positive response from Fatah. In a political statement issued on December 10, 1966, Fatah welcomed the "initiative of the PLO to support immediate Palestinian fida'i activities and to discard its earlier reservations."[16]

Against the background of Fatah's positive reaction, Shuqayri renewed talks with the movement's leaders with a view to finding a formula for cooperation, his goal being to bring Fatah under the auspices of the PLO. These meetings took place during the second half of 1966 and early 1967. In addition to representatives from the PLO (including Shafiq al-Hut) and Fatah (Arafat and Khalil al-Wazir), participants included representatives of the Palestinian section of the Ba'th Party and the Palestinian section of the ANM (Ahmad al-Yamani). Some of these meetings took place in Damascus with Egyptian mediation.

In January 1967, Hani al-Hasan, a Fatah founder and leader, met with Shuqayri in Cairo to explore his intentions. Shuqayri proposed to Hasan that the PLO and Fatah coordinate their guerrilla activities and promised material assistance for Fatah. He invited Fatah leaders to join the PLO under his leadership and promised that the PLO would see to all the fida'i needs. Fatah's response to Shuqayri's proposal was that Fatah should be the axis around which other organizations congregate. Fatah also argued that fida'i activities should be coordinated by Fatah itself in Damascus under the name "al-'Asifa" alongside the name of the group carrying out the operation. The PLO would serve as a public relations vehicle for disseminating Fatah statements.[17] Fatah was not actually interested in partnering with the PLO but rather in having a decisive influence over the organization and its leadership in due course.

Shuqayri's Response to Criticism: Imaginary Revolution

The shift in the PLO's position on fida'i activities and the severe crisis between Shuqayri and Jordan that erupted after the raid on Samu' (on November 13, 1966) combined to improve Shuqayri's standing in the Palestinian arena and within his organization. But these factors were not enough to prevent members of the Executive Committee and nationalist Palestinian circles from renewing their criticism of him for his management of the PLO and his practice of making decisions without consulting the Executive Committee. According to Shafiq al-Hut, "Shuqayri paid no attention to our suggestions, rejected our critiques of him, and took an excessive amount of unilateral and despotic measures or decisions." He added, "We discovered that the third Executive Committee, whose [composition] resulted from the spirit of the third PNC, was not satisfactory [for Shuqayri], given that he refuses to accept any of its requests." The third Executive Committee "did not spare any effort in pursuing the recommendations of the third PNC, especially in all matters related to 'popular organizing,' the PLA, public relations, and so on. In the meantime the Samu' catastrophe took place and relations between the PLO and Jordan tapered, the crisis within the PLO intensified, and Shuqayri's sense of isolation increased. In December 1966, Shuqayri launched an imaginary revolution."[18] Similar criticism was leveled against Shuqayri in the Lebanese press, especially in newspapers aligned with the Arab Nationalists Movement.

Shuqayri's response to the criticism was unexpected. He made extravagantly showy gestures that are hard to attribute to anything other than a state of hysteria and personal pressures that he found hard to bear. Shuqayri's gestures eventually achieved the opposite of what he sought: rather than improving his image and reinforcing his leadership and standing, they contributed to his downfall.

At an Executive Committee meeting on December 14, 1966, Shuqayri used the uproar that erupted across Jordan after the Samu' raid to persuade participants to authorize him "to appoint a new Executive Committee that would serve national objectives in light of the difficult phase that our stolen [Filastin] cause is undergoing."[19] Members of the Executive Committee, especially the Nationalists among them, realized that Shuqayri's intention was to create an Executive Committee that would serve as a collective form of leadership. They saw this move as a sign that "Shuqayri promised favors" and that this time he intended to fulfill his promises.[20]

Despite Shuqayri's remarks to the Executive Committee on December 14 and the participants' assessment of his intentions, Shuqayri presented another surprise, with a dramatic announcement on PLO Radio on December 27, 1966. In his broadcast, he disclosed his reorganization of the PLO, once again without consulting Executive Committee members. In his statement, Shuqayri said that the PLO was undergoing a "revolutionary" process, especially in terms of support for fida'i activities, and was becoming part of the "Palestinian revolution." While harshly criticizing Jordan, he praised the actions of fida'iyyun "who sacrifice themselves for the sake of Allah and the homeland" and he recalled the two fida'iyyun captured by Israel—Fatah member Mahmud Bakr al-Hijazi and Sakran from Abtal al-'Awda. Shuqayri announced the following measures:

- The establishment of a "Revolutionary Council" (Majlis Thawri Filastini): A Palestinian Revolutionary Council will be established, one that can carry the burden of liberation. A new executive council will be established composed of revolutionaries, to provide a Revolutionary Council for the PLO, which will take it on itself to prepare the people to participate in the liberation campaign, with the PLA as the pioneering [force]. In selecting members, emphasis will be placed on their determined, loyal, and honest representation of revolutionary warfare. The names of Revolutionary Council members will not be publicly announced, nor will details of their workplaces, meetings, decisions, or activities. Several council members have already been selected, and the rest will be soon.
- Reduction of Expenses and Closure of Departments: Henceforth, the PLO will have the following departments: The Department of

Arab Affairs and Foreign Affairs (a merger of two departments), the Department of Islamic World Affairs (a new department); the Department of Public Relations and National Guidance; and the Department of National Fund Affairs.[21]

These organizational changes were Shuqayri's response to complaints leveled against him, including accusations of wasting the organization's funds. The cuts he implemented were most evident in the reduction of PLO departments from eight to four, including the merger of two departments and closure of the Popular Organization Department and Department of Elections and General Affairs. Shuqayri pointed to these changes as evidence of the revolution within the PLO and its transformation into a "revolutionary organization"—no less so than fida'i organizations. The measures also reflected the PLO's severe financial hardship, which resulted from Arab states' not meeting their financial obligations and the cessation of Saudi (and later Jordanian) aid after the spirit of the Arab Summit dissipated.[22]

In addition to these new measures, Shuqayri engaged in a public relations campaign focused on the "revolutionary phase" that, according to him, the PLO and the Palestinian public were undergoing. As a consequence, he raised the expectations that Palestinians and Arab states alike had of him. Their expectations were reflected in the responses of Arab and PLO media outlets. They—as well as PLO offices—began to describe Shuqayri and address him in their correspondence as "Head of the PLO and Chairman of the PLO Revolutionary Council."[23]

On January 2, 1967, a "reliable source in the PLO" (most likely Shuqayri himself) was quoted as saying that "within a few days a Palestinian Revolutionary Council will be formed, which will be joined by a number of real Palestinians from various places, including from Jordan and beyond as well as Palestinian representatives from the occupied land."[24] The PLO newsletter in the Gaza Strip added that "the main mission of the Palestinian Revolutionary Council is to unite fida'i and Palestinian activities."[25]

Despite its criticism of Shuqayri, the ANM refrained from adopting an unequivocal position on Shuqayri's new steps, although it did express some doubt about their content. Its weekly *al-Huriyya* stated, among other things, that "Palestinian circles are waiting with interest to see the practical outcome of Shuqayri's decision regarding the formation of a Palestinian Revolutionary Council as an alternative to the Executive Committee. . . . Shuqayri's decision that membership in the Revolutionary Council will be kept secret makes it easier to elect its members and will keep all opportunistic elements away."[26]

The position of the PLA commander and chief of staff was significant. They criticized Shuqayri, who on the one hand presented the further development of the PLA as a main objective of the announced changes, but on the other hand decided on these changes without consulting the PLA General Command, even going so far as to order cuts in officers' salaries and calling on them to reduce expenses. In a memorandum to Shuqayri, the PLA commander and chief of staff demanded that he establish a temporary leadership body that would convene a number of Palestinians, among whom a Revolutionary Council would be elected.[27] The PLA commander and chief of staff sent Shuqayri a second memorandum on February 9, 1967, this time in the name of the PLA General Command, in which they announced their intention to resign if in the future Shuqayri again issued a statement over the airwaves without consulting with them in advance. In response, Shuqayri met with them that same day and gave his "good word."[28]

The state of management of the PLO was a topic of discussion between Nasir and Shafiq al-Hut in a conversation that took place in late January or early February 1962. Nasir called on Hut "to suspend the struggle with Shuqayri" and added, "You complain about Shuqayri because he talks a lot. . . . It's nothing. . . . Let him talk as much as he wants. We need a little talking, in the hopes of preparing [the circumstances]."[29] Indeed, in the spirit of Nasir's remarks, Hut and the Arab Nationalists made an effort not to burn bridges with Shuqayri despite the criticism they felt regarding him.

Relying on Nasir's backing, Shuqayri produced another surprise, this time astounding not only the PLA General Command, Shafiq al-Hut, and the ANM, but also the entire Palestinian public. A statement he delivered on PLO Radio on February 10, 1967, asserted,

> With Allah's help the PLO's Revolutionary Council has been established. The Revolutionary Council is now an existing reality, a revolutionary reality. Council members promised to maintain secrecy and not publicize their names, meetings, and resolutions, other than as required for the struggle. The Revolutionary Council adopted three important resolutions. Two of these were the following:
>
> 1. Establishment of a "Political Bureau" alongside the Revolutionary Council, to handle general, political, public relations, financial, and organizational matters of the organization (PLO). The members of the Political Bureau will soon be appointed, from among those who have been active in the national sphere.
> 2. Development of the PLA to make it a revolutionary army ready for a war of liberation. It is necessary to develop the PLA in a revolutionary manner in terms of budget, structure, and all its affairs. To achieve this goal, the Revolutionary Council decided to establish a "Liberation Council". . . . The PLA General Command will be represented in the Liberation Council. The Revolutionary Council resolved . . . to direct the PLA budget to revolutionary purpose. . . . The budget cuts will not apply to soldiers' [salaries] because their salaries are low. The cuts will apply to several items of salary and expenses [of officers].[30]

Shuqayri's February 10, 1967, statement is significant in several aspects. He referred to the Revolutionary Council as if it had already been formed and appointed, but he maintained the need for secrecy and added the establishment of a Political Bureau. In so doing, he caused the dissolution of the Executive Committee without actually announcing it and the appointment of a Political Bureau—whose composition and function he did not explain—as an advisory more than an executive body. Shuqayri's approach to the status of the PLA in the context of the new institution—the Liberation Council—and to cuts in the PLO's military entity were a severe blow to its status in matters of command and to the status of its senior officers. The establishment of a Liberation Council would in effect strip the PLA General Command of the few functions it had.

Reactions to Shuqayri's statement argued that the establishment of his announced institutions was illegal and that these institutions contradicted PNC resolutions and the PLO's constitution. Shuqayri dismissed these claims, underscoring that "I take action on all issues within my authority that cannot be delayed . . . without turning to the Executive Committee. Every prime minister and foreign minister operates this way, and so do I. In this way I fulfill my operational duties. Even the chairman of the board of directors of a commercial company has such authority."[31]

In fact, the Revolutionary Council and Political Bureau were fictitious, and Shuqayri's statements and actions in this context were actually lies with no basis in reality. This announcement was another ploy by the PLO chairman designed to prove that the organization had become a "revolutionary fida'i organization" and to remove the Executive Committee members who had criticized him, some of whom had also threatened to resign. Shuqayri thus aspired, as in the past, to manage PLO affairs through his own unilateral decision making, without consultation or approval on the part of the Executive Committee or any other body.

Members of the Executive Committee and the PLA commander justifiably doubted the existence of the Revolutionary Council announced by Shuqayri, despite his remarks about its having convened and passed resolutions. Questions and speculations regarding Shuqayri's actions also began to surface among oppositionist nationalist Palestinian circles, including the ANM and Shafiq al-Hut's network. Among their questions were the following: What is the significance of the Revolutionary Council? What are its powers? Who are its members and what are their qualifications? They also posed questions about the manner in which Revolutionary Council members would be elected or appointed, and to whom the council would be subordinate.[32]

Shuqayri's dramatic announcement of February 10, 1967, caused the crisis within the internal PLO leadership to reach an entirely new level. The dispute between Shuqayri and the opposition grew even sharper and came to be focused between himself and Shafiq al-Hut, who gathered Shuqayri's opponents to his side. On Hut's side were PLA Commander Wajih al-Madani and Chief of Staff Subhi al-Jabi as well as ANM leaders. Eventually, Nasir's intervention was necessary again to prevent the situation from worsening to the point of severely undermining Shuqayri and sabotaging his standing as head of the PLO.

The first to respond to Shuqayri's announcement of February 10 were members of the PLA General Command. They were reacting to the remarks he made that undermined their status. The PLA commander, after consulting with his chief of staff, dispatched a memorandum to the presidents of those states that had PLA units: Nasir of Egypt, Atasi of Syria, and 'Arif of Iraq. In these memoranda, Madani expressed the displeasure of the PLA General Command and its objection to the content of Shuqayri's announcement, in particular, the implied insults against the General Command itself. Madani stated that Shuqayri's actions were illegal, and accordingly the PLA could not obey them. He called on the presidents of Egypt, Syria, and Iraq to intervene and remedy the situation, conveying an implied threat that PLA officers intended to submit their collective resignation if Shuqayri continued violating the National Charter and the PLO constitution. Simultaneously, Madani informed Shuqayri that he refused to obey the latter's instructions because they did not derive from any legal authority.[33]

The opposition that crystallized against Shuqayri this time was more extensive and determined than that of 1965. Its guiding spirit was Shafiq al-Hut, whose engagement gave the opposition more legitimacy and weight, given his role in the Palestinian establishment, special ties with Nasir, and responsibility for the Palestine Liberation Front. In the early phase, immediately after Shuqayri's announcement, Hut adopted a moderate tone in his criticism, avoiding personal attacks. He admitted that "indeed there is a crisis among those in charge of the PLO, but this crisis is rooted in the conduct of a few among those who are in charge of the PLO," and he added an overt hint: "We in the PLO will not agree to submit to any tribal or dictatorial policy."[34] At the same time, Hut continued to view the PLO as a legitimate, representative framework. When an attempt was made on his life, on February 17, 1967, he rejected the possibility that this attempt was connected to differences of opinion between himself and Shuqayri, accusing the Jordanian authorities instead.[35]

The ANM's view of Shuqayri's announcement of a Revolutionary Council was very instructive. It treated Shuqayri's remarks as an expression of genuine intention and interpreted them as practically a return to the "straight and narrow." Its approach essentially sought preservation of the PLO's framework alongside an internal struggle for reform.[36]

In contrast to the relatively moderate response of the ANM, the opposition within the PLO Executive Committee—which included Ahmad al-Sa'di, Ahmad Sidqi al-Dajani, and Shafiq al-Hut himself—sent a protest letter to Shuqayri on February 15, in which it argued that his actions were illegal (this group had already objected to Shuqayri's December 27, 1966, statement of intention to establish a Revolutionary Council). On February 25, these three sent Shuqayri another memorandum detailing their position. Its key points were as follows:

- The details of this Revolutionary Council are unclear.
- The decision constitutes a violation of Article 13 of the PLO constitution and distorts Article 5 of the third PNC recommendations.
- The decision of the Executive Committee chairman (of January 27, 1967) effectively means that only the chairman of the Executive Committee is responsible to the PNC.
- Shuqayri should rescind his decision and begin to assemble an Executive Committee that will serve as the political and practical leadership of the PLO.[37]

Shuqayri's announcements drew protests from senior PLO officials, led to the resignation of others, and exacerbated the organization's leadership crisis. Raji Sahyun, a member of the Executive Committee and director of the Department of Public Relations and National Guidance, protested Shuqayri's actions of December 27, 1966, and submitted his resignation two days after they were announced. On January 28, 1967, Sahyun reaffirmed his protestations and resignation. His resignation letter expressed objection to Shuqayri's moves, describing them as illegal and contrary to the PLO's constitution.[38] On February 6, 1967, Rif'at 'Uda, an Executive Committee member, called on Shuqayri to reopen discussion of the PLO structure and leadership, making it a collective leadership.[39] On February 14, Salah al-Dabbagh, director general of the PLO's Political Department, and Khalil 'Uweida, director of the PLO's Division of Education and Culture, sent a joint memorandum to Shuqayri in which they submitted their resignations.[40] In February 1967, three Executive Committee members resigned: Nimr al-Masri, 'Usama al-Naqib, and 'Abd al-Fattah Yunis. On February 17, Haydar 'Abd al-Shafi sent a letter to Shuqayri warning him about the consequences of his self-aggrandizement and usurpation of power.[41]

In this difficult situation, as he was unable to fulfill the promises he had made on February 10, Shuqayri was forced to abandon his stated plan to form a Revolutionary Council, Liberation Council, and Political Bureau, and to return to the regular constitutional framework of PLO institutions, that is, to assemble an Executive Committee. On February 26, 1967, Shuqayri released a statement describing the new Executive Committee: Ahmad al-Shuqayri—chairman; 'Abd al-Majid Shuman, chairman of the board of directors of the Palestinian National Fund; Wajih al-Madani, commander-in-chief of the PLA; 'Usama al-Naqib, director of the Cairo office and PLO delegate to the Arab League; Jamal al-Surani, secretary of the Executive Committee and responsible for administrative affairs; Hamid Abu Sitta, Popular Organization Department; Khalid al-Fahum Department of Public Relations and National Guidance; and Nimr al-Masri, Political Department.

Following on Shuqayri's announcement, a "reliable PLO source" (probably Shuqayri himself) disclosed that "the Executive Committee in its current composition includes members of the first Executive Committee, that is, Khalid al-Fahum, the commander-in-chief of the PLA, and Hamid Abu Sitta. It also includes members of the second and third Executive Committees, namely, 'Usama al-Naqib, Jamal al-Surani, and Nimr al-Masri." The so-called source added that "this new composition represents unity, and moreover the number of Executive Committee members equals the number of PLO departments."[42]

Shuqayri's announcement and the clarifications provided by the "reliable source" amounted to a last-minute "letter of surrender." The announcement represented near-total capitulation to the demands of the opposition and to Shuqayri's critics in the PLO leadership, such as the PLA commander. In the explanatory commentary provided to Executive Committee members, Shuqayri made every effort to persuade his critics that he had returned to the "straight and narrow" and that he was indeed acting in accordance with the terms of the National Charter, the PLO constitution, and the Executive Committee resolution of December 14, 1966. He was aiming to forestall any legally or constitutionally based criticism of himself. He also emphasized that the new leadership would work as a collective, and to prove that he still supported cutting PLO and PLA expenses, he made sure not to increase the number of PLO departments. Although it had been a tradition to include the PLA commander in the Executive Committee since the formation of the first Executive Committee, undoubtedly this move was also an attempt to appease an important senior official in the PLO. In highlighting his inclusion of members from three previous executive committees, Shuqayri was seeking to prevent criticism of his friends and accusations that he was taking revenge against opposition members. In all, Shuqayri wanted to use the new Executive Committee to demonstrate that everything was back to "business as usual"—that is, the routine that had existed before his announcement of December 27, 1966.

However, one matter on which Shuqayri would not concede remained, namely, his right to appoint the Executive Committee members—in number and name—as he saw fit. He had been granted this right by the second PNC. Moreover, in appointing the members of the new Executive Committee, Shuqayri was settling an account with the opposition by not renewing the membership of three former Executive Committee members: Ahmad al-Sa'di, Ahmad Sidqi al-Dajani, and Shafiq al-Hut.

It now became abundantly clear to everyone that all the "secret" bodies whose establishment Shuqayri had repeatedly announced did not exist in practice. It was also clear that the "new" Shuqayri had not changed his political approach or style of management of the PLO, as affirmed by his not having appointed any figures identified with fida'i organizations or anyone who could stand in active opposition to the Executive Committee. Not long after the new Executive Committee was established, the ANM gave voice to this lack of change. Salih al-Shibil, an ANM activist, wrote, "The framework of the new PLO Executive Committee needs to be expanded so as to include a larger number of revolutionary organizations.... The principle of collective leadership should be implemented and dictatorial tendencies should be avoided."[43] The ANM had, accordingly, reverted to its basic criticism of Shuqayri.

After his "surrender," Shuqayri went on a rampage against his opponents. He fired officials in the Palestinian establishment who had not demonstrated full loyalty to him, and above all he sought revenge against Shafiq al-Hut by expelling him from the Palestinian arena. On May 7, 1967, Shuqayri succeeded in passing a resolution through the Executive Committee reassigning Shafiq al-Hut from his post in Beirut to the position of PLO representative in India. He took this action through the Executive Committee to secure its full backing so that the move would not appear to be motivated by personal revenge, although it was still evident that personal motives played a part. Moreover, there was no PLO representative body in India at the time. There was an office of the Arab League in New Delhi, headed by Clovis Maqsoud, where Hut was meant to serve as attaché.[44]

Not surprisingly, Shafiq al-Hut was unwilling to abide by the decision that he be removed from the position of head of the PLO office in Beirut. He argued that the resolution had been adopted on the basis of personal interests rather than substantive considerations, and that it was "not a purely administrative resolution; there are personal interests behind it, which stem from differences of opinion between him and another current within the PLO headed by Shuqayri."[45] Hut approached the Egyptians, expressing his concern about being transferred and requesting their assistance. He cautioned against Shuqayri's intention of removing "revolutionary elements" from most PLO departments. He also expressed concern about the future of approximately fifty fida'iyyun at his service from the organization Heroes of the Return (Abtal al'-'Awda).

In the end, Shafiq al-Hut was not transferred to India, but the crisis between him and Shuqayri remained unchanged and contributed to the continuing crisis in PLO leadership.

Notes

1. *Filastin* (Beirut), February 23, 1967.
2. Fatah, political announcement, Sawt al-'Uruba, December 23, 1966.
3. *Filastin* (Beirut), July 28, 1966; Bilal al-Hasan, *al-Huriyya*, February 13, 1967; *Filastin*, December 15, 1966.

4. Shafiq al-Hut, *'Ishrun 'Aman fi Munazamat al-Tahrir al-Filastiniyya, 1964–1984* (Beirut: Dar al-Istiqlal, 1986); Shafiq al-Hut, *Al-Filastini Bayna al-Tih wa al-Dawla* (Beirut, 1977).

5. Shafiq al-Hut, *'Ishrun 'Aman*, 70–73.

6. Ibid., 81, 95. For another version, by Hut, of the establishment of the PLF, see Shafiq al-Hut, *Al-Filastini Bayna al-Tih*, 52–58.

7. Shafiq al-Hut, *Haqa'iq 'Ala Tariq al-Tahrir*.

8. PLO Radio, July 15, 1966; *al-Ahram*, July 16, 1966; the Arab media reported that Shuqayri, before announcing the composition of the Executive Committee, had contacted other personalities who declined his offer to join the committee, among them Wadi' Haddad (ANM), Yahya Hamuda, 'Abd al-Khaliq Yaghmur, Da'ud al-Husayni, Qusay al-'Abadla, and Dr. Haydar 'Abd al-Shafi, *al-Jarida*, June 6, 1966; *al-Muharrir*, July 2, 1966.

9. Shuqayri, *al-Huriyya*, September 5, November 21, 1966; *al-Muharrir*, November 21, 1966; PLO Radio, November 27, December 11, 1966, February 10, 1967; *al-Nahar*, June 17, 1966.

10. Shuqayri, *al-Huriyya*, September 5, 1966, and November 21, 1966.

11. Shuqayri, PLO Radio, February 2, 1967.

12. On Abtal al-'Awda, see *Al-Jabha*, mouthpiece of Ahmad Jibril's organization, Al-Jabha al-Sha'biyya li-Tahrir Filastin—Al-Qiyada al-'Amma (Popular Front for the Liberation of Palestine—General Command), no. 10 (1970): 20–21; PLO Radio, January 23, 24, 1967; *al-Muharrir*, October 28, 1966, January 18, 1967; *Kul Say'*, November 5, 1966.

13. PLO Radio, January 23, 1967; on this date, Abtal al-'Awda first announced its action in Bayt Jubrin.

14. Matar, *Hakim al-Thawra*, 117.

15. *Al-Muharrir*, January 18, 1967.

16. Fatah, *Dirasat wa Tajarib Thawriyya*, 210–17; *Sawt al-'Uruba*, December 23, 1966.

17. *Al-Hawadith*, April 28, 1967; *al-'Awda*, mouthpiece of the German branch of the General Union of Palestinian Students, internal publication, June 1967.

18. Shafiq al-Hut, *'Ishrun 'Aman*, 98.

19. *Al-Hawadith*, February 16, 1967.

20. Ibid.

21. Shuqayri, PLO Radio, December 27, 1966.

22. Ben-Gurion Archives, Ben-Gurion Research Institute for the Study of Israel and Zionism, Sede Boker, Israel: Private collection of documents from Egyptian government files in Gaza and from the PLO departments in Gaza, captured by the IDF in the Six Day War, files of the PLO Office in Gaza, report by 'Abd al-Majid Shuman on the financial crisis of the PLO.

23. *Akhbar Filastin* (Gaza), January 2, 1967.

24. Ibid.

25. *Akhbar Filastin* (Gaza), January 23, 1967.

26. *Al-Huriyya*, January 9, 1967.

27. Shafiq al-Hut, *'Ishrun 'Aman*, 98; *al-Hawadith*, February 16, 1967.

28. *Al-Hawadith*, February 16, 1967.

29. Shafiq al-Hut, *'Ishrun 'Aman*, 97; *al-Hawadith*, February 3, 1967.

30. Shuqayri, PLO Radio, February 10, 1967.

31. Shuqayri, *al-Anwar*, February 13, 1967.

32. *Al-Hawadith*, February 16, 1967.

33. Wajih al-Madani, *al-Anwar*, February 13, 1967; *al-Hawadith*, February 16, 1967; *al-Hayat*, February 19, 1967.

34. Shafiq al-Hut, *al-Anwar*, February 15, 1967.

35. Shafiq al-Hut, *al-Hayat*, February 16, 1967; Shafiq al-Hut, *Al-Filastini Bayna al-Tih*, 66; *al-Hawadith*, February 24, 1967; *al-Jumhuriyya*, February 19, 1967; *al-Anwar*, February 18, 1967.

36. *Filastin* (Beirut), February 23, 1967; *al-Huriyya*, February 13, 20, 1967; Habash arrived in Cairo in early February to meet Shuqayri and inform him of the ANM's position regarding the "Revolutionary Council," *al-Hawadith*, February 3, 1967.

37. Shafiq al-Hut, *'Ishrun 'Aman*, 99–100.

38. Ibid.; *al-Hawadith*, February 16, 1967.

39. Shafiq al-Hut, *'Ishrun 'Aman*, 101.

40. Ibid.

41. Ibid., 102.

42. Shuqayri, PLO Radio, February 26, 1967.

43. Salih al-Shibil, *al-Muharrir*, March 9, 1967.

44. *Al-Anwar*, May 13, 1967; *Yawmiyyat Filastiniyya*, vol. 5 (Beirut, December 1967), 438.

45. Shafiq al-Hut, *al-Hawadith*, May 12, 1967.

18 Shuqayri: The End of the Road, June–December 1967

Shuqayri at the Khartoum Summit: His Status Reaches a Nadir

One of the significant consequences of the Six Day War in the context of the Arab-Israeli conflict and the new Palestinian national movement was the emergence of fida'i organizations as the foremost leaders of the new Palestinian national movement, recognized as such by Arab states and in time becoming one of the main parties to the Arab-Israeli conflict as well.

The Arab Summit that convened in Khartoum between August 29 and September 1, 1967, approved a new Arab strategy for a phased resolution of the Arab-Israeli conflict. The summit held that "the monarchs and presidents agreed to unite their political efforts in the international and diplomatic arena to eliminate the trail of aggression and ensure the withdrawal of aggressive Israeli forces from the Arab lands that have been occupied since the aggression of June 5; this [strategy was decided] in the framework of the basic principles to which Arab states are committed, namely, no reconciliation [*sulh*] with Israel or recognition of it, no negotiation with it, and adherence to the right of the Palestinian people to its homeland."[1]

In effect, the Summit identified two phases to the resolution of the Arab-Israeli conflict: Phase 1 would entail "elimination of the trail of aggression" or "liberation of lands occupied" by Israel, that is, "a solution to the 1967 problem." Phase 2 would then pursue "preservation of the sacred right of the Palestinian people to its land," that is, "a solution to the 1948 problem" or the "liberation of Filastin" in the pre–Six Day War sense.

The important shift that took place in Arab strategy after the Six Day War—as compared with the prewar strategy—was the Arab consensus to engage openly in political activities to achieve the objective of the first phase in resolving the conflict, that is, "elimination of the trail of aggression" (of 1967). The Khartoum Summit granted Nasir and Husayn the authorization to conduct political negotiations toward this end and, by implication, to engage in political activities aimed at achieving the objective of the second phase ("a solution to the 1948 problem"), subject to the conditions laid down in the summit resolutions.

Jordan's participation in the Six Day War enhanced King Husayn's prestige in the kingdom and in the Arab world, and consequently he was welcomed as a hero and national leader at the Khartoum Summit. Indeed, he received more admiration and support than he had seen since assuming the throne. He became Nasir's most loyal ally almost until Nasir's dying day and nearly "stole the show" at the summit. In the immediate aftermath of the Six Day War, Husayn viewed the return of the West Bank to his kingdom as his government's top priority, and Nasir supported this approach.

In contrast to Husayn, whose status had been enhanced, Shuqayri was so marginalized in the aftermath of the Arab defeat in the Six Day War that his invitation to the Khartoum Summit was "forgotten." In his memoirs, he describes how he imposed himself on the summit and succeeded in influencing its resolutions, such that the summit approved the "three noes" proposed in his memorandum to the conference.[2]

Shuqayri was fighting a losing battle. Sensing that his expulsion from the Palestinian-Arab political arena was only a matter of time, he decided to try to shed the image that had attached to him up to the war and to prove that he did not blindly follow Arab heads of states. He adopted provocative stances against them, even opposing Nasir's positions on issues. During the Khartoum Summit, to the surprise of Arab heads of state, he presented an extreme, uncompromising stance, to the point that he walked out of the summit's final session in protest when his position was not accepted. These gestures did not improve his standing: the Arab world after the Six Day War was deeply affected by its defeat and viewed Shuqayri himself as one of the indicators of this defeat. Its main concern at the time was to bring about Israel's withdrawal from the occupied territories. The Palestinian cause had not yet been granted its new status in the Arab arena.

Shafiq al-Hut participated alongside Shuqayri in the Khartoum Summit, and in his memoirs he recalls,

> Shuqayri was at least as vicious toward the monarchs and presidents as they were toward him, even more so.... It was impossible to distinguish between [the treatment of] Shuqayri the person and [the treatment of] Shuqayri as head of the PLO.... I admit that at times I was surprised, when he reacted to major and minor matters alike, and I also thought he was being extreme and knew it. In addition I felt that his language was more along the lines of [literary] flowery prose than circumstances could take, and that it was far removed from the unimpassioned language of numbers and facts.... I came to believe that there was no alternative other than a new order in the Arab homeland and the Palestinian arena.[3]

Shuqayri opened his programmatic speech at the summit on August 30, 1967, "with improvised comments in which he expressed his bitterness over the positions of several Arab capitals toward the PLO, using sophisticated language to hint at a few of the Arab leaders who had criticized him personally. He expressed his willingness and readiness to do whatever was required of him for the sake of the Palestinian cause and people."

Shuqayri's speech (which actually followed the text of the written memorandum he had submitted to the summit) presented the PLO plan. Shuqayri proposed the following six principles regarding the essence of the Palestinian cause:

> No reconciliation [*sulh*] and no coexistence with Israel; refusal [*rafd*] to negotiate with Israel and nonrecognition of the previous occupation [of 1948]; rejection of any arrangement that would undermine the Palestinian cause or lead to its elimination; no concession on the Gaza Strip, the West Bank, or the al-Hama region, and special emphasis on the Arab character of Jerusalem; no separate Arab state acceptance of a solution to the Filastin problem, whether within or beyond the framework of international talks at the UN; continuous, ongoing emphasis [*tarkiz*] in Arab and international circles on the fact that even if Filastin is a fateful Arab issue, the Palestinian people have the primary rightful claim to its homeland and it will determine its own fate.[4]

Shuqayri concluded his speech by saying that "the continued existence of the PLO is first and foremost a Palestinian and Arab national need" and that the dissolution of the PLO and disbanding of the PLA would be a pan-Arab national catastrophe.[5]

In contrast to the fiery style of his other speeches, Shuqayri's speech at the summit was carefully worded and devoid of belligerent commentary. Shuqayri himself remarked that he had deliberately prepared his speech in the form of a written memorandum because he had selected his words carefully and decided to adhere to them (with the exception of the introduction, which he improvised) so that "no one would think that [his] emotions were doing the talking."[6]

The reactions of Arab leaders to the substance of Shuqayri's memorandum essentially reflected their attitude toward Shuqayri himself: they ignored it. No one, not even Nasir, responded. Tension permeated the venue, and the chairman quickly brought the session to a close.[7]

In light of Shuqayri's position, when it became clear that he aimed to thwart King Husayn's political efforts to reclaim the West Bank, a heated argument erupted between Shuqayri and Husayn. The latter was fully supported by Nasir, who was compelled to intervene when the argument intensified.[8]

The final session of the summit took place on the morning of September 1, 1967, when the draft proposals were approved. Shuqayri had intended to boycott the session, but the heads of the Sudanese and Iraqi delegations convinced him to return to the talks, telling him that they were adopting the following principles: no separate Arab state acceptance of a political solution to the problem of Filastin, and no acceptance of a solution unless it had been thoroughly discussed and approved by an inclusive, authorized Arab gathering that included the PLO.

In the meantime, in a separate discussion, the foreign ministers continued trying to reach an agreement on the formulation of a final summit resolution. Their intention was to avoid making any mention of the demands of "no peace" and "no separate solution" with Israel and to avoid mention of the need for an all-inclusive Arab gathering with the participation of the PLO in order to discuss a solution to the conflict. Shafiq al-Hut, who represented the PLO in this discussion, insisted on the inclusion of these articles. But when the draft resolution was presented to the full assembly for summit approval, it turned out that these articles had not been included. Shuqayri again demanded they be included, and when it became apparent to him that his proposals would not be accepted, he dramatically left the session. Eventually, the summit did, as noted, accept the suggestion regarding "no peace" with Israel, but it did not include the second article regarding "no separate solution" because of Husayn's fierce opposition.[9]

After the summit's concluding statement was published on September 1, 1967, Shuqayri issued a statement "to the Palestinian people and the Arab nation" in which he explained why he had walked out of the summit's final session:

> The main reason is [that] the PLO submitted a memorandum to the summit, which included six fundamental principles on which any solution to the problem of Filastin must be based. The memorandum noted that no Arab state has the right to agree on a separate solution to the Filastin problem. It was emphasized that the Filastin problem is a fateful pan-Arab problem and that no political solutions are acceptable unless all Arab states agree to them at an inclusive, authorized gathering with the participation of the PLO. Yet the summit did not agree to the PLO proposal. [Therefore] the PLO delegation had no alternative but to withdraw from the summit, thereby expressing its disagreement with the conclusion reached by the summit regarding the problem of Filastin.[10]

Shuqayri's aggressive conduct during the Khartoum Summit was in effect his "swan song." It became clear that this summit was the end of the road for him.

The Crisis of Leadership Peaks: June–December 1967,

The transformation of fida'i organizations into the dominant factor in the Palestinian arena marked the start of a process in which these organizations became, in effect, the leaders of the new Palestinian national movement. As a result of Fatah's renewal of the "armed struggle" against Israel in August 1967, the Arab masses began to regard fida'i organizations as redeemers of Arab honor, which had suffered a blow with the defeat of regular armies. These organizations represented Palestinian liberation from the chains of the Arab Summit and the conditions that prevailed in the Arab arena during the Shuqayri era. The PLO and Shuqayri as its leader were overshadowed by the meteoric rise of these organizations, as attention increasingly shifted toward the "Palestinianness" of the new Palestinian national movement. Simultaneously, fida'i organizations became more cohesive. Several small organizations joined Fatah, and three groups joined efforts to form the Popular Front for the Liberation of Palestine on December 7, 1967.

With the rise to power and increasing popularity of fida'i groups outside of the PLO, the salient questions that surfaced in Palestinian circles, among Executive Committee members, among Palestinian organization leaders, and within the Palestinian intelligentsia were the following: Where is the PLO headed? Is its existence still justified when it is identified with Shuqayri himself? Who should serve as its leadership and how should it be constituted? And what is to become of Arab financial support for the PLO? An Arab and Palestinian consensus emerged that after the war the PLO could not continue in the same manner and with the same leadership and that substantive change was needed.

The crisis in Palestinian leadership, which worsened after the Six Day War, should be viewed as an extension of processes and events that took place during the year preceding the war. The outcome of the war exacerbated these processes and events and led to their full materialization. The belief that it was not possible to change the PLO as long as Shuqayri was at the helm gained ground. Shuqayri's key problem continued to be his inability to disengage from the Arab arena generally and Egyptian support specifically, which he assumed still existed, at least until the Khartoum Summit. He continued acting and working as if the Arab and Palestinian arenas had not undergone substantial changes as regards the Palestinian cause, presumably because he realized that any fundamental change in the PLO and its leadership would mean an admission of failure. Moreover, in Shuqayri's view, transformation of the PLO into a fida'i organization would mean imitating what already existed, and the original would always be better. Accordingly, Shuqayri adhered to his approach and continued making the same mistakes in which he had "specialized" before the war. Under these circumstances, it is no wonder that even his idol Nasir disappointed him. After the war, Nasir placed his bets on a new "Palestinian horse"—the Palestinian Resistance (al-Muqawama al-Filastiniyya)—as the fida'i organizations were called, and he began to regard Fatah as the organization that could and should lead the Palestinian movement. He pressed Fatah leaders to merge with the PLO and turn it into an umbrella group of fida'i organizations, and eventually they did indeed merge.

Shuqayri was well aware of the situation with respect to the organization and to himself personally in the aftermath of the war and especially after the Khartoum Summit. He admitted that after the summit he put an end to political cooperation with Arab states and that since the war he had "forced himself to keep quiet, unless circumstances strongly compelled him to take a stance."[11]

There were two salient schools of thought among Palestinian leaders and activists regarding the desired course of action and the best path for the PLO to take after the Six Day War: The first school of thought espoused the Palestinization of the struggle and the separation of Palestinian activity from Arab activity. This position stemmed from disappointment with the united Arab operation that led to Israel's occupation of the West Bank and Gaza Strip, "which placed the Palestinian people face-to-face with the enemy." The second school of thought espoused the opposite approach: Arabization of the Palestinian struggle. The starting point for this school of thought was the belief that after the Israeli conquest, the Palestinian cause had become a pan-Arab cause in which the Palestinian people no longer had a special role that would distinguish it from any other Arab people.[12]

Shafiq al-Hut was of the opinion that both perspectives were extreme and neither was free of emotional motives. He offered another perspective, which was actually a "merger of the two perspectives and is more logical and objective." He termed this third approach "the Palestinian revolutionary Arab current." Shafiq al-Hut concluded that "the PLO should not be disbanded but, rather, it should be reconstituted in a new form."[13] His perspective was important because it became the central, dominant school of thought among Arab and Palestinian leaders, particularly in Egypt, which supported the continuing existence of the PLO as an umbrella group of Palestinian organizations dedicated to armed struggle against Israel, foremost among them Fatah. Undoubtedly, Shafiq al-Hut's articles and the perspective he presented therein helped convince Fatah leaders to merge into the PLO framework in the manner he proposed and eventually transform their movement into the backbone of the Palestinian establishment.

Even though Shuqayri was aware of his personal standing and the status of the PLO in the Arab and Palestinian arenas after the war, he did not draw the relevant conclusions on a personal level. He did not want to withdraw from the political arena during a low point, arguing that he "does not want such a move to be interpreted as escaping" and that if he does withdraw he would want his resignation to be an expression of his "taking responsibility." He wanted to be written into Palestinian history in a positive light, but once again his actions took him in the opposite direction. Although he announced the "abandonment of political matters and a focus on revolutionary activity" and "abandonment of action at the official level in favor of action at the popular level, far removed from Arab states," in practice he did not have the means to do so, lacking the popular support he had enjoyed during 1964 and 1965. The only tool he had—the Executive Committee—no longer listened to him.[14]

Shuqayri was a completely changed man after the Six Day War. The Arab defeat shocked him, as it did the other Arab leaders, but he was possibly the hardest hit. It was hard for him to accept the new reality in the Arab and Palestinian arenas and the loss of the Palestinian land and population that constituted his raison d'etre. His remarks at the Khartoum Summit and his provocation of Arab state leaders, to the point that the PLO was not mentioned in the concluding statement and resolutions, are evidence of his changed state. His own declarations and announcements, although more moderate than those that preceded the war, were also an indicator.

Shuqayri reached the conclusion that the only way he could survive was to align himself with the "armed struggle" and fida'i action in both word and deed, at least in terms of appearances. The restrictions he had faced in this regard before the war no longer existed. Indeed, Arab states began competing among themselves to support fida'i actions, with Egypt at the forefront. In effect, Egyptian media turned into the mouthpiece of fida'i organizations.[15]

The first phase in the transformation of Shuqayri's position on fida'i action, which lasted until early December 1967, was characterized by statements ascribing a revolutionary, fida'i image to the PLO as custodian of fida'i organizations and provider of an organizational framework for these groups. PLO radio began praising and extolling fida'i actions, and Shuqayri himself emphasized that the PLO had left the Khartoum Summit "with a view to armed struggle."[16] In interviews and in the many statements he issued after the summit, Shuqayri frequently mentioned his strong support for armed struggle and the "unity of fida'i activities across all the organizations" under the flag of the PLO. In his opinion, "the armed struggle that the Palestinian people are carrying out on their occupied land is the first phase of the popular Palestinian war."[17]

Shuqayri gave his audience the impression that the PLO was presumably leading the "popular Palestinian struggle" by organizing the resistance to Israeli occupation of the Gaza Strip and West Bank and through assistance in the arming, funding, and training of fida'i organizations. Moreover, he even attributed guerrilla actions to the PLO. For example, on December 3, 1967, he claimed that "the PLO is now at the center of the campaign and is managing the Palestinian struggle directly, through military and material means," further asserting that "the PLO has smuggled officers and soldiers into occupied Filastin; it smuggles in weapons and provides the national forces with the funds needed to confront the enemy. The PLO is leading the armed struggle within Filastin."[18] In presenting the PLO as the framework for fida'i organizations, including Fatah, Shuqayri argued on November 24, 1967, that "the Palestinian fida'i movements are supported materially, militarily, and through propaganda by the PLO. We are all working to expand and organize these activities. Regarding Fatah, they are members of the PLO and members of the PNC. . . . We agree with Fatah politically and ideologically, in terms of the goal and [matters of] planning."[19] On other occasions, Shuqayri declared, "All fida'i organizations belong to the PLO, and the PLO belongs to all organizations of the struggle,"[20] and "The Palestinian fida'i movements are now all united under the flag of the PLO and have begun to act as a single front."[21]

The second phase of the shift in Shuqayri's position on fida'i activity led to a December 7, 1967, announcement on PLO Radio regarding the establishment of a "Revolutionary Command Council for the Liberation of Filastin" (Majlis Qiyadat al-Thawra li-Tahrir Filastin), which soon turned out to be a fictitious, nonexistent entity. The context for this announcement was the activity of a group of intelligentsia, including Walid al-Khalidi, who joined efforts to solve the Palestinian leadership crisis by bringing Palestinian organizations together—the PLO on the one hand and fida'i groups on the other—to "unite the revolutionary Palestinian struggle on a methodical basis." The members of the group called themselves the "Executive Authority in Support of the Palestinian Revolution" (al-Hay'a al-'Amila li-Da'm al-Thawra al-Filastiniyya), and their assessment was that "having friendly relations with the leaders of various Palestinian organizations, they would be able to play a significant part in bringing the perspectives of the groups closer together."[22]

In describing the aim of this group, Walid al-Khalidi said (on November 27, 1967), "There is no alternative to substantive change within the Palestinian leadership and to the formation of a central body to be called, for example, the 'High Committee for Emergency Affairs.' This council would include representatives from all organizations that are active both within and outside of the occupied land. We will propose to Ahmad al-Shuqayri that he resign from his position as head of the PLO, in order to establish the High Committee for Matters of Emergency."[23]

This group of intelligentsia (al-Hay'a al-'Amila) decided to initiate its contacts with Palestinian organizations by starting with the PLO "because of its official status, and taking into account its financial and public relations potential." Indeed, at a meeting with Shuqayri, they raised the idea in general terms and asked his opinion regarding a plan aimed at viewing the PLO as "an institution in a state of emergency, something that requires making radical changes in the apparatus." Delegation members suggested that al-Hay'a al-'Amila, which they represented, would establish contact with Palestinian organizations of "fighters" and other organizations to present its plan. The aim would be to hold a conference of representatives from these organizations alongside PLO representatives in the framework of an "Emergency High Council" that would be responsible for coordination among the groups. If the coordination phase is successful, the secret "Emergency High Council" would be followed by another council, to be called the "National Council of the Revolutionary Command" (al-Majlis al-Watani li-Qiyadat al-Thawra).

Ghassan Kanafani, who reported on the meeting, noted that Shuqayri welcomed the plan and expressed his willingness to implement it. He asked the delegation to initiate contact with the other Palestinian organizations to secure their agreement and then to begin implementing the plan. According to Kanafani, the delegation set out to visit Arab capitals to meet with the various Palestinian organizations. But just twenty-four hours after leaving Cairo, its members heard on the radio that Shuqayri had established the "National Council of the Revolutionary Command" after—according to the broadcast—"holding talks with active Palestinian organizations and after convening a military conference in the occupied territories." Shortly thereafter, a military statement by this National Council was issued as well. Ghassan Kanafani concluded his observations by noting that "this move was in effect the straw that broke the camel's back regarding Shuqayri."[24]

Shuqayri's statement, as described by Kanafani, was issued on December 7, 1967, on PLO Radio and directed at "the Palestinian Arab people and the Arab nation." The statement said,

> In response to the PLO call to unite the armed struggle under a single command in the framework of one military plan, a military conference was convened within the homeland, which included the leaders of the fida'iyyun who are fighting throughout the land. After discussing the difficult phase that the sacred cause is undergoing, the conference adopted the following resolutions [among others]:
> 1. The course of armed struggle and a popular war of liberation is the only way to liberate Filastin. Toward this end the conference declared the formation of a military council that will be called the "Revolutionary Command Council for the Liberation of Filastin" (Majlis Qiyadat al-Thawra li-Tahrir Filastin).
> 2. The council expresses full confidence in the PLO as the leader of the [Palestinian] people's struggle and representative of its national aspirations.[25]

It is hard to avoid the conclusion that this move on Shuqayri's part was motivated by the action of the Executive Authority in Support of the Palestinian Revolution. There is a great deal of similarity between the authority's plan as previously described, the details of which were conveyed to Shuqayri, and his statement about establishing a Revolutionary Command Council. Shuqayri wanted to demonstrate that he was acting in the spirit of the time and in accordance with his declarations about "uniting organizations" with the PLO serving as their umbrella group. It is reasonable to conclude that Shuqayri sought to take this "preventive" measure by preempting the practical measures of the authority while also taking advantage of the public relations tools available to him. Presumably, he saw the authority's activities as a threat to his standing and an indication of its members' intent to remove him from his position and transfer Palestinian leadership to fida'i organization leaders. Thus he not only sabotaged the committee's mission but also sparked the ire of his remaining supporters and those who hoped that he had changed his ways. Through this and later announcements supposedly issued by the Revolutionary Command Council, he "broke the camel's back" in Kanafani's words. This started a "snowball effect" that rapidly increased until it led to his resignation on December 24, 1967.

In the context of his efforts to improve his standing after the Arab Summit in Khartoum, Shuqayri tried to renew his contacts with Fatah, but without success. Fatah, for its part, had already resumed its actions on the ground on August 27, 1967, and was gaining in popularity and earning recognition of its status as the foremost Palestinian organization.

Fatah aspired to lead the new Palestinian national movement, and not as the PLO's partner. It therefore increased its criticism of and attacks against the PLO and Shuqayri personally, and it rejected Shuqayri's suggestion that the PLO have "political and propaganda responsibility" while the other Palestinian organizations have responsibility for the "operational aspect of activities." In a newspaper interview, Shuqayri explained his difference of opinion with Fatah by pointing to Fatah's refusal "to provide details about its units and armaments, for reasons of security and ideological motives." According to him, "we tried to overcome this obstacle by proposing to divide the targets or agree on a geographical division of military actions, but were unable to reach a positive result."[26]

Encouraged by its own successes and by the growing criticism of Shuqayri, Fatah intensified its attacks against him, with the aim of causing his withdrawal or dismissal from the political arena. In doing so, Fatah was forceful and merciless. On November 13, 1967, Fatah launched an aggressive attack on the PLO, calling on the organization to transfer its funds to the al-'Asifa fida'iyyun. In addition, it called on PLA fighters to join the forces of al-'Asifa. The movement's newsletter asserted that "Shuqayri's organization has become corrupt and is unfit to represent the Palestinian people" and that "the PLO is in effect a relic of time gone by."[27]

Undoubtedly, Fatah's attack on the PLO constituted a new, more intensive phase in Fatah's attack on Shuqayri and the organization he headed. The call to PLA personnel to join Fatah was intended to encourage a process that was in fact already under way—the desertion by soldiers from PLA battalions in Syria and in particular from the Iraqi 421st PLA battalion stationed in Jordan, their enlistment in fida'i organizations, and their infiltration into the West Bank to carry out attacks.

On December 9, 1967, Fatah issued another harsh statement, in which it refuted Shuqayri's December 7 announcement, "supposedly issued in the name of 'the Revolutionary Command Council for the Liberation of Filastin' stating that a military conference had taken place within the occupied land, and so on." In its statement Fatah asserted that "the General Command of the al-'Asifa forces declares that it has no knowledge of such a conference or of the establishment of such a council. It warns against these repeatedly used means—[that is,] purported operations that were never undertaken or conferences that never took place."[28]

On December 13, 1967, the Palestinian National Liberation Front issued a statement along the lines of Fatah's earlier one, noting that "the spirit in which the PLO was founded and the contradictions that emerged between its stated goals and the means used to achieve them have given it a negative image that cannot serve as a framework for revolutionary Palestinian action. The methods employed by the PLO's leadership in its recent announcement regarding a meeting of the 'Revolutionary Command Council' have nothing to do with the Palestinian revolution."[29]

The End of the Road: Shuqayri Resigns

Shuqayri's standing had reached a new low. The demands for a fundamental change in the PLO and for the removal of Shuqayri as its leader were growing. In addition, it was evident that reorganization was under way among fida'i groups, a salient manifestation of which was the establishment of the Popular Front for the Liberation of Palestine (al-Jabha al-Sha'biyya li-Tahrir Filastin). Simultaneously, doubts about the validity of Shuqayri's announcements steadily increased, as did lack of confidence in him personally. By early December 1967, Egyptian media outlets were already ignoring Shuqayri completely, shifting their enthusiastic support to fida'i organizations and calling on them to unite. All these factors "turned the PLO under Shuqayri's leadership into an organization on the verge of annihilation."[30]

Shuqayri still refused to draw the necessary conclusions on a personal level and remove himself. Consequently, in an unprecedented move, seven members of the PLO Executive Committee sent a memorandum to Shuqayri (probably on December 18, 1967), demanding his resignation. These seven were 'Abd al-Khaliq Yaghmur, Bahjat Abu Gharbiyya, 'Usama al-Naqib, Yahya Hamuda, Wajih al-Madani, Nimr al-Masri, and Yusif 'Abd al-Rahim. Their memorandum asserted that in reviewing the status of the PLO, it became apparent to them that "unless the necessary steps are taken, the PLO could collapse." The memorandum concluded, "We hereby declare that there is no alternative other than your removal from the position of chairman of the Executive Committee, in order to allow the Executive Committee, in cooperation with active Palestinian organizations and bodies, to establish a collective leadership of the PLO that will represent the will and aspiration of the people. We place responsibility on you for the consequences of refusing to accede to this national demand."[31]

Following the Executive Committee members' demand that Shuqayri resign, the Popular Front for the Liberation of Palestine issued a statement supporting this demand on December 18. Similar statements were issued by the General Union of Palestinian Students, Palestinian labor unions, and other Palestinian organizations such as the Palestinian National Liberation Front.[32] Shafiq al-Hut also joined the chorus of groups that were demanding Shuqayri's immediate resignation.

Shuqayri's heart effectively hardened in reaction to these demands, and his response was swift. On December 19, he announced the establishment of a reduced Executive Committee, without the participation of the seven members who demanded his removal, pointing to the dire financial circumstances of the PLO as the reason for this reduction. Shuqayri further announced that there would be "cuts in the salaries of officials and in their number, as well as a reduction in the [number of PLO] offices in Arab countries." In this context, he also decided, in his words, to reduce the number of Executive Committee members to seven, as follows: Ahmad al-Shuqayri (chairman), Jamal al-Surani, Hamid Abu Sitta, Khalid al-Fahum, Sa'id al-'Azzi, 'Abd al-Majid Shuman, and Majdi Abu Ramadan—all close colleagues and supporters of Shuqayri.[33]

Shuqayri took the additional measure of sending a memorandum to the secretary general of the Arab League, the Foreign Ministry of Egypt, and Arab embassies in Cairo. In it he attempted to refute the criticism leveled against him by citing legalistic and formalistic excuses for his actions, some of which he had invoked in the past.[34]

The Egyptian press, which had shifted its support from Shuqayri to fida'i organizations, further fueled the fire of the campaign calling for his resignation. It prominently reported on anti-Shuqayri activities within the PLO and on Palestinian organizations' demands that he resign. This news coverage was a blatant hint directed at Shuqayri. For example, on December 22, *al-Ahram* and *al-Jumhuriyya* published details about the emergence of the crisis in the PLO, stressing that "Shuqayri is still stubbornly refusing to resign his position as chairman of the PLO."

The Egyptian press continued and even intensified its pressure. On December 23 and 24, its main headline stories focused on the crisis and on the demands for Shuqayri's resignation. Representatives from Fatah, the Popular Front for the Liberation of Palestine, and other organizations arrived in Cairo to discuss the crisis and formulate a position regarding the demand that Shuqayri resign. The Palestinian National Liberation Front and Tala'i' al-Fida' joined other organizations in demanding Shuqayri's resignation and dissolution of the Executive Committee.[35] On December 24, all the Palestinian organizations—Palestinian unions and associations, the fida'i organizations, and independents—reached a consensus calling for Shuqayri's resignation, for the establishment of a new Palestinian National Council, and for a change in the character of the PLO while maintaining its structure.

The pressure on Shuqayri to resign intensified when 'Abd al-Majid Shuman joined the seven Executive Committee members who were demanding his resignation, thereby forming a majority of eight members who favored resignation.

In addition, on December 22, the Palestinian National Fund informed banks that they should not honor checks signed by Shuqayri.[36]

In an effort to escape his fate, Shuqayri sent out feelers to a number of Arab states to see if they would convene a meeting of the PNC on their own territory, with the aim of re-establishing public confidence in himself. Because of the consensus that had taken shape against him among Palestinians, the Arab states' responses were not positive. Such a gathering would also have been impossible given that most PNC members were located in the occupied territories.[37]

Apparently, Shuqayri finally decided to resign after discussions with the Egyptian leadership led him to understand that he no longer had its support. On December 19, Shuqayri met with Vice President Husayn al-Shafi'i, but the decisive meeting took place on December 23, with Vice President Zakariyya Muhyi al-Din, when Shuqayri sought to ascertain Egypt's basic position. The official stance as presented to him was a "neutral position," according to which "the Palestinian people will determine the question of resignation or nonresignation," and it was made clear to him that he could not expect official support or opposition on Egypt's part in this regard.[38] Shuqayri understood the significance of this "neutral" Egyptian position, especially given that—in contrast to the supportive position to which he had been accustomed in the past—this new unofficial position was reflected in the Egyptian press as well.

On December 24, 1967, the PLO Executive Committee convened, in a decisive meeting that included eleven of its fifteen members. Aside from Shuqayri, those present included Liwa' (Brigadier-General) Wajih al-Madani, 'Usama al-Naqib, Nimr al-Masri, Bahjat Abu Gharbiyya, Yusif 'Abd al-Rahim, Yahya Hamuda, Rif'at al-Nimr, 'Abd al-Khaliq Yaghmur, Hamid Abu Sitta, Jamal al-Surani, and Majdi Abu Ramadan. Those absent were 'Abd al-Majid Shuman (who was represented by Rif'at al-Nimr), Khalid al-Fahum (who remained in Syria), and Sa'id al-'Azzi (who was in Jordan). During the meeting 'Usama al-Naqib, fearing that Shuqayri would delay submission of his resignation, threatened that if he refused to resign, his opponents would have no choice but to take over the broadcast station (PLO Radio) and the PLO's central office within half an hour, with the assistance of supporters (reportedly, groups of laborers had already been mobilized in preparation for these takeovers).

Shuqayri responded by asserting that his resignation would not have legal validity because it required convening the PNC. His opponents replied that the formal procedure was irrelevant when a majority of the Executive Committee and various unions and associations were demanding his resignation, and that, in any event, it was not possible to convene the PNC, most of whose members were located in the West Bank and Gaza Strip. The PLA commander, Wajih al-Madani, presented a short report detailing the harm caused by Shuqayri's announcement regarding the establishment of the Palestinian Revolutionary Command

Council. On conclusion of the discussion, Shuqayri submitted his resignation from the position of PLO Executive Committee chairman to the committee and his resignation as the representative of Filastin in the Arab League to the league's secretary general.[39] After affirming Shuqayri's resignation, the Executive Committee appointed Yahya Hamuda as the acting chairman of the committee.

On concluding its meeting, on December 25, the Executive Committee issued the following statement, in which it set the objectives for PLO activities during the "current stage":

- Establishment of a National Council that will represent the will of the people and from which a collective, agreed-on leadership will be formed
- Unification and advancement of the armed struggle
- Achievement of national unity
- The harnessing of national potential
- A clean-up of PLO bodies[40]

The intention was to establish a new PNC and to reconstitute the Executive Committee to reflect the changes that had taken place in the Palestinian arena, where the dominant factor now was fida'i organizations—that is, the new generation of Palestinians. Toward this end, the Executive Committee established a subcommittee headed by Yahya Hamuda, whose mandate was to hold talks with Palestinian organizations for the purpose of implementing the objectives just presented.

* * *

"No great Arab politician has ever bowed his head and conceded that a new era had begun, then subsequently left politics through the door before being tossed out through the window."[41] Shuqayri was no exception in this sense, even if he was not a "great Arab politician." He was no less a revolutionary in his opinions than were his fida'i successors, but his greatest problem was the vast gap between his many words and his actual deeds. This gap was filled by the support he received from Egypt. During the first half of the period from the founding of the PLO to the Six Day War, he enjoyed the support of Palestinians and enjoyed credit in the Palestinian arena, but during the latter half of this period he relied primarily on Egyptian support and the changed political circumstances in the Arab arena. The cessation of Egypt's support after the Six Day War effectively brought Shuqayri's political career to an end. Although in his memoirs Shuqayri sought to justify his failings and pin them on "inter-Arab circumstances," these do not diminish his own contribution to his failure. The PLO under his leadership was branded by his personal mark. The equation he formulated, namely, "the PLO equals all Palestinians," became in practice "the PLO equals Shuqayri." During his rule, and in particular from 1965 onward, Shuqayri created a crisis of Palestinian leadership that came to an end only when he resigned.

Shafiq al-Hut, who remained an associate of Shuqayri's throughout the latter's chairmanship, observes the following regarding the challenges Shuqayri faced in the Palestinian arena:

> The burden of "the leader" stems from his having no "authority" or "alternatives" when all look to him as if he had a magic wand that with one wave could create a miracle. The Palestinian people are a difficult people—generous, but consisting entirely of leaders and presidents. [They are an impatient people who] seek immediate liberation, not realizing that even flying a Palestinian flag over one of the PLO offices requires a prolonged struggle with the host state. Arab skies were filled with poles that carried the state flags yet were too narrow to fly the flag of Filastin. The path to the founding of the PLO was treacherous and riddled with obstacles, but Shuqayri symbolized the perspective [the thinking] that clashed with that of the generation that came after the Nakba. Because of his age and political makeup, [Shuqayri] was far removed from this new generation that emerged into the Palestinian arena, and it hated him.[42]

Notwithstanding his scheming, cunning, and leadership problems, Shuqayri made an important contribution to the Palestinian national movement by founding the PLO and turning it into the Palestinians' representative organization. The establishment of the PLO and the emergence of fida'i organizations shortly thereafter changed the contours of the "Palestinian problem" and enabled the new Palestinian national movement and its leaders, Shuqayri's successors, to keep this issue on the Arab, Israeli, and international agendas and to direct it toward its objective—the establishment of an independent Palestinian state.

Notes

1. On the debates at the Khartoum Arab Summit and its resolutions, see Shemesh, *Arab Politics*, 241–49; Shafiq al-Hut, *'Ishrun 'Aman*, 252–53; *al-Ahram*, September 2, 1967; 'Abd al-Majid Farid, *Min Mahadir 'Ijtima'at 'Abd al-Nasir al-'Arabiyya wa al-Duwaliyya, 1967–1970* (Beirut: al-Mu'assasat al-Abhath al-'Arabiyya, 1979), 90–94, 96–98, 102; Shuqayri, *Al-Hazima*, 214–16.
2. "Ahmad al-Shuqayri, Dhikrayat 'An Mu'tamar al-Qimma fi al-Khartoum," *Shu'un Filastiniyya*, no. 4 (September 1971): 90–99; Shafiq al-Hut, *'Ishrun 'Aman*, 112–18.
3. Shafiq al-Hut, *Al-Filastini Min al-Tih*, 70–71.
4. Shafiq al-Hut, *'Ishrun 'Aman*, 142
5. Shuqayri, *Al-Hazima*, 190–97; Shafiq al-Hut, *'Ishrun 'Aman*, 142–48.
6. Shuqayri, *Al-Hazima*, 190.
7. Shafiq al-Hut, *'Ishrun 'Aman*, 148.
8. Shuqayri, *Al-Hazima*, 212–13; Shafiq al-Hut, *'Ishrun 'Aman*, 156–57.

9. Shafiq al-Hut, *'Ishrun 'Aman*, 175–76; Shuqayri, *Al-Hazima*, 212–13.
10. Shuqayri, *Al-Hazima*, 228–29; PLO Radio, September 2, 1967; *al-Hayat*, September 3, 1967; Shuqayri, *Dhikrayat*.
11. Shuqayri, *al-Hawadith*, October 13, 1967.
12. This analysis was put forth by Shafiq al-Hut, *al-Muharrir*, September 25, 1967; see also *al-Hayat*, no. 6, September 30, 1967.
13. Shafiq al-Hut, *al-Muharrir*, September 25, 1967.
14. Shuqayri, *al-Hawadith*, October 13, 1967.
15. See newspapers and Cairo Radio from early December 1967, including *al-Ahram*, December 5, 1967.
16. Shuqayri, PLO Radio, November 2, 1967; PLO Radio, commentaries, October 11, 16, 17, 1967.
17. Shuqayri, press conference, PLO Radio, October 14, 1967.
18. Shuqayri, *al-Anwar*, December 3, 1967.
19. Shuqayri, PLO Radio, November 24, 1967.
20. Shuqayri, *al-Liwa'* (Beirut), October 20, 1967.
21. Shuqayri, PLO Radio, October 19, 1967.
22. *Al-'Usbu' al-'Arabi* (Beirut), November 27, 1967; *al-Huriyya*, November 25, 1967; *al-Anwar*, November 22, 1967 (Ghassan Kanafani); *al-Muharrir*, December 21, 1967.
23. Walid al-Khalidi, *al-'Usbu' al-'Arabi*, November 27, 1967.
24. Ghassan Kanafani, *al-Anwar*, December 22, 1967.
25. Shuqayri, PLO Radio, December 7, 1967.
26. Shuqayri, *al-Hawadith*, October 13, 1967.
27. *Al-Yawm*, November 14, 1967, citing Fatah's organ *al-'Asifa*, November 13, 1967.
28. Fatah, *Watha'iq 'Askariyya*, vol. 1 (Beirut, 1968), 243–44, announcement by Fatah, December 9, 1967.
29. *Al-Hayat*, December 14, 1967.
30. Bilal al-Hasan, *al-Huriyya*, December 11, 1967.
31. For the text of the memorandum, see *al-Muharrir*, December 19, 1967.
32. *Al-Huriyya*, December 25, 1967; *al-Anwar*, December 19, 22, 24, 1967; *al-Nahar*, December 20, 22, 1967; *al-Muharrir*, December 19, 1967.
33. Shuqayri, PLO Radio, December 19, 1967.
34. PLO Radio, December 23, 1967; *al-Muharrir*, December 23, 1967.
35. *Al-Hayat*, December 24, 1967; *al-Anwar*, December 25, 1967.
36. *Yawmiyyat Filastiniyya*, vol. 1 (Beirut, June 1968), 411, 416; Bo'az, "Political Biography," 155.
37. *Al-Muharrir*, December 21, 1967; *al-Hayat*, December 21, 1967; *al-Huriyya*, December 25, 1967.
38. *Al-Anwar*, December 25, 1967.
39. Ibid.
40. PLO Radio, December 25, 1967.
41. From an article by an "Arab Historian," *al-Huriyya*, May 16, 1966.
42. Shafiq al-Hut, *Al-Filastini Bayna al-Tih*, 63–64.

Conclusion

THIS BOOK PRESENTS the 1950s as significantly more active and important years in the history of the Arab Middle East and Palestinian national movement than Israeli and Arab historians have considered them to be. The processes that took place during the 1950s made those years a period of political developments and Palestinian national revival, against the background of formative developments taking place in the Arab world—a far cry from the narrative of political dormancy and national stagnation that historians have presented in the past. Toward the end of this decade and the early 1960s, the Arab world reached a stage of relative stability and consolidation of its regimes, following the political unrest and turbulence of the aftermath of the 1948 Arab-Israeli War and the rise to power of new regimes in nearly all the leading Arab states.

While these changes were taking place in the Arab Middle East, the Palestinian problem was turning into the central issue in Arab discourse. It underwent a significant transformation, as detailed in this book, a transformation that was in essence a process of "Arabization" ('Uruba). Besides the relative stabilization and consolidation of Arab regimes, this period was characterized by a crisis in Palestinian leadership, which afflicted Palestinian society (and the entire Arab world) from the mid-1930s onward, peaking precisely at the moment when there was a need for recognized Palestinian leadership that could decisively determine the fate of the Palestinian national movement. This crisis of leadership, as we have seen, did not prevent a national reawakening but, on the contrary, catalyzed the formation of a new national movement under a new leadership, which would lead the future struggle for Palestinian self-determination. As such, it is reasonable to conclude that the leadership vacuum that prevailed after 1948 was filled by the Palestinian national awakening, which in turn generated a new, authentic, charismatic, and authoritative leadership. The main theme of this book, accordingly, is that despite the failings of the traditional Palestinian leadership and the accompanying leadership crisis, a Palestinian national awakening took place that was able to endure and withstand the most severe crises, even after the defeat and collapse of the traditional frameworks of the Palestinian national movement in the aftermath of the Nakba.

Developments in the Palestinian arena correlated well with the political processes that took place in the Arab world during the 1950s. The Palestinian national reawakening, or national revival, may be seen as a direct outcome of the processes then shaping the Arab Middle East, just as the rise of Nasirism, the Ba'th, and other nationalist movements were a product of the time. It is no wonder that during this period the Palestinian cause became the most important component of Arab nationalism as formulated by Nasir. Nasir drew the rest of the Arab world to this cause, until eventually it became the main element of Arab nationalism, thereby contributing to the dominance, influence, importance, and centrality of the Arab-Israeli conflict, which steadily intensified until it led to the eruption of the Six Day War. The Palestinian national cause became the core issue of the conflict. Consequently, the power, intensity, and endurance of the new Palestinian national movement also increased.

The mufti's leadership and his failings became a source of trauma for Palestinians and the leaders of the Palestinian national movement who emerged in the mid-1960s, especially after the Six Day War. The mufti's leadership served as a model of how not to lead the Palestinians during a period of national reawakening. Indeed, fida'i leaders, who piloted the new Palestinian national movement, tried to learn the lessons of this bitter experience while also harshly criticizing the mufti's course of action. They were especially critical of his rejection of every proposal that did not entail Palestinian rule over all of Filastin, that is, his refusal to accept "partial solutions." The willingness of David Ben-Gurion, leader of the Jewish *yishuv*, to accept the UN partition plan was cited as a positive example in support of the proposal to establish "Palestinian rule over any liberated Palestinian territory" (the phased plan), which was approved later by the twelfth PNC in June 1974. Fatah's leadership rejected positions "that were characteristic of the traditional leadership during the course of fifty years," and Abu Iyad objected to the mufti's negative positions.[1] In his words, "By studying and analyzing the conduct of our predecessors who led the Palestinian movement, we realized that there was a negative course of conduct that we wanted to avoid. We realized that our predecessors during the years 1917–47 rejected any option that did not offer everything, and in so doing they participated in implementing the Zionist plan. . . . Why did Palestinian leaders not agree to a temporary solution (partition), as did the Zionist authorities, based on the establishment of a state in part of the national territory granted to them by the UN?"[2]

The mufti played the part of heroic leader of the Palestinian national awakening during the British Mandate. He was responsible for the achievements and the failures resulting from this awakening, and particularly for the extremist, violent position it adopted. In retrospect, it appears paradoxical that the Palestinian leadership crisis began during the glory days of his influence, which lasted for eight years (1929–37). Moreover, his influence on the domestic Palestinian arena was decisive and ever-present throughout the Mandate era, despite his absence during World War II and his support for the Nazi regime. In this sense, a great discrepancy existed between the mufti's status among the Palestinian population and his status among Arab countries or at least their leaders. His survival as a leader can also be attributed to the lack of a potential successor who could rival him in terms of status, personality, and charisma.

From a perspective of more than half a century, one may conclude that alongside the mufti's failings and the disaster he visited on the Palestinians—as Arab, including Palestinian, historians agree—he should also be credited with contributing to the development of a Palestinian national movement and placing the Palestinian national cause on the Arab and Palestinian agendas during the 1930s and 1940s.

The new Palestinian national movement that emerged in 1965 in the form of fida'i organizations was, in fact, an extension of the Palestinian movement led by the mufti and thus created a historical continuity between them. This new movement also included different components and a new generation of Palestinian leaders who represented the Sons of the Nakba. The deeds and failures of the old, traditional Palestinian leadership, which followed the Husaynis' school of thought, served as lessons for the new Palestinian movement's leaders. The legacy bequeathed to them by the mufti included the armed struggle and the vision of a Palestinian state on the entire territory of Mandatory Palestine.

The second half of the 1950s and, more specifically, the period between December 1955 and April 1957, was unquestionably a decisive period in the history of the Hashemite Kingdom of Jordan leading up to the Six Day War. This period of ongoing crisis touched on all aspects of domestic policy and foreign inter-Arab policies of the kingdom. It would not be an overstatement to say that for King Husayn these years were the formative period in shaping his regime, including both domestic and foreign policies, since his rise to power in 1953. Indeed, Jordan after April 1957 differed in many aspects from Jordan before the crisis. King Husayn emerged from this crisis with a stronger regime and more confidence, and it is safe to say that the experience matured him. At the same time, through this crisis the West Bank Palestinians demonstrated their influence and standing as a political force within the domestic Jordanian arena, a force that grew steadily stronger in the crises that followed—in April 1963 and November–December 1966.

Palestinian and other researchers view the founding of the PLO as a turning point in relations between the West Bank Palestinian population and the Hashemite regime of Jordan.[3] According to one assessment, "The process of unification as termed by Jordan [that is, Jordanization] was relatively successful, until the founding of the PLO in 1964. After that event, the Jordanian-Palestinian union became increasingly shaky."[4] I disagree with this assessment. In my opinion, the process of Jordanization was ineffective from the outset, and it failed in every aspect in relation to the aims of Jordan's rulers, namely, the assimilation of the Palestinian population into the Jordanian identity and erasure of the historical

Palestinian past through the creation of a "melting pot" in which a new Jordan would take shape and represent the Palestinian cause, in the sense that "Jordan is Filastin and Filastin is Jordan." The inevitable conclusion is that the West Bank Palestinians never abandoned their Palestinian identity or their past, and they retained a collective memory throughout this period. Expressions of Palestinian identity increased over the years and with every recurring confrontation between the regime and this population. The founding of the PLO and emergence of Fatah further catalyzed the Palestinization process but were not its source. The process had been under way all the while and reached a peak during the events following the Samu' operation.

The following conclusions emerge from this analysis: First, throughout the years, an explosive atmosphere prevailed in the West Bank, culminating, as noted, in the riots that erupted after the Samu' operation. The emergence of Fatah added fuel to this explosive situation. Administrative and security measures on the part of the Jordanian regime, and in particular the loyalty of the army, prevented an outburst in the West Bank that would have destabilized the kingdom domestically or turned into violent popular resistance. This continuing explosive situation would have led, in time, to one of two outcomes: either Jordan would become a Palestinian state ruled by a Palestinian majority, or the West Bank would disengage from the East Bank to become an independent, autonomous Palestinian entity. The outcome of the Six Day War and Israel's conquest of the West Bank eventually determined the latter's fate, taking it in the direction of disengagement from the East Bank—politically as well as physically. Only much later did King Husayn officially recognize this development, in July 1988, when he announced the severing of any vestige of administrative or legal ties between the West Bank and the kingdom of Jordan.

Second, paradoxically, the process of gradual disengagement of the West Bank from the East Bank, which eventually resulted in full disengagement, began with the annexation itself. The Palestinians' mistrust of the Hashemite regime, which was rooted in the Mandate era, remained and even grew stronger over the years. The consequences of the Six Day War catalyzed this process.

Third, after the Six Day War, it was highly unlikely that West Bank residents would want to return to the kingdom. King Husayn fought over the West Bank, but only in order to maintain hold over the East Bank, that is, the integrity of the kingdom. Accordingly, from the outset Israel's plans and ideas regarding the "Palestinian option" (namely, local rule or autonomy based on an agreement with Israel) and, later, the "Jordanian option" were also illusory and lacked any chance of implementation.

As a result of the political and social processes that Palestinian society underwent from the latter half of the 1950s through the beginning of the 1960s, two dominant, parallel trends emerged in the Palestinian political arena by early

1965: the PLO, founded in 1964, and Fatah, which officially appeared in 1965. Both reflected the Palestinians' aspiration to revive their own entity and assert the Palestinian personality as part of the path to self-determination. The PLO under Shuqayri's leadership embodied the Palestinian entity that relied on Arab patronage generally and Egyptian patronage specifically, while exhibiting clear signs of Palestinian nationalism in the form of an active opposition to Shuqayri and to the PLO's Arab patronage. Fatah, in contrast, challenged the Arab-Egyptian strategy and the composition and perspective of the PLO under Shuqayri, and it actively pursued the "armed struggle" by carrying out guerrilla operations against Israel. Although Fatah's guerrilla actions before the Six Day War on behalf of the "liberation of Filastin" did not contribute substantively toward this objective, they did contribute to the deterioration of the regional situation to the point of war. These two trends proceeded in parallel, as it was almost impossible for them to overlap without one of them absorbing the other.

The founding of the PLO and the emergence of fida'i organizations, foremost among which was Fatah, constituted a historic turning point in the progression of the Palestinian cause. There arose a new Palestinian political generation, which was also described as the Generation of Liberation (Jeel al-Tahrir) and was destined to lead the new Palestinian national movement. This generation was raised on Arab nationalism, as formulated by Nasir and informed by his disappointment with the dissolution of the Egyptian-Syrian union. This generation also challenged the old Palestinian leadership, whose "last of the Mohicans" was Shuqayri. When it appeared that Shuqayri's fate had been sealed, other leaders of Palestinian organizations began to ponder the value of disbanding the PLO. Fatah and other fida'i organizations started weighing the benefits of preserving the PLO framework, which included a mechanism and means of operation, and had earned the recognition of the Arab world. Thus it was decided to retain the framework but change its representational composition. Within only three years of its appearance on the scene, Fatah succeeded in establishing its presence among Palestinians, making itself the most prominent of the organizations and directing the future course of the Palestinian national movement.

To his credit, Shuqayri did make an important contribution to the new Palestinian national movement—founding the PLO out of nothing. One would be hard-pressed to identify another Palestinian political figure capable of filling this difficult role or better suited to it, considering the political conditions prevalent in the Arab and Palestinian arenas at the time. In this sense, Nasir's choice of Shuqayri proved to be the right one. He symbolized the lowest common denominator on which Arab states could agree for the sake of "an organization of the Palestinian people." He carried out this mission skillfully, enthusiastically (at times overly so), and successfully. The alternatives to Shuqayri, namely, fida'i organizations, were admittedly capable of founding the PLO or any other umbrella framework, but this process would have taken several more years, perhaps only culminating after the Six Day War. Egypt, with Shuqayri's help, shortened the process. Thus, the fida'i organizations received a ready-made package, for which they are beholden to Shuqayri.

* * *

What lessons and insights does this book offer with respect to the Palestinian national movement and its leadership from our historical perspective of sixty years, and knowing what we know today about the impact of those developments in the Arab-Israel conflict and Palestinian national cause that were surveyed here?

The first insight is that Palestinian society greatly surprised not only the Israeli political system—especially all the assessment apparatuses of the Israeli intelligence community—but also the Arab world. An extensive review of assessments by the Israeli intelligence community and academic experts from the 1950s and 1960s indicates that nearly all of the processes that took place were not anticipated, including developments within Palestinian society and undercurrents that led to the emergence of a deep-rooted national movement. These assessments regarded the founding of the PLO and activities undertaken by Shuqayri and the Palestinians—such as the convening of the PNCs—as Arab activities and lip service aimed at placating the Palestinians and shirking responsibility toward the Palestinian cause. Even during a later stage of the Palestinian national awakening—in the 1960s and especially after the Six Day War—fida'i organizations were viewed as no more than "military" or "armed" groups whose suppression would mean not only their end but also the end of the national awakening in territories captured by Israel in 1967 and elsewhere. The concept of a Palestinian national movement struggling toward self-determination in Filastin was unmentionable, and anyone who tried to raise this possibility was marginalized. Even Yehoshafat Harkabi in all his writings about Palestinians refrained from mentioning the existence of a Palestinian national movement striving for self-determination, and in this sense he toed the establishment line.

Moreover, under these circumstances, it is no wonder that the illusion of the Jordanian option took shape among the Israeli political leadership and among some academics. The inevitable conclusion of this book is that the Jordanian option was never realistic or executable. It was an illusion adopted by those who wanted to see it as a solution to the Palestinian national problem. Proposals that advanced the concept of the Jordanian option as a solution to the Palestinian national problem reflected a misunderstanding or nonrecognition of the sociopolitical developments within Palestinian society, in spite of clear indications of its national awakening. These indications appeared initially in press publications and later in the founding of the PLO, the emergence of other Palestinian organizations, and their struggle against the Jordanian regime regarding the representation of the Palestinian people and the annexation of the West Bank.

In addition, Arab involvement in the question of Palestine steadily increased from the moment the Jewish Zionist–Palestinian Arab conflict broke out in the late nineteenth century. It further intensified during the Mandate period and especially after the 1948 war, when it took the form of the Arab-Israeli conflict. The Arab involvement began with declarations of support for the demands of Palestinian Arabs, then took forms of opposition to the Balfour Declaration, that is, financial assistance and weaponry, engagement in the "Arab Revolt" of 1936–39, and support for the Palestinian movement's armed struggle, culminating in full military intervention to prevent the establishment of the state of Israel. Ultimately, the Jewish Zionist–Palestinian Arab conflict turned into the all-inclusive Arab-Israeli conflict. The course of the Palestinian cause thus reached the peak of its "Arabness" ('Uruba)—a process that entailed a pan-Arab commitment to the Palestinians. Resolution of the Palestinian national problem became essentially a personal matter for every Arab, not just every Palestinian.

In this context, the Israeli establishment in all its official manifestations did not learn the lesson of the Gordian knot that had formed between the Arab-Israeli conflict and the Palestinian-Israeli conflict. It took Israel's leadership a long time to understand this knot and its many implications. Assessments and actions by the Israeli establishment followed rather than preceded events and reflected a profound lack of understanding regarding all Arab world developments that touched on the Arab-Israeli conflict. At times, political phenomena or events relating to the conflict were interpreted from a narrow and superficial perspective, without an in-depth understanding of the Arab world's stance and intentions regarding Israel, without an appreciation of political and social processes, and without a thorough analysis of the Arab position regarding the conflict. This book reveals that the Arab world believed that Israel aspired to expand territorially at the Arabs' expense and to wipe the Palestinian cause off the agenda. This misunderstanding of the Arab world was the fundamental reason that the Israeli establishment was frequently surprised by Arab or Palestinian political and military actions.

The book also underscores the depth and centrality of the Nakba in the collective Arab memory generally and the Palestinian memory specifically. The memory of the Nakba was passed along, from the generation of the Nakba to the generation of the Sons of the Nakba, then to the generation of the Intifada, and from them to the generation of Palestinian independence. It is safe to say that the Nakba became a central theme in Arab and Palestinian perspectives on the Palestinian national issue and, accordingly, on any resolution of the Palestinians' national cause. Perspectives on the vision of "return" ('awda) and the concept of "liberation" are also integrally linked to this theme.

The outcome of the Six Day War infused the concept of 'awda with new meaning, as the territory of the West Bank, which had been part of an Arab state, became physically transformed into Palestinian territory under Israeli occupation. In this context, the term "liberation of Filastin" also acquired a new meaning: whereas before the war the concept of *'awda* had represented the refugees' return to their places of residence inside Israel, now there was a new alternative—that of return to the territory of Filastin under Israeli occupation. The new meaning of the phrase "liberation of Filastin" eventually facilitated acceptance of the PLO's "phased plan" in June 1974, according to which national Palestinian rule would be established "on any liberated Palestinian territory" (that is, the West Bank and the Gaza Strip). Later it also facilitated the PLO's acceptance of the principle of a Palestinian state in the territories of the West Bank and Gaza Strip, along the borders of June 5, 1967.

For many years researchers and the establishment in Israel misunderstood or ignored the far-reaching impact of the Nakba on Arab leadership, especially the leadership that emerged during the 1950s and 1960s. The impression one forms is that the Arab world was assessed through Israeli eyes and Israeli values, and its actions and stances were often analyzed on the basis of Israeli aspirations and the Israeli view of Arab and Palestinian societies. Of particular salience was the tendency to disparage Arab declarations of support for Palestinians, for the Palestinian cause, and for its resolution. The prevailing assumption was that the Arab position on these issues was intended to serve domestic political interests and had no political validity.

Today we are witness to the emergence of the third generation of the Nakba, which was raised on legacy of the armed struggle of the Sons of the Nakba generation, that is, the Generation of Liberation (Jeel al-Tahrir). The second generation underwent a revolutionary shift in favor of a political solution, namely, the establishment of a Palestinian state in the territories of the West Bank and Gaza Strip, including East Jerusalem. The third generation, which grew up under Israeli occupation, produced the leaders of the first and second intifadas, in 1987 and 2000. This generation may be termed the Generation of Palestinian Independence (Jeel al-Istiqlal)—that is, they represent the generation that is expected to harvest the fruit of the struggle conducted by the Sons of the Nakba generation, beginning with the 1993 Oslo Accords and concluding with the establishment of a Palestinian state.

Two interrelated processes have developed since the 1950s: first, intensification of the Arab-Israeli conflict; and second, the revival of Palestinian nationalism. These two processes fueled and reinforced each other, to the point that the Israeli-Palestinian conflict became the heart and essence of the Arab-Israeli conflict. The parameters for resolution of the Palestinian-Israeli conflict are clear. The new Palestinian national movement is on the path to achieving its objective—self-determination in the form of a state in the territories of the West Bank and Gaza Strip. No Palestinian leader will concede the principles of a solution that were formulated after a decades-long military and political struggle. The solution has become not only a Palestinian-Israeli solution but, by the same measure, an Arab-Israeli solution as well. It is not surprising, therefore, that the Palestinian leadership has sought the agreement of Arab states for every proposed solution, and that it has insisted on the need to reach a pan-Arab consensus on this issue in light of the Arabness ('Uruba) of the problem and the Arab commitment to its resolution.

The context in which the new Palestinian national movement emerged and the successes it has achieved since first visibly appearing on the scene in 1965 indicate that every Palestinian leadership will resolutely uphold the objective of founding a Palestinian state in the territories of the West Bank and Gaza Strip with East Jerusalem as its capital, using all available means. Currently, the Palestinian leadership is focused on the political approach, taking advantage of the support of the international community. A prolonged stalemate in the political process and lack of substantive progress toward its objective are likely to result in the official Palestinian leadership taking unilateral measures and even taking semiviolent action. This move could lead, at a later stage, to genuinely violent action, with the participation of the Palestinian population as well—that is, a new version of Intifada with elements of armed struggle.

Notes

1. Shemesh, *The Palestinian Entity*, 28–29; Abu Iyad, "Afkar Jadida Amam Marhala Ghamida," *Shu'un Filastiniyya*, no. 29 (January 1974): 5–10.
2. Abu Iyad, *Filastini*, 218.
3. See Shu'aybi, *Al-Kiyaniyya*, 126–27; he views the establishment of the PLO as a turning point; see also Sakhnini, "Al-Kiyan al-Filastini."
4. Asher Susser, "Ha-Mshulash Hayisra'eli ha-Falastini ha-Yardeni" [Israeli-Filastinian-Jordanian triangle], in *Shekhenim be-Mavokh* [Neighbors caught in a maze], ed. Joseph Nevo (Tel Aviv: Yitzhak Rabin Center, 2004), 27.

Bibliography

The Bibliography lists sources that are directly cited in the text. State media are included under Media, even where generally regarded as expressing only government policies. Official magazines and other publications of Palestinian organizations are classified under Palestinian Organizations.

Primary Sources

Archives

Ben-Gurion Archives, Ben-Gurion Institute for the Study of Israel and Zionism, Sede Boker, Israel
Collection of reports and surveys prepared by the Israel Defense Forces (IDF), Intelligence Branch, Research and Assessment Department
Private collection of documents and files of the Egyptian government in Gaza, captured by the IDF in the Six Day War
Private collection of documents and files of the Jordanian government in the West Bank (DJG), including Security and Intelligence Services files, 1948–67, captured by the IDF in the Six Day War
Private collection of documents and files of the Palestine Liberation Organization (PLO) offices in Gaza, captured by the IDF in the Six Day War
Foreign Relations of the United States, Washington DC (FRUS)
Israel State Archives, Jerusalem: Papers and documents, 1949–60, Foreign Ministry, Department of Middle East
National Archives of the United Kingdom, London (formerly Public Relations Office [PRO])

Memoirs (Interviews), Books, and Articles

'Abd al-Hadi, 'Awni. *Awraq Khassa*. Edited by Khayriyya Qasimiyya. Beirut: PLO Markaz al-Abhath, 1974.
'Abd al-Nasir, Jamal. *Falsafat al-Thawra*. Cairo: Maslahat al-Isti'lamat, n.d.
Abu Iyad. *See* Khalaf, Salah.
Abu Jihad. *See* al-Wazir, Khalil.
Abu Khatir, Josef. *Liqa'at ma'a Jamal 'Abd al-Nasir*. Beirut: Dar al-Nahar, 1971.
Bin al-Husayn, 'Abdulla. *Al-Takmila min Mudhakirat Hadrat Sahib al-Jalala al-Hashimiyya al-Malik 'Abdulla Bin al-Husayn*. Jerusalem: al-Matba'a al-Tijariyya, 1951.
Darwaza, 'Izzat. *Mudhakkirat*. vol. 1. Beirut: Dar al-Gharb al Islami, 1993.
Hawatma, Na'if. *Na'if Hawatma Yatahaddath*. Edited by 'Imad Naddaf. Damascus: Dar al-Katib, 1997.
al-Husayni, Amin. *Haqa'iq 'An Qadiyat Filastin*. Cairo: Maktab al-Hay'a al-'Arabiyya al-'Ulya li-Filastin, 1954.
al-Husayni, Amin. *Haqa'iq 'an Qadiyyat Filastin*. 3rd ed. Cairo: Dar al-Kitab al-Arabi, 1977.

———. "The Mufti's Memoirs." *'Akhir Sa'a* (weekly), September 20, 1972, September 27, 1972, November 8, 1972, November 29, 1972, December 11, 1972.
Hussein (Husayn), King (of Jordan). *Mihnati ka-Malik*. Amman, (translated into Arabic by) Ghalib Tuqan, 1978.
———. *Uneasy Lies the Head*. London: Heinemann, 1962.
al-Hut, Shafiq. *Al-Filastini Bayna al-Tih wa al-Dawla*. Beirut: PLO Markaz al-Abhath, 1977.
———. *'Ishrun 'Aman fi Munazamat al-Tahrir al-Filastiniyya, 1964–1984*. Beirut: Dar al-Istiqlal, 1986.
Khalaf, Salah (Abu Iyad). *Filastini Bila Hawiyya*. Kuwait, n.d.
Kirkbride, Alec. *From the Wings: Amman Memoirs 1947–1951*. London: Frank Cass, 1976.
Matar, Fu'ad. *Hakim al-Thawra*. London: Highlight Publications, 1984.
Shakur, 'Ammad, and Khayriyya Qasimiyya. "Muqabalatayn ma'a al-Haj Amin al-Husayni." *Shu'un Filastiniyya* 26 (August 1974): 12–18.
al-Shuqayri, Ahmad. *'Ala Tariq al-Hazima* 2. Beirut: Dar al-'Awda, 1972.
———. *'Ala Tariq al-Hazima, ma'a al-Muluk wa al-Ru'asa'*. Beirut: Dar al-'Awda, 1972.
———. *Arba'un 'Amman fi al-Hayat al-'Arabiyya wa al-Duwaliyya*. Beirut: Dar Al-Nahar, 1969.
———. "Dhikrayat 'An Mu'tamar al-Qimma fi al-Khartoum." *Shu'un Filastiniyya* 4 (September 1971).
———. *Al-Hazima al-Kubra ma'a al-Muluk wa al-Ru'asa'*. Vols. 1 and 2. Beirut: Dar al-'Awda, 1973.
———. *Hiwar wa Asrar ma'a al-Muluk wa al-Ru'asa'*. Beirut: Dar al-'Awda, 1970.
———. *Kalimat 'Ala Tariq al-Tahrir, 1965*. Gaza: Dar Akhbar Filastin, 1966.
———. *Al-Kiyan al-Filastini*. App. 3, submitted to the second Arab Summit, September 1964.
———. *Min al-Qimma 'Ila al-Hazima ma'a al-Muluk wa al-Ru'asa'*. Beirut: Dar al-'Awda, 1971.
Ta'i', Ahmad Farraj. *Safahat Matwiyya 'An Filastin*. Cairo: Dar Matabi' al-Sha'b, 1964.
al-Wazir, Khalil (Abu Jihad). *Harakat Fatah, al-Nushu', al-Irtiqa', al-Tatawwur, al-Mumathil al-Shar'i, al-Bidayat* 1. Internal publication, n.p., January 1986.

Official Documents

THE ARAB LEAGUE SECRETARIAT (MAZABIT JALASAT AL-JAMI'A AL-'ARABIYYA)

Jami'at al-Duwal al-'Arabiyya. *Al-Amana al-'Ama, Fahras Muqarrarat Majlis al-Duwal al-'Arabiyya min al-Dawra al-'Ula Hatta al-Dawra al-Tasi'a 'Ashara, June 1945–September 1953*. Cairo, n.d.
———. *Al-Mahadir al-Khitamiyya li-Jalasat Dawr al-'Ijtima' al-'Adi al-Thani li-Majlis al-Jami'a, 31 October 1945–14 December 1945*. Cairo, 1949
———. *Mazabit Jalasat Dawr al-'Ijtima' al-'Adi al-Thalith li-Majlis al-Jami'a, 25 March 1946–13 April 1946*. Cairo, 1946.
———. *Mazabit Dawrat al-'Ijtima' al-Rabi' Ghayr al-'Adiya, 8 June 1946–12 June 1946*. Cairo, 1946.
———. *Mazabit Dawr al-'Ijtima' al-'Adi al-Sabi' li-Majlis al-Jami'a, 7 February 1948–22 February 1948*. Cairo, 1948.
———. *Mazabit Jalasat al-Dawratayn al-Thamina wa al-Tasi'a, 12 March 1948, 30 October 1948–15 November 1948*. Cairo, 1948.

———. *Al-Amana al-'Ama, Mazabit Jalasat Dawr al-Ijtima' al-'Adi al-Hadi 'Ashar li–Majlis al-Jami'a, 17 October 1949–15 February 1950*. Cairo, n.d.
———. *Al-Amana al-'Ama, Mazabit Jalasat Dawr al-Ijtima' al-'Adi al-Thani 'Ashar li-Majlis al-Jami'a, 25 March 1950–17 June 1950*. Cairo, n.d.
———. *Al-Amana al-'Ama, Mazabit Jalasat Dawr al-Ijtima' al-'Adi al-Thalith 'Ashar li-Majlis Jami'at al-Duwal al-'Arabiyya, 23 October 1950–2 February 1951*. n.p., n.d.
———. *Al-Amana al-'Ama, Mazabit Jalasat Dawr al-Ijtima' al-'Adi al-Rabi' 'Ashar li-Majlis Jami'at al-Duwal al-'Arabiyya, 17 March 1951–19 May 1951*. n.p., n.d.
———. *Al-Amana al-'Ama, Mazabit Jalasat Dawr al-Ijtima' al-'Adi al-Khamis 'Ashar li-Majlis Jami'at al-Duwal al-'Arabiyya, 3 October 1951–13 October 1951*. n.p., n.d.

Arab States

Egypt
Farid, Abd al-Majid. *Min, Mahadir Ijtima'at 'Abd al-Nasir al-'Arabiyya wa al-Duwaliyya.* Beirut: al-Mu'assasat al-Abhath al-'Arabiyya, 1979.
Al-Nizam al-Dusturi li-Qita' Ghaza. *Al-Jarida al-Rasmiyya*, no. 75, March 29, 1962.
"Al-Qanun al-Asasi lil-Mantiqa al-Waqi'a Tahta Raqabat al-Quwwat al-Misriyya." *Al-Jarida al-Rasmiyya*. Statute no. 225, 1955.
Al-Waqa'i' al-Filastiniyya, al-Jarida al-Rasmiyya li-Qita' Ghazza. Vol. 1, 1948–56. Cairo, 1957.

Iraq
Taqrir Lajnat al-Tahqiq al-Niyabiyya fi Qadiyyat Filastin. Baghdad, 1949.

Jordan
Mawqif al-Urdun Min Matalib Ra'is Munazamat al-Tahrir al Filastiniyya. Ministry of Foreign Affairs, December 6, 1965.
Al-Urdun wa al-Qadiyya al-Filastiniyya wa al-'Ulaqat al-'Arabiyya. Amman, 1964.
Al-Urdun wa Qadiyyat Filastin. Husayn's speech, January 5, 1966. Official brochure, Ministry of Information, Amman.

Syria (Ba'th)
'Abr Bayanat Qiyadatihi al-Qawmiyya, 1963–1966. Beirut, October 1971.
'Abr Mu'tamaratihi al-Qawmiyya, 1947–1964. Beirut, June 1971.
Al-Ba'th wa Qadiyyat Filastin. Vol. 3, 1955–59. Beirut: Dar al-Tali'a, 1974.
———. Vol. 4, 1959–64. Beirut: Dar al-Tali'a, 1974.
———. Vol. 5, 1964–69. Beirut: Dar al-Tali'a, 1975.
Al-Manhaj al-Marhali li-Thawrat al-Thamin 'Ashar. Approved by the Extraordinary Regional Congress, June 1965. Ministry of Information, Damascus, July 22, 1965.
Nidal al-Ba'th. Old series, vol. 4. *Al-Qiyada al-Qawmiyya, 1955–1961*. Beirut, 1964.
———. Vol. 7. *Al-Qutr al-'Iraqi, 1958*. 2nd ed. Beirut, February 1972.
———. Vol. 8. *Al-Qutr al-Lubnani, 1951–1961*. Beirut, March 1972.
Nidal Hizb al-Ba'th al-Arabi al-Ishtiraki. New series. *'Abr Bayanat Qiyadatihi al-Qawmiyya, 1955–1962*. Beirut, June 1971.

PALESTINIAN ORGANIZATIONS

Fatah

Al-'Awda (West Germany).
Dirasat wa Tajarib Thawriyya. n.p., n.d.
Filastinuna. Beirut (monthly), October 1959–November 1964.
Ideological Notebook. Cairo University, 1958. (This student notebook, in which one of Fatah's founders outlined the ideology of Fatah, was captured by IDF soldiers during the raid on Beirut in April 1973. It is presumed that the notebook was written by Yusif al-Najjar or Kamal 'Udwan, both of whom were killed in this operation.)
Kifahuna al-Musallah. Brochure no. 10, n.d.
Limadha Ana Fatah. The Second Program, "Al-Tala'i' al-Thawriyya," and the Third Program, "Harb al-Tahrir al-Sha'biyya," n.d.
Limadha Hiya Harb Tawilat al-Amad. Brochure no. 9, n.d.
Mafahim Asasiyya. August 1972 (for members only).
Maktab al-Ta'bi'a wa al-Tanzim. Al-Tala'i' al-Thawriyya. Pamphlet no. 7 of the Fatah Political Cadres' Course, Second Program, n.p., n.d.
———. Al-Thawra al-Filastiniyya wa Marahil Tatawwuriha. Internal publication no. 106, n.p., March 31, 1969.
———. Min 'Ikhlaqiyyat al-Muqatil al-Thawri. Pamphlet no. 4. The Young Fighter Library, n.p., n.d.
Mawaqif wa Muntalaqat Thawriyya. n.p., n.d.
Al-Milad wa al-Masira. n.p., n.d.
Min Muntalaqat al-'Amal al-Fida'i. Pamphlet no. 1 in the series Dirasat wa Tajarib Thawriyya, August 1968.
Al-Mudhakira 'Ila Muluk wa Ru'asa' al-Duwal al-'Arabiyya. In the series Dirasat wa Tajarib Thawriyya, September 7, 1965.
Mudhakira 'Ila Mu'tamar Ru'asa' al-Hukumat al-'Arabiyya. In the series Dirasat wa Tajarib Thawriyya, June 4, 1966.
Nabdha Ta'rikhiyya 'an Harakat Fatah. Pamphlet no. 2 for the Cadres' Course, 1968.
Al-Qiyada al-'Amma li-Quwwat al-'Asifa. Al-Mudhakira al-Marfu'a min al-Qiyada al-'Amma li-Quwwat al-'Asifa 'Ila Ra'is wa A'da' al-Majlis al-Watanui al-Filastioni fi al-Qahira fi Dawratihi al-Thaniya, 28 May 1965. n.p., n.d.
Al-Tajriba al-Kubiyya. Pamphlet no. 6 in the series Dirasat wa Tajarib Thawriyya, n.p., August 1967.
Al-Tajriba al-Siniyya. Pamphlet no. 4 in the series Dirasat wa Tajarib Thawriyya, n.p., August 1967.
al-Thawra (magazine of the Fatah organization in Lebanon, for members only).
Al-Thawra al-Filastiniyya, Ab'aduha wa Qadayaha, 'Aduwun Qawiyun Lakinnahu Laysa Usturiyyan. Two-part pamphlet in the series Dirasat wa Tajarib Thawriyya, n.p., n.d.
Al-Thawra al-Filastiniyya al-Musallaha wa Marahil Tatawwuriha. Internal publication no. 106, December 31, 1971.
Al-Thawra al-Vietnamiyya. Pamphlet no. 5 in the series Dirasat wa Tajarib Thawriyya, n.p., August 1967.
Al-Thawra wa al-'Unf, Tariq al-Nasr. Pamphlet no. 3 in the series Dirasat wa Tajarib Thawriyya, n.p., August 1967.

'Udwan, Kamal. *Muhadara*. Brochure for First Cadres' Course, August 16, 1972 (for members only), August 1972.
Wahdat al-Thawra al-Filastiniyya. Pamphlet no. 9 in the series Dirasat wa Tajarib Thawriyya, n.p., n.d.
Watha'iq 'Askariyya. Pt. 1. Beirut, 1968.

Palestine Liberation Organization (PLO)

Al-Dawra al-Thalitha lil-Majlis al-Watani al-Filastini. Gaza, May 20–24, 1966.
Al-Majlis al-Watani- al-Dawra al-Thaniya. Cairo, May 31–June 4, 1965.
Al-Mithaq al-Qawmi al-Filastini, al-Nizam al-Asasi. n.d.
Munazamat al-Tahrir al-Filastiniyya. *Al-Mithaq al-Watani al-Filastini*. Official publication. Cairo, 1964.
Al-Mu'tamar al-Filastini al-Awal. Cairo, May 28–June 2, 1964.

Palestinian Democratic Front for the Liberation of Palestine (PDFLP)

Malamih Tatawwur al-Nidal al-Filastini. n.p., n.d.
Al-Taqrir al-Siyasi al-Asasi li al-Jabha al-Sha'biyya li Tahrir Filastin. n.p., August 1968.

Popular Front for the Liberation of Palestine (PFLP)

Badr, Adnan. " Sab' Sanawat li al-Jabha al-Sha'biyya li Tahrir Filastin ." *Al-Hadaf*, Beirut, December 14, 1974.

ISRAEL

Documents on the Foreign Policy of Israel. Vol. 8. Edited by Yemima Rosenthal. Israel State Archives, Jerusalem: Ha-Madpis Ha-Memshalti, 1995.

UNITED NATIONS

United Nations Relief and Works Agency for Palestine Refugees in the Near East (UNRWA), *Annual Report 1959 of the Director of UNRWA*, July 1, 1958–June 30, 1959. UN General Assembly, 14th Sess., Supp. 14, UN Doc. A/42/3.

Media

RADIO

Egypt: Cairo Radio, Sawt al-Arab
Fatah: Sawt al-'Asifa
Iraq: Baghdad Radio
Jordan: Amman Radio, Ramalla Radio
Lebanon: Beirut Radio
PLO: Sawt Filastin
Syria: Damascus Radio, Sawt Filastin
United Kingdom: Al-Sharq al-Adna

The Press

Denmark
Politiken

Egypt
al-Ahram
al-Akhbar
Akhbar al-Yawm
Akhir Sa'a
al-Jumhuriyya
al-Masa'
al-Musawar
Ruz al-Yusif
al-Sha'b
al-Tali'a

Gaza
Akhbar Filasatin
Nidal al-'Awda
al-Raqib

Iraq
al-Akhbar
al-Jumhuryiyya
al-Thawra
al-Thawra al'Arabiyya
al-Zaman

Jordan
Akhbar al-Usbu'
al-Difa'
Filastin
al-Jihad
al-Manar

Lebanon
al-'Ahad
al-Ahrar
al-'Amal
al-Anwar
Filastin (AHC)
Filastin (al-Muharrir)
al-Hawadith
al-Hayat

al-Huriyya
al-Jarida
al-Kifah
Kul Shay'
al-Liwa'
al-Muharrir
al-Nahar
al-Sahafa
al-Sayyad
al-'Usbu' al-'Arabi
al-Yawm

Palestine
Filastin

Syria
al-Ba'th
al-Ishtiraki
al-Thawra

United States
New York Times

Secondary Sources
Books and Reports

'Abd al-Hadi, Mahdi. *Al-Mas'ala al-Filastiniyya wa Mashari' al-Hulul al-Siyasiyya 1934–1974*. Beirut: al-Maktaba al-'Asriyya, 1975.
Abu Shilbaya, Muhammad. *Al-Tariq 'Ila al-Khalas wa al-Huriyya, wa al-Salam*. Jerusalem: Matabi' al-Sha'b al-Tijariyya, 1972.
al-'Alami, Musa. *'Ibrat Filastin*. Beirut: Dar al-Kashaf, 1949.
'Alush, Naji. *Al-Masira 'Ila Filastin*. Beirut: Dar al-Tali'a, 1964.
Ankori, Gannit. "Exile and Memories: Art after 1948." In *Palestinian Art*. London: Reaktion Books, 2006.
al-'Arif, 'Arif. *Al-Nakba, Nakbat Bayt al-Maqdis wa al-Firdaws al-Mafqud, 1947–1952*. 6 vols. Sidon: al-Maktaba al-'Asriyya, 1956–60.
Ayyub, Salah. *Al-Qassamiyyun, Lamahat Matwiyya 'An Tarikh al-Nidal al-Filastini*, al-Jabha al-Sha'biyya li Tahrir Filastin- al-Qiyada al-'Amma, n.p., n.d.
Ayyub, Samir. *Al-Bina' al-Tabaqi lil-Filastiniyyin*. Beirut: Dar al-Hadatha, 1984.
'Azzam, Samira. *Al-Sa'a wa al-'Insan*. Beirut: al-Mu'assasa al-Ahliyya, n.d.
Ballas, Shim'on. *Hassifrut ha-'Arvit be-Sel ha-Milhama* [Arabic literature under the shadow of the war]. Tel Aviv: Am Oved, 1978.
Barout, Muhammad Gamal. *Harakat al-Qawmiyyin al-'Arab*. Damascus: al-Markaz al-'Arabi le al-Dirasat al-'Istiratijiyya, 1997.
Ben Porat, Yoram, 'Immanuel Marks, and Shim'on Shamir, *Mahane Plitim be-Gev ha-Har* [Refugee camp on the hillside]. Tel Aviv: Moshe Dayan Center, 1974.

Brand, Laurie A. *Palestinians in the Arab World: Institution Building and the Search for State.* New York: Columbia University Press, 1988.

Bo'az, Arie. "Biografia Politit shel Ahmad al-Shuqayri" [Political biography of Ahmad al-Shuqayri]. MA thesis, Tel Aviv University, March 1987.

Carmon, Yig'al. "Mufti Yerushala'im, Haj Amin al-Husayni, ve-Germania ha-Nazit be-Tkufat Milhemet ha-Olam ha-Shniyya" [The mufti of Jerusalem, Haj Amin al-Husayni, and Nazi Germany during World War II]. MA thesis, the Hebrew University of Jerusalem, 1988.

Clapp Mission. *Final Report of the UN Economic Survey Mission for Middle East.* Pt. 1: *The Final Report and Appendices*, December 28, 1949, UN Doc. A/AC/25/6.

Cohen, Amnon. *Political Parties in the West Bank under the Jordanian Regime, 1949–1967.* Ithaca, NY: Cornell University Press, 1982.

al-Dabbagh, Mustafa. *Biladuna Filastin.* Beirut: Dar al-Tali'a, 1965–66.

Dann, Uriel. *King Hussein and the Challenge of Arab Radicalism.* Oxford: Oxford University Press, 1989.

Darwaza, Muhamad 'Izzat. *Al-Qadiyya al-Filastiniyya.* Vol. 2. Sidon: al-Maktaba al-'Asriyya, 1961.

al-Dur, Niqola. *Hakadha Da'at wa Hakadha Ta'ud.* Beirut: Dar al-Hawadith, 1963.

Efrat, Moshe. *Haplitim ha-Filastinim-Mihkar Kalkali ve Hivrati, 1947–1974.* [Economic and social reseach 1947-1974]. Research Report no. 10, Tel Aviv University, September 1976.

———. "The Palestinian Refugees: The Dynamics of Economic Integration in Their Host Countries." Discussion paper, Israel International Institute for Applied Economic Policy Review, September 1993.

Elpeleg, Zvi. *Ha-Mufti ha-Gadol* [The grand mufti]. Tel Aviv: Ministry of Defense, 1989.

Fawzi, Muhammad, and 'Umar Rushdi. *Al-Sihyoniyya wa Rabibtiha'Isra'il.* Cairo: al-Kulliyya al-Harbiyya, 1962.

Francus, Anya. *Al-Filastiniyyun.* Beirut: Dar al-Nahar, 1969.

Frochter-Ronen, Iris. "Jordan and the Palestinian Challenge: Jordan's Handling of the Palestinian Issue as Part of the Consolidation of its Own National Identity and as Reflected in Jordanian Textbooks, 1964–1994." PhD diss., University of Haifa, July 2003 (Hebrew).

Goren, Asher. *Ha-Liga ha-'Aravit, 1945–1954* [The Arab League, 1945–1954]. Tel Aviv: Ma'yanot, 1954.

Harkabi, Yehoshafat. *Arab Attitudes to Israel.* Jerusalem: Israel Universities Press, 1976.

———. *Haffalastinim Me-Tardima le-Hit'ororut* [The Palestinians from dormancy to awakening]. Jerusalem: Magnes, 1975.

Hashad, Adli. *Sha'b Filastin fi Tariq al-'Awda.* Cairo: al-Dar al-Qawmiya, 1964.

al-Hawari, Nimr. *Sir al-Nakba.* Nazareth, 1955.

Hirschowitz, Lukas. *Ha-Reich ha-Shlishi ve-ha-Mizrah ha-'Aravi* [The Third Reich and the Arab East]. Merhavia: Sifriat Poalim, 1965.

———. *Al-Fikr al-Siyasi al-Filastini, 1964–1974.* Beirut: PLO Markaz al-Abhath, 1980.

Husayn, Hasan Khalil. *Abu Iyad-Salah Khalaf, Safahat Majhula min Hayatihi.* Amman, 1991.

al-Hut, Bayan Nuwayhid. *Al-Qiyadat wa al-Mu'assasat al-Siyasiyya fi Filastin, 1917–1948.* Beirut: Mu'assasat al-Dirasat al-Filastiniyya, 1986.

al-Hut, Shafiq. *Haqa'iq 'Ala Tariq al-Tahrir*. Beirut: PLO Markaz al-Abhath, 1966.
Israel Foreign Ministry. *Ba-Mahane ha-'Aravi, Sikum Yedi'ot* [Summary of information], December 28, 1947, January 11, 1948, January 18, 1948, and *Intelligence Report*, January 17, 1948 (Hebrew).
———. *Intelligence Report*, January 17, 1948 (Hebrew).
———. Middle East Department, Daily Summary of Arab Radio Stations (Hebrew).
———. Research Department, Daily Summary of Information, July 19, 1948, July 23, 1948 (Hebrew).
al-Kayali, 'Abd al-Wahab. *Al-Qadiyya al-Filastiniyya, 'Ara' wa Mawaqif, 1944–1967*. Beirut, 1973.
Kaziha, Walid. *Revolutionary Transformation in the Arab World*. London: St. Martin's Press, 1975.
Khalidi, Walid. "The Arab Perspective." In *The End of the Palestine Mandate*, edited by William Roger Louis and Robert W. Stookey. London: Tauris, 1986.
al-Kilani, Haytham. *Al-Istiratijiyyat al-'Askariyya lil Hurub al-'Arabiyya—al-Isra'iliyya, 1948–1988*. Beirut: Markaz Dirasat al-Wahda al-'Arabiyya, 1991.
al-Kubaisi, Basil. *The Arab Nationalists Movement, 1951–1971: From Pressure Group to Socialist Party*. Washington, DC: ProQuest Dissertations Publishing, 1971.
al-Majali, Hazza'. *Qissat Muhadathat Templer*. n.p., n.d.
Al-Mawsu'a al-Filastiniyya. Pt. 1. Damascus: al-Hay'a al-Mawsu'a al-Filastiniyya, 1984.
Al-Mawsu'a al-Filastiniyya. Pt. 2. Vol. 3. Beirut: al-Hay'a al-Mawsu'a al-Filastiniyya, 1990.
Middle East Record. Vol. 1, 1960; Vol. 2, 1961; Vol. 3, 1967; Vol. 4, 1968. Tel Aviv: Shiloah Institute.
Muhsin, Ibrahim. *Harakat al-Qawmiyyin al-'Arab min al-Fashiyya 'Ila al-Nasiriyya*. Beirut: Dar al-Tali'a, 1970.
Muslih, Muhammad. *The Origins of Palestinian Nationalism*. New York: Columbia University Press, 1988.
Mutawi, Samir. *Jordan in the 1967 War*. Cambridge: Cambridge University Press, 1987.
al-Naqqash, Raja'. *Mahmud Darwish—Sha'ir al-Ard al-Muhtala*. 3rd ed. Cairo: Dar al-Hilal, 1971.
al-Nashashibi, Nasir al-Din. *Tadhkarat 'Awda*. Beirut: al-Mat ktab al-Tijari, 1962.
Nevo, Joseph. *'Abdulla ve-'Arviyei Eretz Yisra'el* ['Abdulla and the Arabs of Palestine]. Tel Aviv: Papyrus, 1975.
———. "Ha-Hitpathut ha-Politit shel ha-Tnua'a ha-Le'umit ha-'Aravit ha-Falastinit, 1939–1945" [The political development of the Palestinian Arab National Movement, 1939–1945]. PhD diss., Tel Aviv University, 1977.
Pappe, Ilan. *Asulat ha-Aretz: Mishpahat al-Husayni* [The aristocracy: The Husaynis, a political biography]. Jerusalem: Musad Bialik, 2002.
Porath, Yehoshua. *The Emergence of the Palestinian-Arab National Movement, 1918–1929*. London: Frank Cass, 1974.
———. *Ma'avak Ha'Aravim Hafalastinim, 1918–1939: Kovetz Te'udot* [The Palestinian-Arab struggle, 1918–1939: Collected documents]. Jerusalem: the Hebrew University of Jerusalem, 1981.
———. *The Palestinian-Arab National Movement: From Riots to Rebellion, 1929–1939*. London: Frank Cass, 1977.

al-Qamhawi, Walid. *Al-Nakba wa al-Bina' fi al-Watan al-'Arabi.* 2nd ed. Beirut: Dar al-'Ilm le al-Malayeen, 1962.

al-Qasim, Anis. *Min al-Tih 'Ila al-Quds.* Tripoli: Dar al-Nashr, 1965.

Qura, Nazih. *Ta'lim al-Filastiniyyin—al-Waqi' wa al-Mushkilat.* Beirut: PLO Markaz al-Abhath, 1975.

Rabinovich, Itamar. *Hashalom Shehamak: Yahse Yisra'el-Arav, 1949–1952* [Elusive Peace: Israel-Arab relations, 1949–1952]. Tel Aviv: Keter, 1991. Published in English as *The Road Not Taken: Early Arab-Israeli Negotiations.* New York: Oxford University Press, 1991.

al-Sawafiri, Kamil. *Al-Shi'r al-'Arabi al-Mu'asir fi Nakbat Filastin.* Cairo: Matba'at Nahdat Misr, 1963.

Sayigh, Yezid. *Armed Struggle and the Search for State: The Palestinian National Movement, 1949–1993.* Oxford: Clarendon Press, 1997.

Sela', Avraham. *Memaga'im le-Masa u-Mattan* [From talks to negotiations]. Tel Aviv: Moshe Dayan Center, 1985.

Shabib, Samih. *Hukumat 'Umum Filastin Muqadamat wa Nata'ij.* Algiers, 1988.

Shahrabani, Na'im. *Hassikhsukh Ha-'Arbi Yisraeli: Bibliografya shel Sfarim ve-Pirsumim be-'Arvit* [The Arab-Israeli conflict: Bibliography of Arabic Books and Publications]. Jerusalem: Truman Institute, the Hebrew University of Jerusalem, 1975.

al-Sha'ir, Muhammad. *Al-Harb al-Fida'iyya fi Filastin.* Beirut: PLO Markaz al-Abhath, 1967.

Shemesh, Moshe. *Arab Politics, Palestinian Nationalism and the Six Day War: The Crystallization of Arab Strategy and Nasir's Descent to War, 1957–1967.* Brighton, UK: Sussex, 2008.

———. *Meha-Nakba la-Naksa* [From the Nakba to the Naksa]. Sede Boker: The Ben-Gurion Research Institute for the Study of Israel and Zionism, 2004.

———. *The Palestinian Entity, 1959–1974: Arab Politics and the PLO.* 2nd ed. London: Frank Cass, 1996.

Shlaim, Avi. *Collusion across the Jordan: King Abdullah, the Zionist Movement, and the Partition of Palestine.* Oxford: Clarendon Press, 1988.

al-Shu'aybi, 'Isa. *Al-Kiyaniyya al-Filastiniyya, 1947–1977.* Beirut: PLO Markaz al-Abhath, 1979.

al-Shuqayri, Jamal. *Al-Kiyan al-Filastini.* n.p., n.d.

al-Tal, Sa'id. *Al-Urdun wa Filastin, Wajhat Nazar 'Arabiyya.* Amman: Dar al-Liwa' le al-Sahafa wa al-Nashr, 1986.

Tuqan, Qadri Hafiz. *Ba'da al-Nakba.* Beirut: Dar al-'Ilm le al-Malayeen, 1950.

Turki, Fawaz. *The Disinherited: Journal of a Palestinian Exile.* London: Monthly Review Press, 1972.

Yasin, Subhi. *Tariq al-'Awda 'Ila Filastin.* Cairo, 1961.

Al-Yawmiyyat al-Filastiniyya. Vol. 2. Beirut: PLO Markaz al-Abhath, December 1966.

Yisraeli, David. *Ha-Reich ha-Germani ve-Eretz Yisra'el, Be'ayot Eretz Yisra'el ba-Mediniut ha-Germanit ba-Shanim, 1889–1945* [The German Reich and Palestine: The problems of Palestine in German policy 1889–1945]. Ramat-Gan: Bar-Ilan University, 1974.

Yusif, Shehada. *Al-Waqi' al-Filastini wa al-Haraka al-Niqabiyya.* Beirut: PLO Markaz al-Abhath, 1973.

Zak, Moshe. *Husayn 'Ose Shalom* [Husayn makes peace]. Ramat-Gan: Bar-Ilan University Press, 1996.

Zurayq, Qustantin. *Ma'na al-Nakba*. Beirut: Dar al-'Ilm le al-Malayeen, 1948.
———. *Ma'na al-Nakba Mujddadan*. Beirut: Dar al-'Ilm le-al-Malayeen, 1967.

Articles and Book Chapters

Abu-Lughod, Janet. "The Demographic Transformation of Palestine." In *The Transformation of Palestine: Essays on the Origin and Development of the Arab-Israeli Conflict*, edited by Ibrahim Abu-Lughod. Evanston, IL: Northwestern University Press, 1971.

Barakat, Halim. "Hannikur ve-Hammahpekha ba-Hayyim ha-'Arbiyim" [The alienation and the revolution in the Arab Life], *Mawaquf* (Beirut), no. 5 (July–August 1969). In *Arab ve Israel* [Arab and Israel], edited by Yehushafat Harkabi, vol. 1. Tel Aviv: Am Oved, 1974.

Bruhns, Fred C. "A Study of Arab Refugee Attitudes." *Middle East Journal* 9, no. 2 (1955).

Carpi, Daniel. "Ha-Mufti shel Yerushala'im, Amin al-Husayni ve-Pe'iluto ha-Medinit be-Yeme Milhemet ha-'Olam ha-Shniyya" [The mufti of Jerusalem, Amin al-Husayni, and his political activities during World War II], *Hasiyyonut* 9 (1984).

al-Dabbagh, Salah al-Din. "Haq al-Sha'b al-Filastini bi-Ardihi wa al-'Awda 'Ilayha." *Shu'un Filastiniyya* 41–42 (February 1975).

Dann, Uriel. "The Foreign Office, the Baghdad Pact and Jordan." *Asian and African Studies* 21 (November 1987).

Galtung, Ingrid, and Johan Galtung. "Some Factors Affecting Local Acceptance of a UN Force: A Pilot Project from Gaza." *International Problems* (Israel) 1–2 (1966).

Ghantus, Lutf. "'Athar al-Tarkib al-Tabaqi fi al-Qadiyya al-Filastiniyya." *Dirasat 'Arabiyya* (December 1965).

Harkabi, Yehoshafat. "The Palestinians in the Fifties and Their Awakening as Reflected in Their Literature." In *Palestinian Arab Politics*, edited by Moshe Ma'oz. Jerusalem: Academic Press, 1975.

Kanafani, Ghassan. "'Thawrat 1936–1939 fi Filastin, Khalfiyyat wa Tafaseel wa Tahlil." *Shu'un Filastiniyya* 6 (January 1972).

Khalaf, Salah. "Afkar Jadida Amam Marhala Ghamida." *Shu'un Filastiniyya* 29 (January 1974).

Khalul, Faysal. "Harakat al-Qawmiyin al-'Arab, Qira'a Jadida li-Tajriba fi Dhimmat al-Tarikh." *al-Fikr al-'Arabi* 28 (July–August 1982).

Mannheim, Karl. "The Problem of Generations." In *Essays on the Sociology of Knowledge*, (by Karl Mannheim) edited by Paul Kecskemeti. London: Routledge & Kegan Paul, 1959.

Musa, Shehada. "Hawl Tajribat al-Ittihad al-'am li-Talabat Filastin." *Shu'un Filaastiniyya* 5 (November 1971).

Nevo, Joseph. "Ha-Tnua'a ha-Le'umit ha-'Aravit ha-Falastinit be-Milhemet ha-'Olam ha-Shniyya" [The Arab-Palestinian National Movement during the Second World War]. In *Ha-Tnu'a ha-Le'umit ha-Falastinit: Me-'Imut le-Hashlama?* [*The Palestinian National Movement: From Confrontation to Reconciliation?*], edited by Moshe Ma'oz and Benjamin Z. Kedar. Tel Aviv: Ministry of Defense, 1996.

Pa'il, Me'ir. "Hafka'at ha-Ribonut ha-Medinit 'al Falastin mi-yede ha-Falastinim 'al yede Medinot Arav bi-Tkufat Milhemet ha-'Asma'ut 1947–1948" [Expropriation of political sovereignty over Palestine from the Palestinians by Arab States during the War of Independence, 1947–1948]. *Hasiyyonut* 3 (1974).

Sakhnini, 'Isam. "Al-Filastiniyyun fi al-'Iraq." *Shu'un Filastiniyya* 13 (September 1972).
———. "Al-Kiyan al-Filastini 1964–1974." *Shu'un Filastiniyya* 41–42 (February–March 1975).

———. "Nashrat al-Tha'r-Qira'a fi Muqaddimat al-Fikr al-Muqawim." *Shu'un Filastiniyya* 21 (May 1973).

———. "Tamthil al-Sha'b al-Filastini wa Munzamat al-Tahrir al-Filasiniyya," *Shu'un Filastiniyya* 15 (November 1972): 27.

Sayigh, Rosemary. "Palestinian Camp Women as Tellers of History." *Journal of Palestine Studies* 27, no. 2 (1998).

Sela', Avraham. "Ha-'Aravim ha-Falastinim be-Milhemet 1948" [The Palestinian Arabs during the 1948 War]. In *Ha-Tnu'a ha-Le'umit ha-Falastinit: Me-'Imut le-Hashlama?* [The Palestinian National Movement: From confrontation to reconciliation?], edited by Moshe Ma'oz and Benjamin Z. Kedar. Tel Aviv: Ministry of Defense, 1996.

Sha'ath, Nabil. "High Level Palestinian Manpower." *Journal of Palestine Studies* 1, no. 2 (1972).

Shabib, Samih. "Muqadamat al-Musadara al-Rasmiyya lil-Shakhsiyya al-Wataniyya al-Filastiniyya, 1948–1950." *Shu'un Filastiniyya* 129–131 (August–October 1982).

Shemesh, Moshe. "The IDF Raid on Samu': The Turning Point in Jordanian Relations with Israel and the West Bank Palestinians." *Israel Studies* 7, no. 1 (2002).

———. "Prelude to the Six Day War: The Arab-Israeli Struggle over Water Resources." *Israel Studies* 9, no. 3 (2004).

Shlaim, Avi. "The Rise and Fall of the All-Palestine Government in Gaza." *Journal of Palestine Studies* 20, no. 1 (1990).

Sirhan, Basim. "Shuhada' al-Thawra al-Filastiniyya." *Shu'un Filastiniyya* 9 (May 1972).

Susser, Asher. "Hamshulash Hayisra'eli-Hafalastini-Hayardeni" [The Israeli-Filastinian-Jordanian triangle]. In *Shekhenim be-Mavokh* [Neighbors caught in a maze], edited by Joseph Nevo. Tel Aviv: Yitzhak Rabin Center, 2004.

al-Ta'ma, Salih. "Al-Mas'ala al-Filastiniyya fi al-Adab al-'Arabi al-Hadith." *Shu'un Filastiniyya* 12 (August 1972).

Tibawi, A. L. "Visions of the Return: The Palestine Arab Refugees in Arabic Poetry and Art." *Middle East Journal* 17, no. 5 (1963).

Turki, Fawaz. "To Be a Palestinian." *Journal of Palestine Studies* 2, no. 11 (Spring 1974).

Name Index

Abadla, Qusay, 229
'Abbas, Mahmud (Abu Mazen), 107, 137–138
'Abd al-Baqi, Ahmad Hilmi, 13–15, 17, 25–26, 28–30, 40–41, 41n9, 44–50, 52, 57n9, 60–63, 223
'Abd al-Fattah, Yunis, 258, 266
'Abd al-Hadi, 'Awni, 13, 17, 21n15, 21n17, 21n26, 21n29, 21n31, 25, 28, 41n9, 41n12, 42n15, 42n17, 46, 49, 63, 73n2, 73n8,
'Abd al-Hadi, 'Isam, 217
'Abd al-Hadi, Na'im, 184
'Abd al-Hamid, Ha'il, 137, 138
'Abd al-Hamid, Yasin, 248
'Abd al-Karim, 'Adil, 138
'Abd al-Karim, Hamad, 130
'Abd al-Khaliq, Yaghmur, 217, 229, 245, 269n8, 281, 283
'Abd al-Latif, Salah, 13, 15, 17, 25, 26
'Abd al-Majid, Shuman, 229, 245, 248, 258, 266, 269n22, 282, 283
'Abd al-Muhsin, Abu Mayzar, 256
'Abd al-Nabi, Hafiz, 217
'Abd al-Nasir, Jamal, 19n5, 67, 82, 86, 102n7, 102n8, 102n9, 102n10, 102n11, 102n12, 106, 110, 111, 129, 132, 135, 138, 145, 147, 167, 168, 172, 179, 182, 184, 188, 190, 192, 196, 203, 204, 223, 227, 229, 230, 232, 234, 235n10, 240, 242, 245, 247, 248, 253n25, 254, 256, 257, 263, 265, 271–273, 275, 285n1, 288, 291
'Abd al-Qadir, Salih, 186
'Abd al-Rahim, Samir, 238, 252n4
'Abd al-Rahim, Yusif, 281, 283
'Abda, Yusif,. 217
Abdulla, king of Jordan, xii, 5, 14, 32, 42n30, 44, 47–48, 51–56, 61, 65, 67, 70–71, 125–126, 165–166, 172, 184, 230
al-'Abdulla, Radi, 194, 210
Abqaryus, Michel, 46, 49, 63
Abu 'Alan, Isma'il, 217

Abu Gharbiyya, Bahjat, 217, 229, 245, 248, 281, 283
Abu Ghazala, Hatim, 200–201, 203n4
Abu Ghosh, Musa, 217
Abu Hijla, 'Abd al-Majid, 178
Abu al-Huda, Tawfiq, 173
Abu Iyad. See Khalaf, Salah
Abu Jihad. See al-Wazir, Khalil
Abu-Lughod, Janet, 90, 103n25
Abu Mazen. See 'Abbas, Mahmud
Abu Nuwar, 'Ali, 190, 192–194
Abu Nuwar, Ma'an, 193
Abu Ramadan, Majdi, 282–283
Abu al-Sa'ud, Shaykh Hasan, 40
al-'Abushi, Fahmi, 217
Abu Shrara, Majid, 137
Abu Sitta, Hamid, 229, 267, 282–283
Abu Sitta, Ibrahim, 248, 257
Abu al-Su'ud, Tawfiq, 211
Abu al-Su'ud, Yasir, 211
'Aflaq, Michel, 143
al-Ahmad, Najib, 201, 203n4
al-'Alami, Musa, 16, 19n4, 24, 26, 41n2, 41n9, 89, 103n22, 187, 223
al-'Alami, Zuhayr, 146, 231
'Alush, Naji, 79, 102n2
al-'Amad, Muhammad, 178
'Amir, 'Abd al-Hakim, 131, 181
al-'Anabtawi, Fa'iq, 177–178
al-'Anabtawi, Mundhir, 246
al-'Anabtawi, Salah, 126, 167, 217, 232–233
Andrews, Lewis, 14, 58n22, 58n29
Ankori, Gannit, 99, 104n58, 104n59, 104n60, 104n61
Antonius, George, 15–16
'Aql, Amin, 46, 49, 62–63
'Aql, Basil, 246
Arafat, Yasir, 107–108, 135–136, 138–140, 145–146, 231, 260
'Arif, Abd al-Rahman (of Iraq), 265

Ashton, Nigel, 176
'Ashur, Yahya, 135, 138
'Atalla, 'Atalla, 107
Atasi, Hashim Khalid, 265
'Awad, 'Awad Mahmud, 200–201
Ayyub, Samir, 113, 122n17
'Azzam, Samira, 101, 105n67
'Azzam, 'Abd al-Rahman, 15
al-'Azzi, Sa'id, 248, 257, 282–283

Bakr, Ibrahim, 217
Bakr, Sayyid, 248
Bal'awi, Fathi, 135
Bal'awi, Hakam, 107
Barakat, Fa'iq, 217
Barakat, Halim, 100, 104n62
al-Barazi, Muhsin, 52
Baydun, Mustafa, 131
Ben-Gurion, David, 288
Bennike, Vagn, 175
Bernadotte, Folke, 47, 50; Bernadotte plan, 45, 50
Bin Jamil, Sherif Husayn Nasir, 165, 202, 203n7
al-Bitar, Salah, 143
Bruhns, Fred, 92, 95, 104n35, 104n44
Bsiso, Mu'ayn, 99
Burns, Eedson Louis Millard, 181, 187
Bustami, Bashir, 217

Churchill, Winston, 165

al-Dabbagh, Mustafa, 79, 97, 102n2, 104n48
al-Dabbagh, Salah, 122n28, 266
al-Dajani, Ahmad Sidqi, 258, 265, 267
al-Dajani, Burhan, 245, 253n24
al-Dajani, Kamal, 26
Darwaza, Muhammad 'Izzat, 8, 15, 17, 21n13, 21n14, 21n15, 21n16, 21n17, 21n23, 21n26, 26–27, 31–33, 39–41, 41n9, 41n12, 42n18, 43n41, 43n42, 45, 57n3, 57n4, 57n8, 57n10, 57n12, 57n13
Darwish, Is-haq, 40
Da'ud, Sam'an, 184
al-Dazdar, 'Is-haq, 211, 217, 245
al-Dur, Niqola, 79, 102n2, 104n63, 229, 256

Efrat, Moshe, 90–91, 103n24, 103n27, 122n20, 174n2

Fahmi, Ahmad, 98
al-Fahum, Khalid, 229, 267, 282–283
al-Fa'iz, 'Akif, 230
Falaha, Mahmud, 138
Fanon, Frantz, 121
al-Fara, Qasim, 153
al-Farhan, Ahmad, 217
Farraj, Ibrahim, 62
Farraj, Ya'qub, 13
Faruq king of Egypt, 44, 51–52, 57n1, 63, 67
Fawzi, Mahmud, 23
Faysal I of Iraq, 7
Frayj, Futi, 49, 62–63

Galtung, Ingrid, 95–96, 104n45
Galtung, Johan, 95–96, 104n45
Ghannam, Ibrahim, 99
Ghantus, Lutf, 79, 102n2, 103n30, 104n34, 117, 122
Ghazala, Da'ud, 233
Ghazi king of Iraq, 14
Ghosha, Subhi, 126
al-Ghuri, Amil, 26, 29–30, 32, 35, 46, 57n5, 57n9, 67–69, 74
al-Ghusayn, Ya'qub, 13, 15, 17, 25–26, 28
Giáp, Võ Nguyên, 121
Glubb Pasha (John Bagot Glubb), 57, 128, 175–176, 182, 190

Habash, George, 109, 121n4, 124–132, 149n9, 149n17, 150n20, 150n24, 150n27, 150n33, 258–259, 270n36
Hadad, Wadi', 109, 124, 126–128, 130–133, 149n12
Hafiz, Mustafa, 180
Hamad, Khayri, 250
Hamdalla, Hafiz, 177
al-Hamud 'Abd, al-Fatah, 137
Hamuda, Yahya, 269, 281, 283–284
Hanun, Hilmi, 217
Hanun, Kamal, 28
Harkabi, Yehoshafat, xii, 79–80, 102n1, 102n2, 102n3, 102n6, 104n62, 292

al-Hasan, Bilal, 131, 268n3, 286n30
al-Hasan, Hani, 107, 137–138, 260
al-Hasan, Khalid (Abu al-Saʿid), 122n16, 137–138, 231
Hasana, ʿAli, 46, 49, 63, 184
Hashemite family, xii, xiv, 7, 52, 54, 60, 72, 86, 90, 138, 165–166, 168–169, 172–173, 178–179, 184, 190, 194, 196, 198, 202–203, 205, 212, 214, 218, 228, 234, 289–290
Hashim, Ibrahim, 188–189, 192
Hawatma, Naʾif, 109, 120, 126, 128, 132, 149n13
al-Hijazi, Mahmud Bakr, 261
Hijja, Muhammad, 210
Hijja, Ramadan, 217
Al-Hindi, Amin, 132
al-Hindi, Hani, 124–126, 128, 131–132
al-Hindi, ʾUsama, 131
al-Hiyari, ʿAli, 239, 248
Hurani, Akram, 143
al-Hurani, Faysal, 142, 150n56, 151n59, 151n62, 235n18, 252n4
al-Hurani, Nafid ʿAbd al-Majid, 238–239
Husayn, king of Jordan, xiv, 86, 165–166, 170, 178, 185–188, 190, 192–194, 196, 199, 202, 204–206, 208, 214, 219–220, 225–230, 232, 254, 271, 273, 289–290
al-Husayni, ʿAbd al-Qadir, 120, 135
al-Husayni, Daʾud, 248, 269n8
al-Husayni, Faruq, 229
al-Husayni, al-Haj Amin (the Mufti), xi–xii, 1, 3–18, 20n9, 21n19, 21n27, 23, 27, 30–41, 42n30, 43n40, 44–54, 56, 57n5, 57n6, 57n9, 57n15, 58n24, 60, 63–73, 74n17, 74n19, 74n22, 74n26, 74n27, 74n28, 74n30, 80, 130, 153, 185, 229, 232–233, 288–289
al-Husayni, Jamal, 13, 15, 17, 26–30, 35, 39, 41n12, 46–47, 49, 56, 60, 63
al-Husayni, Musa Kazim, 6, 8–9, 11–13
al-Husayni, Rajaʾ, 46, 49, 62–63
al-Husayni, Tawfiq Salih, 25–26
Husayni family, xii, 3–4, 9–10, 17–18, 19n6, 23, 25–26, 28, 30–31, 36, 39–40, 41n9, 70, 289
al-Hut, Bayan Nuwayhid, xii, 4, 8–11, 13, 15–17, 19n3, 20n7, 20n11, 20n12, 20n13, 21n14, 21n15, 21n16, 21n17, 21n18, 21n20, 21n22, 21n23, 21n24, 21n26, 21n28, 21n29, 21n30, 21n33, 21n34, 22n38, 22n40, 37, 39, 41n1, 41n2, 41n4, 41n10, 42n14, 42n17, 42n18, 42n22, 42n24, 42n30, 42n31, 42n32, 42n35, 42n36, 43n37, 43n38, 43n39, 43n41
al-Hut, Mahmud, 98
al-Hut, Shafiq, 111, 122n9, 122n24, 236–237, 241, 250, 252n1, 252n12, 252n13, 256–260, 263–265, 267–268, 269n4, 269n5, 269n6, 269n7, 269n18, 269n27, 269n29, 270n34, 270n35, 270n37, 270n39, 270n45, 272, 274, 276, 281, 285n1, 285n2, 285n3, 285n4, 285n5, 285n7, 285n8, 286n9, 286n12, 286n13, 286n42

Ibrahim, Muhsin, 131, 150n18, 188–189
Ibrahim, Rashid al-Haj, 15
al-Ifranji, Muhammad, 242
ʿIsa, Salah, 155

Jaber, Salih, 32–33, 42n20, 42n23, 42n26, 52
al-Jabi, Subhi, 265
al-Jaʿbri, Sidqi, 217
al-Jaburi, Hamid, 124
Jarar ʿAbd, al-Rahim, 177
al-Jayusi, Salma, 95, 99
Jibril, Ahmad, 108, 120, 144, 259, 269n12
Jumaʿa, Shaʿrawi, 131

al-Kaʿkabani, Salih, 138
al-Kalouthi, Fathi, 211
al-Kalouthi, Fuʾad, 211
Kamal, Shawkat, 178
Kanafani, Ghassan, 123n34, 239, 252n7, 252n10, 253n39, 278–280, 286n22, 286n24
Kanʿan, Ahmad, 217
Katan, Henry, 45, 61
al-Katib, Hasan, 188
al-Kayali ʿAbd, al-Wahab, 143
al-Kaylani, ʿAbd al-Khaliq, 211
al-Kaylani, Rashid ʿAli, 54
al-Khadra, Subhi, 33
al-Khafish, Husayn, 178
Khalaf, Salah (Abu Iyad), 86, 88, 103n16, 103n19, 103n20, 107, 111–112, 121, 122n7, 122n10, 122n13, 123n36, 123n40, 134–135, 137–138, 146, 150n36, 235n18, 243, 252n16, 288, 295n1, 295n2,

Name Index

al-Khalidi, Husayn Fakhri, 13, 15, 17, 21n23, 22n40, 25–26, 28–30, 39–40, 41n1, 42n14, 42n17, 42n18, 43n38, 43n41, 45–46, 49
al-Khalidi, Mahmud, 138
al-Khalidi, Rasim, 211
al-Khalidi, Walid, 57n1, 245, 278, 286n23
al-Khatib, Ahmad, 124
al-Khatib, Anwar, 186–187
al-Khatib, Husam, 138
al-Khatib, Rashad, 217
al-Khatib, Ruhi, 169, 217
Al-Khatib, 'Umar, 211
al-Khatib, Ziyad, 67
Khouri, Tawfiq, 137, 140
Kirkbride, Alec, 54–56, 57n10, 58n30, 58n32, 58n33, 58n34, 59n36
al-Kubaysi, Basil, 128

al-Lababidi, Rafiq, 62

al-Madani, Wajih, 229, 248, 258, 265–266, 269n33, 281, 283
al-Madi, Falah, 217, 229
al-Madi, Mu'in, 31–33, 35, 40, 49
Mahir, 'Ali, 16, 21n32
al-Majali, Hazza', 185–188, 194, 195n5, 197
Makhyun, 'Abd al-Rahman, 180
Mannheim, Karl, 90–91, 103n28, 106, 121n1
Maqsoud, Clovis, 268
Mardam, Jamil, 24–26, 28, 33, 57n1
al-Masri, Hikmat, 66, 69, 167, 182, 192, 198, 217, 230, 232–233
al-Masri, Ma'zuz Haj, 167, 197
al-Masri, Nash'at, 197
al-Masri, Nimr, 258, 266–267, 281, 283
Maswada, Rashad, 177
al-Mufti, Sa'id, 184, 192
Muhammad the Prophet, 98, 109
Muhyi al-Din, Zakariyya, 283
al-Mustafa, Najib, 177
Mustafa, Salah, 181
Mutawi, Samir, 219–220

al-Nabulsi, Sulayman, 188, 192–193, 198, 201, 203n4, 217, 230
al-Nahas, Mustafa Pasha, 16, 23, 61–62
al-Najar, Yusif Muhammad, 107, 135, 137
al-Naqib, 'Usama, 130, 258, 266–267, 281, 283
al-Nashashibi, 'Azmi, 184
al-Nashashibi, Nasir al-Din, 66, 79, 102n2
al-Nashashibi, Raghib, 10–13, 17–18, 26, 39
al-Nashashibi family, 10, 12, 16–17, 19n6, 21n21, 30
Nasim, Muhammad, 131
Nasr, Salah, 131
al-Natsha, Rafiq, 107, 231
Na'was, 'Abdulla, 186
Nevo, Yosef (Joseph), 17, 20n6, 22n37, 22n39, 22n40, 41n9, 295n4
al-Nimr, Rashid, 197
al-Nimr, Rifa't, 283
al-Nuqrashi, Mahmud Fahmi, 33, 51–53, 58n20
Nusayba, Anwar, 49, 63
Nusayba, Hazim, 217, 219

al-Pachachi, Hamdi, 35, 42n29, 42n30
al-Pachachi, Muzahim, 52–54
Porath, Yehoshua, 8, 16, 19n6, 20n8, 20n12, 21n13, 21n15, 21n16, 21n17, 21n19, 21n21, 21n22, 21n25, 21n26, 21n27, 21n28, 22n35, 22n36

al-Qadumi, Faruq, 107, 137–138
al-Qadumi, Hani, 231
al-Qamhawi, Walid, 19n4, 79, 102n2, 229, 232–233, 245, 248, 250
Qamhawi, Zahi, 130
Qarman, 'Izzat, 217
Qasim, 'Abd al-Karim, 66–67
al-Qasim, Anis, 91, 100, 102n2, 103n31, 104n64, 117, 122n24, 122n26
al-Qassam, 'Iz al-Din, 119–120, 140
Qays, Abu 'Adnan, 127
al-Qishawi, Abu Mu'in, 242
al-Qudwa, Musa, 242
Quray', Ahmad, 137
al-Quwatli, Shukri, 223

Ramadan Pasha, 29
Rashid, Harun Hashim, 95
al-Rawi, Najib, 62
al-Rayis, Munir, 156

al-Razzaz, Munif, 143
Rida, Mamduh, 64–65, 74n17
al-Rifa'i, Samir, 189, 195n11, 199–202, 203n3, 203n6
Rif'at, Kamal, 180
al-Rimawi, 'Abdulla, 177, 182, 194
al-Rimawi, Qasim, 229
Rok, Alfred, 13, 15, 17
Rommel, Erwin, 6
Rsheidat, Najib, 217, 239, 248
Rsheidat, Shafiq, 188
al-Rusan, Mahmud, 194

Saba, Fu'ad, 15, 17
Sabri, 'Ali, 180
Sabri, Husayn, 217
al-Sabrini, Hilmi, 138
al-Sa'di, Ahmad, 258, 265, 267
Safwat, Isma'il, 34, 36–38
al-Shami, Ja'far, 217
Sahyun, Raji, 257, 266
Sahyun, Yusif, 26, 46, 49, 63
Sa'id, Ahmad, 83
al-Sa'id, Nuri, 17, 61, 125–126
al-Sakakini, Khalil, 49
Sakhnini, 'Isam, 19n2, 86, 103n17, 123n38, 149n12, 220n7, 295n3
Sakran, Sakran, 261
al-Saksak, 'Abd al-Rahman, 229, 253
Salah, Walid, 182–183
Salah al-Din, Muhammad, 62, 110
Salam, Sa'ib, 28–30
Salim, Ahmad, 152
Samuel, Herbert, 65
Saraj al-Din, Fu'ad, 63
Sarraj, Abdel Hamid, 131
Sa'ud, king of Saudi Arabia, 14, 68, 73
al-Sayigh, Fa'iz, 248
Sayigh, Yezid, 75n34, 130, 143–144, 149n1, 149n3, 149n5, 149n6, 149n10, 150n23, 150n25, 150n27, 150n28, 150n30, 150n39, 150n47, 150n49, 151n63
Sha'ath, Nabil, 107, 114, 116, 122n19, 122n23
Sha'ban, Sami, 246
'Abd al-Shafi, Haydar, 160–161, 162n14, 162n15, 162n16, 162n17, 229, 245
al-Shafi'i, Husayn, 283

al-Sha'ir, Muhammad, 120, 123n35
al-Shak'a, 'Adil, 178
al-Shak'a, Walid, 167, 177, 182, 186, 197–198, 230, 232–233
Shammout, Ismail, 99
Sharaf, Sami, 131
Sha'ur, Yasri, 217
al-Shawwa, Rushdi, 153–154
al-Shibil, Salih, 124, 128, 268, 270n43
al-Shihabi, Zlikha, 217
Shishakli, Adib, 126
al-Shu'aybi, 'Isa, 75n33, 130, 149n2, 150n22, 150n26, 150n37, 156, 161n7, 219, 220n7, 295n3
al-Shuqayri, Ahmad, xi, xv, 16, 22n35, 27, 45, 66, 68–70, 72–73, 75n32, 75n35, 85–87, 133, 148, 150n32, 161, 165, 169, 195, 198, 204–208, 213–214, 217, 219, 221, 223–234, 234n1, 234n3, 234n4, 234n5, 234n6, 234n10, 234n11, 234n12, 234n14, 234n20, 234n21, 236–251, 252n2, 252n3, 252n6, 252n12, 252n15, 252n20, 253n22, 253n24, 253n27, 253n28, 254, 257–268, 269n8, 269n9, 269n10, 269n11, 269n21, 269n30, 269n31, 270n36, 270n42, 271–285, 285n1, 285n5, 285n6, 285n8, 286n9, 286n10, 286n11, 286n14, 286n16, 286n17, 286n18, 286n19, 286n20, 286n21, 286n25, 286n26, 286n33, 291–292
al-Shuqayri, As'ad, 223
al-Sulh, Riyad, 32, 35
al-Sulh, Taqi al-Din, 24–25
al-Suqi, Husni, 217
al-Surani, Jamal, 248, 257, 266–267, 282–283
al-Surani, Musa, 153
al-Sururi, Ahmad, 248
al-Suwaydi, Tawfiq, 24
Sweid, Munir, 138

Ta'i', Ahmad Farraj, 40, 42n36
al-Takruri, Yusif, 217
al-Tal, Sa'id, 219, 220n9,
al-Tal, Wasfi, 199, 204, 206–208, 218–219
al-Tamimi, Rafiq, 26, 35, 40
al-Tamimi, Subhi, 211
Tannus, 'Izzat, 16, 27
al-Taziz, Ali, 217

Templer, Gerald Walter Robert, 184–185, 195n5
Tibawi, A. L., 97–98, 104n51, 104n55, 104n57, 104n58
Tuqan, Fadwa, 94
Tuqan, Qadri, 19n4, 89, 103n23, 171, 174n5, 176–178, 217, 230, 233
Tuqan, Sulayman, 25, 28, 46
Turki, Fawaz, 95–96, 100–102, 104n43, 104n47, 104n66, 105n68, 105n70, 117, 122n25

'Ude, Rif'at, 246
'Udwan, Kamal, 103n18, 107, 135, 137, 231, 235n18
'Uweida, Khalil, 266

al-Wazir, Khalil (Abu Jihad), 72, 75n34, 108, 110, 112, 119–120, 122n6, 122n11, 122n30, 134–140, 150n37, 150n40, 150n41, 150n42, 150n43, 150n44, 150n48, 150n51, 150n53, 231, 260
Weizmann, Chaim, 65

al-Yahya, Muhammad Tawfiq, 217
al-Yamani, Ahmad, 127, 130, 258–260
al-Yamani, Muhammad, 259
al-Yashruti, Khalid, 143, 256
Yasin, Subhi, 79, 102n2

Za'nun, Salim, 135, 138
al-Zaru, Nadim, 217
Zedong, Mao, 121
al-Zirikli, Khayr al-Din, 25
Zu'aytir, Akram, 21n13, 21n15, 21n16, 49, 61, 167
Zurayq, Qustantin, 19n4, 88–89, 103n21, 124

Subject Index

1936–39 revolt, 5, 13–15, 50, 119–120, 123n34, 140, 293

1948 Arab-Israeli War, xi–xiii, 3–4, 19n2, 23, 42n25, 45, 71, 73, 79–81, 83–84, 87–91, 93–94, 96, 107–108, 120, 124, 135, 152, 287, 293; Nakba, xiii, 4–5, 19n4, 40, 42n22, 42n24, 57n7, 57n12, 57n13, 58n25, 74n14, 79–80, 83, 88–90, 94, 96, 98–100, 102n2, 103n21, 103n23, 104n42, 106, 110, 117, 127, 141, 145, 156, 255, 285, 287, 293–294; "Sons of the Nakba" (Jeel Abna' al-Nakba), xiii, 106–107, 110–113, 118–119, 140, 289, 294. *See also* "Generation of Liberation" (Jeel al-Tahrir)

al-*Ahram* (newspaper), 74n16, 103n9, 153, 161n3, 161n5, 161n8, 162n10, 162n12, 212n6, 235n5, 235n11, 252n12, 253n25, 253n37, 269n8, 282, 285n1, 286n15

Akhbar Filastin (weekly), 159, 252n12, 269n23, 269n25

Akhbar al-Yawm (weekly), 74n16, 153, 159, 161n2

Algeria, 100, 109, 121, 131, 134, 138–139, 142, 198, 246, 256; Algerian revolt (1954–62), 120–121, 131, 139, 142, 160

Allies states, 6, 16

All-Palestine Government, 31, 44–45, 47–54, 56, 57n10, 57n35, 60–63, 72–73, 79, 136, 153, 155

Anglo-Jordanian Treaty, 55, 171, 184, 192

al-*Anwar* (newspaper), 66, 252n2, 252n3, 252n11, 252n20, 269n31, 269n33, 269n34, 270n35, 270n44, 286n18, 286n22, 286n24, 286n32, 286n35, 286n38

Arab Higher Authority (al-Hay'a al-'Arabiyya al-'Ulya), 7, 28, 30–32, 35–37, 39–40, 45–48, 58n24, 60, 63–65, 67–69, 130, 232

Arab Higher Committee (AHC, al-Lajna al-'Arabiyya al-'Ulya), 7, 11–17, 25–31, 33, 41n9, 41n12

Arab Higher Front (al-Jabha al-'Arabiyya al-'Ulya), 28, 30

Arab–Israeli conflict, xi, 4, 71, 79–83, 85–86, 89, 102n6, 103n13, 103n25, 141, 172, 179, 196, 236, 240, 251, 257, 271, 288, 292–294

Arab League, 6–7, 15, 20n10, 23–31, 33–35, 37–38, 44, 46–48, 55–56, 60–65, 67, 70–72, 81, 85, 102n5, 130, 146, 148, 155, 161, 168, 177, 196, 198, 223–224, 226–227, 234, 238, 243, 248, 266, 268, 282, 284; Alexandria Protocol, 24; 'Aley conference (October 1947), 32; Cairo conference (December 1947), 34; League Charter, 24, 41, 61; League Council, 24, 27–28, 36, 42n30, 45–46, 60, 62–65, 69, 74n16, 144, 154, 196, 223–224; Permanent Military Committee, 37–38, 42n30, 42n31; Political Committee; 35, 44, 46, 53; Sawfar meeting (September 1947), 32, 42n20; secretary general, 15, 27, 33, 46–47, 61–62, 81, 223–224, 226, 282, 284; Summit, 204, 249–251, 254, 262; First summit (January 1964), 69, 85, 133, 161, 223–227, 230–232; Second summit (September 1964), 229, 234, 235n3; Third summit (Khartoum summit, September 1967), 237, 243–244, 249, 271–277, 280, 285n1

Arab Liberation Front, 118

Arab Nationalists Movement (ANM), xiii, 74n30, 86, 106, 109–110, 124–133, 135, 141, 144–145, 147, 149n1, 150n32, 154, 168, 171–172, 201, 207–208, 213, 227, 229, 231–232, 241, 244–246, 254–256, 258–265, 268, 269n8, 270n36; Filastin Committee, 130–131, 133; Leadership Committee for Palestinian Action (al-Lajna al-Qiyadiyya lil-'Amal al-Filastini fi al-Haraka), 132–133

Arab Palestinian Liberation Front (Jabhat al-Tahrir al-'Arabiyya al-Filastiniyya), 244

315

Subject Index

Arab Salvation Army (Jaysh al-Inqadh), 54, 125
Arab states, xii, 3–6, 14–18, 24, 28, 31–37, 44–45, 47–48, 50, 52, 54–55, 58n34, 60–61, 63, 65, 68–71, 73, 80–83, 85, 87–88, 90, 94–95, 110–111, 113–114, 118, 120, 127, 131, 134, 140, 143, 155, 165, 171, 180, 182, 189, 214, 216, 224–226, 237–238, 243, 254, 262, 271, 274–277, 283, 287, 291, 295. *See also by country name*
Arab Youth (al-Shabab al-'Arabi), 127, 229
Association Opposing Peace with Israel (Haya'at Muqawamat al-Sulh ma'a 'Isra'il), 126–127
Austria, 138, 145, 147
Axis States, 18

Baghdad Pact, xiv, 129, 170, 180, 184–187, 189, 192, 195n5, 195n6
Balfour Declaration, 5–6, 8–9, 11, 80, 89, 293
al-Ba'th (newspaper), 230, 235n17
Ba'th Party, 68, 86, 124, 137–138, 140–14, 151n57, 151n58, 151n61, 168, 171–172, 185–186, 199, 201, 207–208, 213, 229–230, 232–233, 244, 246, 255–256, 260, 288; Ba'th coup (1963) 66, 144, 198–199; Ba'th National Command, 141–144, 235n17
Bedouin, 15, 126, 165, 199
British Mandate, xii, 4–9, 11, 13–18, 31, 35–37, 42n19, 44, 48–50, 52–55, 57n10, 58n18, 65, 69, 71, 73, 89, 119, 125, 165, 168, 171, 223, 288

Cairo agreement (March 1966), 207, 212n1, 249
China, 139, 146, 242
Chinese Endeavor (pamphlet), 121
Commission of Experts on Filastin, 65
Communism, 124, 138–139, 154, 161, 168, 172, 185, 192–193, 201, 207–208, 213, 246
Cuban Endeavor (pamphlet), 121

Democratic Front for the Liberation of Palestine, 108–109, 120, 122n33, 127
al-Difa' (newspaper), 74n31, 168, 235n15, 252n8

East Bank, xiv, 91, 108–109, 169–170, 173, 186, 198, 215, 219, 290

Egypt, xii, xiv–xv, 3, 5–6, 15, 17–18, 23, 30, 33, 35, 39–40, 44, 47–54, 56, 58n20, 58n24, 60–67, 69–72, 74n16, 81–86, 90, 96, 106–107, 109, 112, 114, 116, 125–126, 129–133, 136–138, 140–143, 145–148, 150n38, 152–161, 161n6, 162n13, 163, 165, 167–168, 170, 172, 176, 179–185, 187–188, 190–195, 196, 198–199, 202, 214–215, 217–219, 223–230, 236–237, 240–241, 243, 246, 249, 252n20, 254–260, 265, 268, 269n22, 275–277, 281–284, 291–292; Cairo, 24–27, 29–30, 32–35, 38, 40, 48–49, 52–53, 58n24, 60–63, 65, 68, 72, 101, 127, 132, 134, 136, 145–147, 151n71, 153–155, 158, 182, 207, 215–216, 223, 230, 243, 246, 248, 260, 266, 270n36, 279, 282; Cairo Radio, 58n27, 102n8, 102n10, 102n11, 102n12, 160, 162n15, 162n17, 162n18, 215, 286n15; Cairo University, 87, 103n18, 112, 135, 137, 145; military coup (1952), 154; Straits of Tiran 81, 83; Suez Canal 81, 86, 135, 192
Egyptian-Syrian union, 84, 112, 131, 142, 146, 156, 168, 291
"Emergency High Council", 278
"Eternal Palestinian republic" (*khalida*), 67, 74n21, 196
"Executive Authority in Support of the Palestinian Revolution" (al-Hay'a al-'Amila li-Da'm al-Thawra al-Filastiniyya), 278–279
Executive Committee (al-Lajna al-Tanfidhiyya), 6

Facts about the Path to Liberation (*Haqa'iq 'Ala Tariq al-Tahrir*, pamphlet), 256
Fatah (Harakat al-Tahrir al-Watani al-Filastini), xiii, xiv, 72, 75n34, 80, 85–87, 97, 103n18, 106–114, 118, 120–121, 121n3, 122n8, 122n12, 122n14, 122n15, 122n16, 122n18, 123n39, 123n41, 123n42, 123n43, 123n44, 124, 133–141, 144–147, 150n34, 150n35, 50n37, 150n38, 150n46, 160, 172, 204, 209–212, 213–214, 217, 227, 229, 231–232, 235n18, 236–237, 240–244, 246–247, 251, 254–257, 259–261, 268n2, 274–277, 280–282, 286n27, 286n28, 288, 290–291
Fida'i Arab Batalions (Kata'ib al-Fida' al-'Arabi), 125–126
Fida'iyyun, xiii, xv, 4, 66, 80–81, 85–86, 99, 107–108, 117–121, 122n8, 123n35, 124–126,

133, 140, 159, 172, 179–184, 190–193, 195n1, 209–214, 216–217, 237, 240, 242–244, 249, 251, 254–262, 264, 268, 271, 274–275, 277–282, 284–285, 288–289, 291–292
Filastin (magazine), 58n24, 68, 74n28, 74n31, 255
Filastin (newspaper), 20n9, 189, 195n9, 235n8, 252n20, 253n33, 268n3
"Filastin Segment" (radio program), 94, 159–160, 162n17, 162n18
Filastinuna Nida' al-Hayat (magazine), xiv, 97, 109, 112, 119, 134–135, 137–141, 150
Front de Libération Nationale (FLN), 21, 138, 142
Front for Sacrificial Operation (Jabhat al-'Amal al-Fida'i), 244

Gaza Strip, xii, xiv, 5, 45, 48, 50–52, 55–56, 57n10, 58n24, 70–72, 79, 81, 87, 90–91, 94–97, 104n45, 107, 128, 131, 134–138, 142–143, 147, 151, 152–161, 161n6, 162n13, 180, 182–183, 190–191, 194, 196, 227–229, 242, 244, 248–249, 252n20, 253n34, 256–257, 262, 269n22, 273, 276–277, 283, 294–295
General Union of Palestinian Students (GUPS), xiv, 124, 129, 135, 144–149, 151n65, 269n17, 281
Generation of Liberation (Jeel al-Tahrir), 90, 106–107, 291, 294
Generation of Palestinian Independence (Jeel al-Istiqlal), 293–294
Germany, 17–18, 107, 137, 139, 145, 147; Nazi Germany, 6, 18, 20n9, 31
Great Arab Revolt (1916-18), 165
Great Britain, 16, 18, 35, 50–52, 54–55, 89, 125, 187, 189, 193

al-Hawadith (weekly), 74n27, 162n14, 236, 252n1, 255–256, 269n17, 269n19, 269n27, 269n28, 269n29, 269n32, 269n33, 270n35, 270n36, 270n38, 270n45, 286n11, 286n14, 286n26
al-Hayat (newspaper), 74n22, 74n28, 74n29, 74n31, 161n8, 171, 174n5, 210, 212n5, 252n11, 252n15, 252n20, 253n22, 253n23, 253n33, 255, 269n33, 270n35, 286n10, 286n12, 286n29, 286n35, 286n37

Heroes of the Return (Abtal al-'Awda), 256, 258–259, 261, 268, 269n12, 269n13
al-Huriyya (newspaper), 74n19, 252n7, 252n19, 253n38, 255, 262, 268, 269n9, 269n10, 269n26, 270n36, 286n22, 286n30, 286n32, 286n37, 286n41

India, 246, 268
Indonesia, 246
International Student Congress, 146
International Union of Students, 146
Intifada, 178, 219, 293–295
Iraq, 7, 15, 17–18, 23, 31–35, 37–38, 42n20, 46–47, 52–56, 61–62, 66–68, 74n24, 90, 124–125, 128–129, 144, 147, 161, 165, 170, 174n1, 187, 189, 192, 196, 198, 265, 273, 280; Baghdad xiv, 15, 53, 67–68, 74n20, 74n21, 74n24, 74n25, 74n26, 127–128, 143, 151n61, 252n15; Coup of July 1958, 66, 129
Islamic Liberation Party, 233
Israel, State of, xii, xv, 3–5, 42n28, 45, 47–48, 50, 54–56, 57n7, 60, 67, 70–71, 79–85, 87, 89–91, 96–97, 101, 102n6, 108, 111, 114, 116, 119–120, 125–127, 130, 132–134, 140, 143, 148, 153–154, 156, 158–159, 169–173, 175, 177–178, 179–184, 187–189, 191–194, 209–212, 213–214, 219, 220n1, 237, 239–243, 251, 254–259, 261, 271–274, 276–277, 285, 290–294; Israel's National Water Carrier xiii, 80, 134
Israel Defense Forces (IDF), xiv, 74n28, 86, 102n4, 103n15, 103n18, 108, 150n52, 151n71, 158, 161n6, 162n11, 162n13, 172, 175–176, 180, 182, 189, 191–192, 195n1, 195n7, 213, 220n1, 252n20, 254, 269n22
al-Istiqlal party, 13, 33, 40–41

Jaffa, 9, 15, 20n8, 82, 94, 97–98
al-Jarida (newspaper), 66, 252n18, 252n20, 255, 269n8
Jelazoon (refugee camp), 92, 103n32, 109
Jerusalem, 8–12, 23, 25, 28, 30, 39–40, 44, 48–50, 55–56, 69, 82, 98, 128, 135, 165, 169, 173, 174n3, 174n4, 178, 182–183, 185–189, 198, 200–201, 203, 208, 210–211, 213–215, 217–218, 223, 226, 234, 248, 273, 294–295; Dome of the Rock, 186, 188; al Haram al-Sharif, 14–15

Jerusalem Congress. *See* Palestinian National Council (PNC)
Jewish Agency, 6, 20n8, 239, 243
al-Jihad (newspaper), 168, 252n5, 252n6, 252n20, 253n31, 253n32
Jordan, xii, xiv-xv, 3-4, 7, 15-16, 18, 19n1, 31-34, 37, 44-48, 50, 52-56, 57n10, 58n31, 60-63, 66-72, 74n28, 81, 85-86, 90-91, 97, 103n15, 108-109, 117, 124-132, 135, 138-139, 142-143, 148-149, 150n52, 154, 157-160, 165-173, 174n1, 174n7, 175-195, 195n5, 195n6, 196-203, 203n1, 204-212, 213-220, 220n1, 220n8, 224-234, 238-239, 243-244, 248-251, 252n20, 253n37, 254-255, 260-262, 265, 271, 280, 283, 289-290, 292, 295n4; Amman, 54-56, 57n10, 58n30, 58n32, 58n33, 58n34, 58n36, 94, 96, 126-127, 129, 138, 166-167, 174n1, 179, 181-182, 184-187, 189-190, 193, 197, 200-201, 203n3, 203n5, 203n6, 203n7, 211, 212n3, 230, 233-234, 239, 248; Hashemite Kingdom, xii, xiv, 7, 52, 54, 60, 72, 86, 90, 138, 165-169, 172-173, 178-179, 184, 190, 194, 196, 198, 202-203, 205, 212, 214, 218, 228, 234, 289-290; House of Representatives, 167, 169-171, 173, 176-177, 182, 186-187, 189, 191-193, 195n12, 196, 200-203, 210, 214, 218, 228; Jordanian Legion, 44, 183-185
al-Jumhuriyya (newspaper), 66, 74n19, 162n10, 162n14, 215-217, 220n3, 252n20, 270n35, 282

Khartoum Summit. *See* Arab League: Third Summit
al-Kifah (newspaper), 66, 150n21, 252n4, 252n12, 252n15, 252n20, 252n21
Al-Kifah al-Musallah — Tariq al-'Awda (pamphlet), 138
Kuwait, 66, 109, 124, 129, 133-134, 136-139, 161, 211, 229, 231, 242, 256

Lebanon, 3, 15-17, 28, 32, 35, 47, 50, 52, 65-66, 68, 81, 88, 90-91, 113-114, 127, 129-135, 141-144, 151n57, 151n58, 152, 160-161, 162n14, 180, 191, 194, 223, 229, 231, 235n18, 238, 240, 256-259; Beirut, xiv, 15, 40, 57n11, 57n14, 68-69, 96, 100-101, 103n18, 114, 125-126, 128, 131-132, 137, 140-141, 143, 146, 160, 230, 236, 240 248, 256, 258-259, 268; Beirut Arab University, xiii, 63, 126; Civil war (1958), 88, 141; University of Beirut, 98, 114, 124, 129, 145
Libya, 231, 257
London congress, 16

Majlisiyyin (the mufti's supporters), 10, 12
al-Mu'arada (oppositionist group to the Majlisiyyin), 10, 12
al-Muharrir (newspaper), 103n20, 212, 215, 255, 269n8, 269n9, 269n12, 269n15, 270n43, 286n12, 286n13, 286n22, 286n31, 286n32, 286n34, 286n37
al-Muntada al-'Arabi (Arab cultural club), 126
Muslim Brotherhood, 51, 58n20, 128, 135-137, 154, 171-172
Muslim-Christian Associations, 7, 20n12

Al-Nahar (newspaper), 252n20, 255, 269n9, 286n32
National Bloc (al-Kutla al-Wataniyya), 13
"National Council of the Revolutionary Command," 279
National Defense Party (Hizb al-Difa' al-Watani), 13-15, 17-18
National Front for Liberation (al-Jabha al-Wataniyya lil-Tahrir), 244
Near East Radio (al-Sharq al-Adna), 49, 57n14, 177, 178n1
North Korea, 139

Orthodox Executive Committee, 49
Oslo Accords (1993), 294

Palestine Liberation Front (PLF, Jabhat al-Tahrir al-Filastiniyya), 118, 144, 209, 227, 229, 244, 254, 256, 258-259, 265, 269n6
Palestine Liberation Movement (Harakat Tahrir Filastin), 229
Palestine Liberation Organization (PLO), xi, 43, 45, 57n9, 64-68, 71-72, 74n16, 74n21, 75n34, 79, 84-86, 99, 107, 114, 116, 120-121, 122n27, 129-133, 140-142, 144-145, 147-149, 150n32, 151n71, 154, 156-157, 160-161, 165,

168–169, 172, 195, 196–198, 204–210, 212, 212n6, 213–218, 223–234, 235n17, 236–251, 252n12, 252n20, 253n26, 253n30, 253n34, 254–268, 269n8, 269n9, 269n11, 269n12, 269n13, 269n21, 269n22, 269n30, 270n42, 272–285, 286n10, 286n16, 286n17, 286n19, 286n21, 286n25, 286n33, 286n34, 286n40, 289–292, 294, 295n1, 295n3; Executive Committee, 151n71, 226, 231, 238–239, 241, 243, 246–247, 256, 258, 265, 268, 281, 283–284; PLO Radio, 258, 277
Palestinian Arab Congress (al-Mu'tamar al-'Arabi al-Filastini), 7–9, 11, 12, 21n14
Palestinian Arab National Union, 156
Palestinian Arab Party (al-Hizb al-'Arabi al-Filastini), 13, 25
Palestinian entity (*al-kiyan al*-Filastini). *See* Palestine Liberation Organization (PLO)
Palestinian leadership crisis, xi–xii, 13, 23, 70, 87, 237, 254–268, 278, 287–288
Palestinian Liberation Army (PLA), 67, 229, 232, 240, 248, 251, 258–267, 273, 280, 283
Palestinian National Council (PNC), 8, 48–52, 56, 68–69, 148, 169, 205, 207–208, 225–232, 235n8, 236–237, 239, 242, 246, 282
Palestinian National Fund, 245–246, 248, 258, 266, 283
Palestinian National Liberation Front (Jabhat al-Tahrir al-Watani al-Filastini), 138, 244, 281, 282
Palestinian National Liberation Movement, 118, 133
Palestinian National Movement, xi–xiv, 3–9, 11–14, 17–20, 22n39, 22n40, 26, 30–31, 39, 41n9, 46, 69–73, 79–80, 86–88, 90, 97, 106–108, 112–113, 117–119, 133–134, 149n1, 172, 220, 237, 242, 255, 271, 274–275, 280, 285, 287–289, 291–295
"Palestinian National Movement" of the Mufti (Al-Haraka al-Wataniyya al-Filastiniyya), 69
Palestinian national reawakening (1960s), xi, xiii, xv, 4, 13, 23, 71–73, 79–80, 82–83, 85–88, 90, 98–99, 102n1, 106–114, 117–121, 133, 137–138, 145, 149, 172, 190, 219, 237, 255, 271, 274–275, 280, 285, 287–289, 291–292, 294–295

Palestinian national revival (1950s), xi, xiii, 65, 67, 79–80, 84–85, 87, 90, 106, 144–145, 147, 157, 196, 287, 290–292, 294
Palestinian Revolutionary Forces (al-Quwat al-Thawriyya al-Filastiniyya), 244
Pan-Arab National Committee (Lajnat Filastin al-Qawmiyya), 143
Persian Gulf, 135–136
Popular Front for the Liberation of Palestine (PFLP), xiii, 108–109, 118, 120, 122n32, 130, 133, 244, 259, 269n12, 275, 281–282
Popular Liberation Front, 118

Qatar, 137, 229, 231
"al-Qawmiyyun al-'Arab." *See* "al-Shabab al-Qawmi al'-Arabi" (Arab Nationalists Movement)
Qibya raid (October 1953), xiv, 81, 170, 175–176, 178, 219
Quran, 109, 251

Rabat Summit (October 1974), 72, 85
al-Ra'i (newspaper), 127–128
Ramalla Radio, 176, 178n2, 178n3, 187, 195n10, 195n11
al-Raqib (newspaper), 97, 104n49, 104n50
Reform Party (Hizb al-'Islah al-'Arabi), 13, 40
Refugees, xiii–xiv, 62, 64, 69, 79, 81–82, 87–88, 96–98, 103n24, 103n27, 104n35, 104n44, 104n51, 113–118, 120–121, 122n20, 126–128, 138, 140, 154–155, 158, 166–167, 170, 173, 174n2, 177, 183–187, 198, 256, 294; Camps, xiv, 90–95, 100–102, 106–109, 114–115, 117, 126–128, 132, 135, 144, 152, 166, 170, 185–186, 201, 212–213, 232, 256
Return (*'awda*), 87, 93–99, 104n51, 104n55, 104n57, 104n58, 106, 111, 113, 118, 127, 138, 142, 146, 148, 151n61, 160, 168, 173, 228, 232, 256, 258, 268, 293–294
"Revolutionary Command Council for the Liberation of Filastin" ("Majlis Qiyadat al-Thawra li-Tahrir Filastin"), 278–280
Revolutionary Front for the Liberation of Palestine (al-Jabha al-Thawriyya li-Tahrir Filastin), 239, 244

Revolutionary Studies and Endeavors (pamphlets series), 121
Rhodesia, 17, 23, 26, 41n12
Ruz al-Yusif (weekly), 64, 74n16, 74n17, 74n19

al-Sahafa (newspaper), 142, 151
Salvation Army (Jaysh al-Inqadh) of Qawuqji, 54, 125
Samu' raid (November 1966), xiv, 86, 103n15, 169–170, 172, 213, 217–219, 220n1, 254, 260–261, 290
San Remo Conference (April 1920), 8
Sarkhat Filastin (magazine), 139
Saudi Arabia, 14–15, 25, 63, 66, 68, 98, 109, 137, 208, 223, 249–250, 252n20
Sawt al-Arab Radio, 200
Seychelles islands, 14–15
al-Shabab al-'Arabi al-Filastini (Arab Palestinian Youth), 127, 130
"al-Shabab al-Qawmi al'-Arabi" (Arab Nationalists Movement), 128
Shahids, 50
Shu'un Filastiniyya (monthly), 19n2, 20n9, 103n17, 104n41, 120, 121n2, 122n16, 122n28, 123n34, 149n12, 285n2, 295n1
Sinai War (1956), 81–87, 89, 107, 128–129, 136, 154, 172, 179, 192
Six Day War (1967), xiv–xv, 19n5, 69, 74n28, 83, 85, 89, 99, 103n9, 103n14, 108, 133, 150n52, 151n71, 161n6, 162n13, 166, 172, 179, 211–212, 217, 219–220, 226–227, 237, 244, 252n20, 254–255, 269n22, 271–272, 275–276, 284, 288–293
Soviet Union, 171, 192
Sunni, 109
Supreme Muslim Council (al-Majlis al-Islami al-A'la), 7, 9-10, 12, 14
Syria, xiv, 3, 7–8, 14, 25, 28, 33, 47, 50, 52–54, 61, 66, 68–69, 72, 82, 84–86, 90–91, 100, 106, 109, 112, 114–117, 122n20, 124–127, 129–133, 135–148, 156, 158, 161, 165, 167–168, 170, 172, 176, 179–180, 182, 190, 193–194, 198–199, 202, 204, 211, 214, 218–219, 223, 229, 232, 238–239, 249, 254–256, 258, 265, 280, 283, 291; Bloudan, 28–30; Damascus, 7, 21n14, 26, 33, 40, 41n12, 42n30, 68, 94, 96, 114–115, 125–129, 131, 144, 146–147, 194, 260; Deuxième Bureau (intelligence service), 132; Syrian General Congress (1919), 7, 21n14

Tala'i' al-Fida', 282
Tariq al-'Awda (magazine), 256
al-Tha'r (weekly newsletter), 127
This Is Our Plan — Revolution until Victory (pamphlet), 139
Turkey, 17, 183, 185, 187–188
Turkish-Iraqi pact, 189

UN General Assembly, 47, 50, 104n46, 224
Union of Christian Churches, 49
Union of Palestinian Fida'iyyun (Itihad al-Fida'iyyun al-Filastiniyyun), 244
United Arab Command (UAC), 214, 216, 259
United Arab Republic (UAR), 82, 87, 106, 129–131, 143, 146, 155–156, 158, 194, 198, 200, 256
United States, 50–51, 57n10, 145, 187–189, 193, 211
UN partition plan of Palestine, 82, 288
UNRWA (United Nations Relief and Works Agency for Palestine Refugees in the Near East), 90–92, 95–96, 104n46, 115, 117, 126, 128, 187–188
UNSCOP (United Nations Special Committee on Palestine), 32, 42n19
UN secretary general, 50, 191
al-'Urwa al-Wuthqa (association), 124, 126, 128
'Usbat al-Tahrir al-Watani, 39

Vietnamese Endeavor (pamphlet), 121

West Bank, xii, xiv–xv, 4–5, 55–56, 61, 63, 69–72, 86, 90–92, 96, 103n15, 110, 126, 128, 138, 163, 165–173, 174n7, 175–176, 178–183, 185–193, 195, 196–203, 204–212, 213–220, 227–228, 230, 232–234, 235n20, 256, 272–273, 276–277, 280, 283, 289–290, 292–295; West Bank annexation (April 1950), xiv, 70–72, 86, 165–168, 175, 290, 292
Western Wall riots (August 1929), 11

White Paper (1939), 14–16
World War II, xii, 3, 6–7, 14–15, 20n9, 39, 51, 54, 70–71, 79, 91, 111, 223, 288

Yemen, 15, 84, 131, 194
Yishuv, 119, 288
"Yoav" Operation (October 1948), 56

Youth Congress (Hizb-Mu'tamar al-Shabab al-Filastini), 13
Youth of Revenge (Shabab al-Tha'r), 256

Zionist movement, xii, 4–6, 9, 18–19, 50, 65, 68, 71, 79–81, 83–84, 89, 97–98, 101, 111, 119, 125, 127, 140, 216, 288, 293

MOSHE SHEMESH is Professor of Middle Eastern Studies at Ben-Gurion University of the Negev and Senior Fellow at the Ben-Gurion Research Institute for the Study of Israel and Zionism. He served as a senior intelligence officer in the Israeli Defense Forces prior to his academic career. He is author of *Arab Politics, Palestinian Nationalism, and the Six Day War: The Crystallization of Arab Strategy and Nasir's Descent to War, 1957–1967*; *From the Nakba to the Naksa: The Arab-Israeli Conflict and the Palestinian National Problem*, and *The Palestinian Entity, 1959–1974: Arab Politics and the PLO*.

FOR INDIANA UNIVERSITY PRESS

Tony Brewer *Artist and Book Designer*
Dan Crissman *Editorial Director and Acquisitions Editor*
Katie Huggins *Production Manager*
David Miller *Lead Project Manager/Editor*
Dan Pyle *Online Publishing Manager*
Pamela Rude *Senior Artist and Book Designer*
Stephen Williams *Assistant Director of Marketing*